ISLAMISM AND MODERNISM

Modern Middle East Series, No. 24

Sponsored by the Center for Middle Eastern Studies (CMES)

THE UNIVERSITY OF TEXAS AT AUSTIN

ISLAMISM AND MODERNISM
The Changing Discourse in Iran

FARHANG RAJAEE

UNIVERSITY OF TEXAS PRESS
AUSTIN

Requests for permission to reproduce material from this work
should be sent to:
Permissions
University of Texas Press
P.O. Box 7819
Austin, TX 78713-7819
www.utexas.edu/utpress/about/bpermission.html

♾ The paper used in this book meets the minimum requirements of
ANSI/NISO Z39.48-1992 (R1997) (Permanence of Paper).

Library of Congress Cataloging-in-Publication Data

Rajaee, Farhang, 1952–
    Islamism and modernism : the changing discourse in Iran / Farhang Rajaee.
— 1st ed.
        p. cm. — (Modern Middle East series ; no. 24)
    Includes bibliographical references and index.
    ISBN 978-0-292-71678-0 (cloth : alk. paper) — ISBN 978-0-292-71756-5
(pbk. : alk. paper)
    1. Islam—Iran—History.   2. Islam and state—Iran.   3. Iran—Politics and
government—20th century.   4. Iran—Politics and government—21st century.
I. Title.
    BP63.I68R354 2007
    320.5'570955—dc22

                                                                    2007033589

To Guitty

CONTENTS

PREFACE AND ACKNOWLEDGMENTS ix

INTRODUCTION 1

1. The First Generation 27
The Politics of Revival,
1920s–1960s

2. The Second Generation 90
The Politics of Revolution,
1963–1991

3. The Third Generation 151
The Politics of Islamism,
1989–1997

4. The Fourth Generation 193
The Politics of Restoration,
1997–2005

Conclusion 237
The Politics of Oscillation

NOTES 247

REFERENCES 253

INDEX 269

PREFACE AND
ACKNOWLEDGMENTS

In a thoroughly shameful fashion, we have lost confidence and belief in ourselves. In our long history, we had never so easily given in without resistance, or had never been so cheaply "disarmed spiritually."

MOHAMMAD ALI ESLAMI-NADOUSHAN (1362/1993, 110).
A KEEN OBSERVER OF IRANIAN CULTURE AND SOCIETY,
ESLAMI-NADOUSHAN MADE THIS COMMENT IN AN ESSAY IN
1965, WHEN AMERICANIZATION HAD WON THE DAY IN IRAN.

This book narrates the story of the Islamic movement in Iran, a framework of thought and action that began as an alternative to a century of modernization. By the beginning of the twentieth century, Iranians had succeeded in ushering in a genuine "Iranian modernity," in the form of a constitutional polity. Then Iran became hostage to the "Age of Imperialism" (Hobsbawm 1987) as the Middle East became the most "penetrated region" (Brown 1984) in the world. As a result, modernism became the dominant paradigm in Iran, leading to the fragmentation of its cultural homogeneity, an erosion of confidence, and, most importantly, a consequential loss of spirituality. The 1979 revolution promised to restore confidence and arm Iran with a renewed spirituality. Even though all social classes had taken part in the course of events, which had also been influenced by diverse intellectual trends, when the revolution destroyed the monarchy, it was the Islam-minded Iranians who assumed the helm of power. In hindsight, it is clear that this group was the most articulate, mobilized, and organized, and this superior preparedness enabled them to gain the upper hand in 1979. My primary objectives are to explain why that was the case, to canvass their thoughts, and to explain how they turned revolutionary.

This book may also serve as an interpretive essay on Iran's contemporary intellectual history, even though it is not an exhaustive account.[1] It concentrates on the views of those Iranians who reacted to modernism from within the framework of Islamic teaching and who expressed their views using familiar Islamic terms and vocabularies. Their responses to modernism, always diverse, are still evolving. In many ways, they have simultaneously complemented and contradicted one another. Fully aware and appreciative of the fact that this complexity could be ill served by my reductionist approach, I am nonetheless compelled to take it to better comprehend and explain Iranians' responses to modernism. To remain focused, I have selected those approaches that have retrospectively proved to be dominant and epoch-making. Thus, I contend that Islam-minded Iranians have displayed four responses to modernism, corresponding to four generations in the evolution of the Islam-centric discourse in Iran. Only the views and practices of one generation could be termed "Islamism," namely, that of the third generation.

The first generation felt threatened by modernism, and thus took on a defensive posture. In this group's lifetime, what came to Iran in the name of modernity did not espouse modernity's original emancipatory aim, offering instead nothing but hegemonic views and practices. As this hegemonic modernity was being challenged within the West itself, this generation of Islam-minded Iranians became very defensive and removed themselves from politics; they concentrated instead on a cultural defense of their indigenous social and religious life. The first generation criticized the West and was apologetic about its religion. I have termed their effort "revival" because they tried to rebuild Islam in the face of Iranians' strong attraction to modernism.

As world politics polarized during the Cold War, the Islam-minded Iranians whom I refer to as the second generation began taking radical positions against modernism and proposed a revolution that would eradicate what they termed *Gharbzadegi*—a neologism meaning "infected or afflicted by the West." Decolonization stimulated their confidence, which emboldened them to put forward the claim that Islam could provide an alternative to the Western project and replace modernism altogether. I have called the paradigm of the second generation "revolution" because its members formulated an ideology of revolt out of Islam. In the end, this ideology was successful in manipulating the revolutionary climate of Iran, culminating in the Islamic Revolution of 1979.

A revolution, however, is easier to instigate and mobilize than it is to direct, manage, or control. Revolution and revolutionary zeal gave birth to a third generation, which adopted Islamism and radicalism as its ideology and practice. The artificiality of this phenomenon is striking, in that Islamism is neither Islamic nor modern, yet it is both Islamist and modernist. The poverty of Islamist ideology, on the one hand, and the enormous demands of practical necessities, on the other, led to radicalism, terror, and a politics of fear. Intellectuals were hunted, forced into exile, and even murdered; the media was restricted, and many of its outlets banned. Since the early 1990s, globalization and the reconsideration of modernity in light of postmodern sensitivities have given rise to a fourth generation of politicians and thinkers, who defend modernity and advocate a "restoration" of both Islam and modernity. Indeed, the politics of Iran has become the battleground of the third and the fourth generations. For example, the presidency of Mohammad Khatami (1997–2005) symbolized the ascendancy of the fourth generation, while the election of Mahmoud Ahmadinejad in 2005 to that office symbolizes the ascendancy of the third generation.

I was drawn to undertake this study, in part, by an intriguing quotation attributed to one of Khomeini's close friends, Murtaza Faqih, known as Haj Daddash (d. 1993). Apparently, as he entered the residence of his old friend after the latter's victorious return to Iran in February 1979, Haj Daddash uttered the following: "You finally did become a shah, didn't you!" This point was confirmed later by a similar story told to me by one of Khomeini's cousins. I interviewed him about Khomeini's habits and ideals. In the midst of the discussion, he said, "When Muhammad Reza Shah traveled to Qom, I went to Khomeini's home and reported that the Shah was received warmly, and he was delivering a speech in the city. Khomeini lamented this and said, 'Our turn will come also'" (Shams 1990, interview). The statement is striking for several reasons. First, since the establishment of the monarchy in Iran, in about 708 BCE, rarely, if ever, had a religious leader become the actual ruler. Second, Khomeini's desire to become a ruler was contrary to the hitherto generally accepted position of Shi'i political thought, which advocated quietism and abstaining from politics. Third, both Haj Daddash and Khomeini's cousin were referring to incidents that had occurred long before Khomeini became a protagonist in Iranian politics.

Now, a religious leader who was determined to replace the monarchy with an Islamic state had substituted a humble cushion for the Peacock Throne. His modest appearance notwithstanding, this new leader commanded more power than did "the King of Kings and the light of Aryans," Muhammad Reza Pahlavi (ruled 1941–1979), the last king of the Pahlavi dynasty. The new leader came to be known as Imam, Abraham of our Age; the Disseminator of the Elevated School of the House of the

Prophet; the Founder of the Islamic Republic; the Glorious Upholder of the Faith; the Great Awakener of the Century; the Great Savior of the Age; the Greatest Guide; the Guardian of All Muslims; the Guardian Jurisconsult; the Highest Ranking Warrior; the Hope of the World's Oppressed; the Idol Smasher; Leader of the Islamic Revolution; Leader of the Islamic Community; Moses of the Time; the Reviver of Religion in the New Century; the Torchbearer of the Universal Islamic Movement; and the Vanguard of the Global Islamic Movement. What made this change possible? Nationalists and secularists had dismissed the religious establishment as transitory and adopted a patronizing attitude toward it; "religion was, after all, the opium of the people" (M. Milani 1994, 214). Yet in the end, it was Khomeini who took power, not any of the rest.

In 1989, I traveled to Qom, the hotbed of revolution and the city from which Khomeini began his showdown with the monarchy in 1963, to find an answer to why he became the new king and to verify the story with Khomeini's friend. The frail, white-bearded Haj Daddash consented to see me only because close friends of his family had arranged the visit. I patiently went along with the custom of almost an hour of tea drinking and social conversation before I turned the discussion to the social life of Qom in the early days of the twentieth century. I raised my specific question: what was the root of Khomeini's desire to become the new leader of Iran? Clerical solidarity, ambivalence about the intentions of a Western-educated Iranian professor of politics, and a host of other reasons inhibited Khomeini's childhood friend from opening his heart to me. Haj Daddash never told me his reasons for uttering the comment attributed to him, but his ambiguities notwithstanding, I gathered that the story was accurate. Fine, I thought, but one man's desire could not in itself have caused the downfall of a 2,500-year-old monarchy. There must be a more sophisticated explanation, one involving the historical development of Iranian society and culture.

I left the old man's home and wandered about the streets of Qom, retracing the path of the marches that had led to the first clash between the religious class and the monarchy, in 1963. I kept asking myself what had allowed an unknown student from the small town of Khomein to turn this city into a revolutionary hotbed, to mobilize Iranians, to help them overthrow an ancient monarchy, and to assume a position that, as a student, he could only have dreamed about. His experiences in Qom might provide the key to this mystery. This possibility was even more likely, considering that Qom became an important religious and political center only in the mid-twentieth century. During the constitutional movement (1905–1911), Qom was not among the urban centers known for any kind of political or religious activism.

Walking through the campus of the Qom seminary, I remembered the euphoria of the afternoon of February 11, 1979: the Islamic revolutionaries had seized power in the capital, and I was mingling with the crowd on the Tehran University campus. I had begun my graduate studies in the United States only a few months earlier, but I came to feel, within days of the first bloody clash between state and society in September 1978, that I had to return to Iran to observe the unfolding of the revolution for myself; I became a participant-observer on the main battlefield of the revolution, the Tehran University campus. I encountered a prominent secular intellectual there and asked him why Islam-minded Iranians had come to dominate events. He responded, "A clerical coup hijacked the revolution." His allegation of conspiracy was unconvincing, and the question remained unanswered in my mind. I returned to the United States and finished my graduate studies; I read many books on revolution as a social phenomenon, and even wrote my first book on Khomeini (Rajaee 1983), but still I found no satisfactory answer.

Now, almost a decade after the revolution, that question had taken me to Qom. I kept thinking that even if one accepted the claim of a hijacked revolution, that still left unanswered the question of how the protagonists of the Islamic movement in Iran had risen to such prominence in the first place. What explained their resilience in holding on to power in the face of constant revolutionary crises, internal strife, factional infighting, a long conventional war, and international pressures? Many insisted that the "rule of the clergy" had persisted through repression and sheer force. There is substantial truth to such an assertion. However, that explanation is not entirely satisfactory, because force alone never translates into legitimacy, and without legitimacy, no polity can survive. The answer had to be more complicated. Without a doubt, there are conspiracies and conspirators in politics, but conspiracy theory as a scientific paradigm seldom holds up under rigorous logical inquiry.

In a city where all roads lead to the holy shrine of the eighth Shi'i imam's sister, I soon found myself in the proximity of the shrine. Adjacent to the shrine stands the famous Fayziyeh seminary—one of the most prominent Shi'i seminaries built during Safavid rule (1501–1736) and the place where the confrontation between Khomeini and the shah had originally begun. I walked into the courtyard of the seminary, visited the students' quarters, and walked up to the second floor of the library. Sitting on a wooden bench and observing the activities of the turbaned students of this seventeenth-century institute of Islamic learning, I recalled my own student days at Tehran University. As I began mentally reviewing my classes, my thoughts became a bit clearer, and I realized that I should have come across a preliminary answer to my question not in Qom, but much earlier, in my very first days of undergraduate study, in 1971. In a course entitled Introduction to Politics, a French-educated Iranian professor had begun his lecture by defining the concept of the political and presenting a sophisticated spectrum of views from prominent scholars such as Raymond Aron (1905–1983), Harold Laski (1893–1950), David Easton (b. 1917), and others. In hindsight, I now recognize that he did a good job. At the time, his presentation struck me as alien and obscure. I was not able to connect with him, his views, or the insights of the people he was citing. His concentration on the notion of power and polity seemed repressive and unjust.

A young seminary student who had noticed that I did not fit into the milieu disrupted my daydreaming. Ironically, while I wished to talk about the revolution and its roots, he wanted to understand the workings of such international institutions as the United Nations. I quickly gave him a crash course on the development of international organizations, then left.

Passing through the gate of the seminary, I remembered leaving Tehran University after class and wandering around the area of campus where the bookstores are located. At one of the used bookstalls, which were quite common in the 1970s, I browsed through the books lying on the sidewalk, still considering the conceptualization of the political as it might apply to the body politic, of which I was becoming a conscious member. The owner, a short half-bald fellow with a dark mustache, approached me and asked whether I was looking for any particular book. In line with the intellectual fashion of the day, to which I had already become accustomed in my few days on the campus, I responded that I had no particular book in mind, but preferred to read the "socially committed writers." Perhaps the naiveté of a country boy was too obvious to the bookseller, so he said, "What you need is a native voice. Do not listen to those empty leftist jargons. I will sell you a good book, provided you promise me you will not look at it until you are inside your home, and also promise to forget where you got it from." Reluctantly, I agreed to his conditions. The bookseller entered his kiosk and soon emerged again with a book-shaped package, wrapped in the pages of an old newspaper, for which he asked what I thought a high price. Torn between intellectual pretense and poverty, I hesitatingly paid the money, hid the package under my jacket, and walked away without looking back. I was worried that I had been cheated and feared running afoul of the Iranian secret service (SAVAK). Partly to preserve my dignity, but mostly out of fear, I kept my promise and did not open the package until I was at home.

When I did open it, I found a book with a white cover—I later became familiar with white-covered books as a genre. I read the title page: *Gharbzadegi* by Jalal Al-e Ahmad (1923–1969). For now, suffice it to say that I had little idea that this essay would become the most widely read and influential work in twentieth-century Iran. I opened the book and read:

> I say that *Gharbzadegi* [Weststruckness] is like cholera. If this seems distasteful, I could say it's like heatstroke or frostbite. But no; it's at least as bad as saw flies in the wheat fields. Have you ever seen how they infest wheat? From within. There's a healthy skin in place, but it's only a skin, just like the shell of a cicada on a tree. In any case, we are talking about a disease. . . . This *Gharbzadegi* has two heads. One is the West, the other is ourselves who are Weststruck. (1982, 11)

Enthralled, I could not put the book down. I could relate instinctively to the author and the content of his book. I read and reread it all night. My mind was exploding; I was connecting with something that made sense to me. I thought the content of this book faithfully echoed my concerns and those of my "Third World" society. It provided answers to many of my existential questions. I remember thinking that my Western-educated professor, when introducing us to politics, had been talking about a different world, which many Iranians of my generation evidently found alien. The essay not only explained my world in terms I could relate to, but also provided me with an intellectual approach and a theoretical framework for understanding my own existence. Many of my contemporaries felt the same way about this essay. Now, of course, many years later, I feel that my response was a matter of native perception and wholeheartedly share Sheldon Wolin's insightful position that "the Third World understood itself in one way, while [Western] social science understood it in another" (Wolin 1973, 345).

Recalling my youthful experiences, I began to see the reasons for the victory of the Islam-minded Iranians in the revolution, and why the secular intellectuals, nationalists, liberals, Islamic liberals, Marxists, Sovietists, and Maoists, who had played an important role in overthrowing the shah's despotism, had had less influence on what took its place. Writers like the author of *Gharbzadegi* and their successors, the Muslim activists, were better able to communicate with Iranians, particularly the new generation, and were attuned to their concerns, anxieties, and aspirations. They spoke a shared language of complex identity and "imagined community" (Anderson 1983) with the majority. One could not make the same observation about either the secular opposition or the shah and his supporters: both were removed and disconnected from the prevailing cultural milieu. The author of *Gharbzadegi* told me a story that I could relate to, whereas my professor at Tehran University had not, and that story presented a nativist imagined community (though an idealized one) that attracted committed members who were prepared to sacrifice their lives to bring it into being. My task in answering the questions I put to myself in Qom in 1989 became clear: I had to document this discovery. Although the task has not been easy, I have found it rewarding.

It took me many long years to carry out the research for this book, including almost a decade for my thinking to "brew," before I was able to begin the actual writing. In the process, many fine minds and hearts—famous and not so famous, published and not published, acquaintances and friends, former teachers and students—have enlightened, refined, and modified my views and thinking. I am indebted to them all. Some of them have passed away; may the Almighty bless their souls. Others, whom I never had the honor of meeting, indirectly influenced my work, and I cherish their insights and teachings. To name all to whom I owe thanks is not possible.

Here, I will name only those who have contributed directly to the present work. First, I would like to focus on those who have played a very special role—my students. As a teacher, I have found my most satisfying challenges in the classroom, regardless of the country or the culture in which I have taught. I am grateful to all my students, whose questions have forced me to think as clearly as possible. Then there is a fine circle of friends, colleagues, acquaintances, listeners, and critics who cared and encouraged me to grow. Some are very close to my heart, and some deserve special respect. It is justified to list them all in alphabetical order. They are as follows: Fereydun Adamiyat, Fouad Ajami, Saeed Bahmani, Bahman Baktiari, Mehdi Bazargan, Kaveh Bayat, James Bill, Mahmud Boroujerdi, Massih Borujerdi, Tom Darby, Gholamhossien Ebrahimi Dinani, Hamid Enayat, Ali Asghar Faqihi, Ali-Reza Farahmand, Hadi Fatemi, Bahman Fouzuni, Henner Furtig, Mohammad Reza Ghanoonparver, Fatemeh Givechian, John Gurney, Saeed Hajjarian, Albert Hourani, Patrick Jones, Mohsen Kadivar, Mohammad Ali Homayun (Homa) Katouzian,[2] Nasser Katouzian, Baha'odin Khoramshahi, John Lorentz,

Mohammad Masjed-Jame'i, Mohiaddin Mesbahi, William Millward, Seyyed Hossein Moddaressi Tabataba'i, Mostafa Mohaqeq Damad, Behzad Nabavi, Mehdi Nourbakhsh, Nicholas Onuf, James Piscatori, Eugene Price, Yohaness Reissner, Reza Ra'is-Tusi, Ali Asghar Schirazi, Farshad Shariat, Alireza Sheikholeslami, John Sigler, Abdolkarim Soroush, Gholam Vatandoust, and Ibrahim Yazdi.

Finally, I would like to express my gratitude for the support of various institutions. My home institution, Carleton University, in Ottawa, generously provided research grants and time off for writing. The International Development Research Centre, also in Ottawa, provided a scholarship that allowed me to write my book on globalization, and that project helped enormously in clarifying my views on the unfolding of the modern age and the international system. Shawnee State University, in Ohio, provided me with gifts in the spring of 2001, including residence in the international house, close to the university, an office facing the woods, plenty of support, and a relatively light load of teaching, enabling me to seriously begin my writing. I will also mention the libraries that I used in various countries and locations. They include the libraries of Beheshti (National) University in Tehran, Carleton University, the United States Congress, the Mar'ashi Foundation in Qom, the Majlis of Iran, the Modern Oriental Institute in Berlin, Oxford University, Pazhuheshgah Ulum Ensani in Tehran, Shawnee State University, and Tehran University as well as the Berlin Public Library and the Ottawa Public Library.

The work of any author could not be polished and sharpened without the keen eye and the red pen of editors and copy editors. Thanks are due to Ms. Eryn Kirkwood in Ottawa, to Jeanette Herman and Wendy E. Moore at the University of Texas at Austin, and to manuscript editor Lynne Chapman, copy editor Kip Keller (especially), and their colleagues at the University of Texas Press. Finally the careful reading of the anonymous referees proved constructive and important.

I am quite aware that writing any sociohistorical account is in part a creative process. I hope that my knowledge of and respect for events, people, and sources have disciplined my imagination. Despite this consciousness and care, I am sure there are shortcomings for which I am solely responsible.

Two editorial explanations are in order. First, translations of Persian text or interviews into English are mine unless otherwise indicated. Second, Persian words are transliterated according to the system developed by Nasser Sharify in *Cataloguing of Persian Works* (Chicago: American Library Association, 1959).

ISLAMISM AND MODERNISM

INTRODUCTION

The Islamic Revolution of 1357 [1979] was indeed the victory of the project of modernity over that of modernism.

SAEED HAJJARIAN, *AZ SHAHED QODSI TA SHAHED BAZARI;
ORFI SHODAN DIN DAR SEPEHR SIYASSAT* (FROM SACRED
WITNESS TO PROFANE WITNESS: THE SECULARIZATION
OF RELIGION IN THE POLITICAL SPHERE), 1380/2001

On February 1, 1979, an Air France Boeing 747 carrying Ayatollah Ruhollah Khomeini landed at Tehran's international airport. After fifteen years of exile in Turkey, Iraq, and France, he was arriving as the leader of an ongoing revolution. From the airport he went directly to the cemetery where the martyrs of the revolution were buried, and declared: "I will appoint a government, I will crush the present government." He achieved what he claimed: in a few days the age-old Persian monarchy fell and an Islamic government replaced it. Here, the adjective Islamic refers to a particular Shi'i interpretation of politics and polity. *Shi'a* is an Arabic word meaning "party" or "faction." It originated as the name of a group of Muslims who supported the candidacy of Ali (assassinated in 661) to be head of the newly founded Islamic state after the death of the Prophet in 632. Shi'ism was a minority view before becoming the official religion of Iran in the sixteenth century and the foundation of the state after the 1979 revolution. This book captures the intellectual development among the ruling elites who fomented the revolution and have guided postrevolutionary rule.

The revolution took everyone by surprise. Very few thought the regime of the Pahlavis, the most powerful monarchy in the Third World and an "island of stability" in the region, would fall so easily and quickly.[1] It was widely believed that the long-established process of modernization, reforms, and development in Iran would never be threatened by a religious movement that might ultimately succeed in creating a seemingly archaic social and political norm. Moreover, since all segments of Iranian society, regardless of creed or ideology, participated in the upheaval, few expected that a group of hard-core Islam-minded activists would become predominant. How did the ancien régime fall? Why did the dominant political group in the new regime become victorious? A response to these questions would require two completely different books. The historical reasons for the fall of the old regime differ from those for the formation of the new regime—here, the Islamic Republic. The two stories involve diverse protagonists. The present work is interested in the origin of the Islamic Republic and its evolution. It will be concerned with the causes of the fall of the old regime insofar as they help the reader grasp the evolution of Islamic discourse more clearly.

Each of these questions can be, and has been, the subject of independent inquiries, and, indeed, many studies have focused on the reasons for the fall of the Pahlavi monarchy. Surprisingly, though, very few studies have focused systematically on the outcome of the last phase. How did the protagonists of the Islamic movement survive the second half of the revolution? There are many works dealing with the emergence of religionism and even Islamism in general, but fewer works specifically address the Iranian Islamic movement. There is, of course, some good scholarship that focuses on particular groups that participated in the revolution (for example, Abrahamian 1988, Chehabi 1990, and Siavoshi 1990), but none of it looks at the Islamist movement as a whole. Some books published in Iran have attempted to tackle this question, but they are either very descriptive or highly opinionated (for example, Davani 1360/1981 and Rouhani 1362–1364/1983–1984).

The present book is concerned with the second phase of the revolution and its general connotation, meaning, and implications. Those who took power in 1979, with Khomeini as their architect, came from a wider milieu, which had taken shape over decades, and that shape was in turn rooted in a wider intellectual terrain, one developed throughout Muslim history. This book aims also to capture that milieu; it analyzes the origin, formation, development, and fate of the Islamic movement in Iran. At the same time, the incongruity of the establishment of Qom as the most important Shi'i center in the face of the Pahlavi dynasty's radical modernism has to be explained.

Ever since the challenge of modernity disrupted the sociocultural life of the Muslim world, the people of that region have tried to present their own responses to the new challenge. The present study is mainly concerned with those responses, which are presented within a theoretical framework as well as within the historical context and heritage of Islam. The result has been a complex, paradoxical system that appears to share traditional norms, though its content and message are radical. Moreover, Islam comprises a multifaceted body of thoughts and approaches, and this heterogeneity has made some scholars, perhaps hastily, talk about "the failure of political Islam" (Roy 1994). This study portrays these various groupings and their views within the Iranian Shi'i context.

As long as Islam-minded Iranians felt that modernity was helping the people, they supported the forces of modernization, but when "modernism" swept Iran and the region, they instituted movements aimed at resisting it. This book begins with this moment of resistance and captures the various postures the movement has taken. The resistance movement against modernism (the aim of what I call the first generation) began with a quietist political stance combined with gestures of refusal, challenging modernism through what I call a revival of Islam and a refutation of modernism. Later, the extremism of the 1960s gave more confidence to concerned Islam-mined Iranians and radicalized the Muslim world. Activist Muslims of the second generation took more critical views of modernism and modernity, and claimed to present Islamic alternatives to the latter. By making an ideology out of Islam, they gave rise to the Islamic Revolution. Following the victory of the 1979 revolution and the restoration of lost confidence, many hoped that a more sober attitude toward modernity would emerge. Instead, the revolution gave rise to a radical force that turned Islam into an instrument of violence. I call this trend Islamism and radicalism, and its proponents (the third generation) have become an important force in the politics of postrevolutionary Iran. At the same time, the failure of Islamism has given rise to a serious reconstruction of Islam as a faith rather than an ideology, and the goal of the fourth generation has been to combine Islam and modernity by trying "to Islamize modernity." This book captures the views of these four generations of Muslim activists.

Two sets of broad questions guide the discussion throughout this study. First, why did the Islam-minded movement's protagonists gain power in the revolution, when both traditional (the bazaar, the *ulama* [scholars of Islam], and the old nobility) and modern (the middle class, the intelligentsia, and the masses) social forces participated in dethroning the Pahlavis? Second, what is the content of the alternative polity they proposed? Is it viable? Or is it, as labeled by some, an anachronistic restoration of the traditional Muslim polity? In responding to these

3

broad questions, I was guided by the following more specific inquiries: What was the origin of the Islam-minded movement in Iran? When did modernity turn into modernism in Iran, and how did it help give birth to the Islam-minded movement? Were the protagonists politically oriented from the very beginning of their formation? How did they organize themselves? What were their original objectives? How did they evolve into a radical revolutionary group? What was the impact of outside factors? What contributed to their politicization—internally, regionally, and internationally? How sophisticated are their views and theories on various issues pertaining to statesmanship and governance? What are their views on government, the economy, culture, society, foreign policy, and the world system? What is their modus operandi? How will the "New Information Civilization," globalization, and the "multiple worlds of postmodern thinking" of the 1990s and beyond influence their fate?

The interplay of Islam and modernity was my main concern in researching and compiling this work. While the interaction between the two has produced occasions of mutual fecundation and a constructive battle of ideas, their degeneration into isms, i.e., Islamism and modernism, has produced an almost century-long zero-sum battle between opposing worldviews, marked by recurring coups, uprisings, resurgences, and revolutions.[2] The primary reason for this battle is that behind the isms lies a feeling of stasis, a condition void of dynamism, nuance, or imagination.

Any ism denotes an ideology—not a way of approaching the world as a thinking agent, but a seeming certitude that claims to possess all the answers. An ideology is a project with a clear blueprint that requires only mechanical implementation. It provides assurance because it offers easy answers to the most difficult and fundamental questions. Approaching the world through the lens of an ideology renders redundant the human processes of constantly thinking, evaluating, facing hard choices, and balancing. The ideologies of modernism and Islamism are extreme and selective approaches to the understanding of modernity and Islam, respectively. Islamism has betrayed many of the tenets of Islam as a divine message; as a way of life; as a civilization, polity, and state; as a religion; and as a body of thought composed of a moral and ethical system. Modernism has done the same to modernity, to its political and philosophical foundations, and to liberty as its core value. In any society in which Islamism and modernism have taken root, these twin degenerations have wrenched those societies from their past and from their organic development. Modernism became the dominant paradigm in the

TABLE I.1. PHILOSOPHICAL COMPARISON OF ISLAM,
ISLAMISM, MODERNITY, AND MODERNISM

	Islam	Islamism	Modernity	Modernism
Political basis	Faith and freedom	Ideology	Responsibility and freedom	Power
Economic basis	Ingenuity	Expropriation	Ingenuity	Exploitation
Cultural basis	Reasoned obedience	Absolute obedience	Reason	Utilitarian rationality
Goal	Salvation	Homogenization	Emancipation	Gain

Muslim world during the first half of the twentieth century, and Islamism enchanted it in the second half.

It is important to note that both Islam and modernity were responses to the powerful grip of traditionalism. The prophet of Islam brought the message of rescuing individual freedom from the grip of tribalism, just as modernity was an attempt to undermine the hold of the church and the feudal system. Table I.1 canvasses the main features of the categories employed here.

Since Muslims' fate was tied to modernity, their venture in the modern world, particularly from the late nineteenth to the late twentieth century, became linear as well. Thus, at any given historical moment, the dialectical interaction of any pair of these concepts produced the predominant path or paradigm, leading to the generational unfolding of revival, revolution, Islamism, and post-Islamist restoration. Intellectually, Islamism reached its climax in the 1990s and in the disastrous events of September 11, 2001, when self-proclaimed defenders of Islam crashed passenger planes into the twin towers of the World Trade Center and the Pentagon.

I call this event the climax of Islamism because its "defenders" shocked the rest of the Muslim world and awoke Muslims to the fact that their religion had been hijacked, taken hostage, and misused for perverted objectives. Things are beginning to change today: most Muslims live within the paradigms of post-Islamism, and modernism is under attack in the West, where many view the world from postcolonial and postmodern perspectives. Post-Islamists hope to revive the basic tenets of Islam and embrace modernity. They aim for a restoration of "Muslim politics," which they define so as to reconcile the teachings of Islam with the imperatives of the modern technological world. Postmodern sensibilities seem to reject modernism's atomistic fragmentation of the human life-world and the consequent loss of social harmony and cohesion, taking instead a holistic view of human life and paying respect to all human achievements, Western and non-Western. The post-Islamist generation seems to appreciate and utilize the achievements of post-modernity to deconstruct Islamism and its ideology. Indeed, Islamism and modernism are by-products of modernity's advent as a new paradigm in human civilization production. In no part of the Muslim world has this dynamic unfolding been as vivid as in Iran, where, in 1979, a major revolution occurred with the aim of creating an Islamic state and an Islamic alternative to modernity.

ANTECEDENTS TO THE REVOLUTION OF 1979

Existing accounts of the causes of the revolution take various approaches. The most prevalent explains the revolution as a conservative, traditional, and religious response to too much modernization occurring too quickly. Others apply theories such as "social breakdown," "Davis's J-curve," "Marx's theory of revolution," "resource mobilization," and the "conjunctural causal model." For example, Foran applies them not only for analyzing the 1979 revolution but also for discussing Iran's social history from Safavid times to the postrevolutionary period (Foran 1993). He claims, however, that the conjunctural causal model is more applicable than other explanations because it takes several factors into account, most notably the "world system, modes of production, situations of dependency, the nature of state and political culture" (13).

Even here, the main assumption is that outside challenges proved too great for Iranian society to overcome. While this approach seems more comprehensive and promising than others, it requires modification in certain respects. Like most models applied by outsiders, this model imposes an external logic on the unfolding of events in Iranian history. Its positivist outlook treats a complex religious ethos as merely a socio-economic variable. More particularly, it overemphasizes the role of various modes of production; the emphasis on the arrival of a dependent capitalist mode of production misses the enormous cultural and religious underpinnings of the revolution. It seems that what has to be modified in the conjunctural causal model relates to these modes of production and to its emphasis on dependency. As one Iranian scholar, Mashayekhi, rightly points out, economic dependency came very late to

Iran, since "in the early 1960s . . . the dependency problematic was in the formative stage" (Mashayekhi 1992, 93). While all factors are given their due consideration in the current study, the central emphases will be on the fate of "Iranian civilization" and on Iran's perception of itself in its encounter with modernity and industrial civilization.

The revolution occurred because three main currents came together in the late twentieth century. First, the genuine voices of modernization in Iran, so disrupted by the Pahlavi dynasty, were revived, and sought to construct a new inclusive identity for Iranians. The revolution was a call for Iranians to return to their cultural home. Second, a politics of restoration—focused on reversing what I call the "erosion of confidence" (za' f-e esteqlal)—last voiced by Mosaddeq, was once again returning. As a result of the infiltration of Iran by outsiders, which Iranians felt had become total in the 1960s, a powerful plea for nativist restoration became the dominant paradigm in the 1970s. The third current was a shift in the international system, which tolerated and even celebrated various brands of nativism as the information and communication revolutions began turning the world into a global village. While the first and the third trends served as cause and catalyst, respectively, it was the second factor, the politics of restoration, that played the key role. The erosion of confidence was doubtless affected by all those conjunctural causes, but the subjective, mental, and ontological dislocation that forced the Iranian nation to lose an authentic perspective on its existence lay at the heart of the contention between the state and society. Indeed, if a certain degree of dependency dominated the Iranian body politic, it had less to do with economics than with what has rightly been termed "psychological dependency" (Sreberny-Mohammadi and Mohammadi 1994, 11).

The internal logic of Iranian political and social history tells us that Iranians have been haunted by their inability to produce and renew their civilization since the fall of the Safavid dynasty, in 1736. Though they created a state and some governance, and even produced some commanding leaders, such as Nader Shah, who invaded the Indian subcontinent in 1738 (and brought the Peacock Throne to Iran from Delhi), the paucity of their statesmanship and civilization was telling. This lack showed itself clearly when Russia defeated Iran in the wars of 1813–1828, which resulted in an enormous loss of territory. Most subsequent attempts to restore Iranian national pride and independence met with failure: reforms undertaken in the mid-nineteenth century ended with the poisoning of popular nationalist prime minister Mirza Taqi Khan Amir Kabir (1807–1851);

reform attempts from the 1870s through the 1890s ended with the king's assassination in 1896; the attempted reform of constitutionalism ended with fourteen years of crisis and a foreign-assisted coup in 1921; nationalist reforms ended with another foreign-assisted coup and the 1953 exile of Iran's most popular nationalist leader, Mohammad Mosaddeq (1882–1967); and the populist movement of the early 1960s ended with the crushing of movement and the exile of its leader in 1963.

These experiences of protest, rebellion, coup, and revolution attest to a state of anomie in contemporary Iranian life. The main reason for this anomie was the persistence of the notion of an erosion of confidence. No wonder revivalism, the return to indigenous values, and authenticity became persistent themes in Iran's recent past: from Amir Kabir to Khatami, nearly all notable figures in Iranian cultural and political discourse, including Seyyed Jamal Assadabadi (d. 1897), Mirza Hassan Shirazi (d. 1895), the protagonists of constitutionalism, Mohammad Mosaddeq (d. 1967), Jalal Al-Ahmad (d. 1969), Ali Shari'ati (d. 1977), Mehdi Bazargan (d. 1995), and Khomeini (d. 1989), advocated self-reliance and authenticity as the solution to the problems Iran was facing. Of course, each proposed his own particular means of authenticity.

In the early nineteenth century, Iranians first realized that their societal problems stemmed from their outdated state and its modes of economic production. To catch up with the West, a process of reeducation was necessary. Iran had to revise its understanding of life, society, polity, and selfhood. No wonder the first students dispatched abroad were called "the caravan of understanding" (karevan-e ma'refat) (Farman-farmayan 1968 and Mahbubi-Ardakani 1368/1989). Then came systematic attempts at modernizing the country; the first, initiated by Amir Kabir, resulted in the establishment of the first modern-style university in Iran. An across-the-board modernization plan introduced in the 1870s led to a modern form of governance and statecraft. Interesting to note is the fact that in all of these processes, two factors were prevalent. First, the sophisticated social classes of Iran—the religious class (ulama), the nobility (a'yan), the landowners (malekin), and the merchants (bazaar)—all participated in and contributed to the process (Rajaee 1994b). During the constitutional revolution against both arbitrary internal rule and the foreign influence exerted through concessions in the latter part of the nineteenth century, these classes composed the revolutionary coalition. Second, a complicated theoretical and intellectual debate was launched to explain the intricacies of modernity and the difficulty of adopting it to Iran's old ways (Adamiyat 1340/1961).

The road to progress and development was being paved slowly but steadily. By 1900, a group of prominent and skilled intellectuals with long-term plans for the new Iran had emerged. For example, they created civic societies whose main objective was to propagate their project of Iranian modernity. The pages of the proceedings of the first and second parliaments are filled with such debates. Then, under pressure from the chaos and disorder following the postconstitutional revolution, as well as from the impact of World War I and the inability of the young Iranian parliamentary system to cope with mounting economic, political, and social problems, the Iranian polity came to a deadlock. The interference of foreign powers, notably Britain, that were unable to tolerate disorder and chaos on the border of the newly established Soviet Union inspired a coup in 1921, which brought to power Reza Khan, a man with no roots in any of the Iranian social classes.[3] A powerful figure, he centralized governmental authority in Tehran, and the intellectuals who wanted so badly to implement their dreams of a modern Iran saw in him a protector (Dolatababdi 1336/1957, vol. 1).

What these intellectuals did not know was that Reza Khan had his own plans, and he gradually eliminated any competitors, inaugurating himself as Reza Shah Pahlavi, the founder of the Pahlavi dynasty. He hijacked the modernization process already in progress and stripped it of all its intricacies and sophistication. In place of modernization, he inaugurated a project of pseudomodernization (Katouzian 1981), or what I call modernism. Reza Shah fundamentally relied on the army, and the more he consolidated his power, the more he alienated Iran's various social classes. The Pahlavi regime associated itself with outside powers partly because neither Reza Shah nor his son, Mohammad Reza Shah, could derive his political power from any indigenous social force.

The Pahlavi dynasty created a baseless state. Faced with a problem of legitimacy during most of its precarious existence, the regime relied so heavily on foreign interests that they should be considered a component of the Iranian polity during the Pahlavi era. The British helped Reza Shah come to power, and in 1941, when it suited them, they persuaded him to leave for a death in exile and supported the inauguration of his son as the new king. Threatened by the nationalist forces led by Mohammad Mosaddeq, Mohammad Reza Shah asked outsiders for support: in 1953, a British and American coup against Mosaddeq helped restore Mohammad Reza Shah to his position of power. In the wake of the popular uprising of 1979, the American general Robert E. Huyser traveled to Tehran and convinced the shah to leave, never to return.

The Pahlavis' reliance on foreign support had exacerbated the Iranians' lack of confidence, self-identity, and self-respect. The protagonists of the Islamic movement capitalized on this loss of confidence and propagated the notion of "the return to the self," which in their view would restore Iran to its rightful national and international position. This explains the appeal and popularity of Khomeini, even for the most secular and nationalist of Iranians. Today, after almost three decades of Islamic rule and despite a great deal of social and economic hardship, the one positive point to which everyone refers is the restoration of Iranian self-confidence. Thus, while discussing this erosion of confidence as the main cause of the nation's distress, I have tried also to follow social-movement theories carefully. Although I recognize their contribution to our understanding of group behavior and collective actions, the more I investigated the cultural and civilizational aspects of Islamic and Iranian history, the more the internal logic of that part of the world manifested itself. Where common bonds led to common patterns of behavior, I have acknowledged and applied general research tools, and where unique analysis has shown itself to be necessary, I have applied that as well.

FEATURES OF THE ISLAMIC MOVEMENT

Bruce Lawrence, an American professor of religion, correctly observes that without modernity there would be no fundamentalism (Lawrence 1989, 2). While the Islamic movement in Iran is such a trend, not all movements among Muslims can be described as such. Perhaps the observation of Edmund Burke III can guide us. He focuses on two questions with regard to the revival of Islam: Are we talking about *Islamic* political movements? Or *social* movements in Islamic societies?" (Burke 1988, 18; original emphasis). This is an important distinction. The former question applies to the Islamic movement in particular, and the latter to Muslim politics more generally. In modern Muslim history, particularly since the weakening and subsequent dismemberment of the Ottoman, Safavid, and Mughal empires (Hodgson 1973, vol. 3), many devout individuals and groups have been active in the political life of their respective communities, but they were not protagonists of the Islamic movement. At the same time, since the formation of the first Muslim community in Medina in 632, politics has constituted the main part of Muslim discourse. Whatever Muslims have achieved in making sense of their creed and putting it into practice may be termed Muslim politics.

I make such a claim because none of the achievements in the long history of Islam had the adjective "Islamic" in its label. Furthermore, none of the Muslim dynasties called their polities Islamic per se, nor did any of the Muslim scholars identify their works as Islamic. Consider the case of the most famous dynasties, the Abbasids, Fatimids, Moors, Ottomans, Safavids, Mughals, and so on—all of which were named after the family or the dynasty that founded them. Or consider the most famous and authoritative works of theology and philosophy, or even the books of tradition that constitute the main sources of Islamic teaching: *Sahih, Usul al-Kafi, Kitab al-Ershad, Kitab al-Kharaj,* and so forth. This provides us with an interesting indicator. Ever since the encounter of the Muslim world with modernity, and more so in its response to modernism, the term "Islamic" has been adjectively used for everything—Islamic banking, Islamic government, Islamic education, you name it!

What does this tell us? It seems that modernism, with its exclusivist secularism, has threatened the totality of Islam and produced a reaction aimed at defending this totality. The concern is not just with being a good Muslim, which is at the heart of the practice of Islam, but more so with defending Islam itself. The Islamic movement, therefore, is a modern phenomenon whose fundamental impetus has been a defensive reaction to the perceived threat of modernism. A simple, perhaps simplistic, description of activism in the Muslim world would claim that this defensive reaction converts Muslim politics into the politics of the Islamic movement and then into its radical form, Islamism. The protagonists of the Islamic movement are those individuals or groups who feel that modernism has endangered the totality of their religion and that they should respond to this danger. Since reaction to modernity has swept through all religious traditions, the Islamic movement is not isolated, but is rather part of a universal phenomenon. Under the experience of modernity, Muslims reacted as Islam-minded agents, but in response to the ideology of modernism, they became possessive of their heritage and insisted on being Islamic. This peculiar historical interaction between the Muslim world and the modern West has made the responses acutely political, inimical, vociferous, and in some ways bloody. Thus Leonard Binder, a longtime observer of the Muslim world, correctly points out that "no other cultural region is so deeply anxious about the threat of cultural penetration and Westernization" (Binder 1988, 83). We might add that more than any other group in the region, the protagonists of the Islamic movement feel that this penetration has endangered their value systems. They are determined to uphold their religion, and they see the guarding, upholding, enhancing, and propagating of Islam as their duty.

Whereas not all Muslims feel that Islam is under siege, the protagonists of the Islamic movement do feel that way, and this explains their apparent xenophobic and conspiratorial mindset. In short, unlike most Muslims, the protagonists of the Islamic movement are persons or groups who not only are anxious about the fate of their religion, but also feel that it is under siege and are prepared to take action to remedy the situation. They think the best way to do this is to restore their religious tradition. It is possible to make the following five general observations about the movement's protagonists.

First, they feel as though Islam in its totality is in danger from the comprehensive challenge of modernity, but more seriously from the projects of modernism. The latter has infiltrated the Muslim world in various ways, but most specifically by promoting the emergence of Westernized elites who are modernizing and reforming their societies, modeling them after those in the West. The protagonists of the Islamic movement contend that modernism is encroaching on Muslims in various ways, through colonialism, neocolonialism, imperialism, and, more recently, a Western cultural onslaught. Having said this, I am not in any way suggesting that the Islamic movements owe their very existence to modernity. Other Islamic groups have arisen because of other perceived challenges to Islam: the Wahhabi movement in the Arabian Peninsula and the Sanussi movement in North Africa, for example, were organized in response to perceived threats to Islam, though they were mostly concerned with the dangers of internal irreligiosity. Indeed, one could argue that Islamic movements are recurrent phenomena, propagated by concerned Muslims who feel the tenets of their religion have been overlooked (Enayat 1980).

Second, they have turned religion more and more into an exclusively public event and a form of social protest. In such a context, religion has become a doctrine and an ideology with a clear demarcation of "us" against "them." No longer is religion a sophisticated body of rituals, mores, belief systems, ethical values, and moral codes in which an individual has a great degree of maneuverability. For the Islamic movements, religion has become a body of thought that "can be fixed with precision and finality" (Gellner 1992, 2). This is why the Islamic movements emphasize a practical commitment to their understanding of Islam as the precondition for membership in their communities and organizations.

Third, they believe that "it is possible to run a modern, or at any rate modernizing, economy, reasonably permeated by appropriated technological, educational, organization principles, and combine it with a strong, pervasive, powerfully internalized Muslim conviction *and* identification" (Gellner 1992, 22; original emphasis). That is to say, they are not against modernity; they welcome it. What they are against is a modernism that emphasizes a hegemonic narrative of modernity and what it has to offer.

Fourth, their movements are ongoing processes that will not retreat to a quietist role after responding to the challenge of modernism. It seems that all great world civilizations, whether Christian, Chinese, or Indian, have embraced secularization—except for the Muslim world, despite many genuine attempts to do so in the past few centuries, beginning with the Ottoman reforms in 1839 (Berkes 1964). Now that Islamic movements aim to modernize their societies without succumbing to secularism, all they need are organization and sophisticated efforts.

Finally, their movements have taken various forms: cultural activism, intellectual debate, etc. However, two distinct approaches are detectable at present. One, emphasizing the Islamic struggle, calls for resistance, uprising, and revolution; the other calls for reform from below, i.e., educational, social, and cultural reforms. In the past, the religious attitudes of the movements' protagonists have gone through several paradigm shifts, marked by revival, revolution, violence, and restoration.

Who are the protagonists of the Islamic movement? Contrary to the stereotype, they are not frustrated lower-class persons who are simply reacting to a marginal fate. No doubt many of the persons doing the dirty work of the movement have emerged from the marginal strata of society; however, most are sophisticated people committed to revivalism and the making of the Islamic state. I think one can justifiably characterize the majority in the following three ways.

First, they are both secular and puritan. A Muslim activist is neither completely secular, mainly preoccupied with mundane affairs, nor puritanical and obsessed only with the hereafter. He or she is against extreme piety as well as extreme secularity. For him or her, religion is a public event. Since juridical approaches to understanding religious doctrine are more amenable to the "precision and finality" (Gellner 1992, 2) associated with public displays of faith, modern Muslim activists are adamant advocates of a juridical approach to understanding Islam. Hence, the centrality of Islamic-revealed law, *shari'a,* which comprises two main parts: prayer (*'ebada,* regulating man's relation to God for eternal salvation), and transaction (*mo'amela,* regulating man's relations with his fellow man so that worldly transactions, smoothly conducted, will pave the way for eternal salvation). Both are devotional acts, whether one recites the word of God or concludes a business transaction. Here lies the root of the inseparability of religion and politics in Islam. An average Muslim, therefore, by the sheer dictates of his faith, must be both secular—that is, concerned with the profane and serious about worldly affairs—and religious—that is, pious and free from worldly attachment—while remaining aware that "the world is the cultivating ground for the hereafter" (*ad-Donya Mazr'a al-Akhera*). In other words, the average Muslim should be a saint in addition to whatever else he does: a saint-merchant, a saint-soldier, a saint-politician, a saint-doctor, a saint-professor, and so on, combining the idealism of what ought to be with the realism of what actually is.

An important cautionary note is in order. The present Islamic movement should thus be seen as different from the whole sophisticated civilizational milieu and process that Islam has produced. The juridical interpretation of Islam constitutes only one approach to understanding that revealed message. Other trends, such as philosophical, theosophical, mystical, and Gnostic approaches, have provided different outlooks on Islam, and these in many ways contradict the picture presented by contemporary Islamism. For the moment, however, it is the juridical interpretation that has captured the ears and the minds of the masses throughout the Muslim world.

Second, the protagonists of the Islamic movement are modern and even postmodern but not Western. In 1987, when *Time* magazine first named Mikhail Gorbachev, the last leader of the Soviet Union, its "Man of the Year" (he was honored so again in 1989), he was described as a modern but not a Western man. The same can be said about the members of the Islamic movement today.

The early reformers or religionists of the Muslim world either opposed modernity as being contradictory to Islam or else considered Westernization and modernization a process borrowed from the Muslim world. But the Muslim activists at the beginning of the twentieth century took an accommodating position toward the Westernization project advocated by the emerging middle class. They accepted the introduction of the new ways as a lesser evil that would help Muslims fight greater evils (*daf'-e afsad be fassed*), such as tyranny and backwardness. Since the 1960s, however, a new group of Muslim activists has replaced the

14

secular middle class as the main force of modernization. Modernity is a necessity of the present age, the voices of the Islamic movement concluded. Many of them became strong believers in the concept of revolution, despite its being, in essence, the product of a modern worldview. For the ancients, revolution referred to the rotation of the moon and the earth, not to the volitional transformation of the social order. For this kind of transformation to be accepted, there had to be a radical change in the perception of what it means to be human. Life had to become temporal and secular and not subject to a natural order. Revolutionary ideas meant transgressing the accepted order and cosmology. And the notion of revolution was embedded in a larger system of temporal science, instrumental rationality, empirical studies, and critical reason. Contemporary Islam-minded people accept all this, and it is no wonder that most of the protagonists of the Islamic movements began their education and professions in fields other than Islamic studies. Table I.2 shows the educational affiliation of the major modern Islamist leaders.

So far as the influence of a postmodern sensibility is concerned, the case of the fourth generation of the Islamic movement is even more telling. Here the example of Abdolkarim Soroush, a contemporary Iranian reformist, and his followers is very important. His emphasis on the distinction between religion and man's understanding of it resonates with the importance of narratives in postmodern discourse. He acknowledges the existence of a pertinent religious essence but argues that any representation of this essence is simply a narrative, and thus cannot be considered the truth or, therefore, sacred. Also, the prominence of the works of people such as Michel Foucault and Jacques Derrida among contemporary Muslims cannot be overlooked.

Finally, the protagonists of the Islamic movement follow Islamic tradition but are not traditionalists. With the exception of the Islamists—that is, the third generation—members of the Islamic movement emphasize the tenets of Islam but have little tolerance for their traditional interpretation. As the previous table shows, most of the leaders were educated in modern science, and even those who focused on Islamic studies either were self-taught or attended modern universities that offer Islamic studies. For example, neither father of the two prominent modern Muslim radicals, Qutb and Mawdudi, permitted his son to attend traditional religious schools; even Khomeini concentrated on philosophy and mysticism in his studies, not jurisprudence.

The cases of Mawdudi and Khomeini are very interesting because both of them were accepted by the traditional clerical class, yet both

TABLE I.2. EDUCATIONAL BACKGROUNDS OF
THE PROTAGONISTS OF THE ISLAMIC MOVEMENT

Name	Education	Place of Study	Movement
Abdolrahman, Umar	Islamic studies	Egypt	Egypt's Islamism
Bazargan, Mehdi	Thermodynamics	France	Freedom Front (Iran)
Dahshani, Abdolqader	Petrochemical engineering	France	Islamic Salvation Front (Algeria)
Al-Ghanushi, Rachid	Liberal arts	Syria, France	Renaissance Party (Tunisia)
Khomeini, Ruhollah	Jurisprudence, philosophy	Iran	Islamic Revolution (Iran)
Madani, Abbas	Education	France	Islamic Salvation Front (Algeria)
Mawdudi, Abo A'ala	Journalism	India	Jama'at al-Islami (Pakistan)
Qutb, Sayyed	Literature	Egypt, United States	Ikhwan al-Muslimin (Egypt)
Shari'ati, Ali	Sociology	France	Iran's Islamic movement
Soroush, Abdolkarim	Pharmacology, philosophy of science	Iran, England	Iran's Islamic movement
Turabi, Hassan	Law	London, Paris	Sudan's Islamism
Yasin, 'Abd al-Salam	Education	Morocco	Justice and Charity (Morocco)
Yassin, Ahmad	Islamic studies	Egypt	Hamas (Palestinian territories)

Source: Compiled by the author.

opposed the predominance of the traditional approach among the established clergies. Moreover, many of the key voices in the Islamic movement belong to engineers and doctors, most of whom were educated in modern universities, either in the Islamic world or abroad. Even the turbaned clergymen take pride in having obtained an advanced degree from a foreign university. It may seem ironic, but the majority of the Iranians pursuing Islamic studies at McGill University are turbaned mullahs from Qom, even if they do not wear the turban in public—a practice, incidentally, in accordance with the principle of *taqiyyah* (expedient dissimulation). The great intellectual protagonists of contemporary Islamism—Mawdudi, Qutb, and Shari'ati—had enormous contempt for the traditional centers of Islamic teachings.

To sum up: The grave enemy of the contemporary Islamic movement is modernism, i.e., a particular Western narrative of modernity. The hegemonic narrative of modernism disrupted the cultural homogeneity of the Muslim world and afflicted the minds of the people with "Weststruckness"—modern *jahiliya* (ignorance), or "Westamination"—a notion that lies at the heart of the proposed Islamic modern imagined community. Although conservatism, or traditionalism—the rigid interpretation of Islamic tenets—has, in the name of protecting authenticity, blocked the path to any genuine modernization, some parts of the Islamist movement have nonetheless welcomed modern influences.

GENERATIONAL VIEWS AND A POSSIBLE STARTING POINT

Islam-minded Iranians had been active in politics and society since the Safavids made Shi'ism the country's official religion, in the sixteenth century. In the late nineteenth century, when Iran modernized and a secular version of nationality became dominant, these Islam-minded Iranians adopted a strategy of compromise because they claimed that the new, modern ways would help the people. Indeed, they remained actively supportive as long as modernization followed its promise of emancipation, but when modernism began to emerge, they felt threatened and took the successive postures of revival, revolution, radicalism, and restoration that I have described. The protagonists of each posture belong to a generation.

The first generation that shaped Iran's Islamic movement appeared when a strong wave of modernism overtook Iran. Its members felt they had to quietly defend Islam against this onslaught. They avoided politics and worked to consolidate the position of the clerics in the face of what seemed to be a threat to their very existence, and they even tacitly acquiesced in what was going on in the country. They tried to revive their religion and modernize their faith by creating modern institutions. In the process, they introduced a paradigm shift, turning Islam into a sociocultural project.

The second generation of the Islamic movement reacted against Americanization in the 1960s and 1970s and advocated a complete end to

Westernization. Its members relied on the ideologization of Islam. Intellectually, the second generation questioned modernity and reevaluated both it and their faith. They thought they could achieve this through the politics of revolution. The victory of the 1979 revolution inaugurated a new phase, during which one might have expected a moderation of the Islamic movement. Indeed, in December 1982, Khomeini declared the end of the revolution.

Little did he know that revolutions unfold in their own peculiar patterns. It appears that in the postrevolutionary era, two trends manifested side by side. The first, riding the crests of the postrevolutionary tide—the hostage crisis (1979–1981) and the Iran-Iraq War (1980–1988)—gave birth to a generation that further politicized Islam by turning it into an instrument of power and exclusion. Political purges, executions, and radicalism gained currency, and thus was born a third generation, whose views and positions I describe as Islamist and extremist. This generation believed that the sacred ideals of the past had to be re-created in the present, that tradition had to be safeguarded against the modern condition, and that modernity, once eradicated, had to be replaced by Islamism.

The second trend was a moderate approach that sought to quench this revolutionary zeal. Indeed, the failure of Islamism, the consequences of globalization, and the maturation of the children of the revolution brought about the fourth generation, which has invited a rethinking of both Islam and modernity. Its members aim for localization of the global and globalization of the local. They want to restore to Islam its focus on the individual, part of the essence of the original revelation.

Each chapter of this book deals with one of these trends. While the historical unfolding of events provided an occasion for each generation to emerge, the interaction between the challenge of modernity and the response of the Islamic movement provided the substance of each generation's views.

The revivalists remain loyal to Islam, but their understanding of modernity is instrumental; the revolutionaries accept modernity's invitation to institute a secular polity through revolution, but they use Islam as an instrument of activism and revolt. The Islamists have complete faith in instrumental rationality insofar as they make both Islam and modernity instruments of power. The advocates of restoration take Islam and modernity to be two distinct value systems that require special reverence and careful consideration. Figure I.1 captures the four conditions that result from the interactions among modernity, Islam, modernism, and Islamism, the latter pair considered degenerations of the first.

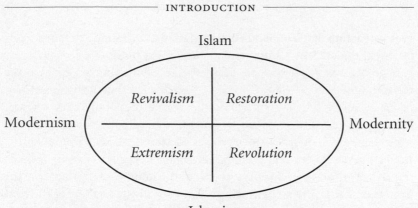

FIGURE I.1. Interactions between Islam and the modern sensibility

When did the Islamic movement begin? Since it is a by-product of Iran's encounter with modernity, it is as old as the process of modernization in Iran. But in fact, it truly began when Islam-minded Iranians became concerned about the pitfalls and negative consequences of modernity. It was then that Islam-minded Iranians became more than conscious of the danger of foreign powers—became paranoid, in fact—and took a defensive posture against modernity's negative impact. Iranian encounters with the modern West date back to the time of the Safavids (1501–1736). Such an encounter, however, was an interaction between powers that were equal, or at least perceived to be equal. Iranians had enormous self-confidence about their culture and mores. The post-Safavid encounters with the West, however, proved to be of a different kind: interactions between a decaying civilization and a dynamic and blossoming culture. Nowhere was this more apparent than in the long war between Iran and Russia in 1805–1828, ending with a disastrous defeat that made Iranians realize that they had to adopt modern ways.

One possible date for the beginning of the Islamic movement, as suggested by an Iranian historian, falls precisely within this period (Davani 1360/1981). Apparently, some contemporary religious leaders expressed concern for the war and even issued a legal ruling (*fatwa*) against Russia. For example, Davani refers to the fatwa of Muhammad Mojahid against the Russians during that war as the beginning of the Islamic movement in Iran. However, this was not the first time a member of the ulama had opposed foreign infiltration. Moreover, Mojahid's effort did not translate into a general and comprehensive movement. Iranian scholar and historian Homa Nateq suggests that Mojahid's fatwa was not even religiously motivated; rather, it had been orchestrated by the shah to attract the support of the people for his unpopular war (Nateq 1368/1990, 34–35).

Another suggested starting point of the Islamic movement was the tobacco crisis in 1890–1891. The story began when the Qajar king, Nasir al-Din Shah (assassinated in 1896), granted a monopoly over the sale and export of tobacco to the British Imperial Tobacco Company for fifty years. The monopoly came to an end after a fatwa attributed to the then highest religious leader of Shi'ism, Hassan Shirazi (d. 1895), forbade the use of tobacco, declaring it to be tantamount to a war against the Vanished Imam. The government had to back down and repeal the concession. While this is one of the most-cited episodes in the fight of Shi'i ulama against local tyranny and European encroachment, it should not be seen as the beginning of the Islamic movement in Iran. Some historians have suggested that this was in fact a clear uprising against a foreign company by the merchant class, using the power and influence of the ulama to further their cause (Adamiyat 1360/1981).

Neither of these dates is very convincing. A more critical moment came when Iranians began to formulate an alternative view to modernity; it was then that Islam-minded Iranians had to explain or justify the position of Islam. I contend that these attempts began with the assassination of the shah in 1896, which marked a clear break with the past; the bullet that penetrated the king's body also shook the cosmological view that had been held by Iranians for centuries. In the aftermath of this event, the Constitutional Movement began constructing a framework for a new polity. All segments of society participated.

Many scholars contend that both events, the assassination and the tobacco protest, were partly instigated by Seyyed Jamal Assadabadi, better known as al-Afghani, who launched a campaign of awareness about the backwardness of Islamic societies. Since Islam-minded Iranians initiated the process of reform in the wake of the assassination, this occurrence should be taken as the beginning of the movement. In practice, however, what al-Afghani was inviting Iranians to do was take active part in their own political life, using Islam as a cultural umbrella. This invitation was congruent with Muslim politics from previous centuries. The advent of the Pahlavi family, as I will show in the next chapter, marked a new phase in Iranian history. Modernity changed to modernism, and Iran was meant to become like the West, rather than grasping modernity on its own terms and localizing it. This transition created a powerful schism that was never repaired. The Pahlavis introduced a battle of worldviews that forced Islam-minded Iranians to begin thinking of isolating themselves from the modernizing process, and later presenting alternative frames of thought and plans of action. Thus, the story of this book begins with the 1921 coup that brought the Pahlavis to power and changed the face of Iran.

APPROACH, ORGANIZATION, AND SOURCES

In this study, I have taken a civilizational approach in which modernity represents the predominant framework of contemporary industrial civilization. When I observe Iran's response to modernity, I also consider the civilizational framework that underlies Iran as a polity. Because of my training in international affairs, I used to take the modern state as my unit of analysis, but there are two difficulties with such an approach. The first is that modernity is about much more than just the modern state; it is also about economics, culture, and imagination. Second, the voices expressing the concerns of the state in Iran did not represent the views of the wider Iranian cultural and the civilizational milieu, whose participants responded to challenges of the sophisticated modernity-based civilization of the West in their own terms. It seems that Iranians understood the potential of the new civilization for both hegemony and emancipation. Iranians associated first France and later America with emancipation, and later they associated first Britain and subsequently America, when the latter became "the Inheritor of Colonialism" (Bahar 1344/1965), with the notion of hegemony. From the nineteenth-century Iranian minister Amir Kabir to the most popular nationalist leader, Mosaddeq, America was seen as a faraway party to be used against imperial Britain or Russia.

A few words are in order about the title, organization, and methodology used in this book. The title captures the dialectical interaction between two parallel trends. One trend is the transformation of European modernity into modernism and the emergence of self-criticizing postmodernity. I make the claim that the modern sensibility, with an emphasis on the free and autonomous self, degenerated into modernism, an ideology of political power and economic gain. The second trend is the transformation of Islam into the Islamic movement and Islamism, and now the emergence of a self-criticizing post-Islamism. I hope this book captures how the unfolding of these trends and their interactions have manifested in recent Iranian history.

The main chapters of the present work are devoted to the generations through which the Islamic movement has interacted with modernism in

Iran. Chapter One shows how and why the first generation of the Islamic movement established a stronghold in the city of Qom and became culturally active while remaining politically quiet. The chapter canvasses the time, life, and views of those who followed the politics of revival. Its followers were dismayed with politics but were active in defending their faith culturally. Chapter Two elaborates on the reasons for the politicization of the movement and the emergence of the second generation, which claimed to present an alternative program to the existing Westernizing regime. This generation was successful in bringing about the destruction of the ancient regime in Iran and the formation of an Islamic Republic. However, its success notwithstanding, the generation reduced Islam to an ideology of revolution for the sake of power, and thus, through its politicization of Iranian society, paved the way for the politics of extremism and radicalism of the third generation, which propagated Islamism with a vengeance. Chapter Three concentrates on the logic behind the use of Islam as a means of violence, radicalism, and revolution. In 1989, Khomeini died in full power, leaving millions of Iranians to mourn for days. His departure coincided with the revision of the 1979 constitution, and for the story of the Islamic movement, the book could end here.

Yet life goes on, and an age of globalization and a world of one civilization and many cultures have set in. Postmodernity and the politics of identity have opened new chapters in many parts of the world, including the Muslim world. There are clear signs that the new generation of Islam-minded Iranians that has emerged is challenging Islamism and is interested in a new form of religiosity. It hopes to combine Islam and modernity. Thus, Chapter Four deals with this latest generation of Muslims, who, first and foremost, have restored their own confidence and feel that they can shape and decide their own fate. Unlike the Islamist religionists, they do not see the world as an us-them dichotomy, and unlike their revolutionary brothers, they do not see life as a constant struggle along a friend-enemy divide. They speak the language of dialogue and inclusion. Their main questions aim at how to survive in a world of complicated and contending ideologies while preserving their complex Iranian-Islamic identity. In the concluding chapter, I argue that Iranian politics has become a competition between the third and fourth generations. While the politics of Iran was dominated by the fourth generation from 1997 to 2005, for example, the election of the new president in Iran in 2005 brought members of the third generation to the center of power. The conclusion captures a general evaluation of the Islamic movement, the meaning of the oscillation in Iranian politics, and makes some generalizations regarding the future of the movement in Iran and the world over.

As to my method for presenting my findings, each chapter has two main sections: one section discusses the context and the other focuses on the voices, whether those of individuals or groups. Some criticisms could be offered against such a division. First, it may appear historicist, suggesting that the context has determined the content and the shape of the voices. I am aware of the danger of crude materialism, and this is not my intention here. However, I hold that the context presents and suggests the challenges and the questions to which conscious members of society feel the need to respond. Thus, a discussion of the context helps identify the chief areas of concern and the irritated souls who responded to them, although I will be as brief as possible. Second, concentrating on certain individuals, institutions, or publications may not reflect the spirit of the time, but, rather, may amount to an artificial construction on my part. For example, it is a fact that the now dominant notion of "the Guardian-ship of the Jurisconsult" (*velayat-e faqih*) does not represent the whole of Shi'i political thought. And as rightly pointed out by the late professor Hamid Enayat, "the idea of the guardianship of the *jurisconsult* belongs to the realm of what the jurists themselves term disputation (*ekhtelaf*) and independent reasoning (*ijtihad*)" (correspondence with the author, 1982). In other words, to treat Khomeini's idea as the dominant paradigm may reduce the sophisticated political thought of Shi'ism to the issue of power and authority only. Also, concentrating on certain individuals and publications, in the words of the late Albert Hourani, "may be too rigid" (correspondence with the author, 1991). Yet, like all researchers, I had to isolate certain events or certain people and their works in order to illustrate the challenges and responses issued by modernity, Islam, and Iran, as observed and responded to by Islam-minded Iranians. I main-tain, however, that the voices discussed here represent the dominant or epoch-making trends in their times.

What the reader may find wanting about all four generations is how preoccupied they are with the "big ideas" of eradicating despotism, im-perialism, and the dialogue of civilizations. Iranian society has been concerned with the issue of justice, i.e., "the house of justice" (*edalat-khaneh*), as it was embodied in the demands of the protagonists of the 1905 constitutional revolution. This concept of justice entailed gender, religious, ethnic, educational, economic, and political equality. Its pro-ponents hoped for a civilizational milieu in which linguistic, religious, ethnic, and cultural diversities were recognized and respected. Iranian women, furthermore, have been speaking out for political participation and equal status in new and revolutionary Iran. Yet Islam-centered discourse lacks any plans or measures to deal with these demands. If there are some, as in the works of Motahhari and Soroush, they are in reaction to existing measures by the powers that be. For example, Motahhari's work on women's issues was produced in response to the discussions in the pages of the popular magazine *Zan-e Ruz* (*Today's Women*) in the sixties, rather than as a serious treatment of gender issues in Iran. Indeed, one could make the same observation about Islamic movements throughout the world. Only the new, postmodern generation of Muslims in the diaspora unapologetically deal with what they have called a "gender, justice, democracy and pluralism deficit" (Safi 2003).

The irony is that in today's Iran women have become a significant voice. How is this explained? One deliberate policy of the Islamic Republic, namely that of sex segregation, has had an indirect effect. Since women and men are supposed to be physically separated, an almost parallel set of structures has evolved. If women cannot be secretaries or if women nurses cannot minister to strange men, one has to encourage members of both sexes to become professionals in order to serve the demands of the growing population. Thus, in every conceivable profession, opportunities are provided for both sexes, leading to an indirect and unanticipated empowerment of women. This indirect effect of an Islam-centered policy is fascinating, but lies beyond the scope of this work.

A few words about sources are in order. To construct my narrative, I have relied on various sources. To understand the evolution of modernity, I looked first to the modernity-postmodernity debate. Fate brought me to Carleton University, in Canada, and as part of my responsibilities in the College of the Humanities, I found myself teaching Samir Amin, Hannah Arendt, Simone de Beauvoir, Jacques Ellul, Michel Foucault, Marshall McLuhan, Karl Polanyi, Edward W. Said, and Charles Taylor. At the same time, I was doing a research project for the International Development Centre in Ottawa, which resulted in my book *Globalization on Trial*. Together, these experiences helped me understand clearly the metamorphoses of modernity.

Regarding sources on the Islamic movement in Iran, I conducted research in the Iranian research and archival institutions created after the 1979 revolution; a large body of documents dealing with the Pahlavi era is preserved there. During my ten years of research and teaching in Iran, 1986–1996, I also interviewed many of the protagonists of the Islamic movement and tried to both participate in and observe events there.

24

To conduct further research, I traveled to Iran in 1998, 2000, 2001, 2004, and 2006 for short-term research and the procurement of sources. These sources are discussed here. (Note: In text citations to sources in Persian, dates are given in AH/AD [*anno Hegirae/anno Domini*] form.)

First, I drew on the resources of the Institute of Cultural Research and Inquiry, or *Mo'assesseye Tahqiqat va Pazhuheshhaye Farhangi,* which holds confiscated private documents, books, and papers of more than one thousand families of the Pahlavi elite, including those of the royal court. The diaries, files, and records of many officials are accessible to researchers. I also made use of other institutions, such as the National Archive, or *Sazemane Asnad-e Meli,* where most official records are preserved. Among these, for example, are the trial proceedings related to the assassination of the prominent intellectual and historian Ahmad Kasravi (1890–1946); these records reveal a great deal about the sociopolitical climate and factional politics in Iran in the aftermath of World War II.

The second body of material comprised long interviews and conversations I had with many people who were either active in the Islamic movements or had known the people at the center of this story. I will mention a few as examples. First, the late Mehdi Bazargan (1907–1995)—the first prime minister of revolutionary Iran and, more importantly, one of the main protagonists of the movement for over half a century—patiently talked with me for almost a decade, from 1986 to his death in 1995, about his career and those of his colleagues. Second, the late Murteza Passandideh, Khomeini's older brother, shared with me many eventful stories of the life of his brother and his involvement in the Islamic movement. Third, Abdolkarim Soroush, the prominent theorist and activist, spoke with me regularly in his office at the Iranian Academy of Philosophy. Finally, Ayatollah Hossein-Ali Montazeri, Hojjatoleslam Mohsen Kadivar, and Saeed Hajjarian generously also gave me their time.

The Iranian custom of *bar-e 'am,* or open house, provided me with another source of information and insights. Throughout the history of Iran, and perhaps that of the Middle East as a whole, men and women of stature, including the monarch and the economic, cultural, and political elites, hold open houses for a few hours every week and welcome anyone who cares to attend. During these social gatherings, there is open discussion on matters related to politics, society, history, and civilization. To name just a few, I attended regularly the *bar-e 'am* of Ostad Mohammad Mohit Tabataba'i, Ayatollah Mohammad Reza Sadr, Ali Akbar Sa'idi Sirjani, Mohammad Javad Mashkur, and Mohammadali

Eslami Nadushan. Recently, some educational and cultural establishments have held institutional open houses, and I attended those of the *Da'rotma'arefe Tashiyu'* (Shi'i Encyclopedia), the *Bonyad-e Tarikhe Iran* (the Foundation for Iranian History), and the *Entesharat-e Farzan* (Farzan Publishing House). I encountered many members of the intelligentsia at these gatherings.

Yet another source of information was the journals, books, and occasional papers published by the various members of the Islamic movement. As examples, I mention *Homayun* and *Maktab-e Islam,* the journals of the Qom religious establishment; *Maktab-e Mobarez* and *Payam Mojahed,* published by the movement abroad; and *Asr-e Ma* and *Mahsreq,* the organs of active political groups. Further, I drew upon the enormous body of research and the voluminous publications on Shi'ism, Iran, and the revolution by both Iranian and non-Iranian scholars and researchers. These studies have been growing rapidly since the Islamic revolution.

ONE

THE FIRST GENERATION

The Politics of Revival, 1920s–1960s

*[We have to] unconditionally accept and promote European
civilization and absolute submission to Europe. . . . Iran has to become
Europeanized in appearance, essence, physical features and spiritual
aspects. There is no other way.*

SEYYED HASSAN TAQIZADEH, EARLY 1900S (QUOTED IN YAHYA
ARYANPOUR, *AZ SABA TA NIMA; TARIKH-E SADOPANJAH SAL
ADAB-E FARSI* [FROM SABA TO NIMA: A HUNDRED YEARS
OF PERSIAN LITERATURE], 1350/1971)

The year 1921 was a decisive one for the Iranian polity. In February, an officer of a Cossack brigade, Reza Khan Mir-Panj, spearheaded a military coup and changed the face of politics in Iran. In March, a clergyman, Sheikh Abdolkarim Ha'eri Yazdi (d. 1937), moved to Qom and changed the religious life of Shi'ism. The first event became instrumental in turning the traditional state into a socially "baseless" state; that is, an attempt was made to Westernize Iran by introducing many modernist reforms into its political, educational, and cultural institutions. The second was instrumental in turning the city of Qom and its seminary into the strongest Shi'i center of schooling and inadvertently into a hotbed of religious revival, revolution, and political activism.

When reforms for developing Iran began in the late nineteenth century, all segments of Iranian society took part in the process. Even the Islam-minded religious class played a significant role in generating public support for the reforms. But as the reforms took on a secularist and modernist tone, the coalition fragmented and each group took its own path. As poetically stated by one observer, an "attempt to brew wine resulted in vinegar" (Faqihi 1995, interview). In other words, the radical changing of the Iranian polity was unbearable for the indigenous segments of the society. State and society parted ways, and in response, the first generation of Islam-centered Iranians took a revivalist approach to their faith. How did this story unfold? What was the response of Islam-minded Iranians?

CONTEXT

Reza Khan's 1921 coup brought the military to the center of politics in Iran, where it stayed until 1979. The new government imposed martial law and arrested most of the existing political elite, but "assured the shah that the coup d'etat was designed to save the monarchy from the revolution" (Abrahamian 1982a, 118). It promised order, stability, and governance to a country that had been haunted by chaos and crisis since the monarchy had been replaced with a constitutional government in 1906. The fifteen years leading to the coup had been so deleterious to many Iranians that they were ready for some degree of order and stability at any price. The biggest price was suppression of the new parliamentary monarchy, which was soon replaced by the military state of Reza Shah, who succeeded in deposing the Qajar dynasty in 1925. Forces of genuine modernity, as opposed to modernism, gained a respite with the outbreak of World War II, when a young and less despotic king assumed power along with Prime Minister Mohammad Mosaddeq. The latter was overtaken, however, by a new version of modernism, this time an American one that encouraged the police state of Mohammad Reza Shah, which lasted until 1979.

The Internal Context: From Modernity to Modernism

The main feature of the Pahlavi (the surname Reza Khan adopted) state, during the rule of both father and son, was that it was baseless. While Iran's initial modernization process had included all segments and social classes, Reza Shah based his power on the army and the support of the outside forces—specifically, Great Britain. His son, Mohammad Reza Shah, relied on the police and the support of an outside force, this time the United States. In the interim early years of Mohammad Reza Shah's rule, between 1941 and 1953, the forces of modernization made some headway, but ultimately failed because of foreign involvement. In a way, one could claim that both father and son disrupted the modernization process of Iran. An analysis of each is in order.

REZA SHAH AND THE FIRST DISRUPTION OF IRANIAN MODERNIZATION

The 1905 constitutionalists put forward a modernization project that was good for the country, but the ruling elites were unable to implement broad reforms. Still, from the return of constitutionalism in 1911 until the 1921 coup, the program presented to the parliament represented genuine modernization within a parliamentary democracy. For example, the following is a list of the policies the prime minister presented to the parliament in 1914: "(1) the abolition of the old feudalistic system of pensions; (2) the speedy completion of the new codes of law; (3) the foundation of a secular law school to train personnel for the Ministry of Justice; (4) the establishment of several schools for girls; (5) the expansion of telegraph lines; and (6) new laws governing telegraphic communications" (cited in Banani 1961, 34). These were all attempts to modernize Iran. Opposition from traditionalist forces, external pressures, and the coming of World War I, however, created enormous impediments to the implementation of these reforms.

In the face of chaos, many people assumed that the emergence of a strong leader could save the nation. Iranian modernizers realized that their constitutional system had resulted in a deadlock. For the forces of both modernity and modernism, some form of coup seemed to present itself as the only alternative to chaos. Note the comment of one protagonist of the time, Mohammad Taqi Bahar, journalist, politician, nationalist poet, and historian, concerning how those who supported general reforms and were against the 1919 British-Iran treaty welcomed some decisive move (Bahar 1323/1944, 50–58). Indeed, he reports that many, including Seyyed Hassan Moddaress (a prominent clergyman of the time), were contemplating a coup (61–64). But the forces of modernization did not foresee that soon they would be supplanted by a new group, which would replace the Iranian project of modernity with one of modernism, or Westernization. This replacement came by way of the 1921 coup, headed by a relatively unknown officer named Reza Khan.

His supporters depicted Reza Khan as a savior. For example, Yahya Dolatabadi, a staunch proponent of Westernization, captured the mood of modernism's supporters: "Iran of yesterday had one step to destruction, and now the Iran of today has one step to happiness. Only one person, Reza Shah, can take that step" (Dolatabadi 1309/1930, 164). The British officers, who supported the forces of modernism in Iran and felt that Iran needed a "strong man," selected him. Iranian historian Cyrus

Ghani wrote: "The weight of reliable evidence indicates that Reza Khan had been hand-picked by an adventurous British General" (Ghani 2000, 165). The coup had to be completed by the spring of 1921 because Britain had decided to withdraw its forces from Iran by then. The British knew that Seyyed Zia al Din Tabataba'i (1888–1969), a journalist and political operator who was anxious to cooperate with the British, was not strong enough to suit their officers on the ground. Tabataba'i became the front man for the coup, while Edmund Ironside (1880–1959) picked Reza Khan and worked to implement the withdrawal of the British forces from Iran "with minimum difficulty and casualties" (Ghani 2000, 107).

Ironside kept a diary that his son later published. Before the coup, he wrote that Iran "needed a strong man to bring her through." He added the following rhetorical question: "When would the strong man come to rule Persia?" (quoted in Ghani 2000, 148). After he was introduced to Reza Khan sometime in January 1921, he concluded that he had found such a man, since in his estimation Reza Khan was a "strong and fearless man" (154). Thanks to Reza Khan's tact, he gave the impression, after coming to power, of continuing the Iranian modernizers' reforms of the previous decades and even of the previous century. For example, on the day of Reza Khan's coronation, he pledged the following: "I will pay special attention to preserving the principle of religion, because it is one of main sources of national integrity. . . . Second, I will do my best for progress of the country" (quoted in *Bist-o-Hasht Hezar Ruz Tarikh-e Iran* 1309/1930, 81). Soon, things began to change radically.

The changes among the elite and the administration proved to be broader than anticipated. The new power supported Westernization and modernism, not modernization, emphasizing power rather than emancipation and freedom. This process began with the manner in which Reza Khan declared his presence in Iranian public life. His very first proclamation after the coup began with the phrase "I order" (*hokm mikonam;* Bahar 1357/1978, 86). What is significant about this is that hitherto not even the most authoritarian kings in the history of Persia had pontificated as such; humility had been the name of the game.

The ancient kings of Persia thought they owed their position of power to the grace of God (*Farah-e Eizadi*), and later, when Islam became the dominant paradigm, they claimed their authority was founded on acting as God's shadow (*Zell al-Allah*) on earth. They mostly described themselves as "the agent" of the higher authority. Hitherto, the pronoun "I" played a small role in the intellectual and political vocabulary of Iran, and this form of assertive individualism was alien to the culture.[1]

Moreover, Reza Khan's measures for exercising and preserving power alienated many people. He declared martial law; forbade all media, associations, and groupings; and threatened severe punishment for anyone who violated his rules.

At the beginning, many thought these were temporary measures used to restore order, but soon the changes took a more permanent form. When Reza Shah finally succeeded in securing the throne for himself, cleric and political activist Seyyed Hassan Moddaress said the following about the change of dynasty: "If the purpose of this change had been only to remove the [Qajar] king and replace him with another one, I would have had no objection to it. It was proved to me that the aim was a radical regime change affecting all sociopolitical spheres, which for better or worse, constituted [a change in] our national identity" (quoted in Maki 1357/1978, 3:313). I might add that this new "national identity" was exclusive and unbalanced.

Reza Shah's longtime figurehead, Prime Minister Mehdiqoli Khan Hedayat, expressed a similar view. Pointing out the abnormality of the new regime's policies, he commented sarcastically that what was done behind the scenes before the coup of 1921 was revealed when "the corner of the curtain was exposed" (Hedayat 1346/1967, 407). He added this important observation: "At the height of these days [during modernism and Westernization], I told the king that modern civilization, which has become famous in the world, has two faces. One is manifested in boulevards and the other one in laboratories. The useful civilization is that of libraries and laboratories. I thought he would get the point, but what emerged was more of the civilization of boulevards" (383).

In short, modernism, taken as a desire for power, wealth, and material gain, replaced the modernity of freedom, dignity, and human reason. Reza Shah was not interested in freedom or democracy. He wanted power and wealth, and after a while, he acquired both. For Reza Shah, parliament was not an organ of the people's will, but a servile functionary; at most, it symbolized the mediation between the government and the governed. At the opening of the new parliament in 1306/1927, he expressed the hope that the "representatives of the people would succeed" in implementing "our intentions," which he equated with "national ideals" (*Saalnaameye Paars* 1927, 2). He repeated the same idea at the opening of the twelfth parliament, in 1318/1939, when he claimed that "his reforms had been established" and that it was everyone's duty, including that of the "parliamentary representatives," to help promote and implement them (*Saalnaameye Paars* 1940, 103).

31

To his credit, Reza Khan did establish order and security, but he failed to follow the difficult path of the Iranian modernizers, of balancing the competing forces of tradition and modernity by building some form of national consensus. Instead, he combined traditionalism and modernism, adopting arbitrary rule from traditionalism and the use of force from modernism. He reportedly told parliament that even when it was not in session, its members should come and see him in Sa'dabad Palace, his residential palace, at least once weekly (*Ettela'at,* 10 Tir 1308/June 1929, 2).

Ironically, Reza Khan was successful in attracting some of the most sophisticated and educated Iranians to his team of ministers. For example, his longtime prime minister was a man of letters, scholarship, and music. The main program that Reza Khan and his ministers followed included the "absolute separation of religious and political forces," and they branded those who opposed it as "conservatives, reactionaries, Akhunds [a pejorative word for clerics], capitalists, aristocrats and oligarchs" (Bahar 1357/1978, 9). The program also included secular nationalism, patriotism, and the adoption of the products of modern advancements, factories, and commodities. In the words of Ann Lambton, a British scholar and longtime observer of Iranian history, "In 1925 Reza Shah assumed power. He made determined efforts to modernize the country and to replace Islam as the cohesive force of society by loyalty to the territorial state. He regarded the religious classes as an obstacle to this policy and, temporarily, effectively suppressed their power" (Lambton 1964, 118).

Lambton's observation was verified and emphasized by Reza Shah himself. Upon dispatching the first group of Iranians to study abroad, he reminded them of their duties: "You are being sent from a monarchical state to a republic so that you may adopt the patriotism of the French as your slogan, particularly learn from them the love of homeland, and return with that feeling to serve your country. I hope my children return with two important achievements: one, patriotism; and the other, scientific discoveries and advancement" (*Saalnaameye Paars* 1928, 37–38). He did not want them to learn about freedom, but about loyalty to the territorial state, applied sciences, and instrumental rationality. However, not everything he wanted came to pass. For example, one of the students sent abroad to study was Mehdi Bazargan, who saw the West differently from how he was asked to, as he said to his father before leaving, "If I stay in Iran I will lose my religion" (1356/1977, 41). What he brought back from Europe was also significant. He underplayed "the scientific discoveries" and emphasized that his "faith and attachment to Islam was increased" there (64). For Reza Shah, the West represented secularism, a strong state, and positivistic science, all of which were easy to adopt and implant; for Bazargan, it was a religious place with intellectual advancements.

Reza Khan should not be blamed for everything; he had local support. The seed of modernism and cultural alienation had been planted in the newly created parliament from the early days of the National Consultative Assembly (*Majlis Shuraye Melli*). From the beginning, supporters of modernity and the gradual adaptation of Iran to modern ways faced the opposing, Eurocentric tendency (*maslak*); the former became known as the Moderates (*Mo'tadel*), while the latter were known as Liberals (*Azadikhah*). The Moderates were headed by prominent merchants and allied with religious leaders who "drew their support from the propertied middle class." The Liberals "represented predominantly the intelligentsia" (Abrahamian 1982a, 88), and were headed by such men as Seyyed Hassan Taqizadeh, who came to symbolize modernism in twentieth-century Iran.

World War I proved detrimental to the nascent parliamentary system in Iran. The crisis in the polity, brought about by what Abrahamian calls the "period of disintegration" (102–118), continued until Reza Khan's coup. The advocates of modernism and Reza Khan found support in each other, and this new order gradually inaugurated the parallel state: one track followed modernity, the other, modernism. The latter group found an important ally in the new military because "Reza Shah relied on the modern army to be the central pillar of his New Order" (136). As British scholar Peter Avery claimed, "Under the banner of New Order material gains took precedence over social responsibility" (Avery 1965, 314). From this time onward, the Iranian polity was fragmented, and the "battle of worldviews" replaced "the battle of ideas."[2] This objective was achieved through a military state—centralized, very powerful, and tightly controlled by the generals. To this end, Reza Shah "merged the 7,000 Cossacks and 12,000 gendarmes into a new army of five divisions totaling 40,000 men" (120). Each division was in charge of one part of the country: the central, western, eastern, southern, and Azerbaijan areas (the last was singled out for the significance of the Azerbaijan province).

To ensure that the army remained loyal, salaries were raised and the army received special health benefits and medical facilities as well as other services. Reza Shah secured the title of army commander for himself. He watched everything carefully without getting into any of the factional politics ravaging the country at the time.[3] Instead, he "was recruiting soldiers and gathering all the weapons in the country. . . . He created strong centers of power in the hands of his generals in faraway

provinces. He was careful not to antagonize the media and would min-
gle with all the politicians, repeatedly reminding them of his service in
bringing order to the country" (Bahar 1323/1944, 29).

Second, he gathered support from among the intellectuals. He found
it, but only among the newly emerging Westernized thinkers, who were
replacing the nineteenth-century Iranian intellectuals of the constitutional movement. They readily echoed Reza Shah's vision of the new
Iran in their works. The following account by Issa Sadiq, one of these
intellectuals, is important to note. Owing to "the emergence of Army
Commander [Reza Khan], I made arrangement to work with him [Min-
ister of Court Ali Akbar Davar] and other friends in order to help the
Army Commander create a powerful government through three means:
(1) to help our supporters get elected into parliament, (2) to publish newspapers, and (3) to form a party from educated youth" (Sadiq 1352/1973,
1:268). Soon, many supporters of Westernization and the modernism
project secured seats in the parliament and, through an alliance with the
conservative members of parliament, forced genuine modernizers out
(Abrahamian 1982a, 120–122).

They did so by forming such political parties as the Radical Party
(*Hezb-e Raadical*), whose main objective was to demonstrate that "the
country had to be reformed from all its roots" (Sadiq 1352/1973, 1:277). The
party's objective was to create a centralized and powerful Iran through
the "separation of religion and politics, creation of a well-disciplined
army and a well-administered bureaucracy . . . transformation of nomads
into farmers . . . and replacement of minority languages throughout Iran
by Persian" (Abrahamian 1982a, 123). Then there was the publication of
a series of newspapers whose main objective was to consolidate Reza
Shah's rule. One was Ali Akbar Davar's paper called *Mard-e Aazaad* (the
Free Man).

In his regular editorials, Davar advocated the total adoption of technology, advancement through modernization from above, and the creation of a powerful state. He understood the West to be a region of power
and wealth, manifested in factories, roads, and infrastructure. As he
wrote in one of his editorials: "The root of Western civilization is not
its schools, libraries, literature and its scholars. These are incidentals.
The root of the civilization of those people who are superior to us is *the
railroad.* . . . Without it, freedom, equality, representation, patriotism,
nation, and the like are unrhymed poems" (*Mard-e Aazaad* no. 11, emphasis added). In another editorial, he stated, "The contemporary Western civilization is the result of the Industrial Revolution. . . . It is useful

to give a definition here. Industrial revolution means the conversion of the old mode of production to the newly invented one. To speak more clearly, changing the shop to a factory" (no. 17). Clearly then, the problem in Iran was not a lack of understanding of the paradigm shift from a cosmological worldview to one founded on human reason, science, and freedom, but was, instead, that materialist modernism became more attractive and also easier to adopt than before.

Given these views, it is no surprise that the hallmark of Reza Shah's rule became the national railroad. It connected north and south, though the more necessary connection was east with west: because of the interests of the British Empire, an east-west railroad that would connect Iraq to Pakistan would be seen as threatening the jewel in the crown, as India was then called, and so would never be permitted. To build the railroad, a government monopoly was established in 1925 on the importation of tea and sugar, and the funds derived from it were earmarked for railroad construction. Close to 1,394 kilometers (about 865 miles) of railroad was built. Road construction and air transportation were also taken up. The other pieces of Davar's understanding of civilization, namely factories, were also built. "Cotton textile factories were established in Mazandaran, Isfahan, and Tehran. The woolen industry was concentrated in Isfahan. . . . And a modern silk fabric factory was set up in [the northern city of] Chalus" (Banani 1961, 139). The most successful sector was sugar refining; eight state-owned factories were built in various parts of the country.

After Reza Shah felt secure in his power, he and his supporters set about establishing mythic underpinnings for their new state. A myth based on patriotism and chauvinistic nationalism was created through the formulation of an ideology, reformation of the educational system, and the creation of new institutions for socialization and indoctrination. For reasons of ideological change, the prevalent religious cosmology had to be replaced. As Abdollah Razi, one of the Westernizing intellectuals, wrote in 1925, "We must respectfully approach the house of the 'unclean and heathen Westerners' and implore them to save us from our ignorance and misery" (quoted in Banani 1961, 24). The savior was to be secular nationalism. Its main components were an emphasis on the Persian language and Aryan ethnicity. To purify the Persian language, the house of culture (*farhangestan*) was established, whose main task was to create new words to replace any foreign-rooted ones that existed in Persian, but in practice, attention was paid mainly to those with Arabic roots.

Some suggested exchanging the Persian alphabet for the Latin one. In fact, many treatises were written to show the superiority of the latter.

For example, Mostafah Fateh wrote *The Path to Progress* with the aim of "identifying the shortcomings of the present alphabet and noting the advantages of the new one" (Fateh 1310/1932, 2). The new Latin alphabet represented the movement for progress and power. How could Iranians refrain from joining such a movement? Moreover, "the new alphabet does not belong to any group or population" (12), which strikes the reader as odd. Such a claim makes language and culture appear neutral, and thus easy to adopt. Educational institutions such as the Shiraz University medical school, where the main language of instruction was English, proved to be instruments for the promotion of Westernization. Interestingly, close to 60 percent of its graduates ended up in Europe or North America (Rajaee 1365/1986, 14).

Tehran University may be the most important educational institution established under Reza Shah. When it was formed in 1935, it was erroneously presented as the first institution of higher learning in Iran. Upon laying the foundation of the university, Reza Shah said, "The establishment of a university is something that the people of Iran should have done a long time ago" (quoted in Banani 1961, 40). No one reminded him that they had. One of the first things that the Iranian modernizers had thought about in the early nineteenth century was how to establish a new institution of higher learning. Part of Amir Kabir's general plan of modernization included a college of modern sciences. The first news of such an attempt appeared in 1850 in the newspaper *Vaqaye Etefaqiye*, which reported on "'a House of Learning' where sciences and industries will be taught" (Mahbubi-Ardakani 1368/1989, 1:255). Indeed, it was established in 1851, and still functions as a high school. Ironically, while Tehran University would help consolidate the power of the new regime, it soon became the stronghold of many modernizing, as opposed to modernist, Iranian intellectuals, who took refuge there. It remained the center of opposition to the Pahlavi regime until the revolution of 1979.

Among the organizations advocating modernism and Westernization, *Sazman-e Parvaresh-e Afkar* (Organization for Catering to People's Thought) should be mentioned. It had branches "all over the country," and their "main duty was to strengthen national unity" (Sadiq 1352/1973, 1:371). Its activities included establishing radio stations and erecting lecture halls, theatres, art schools, and publishing houses. A document in the Iranian national archives revealed that in 1929 alone, a total of 6,663 public lectures were given, the smallest number of which—fewer than 10—were in Qom (Document 108011, *Sazman* files). The speeches made in the various branches of the organization hammered home the main principles of the Westernization myth: a central powerful state, nationalism, the myth of a benevolent authoritarian king, and unquestioning loyalty to the central regime (*Sazman* 1940). They also promoted Western consumer society and material advancements. For example, they propagated the advantages of eating on a table rather than on the floor, of the nuclear family over the extended family, and so on.

Reza Shah managed to create an autocracy in which everyone, including Westernizing intellectuals, was subservient to his will: "By 1933, however, the Majlis had been reduced to no more than a powerless instrument of the state, and almost all the Shah's early advisors (not to mention critics and opponents) had been dismissed, banished, jailed, murdered, or driven into complete subservience" (Katouzian 2000, 186). His rule, however, came to end as European politics crumbled into the destructive events of World War II. The favorable condition of international politics responsible for bringing Reza Shah to power had now taken a different course. The British, finding him intolerable, agreed to keep his family in power only if he agreed to a life of exile in South Africa, which he did. Reza Shah's twenty years of autocracy came to an end as abruptly as his rule had begun.

THE YOUNG MOHAMMAD REZA SHAH AND THE NEW SURGE OF IRANIAN MODERNITY

While awaiting exile, Reza Shah walked around the marble hall of the Golestan Palace, in Tehran, repeating to himself: "They betrayed me, they betrayed me. Where is the army?" (Pahlavi 1327/1948, 6). The pillars of his power, the army and the foreign powers, had withdrawn their support. His autocracy came to an abrupt end, society rejoiced, and a new page began in Iranian history. "The spring of freedom," or in the words of one historian, "the crisis of democracy," had begun (Azimi 1989). Cynicism, fatalism, and a conspiratorial mentality dominated. In hindsight, the new era was neither the spring of freedom nor the crisis of democracy, but rather a new chance for the Iranian modernization project. It came to the surface with enormous energy: "In rupturing the autocracy, the Anglo-Soviet invasion of August 1941 unleashed the pent-up social grievances of the previous sixteen years" (Abrahamian 1982a, 169). Many groups emerged, and more than 500 newspapers and journals began publishing seemingly overnight. The departure of Reza Shah proved decisive for the future of Islamic discourse. The outbreak of World War II added an extra incentive; both proved fortuitous for Islam-minded Iranians.

Mohammad Reza Shah, who ascended the throne on September 16, 1941, was almost twenty-two years old. In the thirty-eight years he was king, he displayed two distinct styles of ruling. The first was to reign and, in the tradition of Iranian political norms, to allow the first minister (*nakhost vazir*) to do the ruling. This lasted until early 1965, when he appointed Amir Abbas Hoveida (1919–1979) to the job but he himself assumed executive power at the head of a baseless police state. During this time, he showed a tendency to assume additional powers at court, but the forces of modernization kept him in check.

With the departure of Reza Shah, all the previously suppressed social and political forces hurried back into the public sphere, as did the forces of modernity. In the 1940s and even the 1950s, power in Iran became decentralized, shifting among the court, the parliament, the cabinet, and newly emerging political groups and forces. At the same time, external powers—Britain and the Soviet Union—occupied Iran and reduced it to an abject state of dependence. Every group tried to consolidate its power in one corner or another. The left took advantage of the Soviet presence and came onto the scene. Conservative forces did the same, as did the nationalists. The new king tried to strengthen his position.

Two developments helped Mohammad Reza achieve his objectives of concentrating power in the court. The first was the crisis that led to the formation of two regional republics, one in Kurdistan and the other in Azerbaijan. The second was the unfolding of the Cold War and the fear of communist advances into Iran, which made the shah even more powerful, to the point that he was able to suppress all dissenting voices in the name of progress and development. The creation of the two separatist republics generated strong nationalist feelings in the rest of the country, giving more ammunition to the Shah in his bid for power. Ja'far Pishevari, who spearheaded the Azerbaijan secession, was elected member of parliament for Tabriz, the biggest city in the Azerbaijan province, but was denied the seat because his credentials were rejected. He reacted by returning to Tabriz and forming the Democratic Party of Azerbaijan (*Firqeh-ye Demokraat-e Azarbaijan*). In its first statement, the party expressed a desire to remain within Iran but demanded distinct status (Abrahamian 1982a, 399). Qazi Muhammad made a similar move in Kurdistan and led Komala, the Committee of the Resurrection of Kurdistan (*Komala Zhian Kurdistan*). Again, although both movements declared their desire to stay in Iran, the ruling elite in Tehran "regarded them as separatists in disguise, opposed to sovereignty, territorial integrity, and prevailing socio-political arrangement in Iran" (Azimi

1989, 136). What made the movements so dangerous was that the Soviet government in September 1945 "decided to sponsor armed rebellions in Azerbaijan and Kurdistan" (Abrahamian 1982a, 398).

The government was faced with what became known as the Azerbaijan Crisis. A new Constituent Assembly was convened to consider the issue, but the only result was the granting of unlimited power to the shah. Ironically, the first people to talk about "the need for a Constituent Assembly" were the editorialists of the Iranian Communist Party. They explicitly argued that "the Azerbaijan Crisis would not be solved until Iran convened a Constituent Assembly" (Abrahamian 1982a, 403). However, sophisticated diplomatic maneuvering by Prime Minister Ahmad Qavam, together with the concerns of the Allies, particularly the United States, about containing Stalin's advance, paved the way for the preservation of Iranian sovereignty; the young shah took credit for it. "The Shah who had assumed active field command of the army," a biography of Mohammad Reza Shah puts it, "suppress[ed] the rebellion once and for all" (Sanghvi 1968, 130). This happened on December 12, 1946, when the shah entered Tabriz with his army. As the biographer rightly puts it, he reached "the first milestone in his long journey" (135) by claiming that the "danger to Iran was averted by a Pahlavi" (133).

These two episodes made a hero of the young monarch, who felt the time was right to increase and extend his power. At the same time, the postwar crisis raised hopes among those Iranians who were aiming for a more centralized and powerful government. For example, an editorial from the period compares the condition of Iran at the time of the 1921 coup with the situation of Iran in 1948–1949: "Those people who openly fought against freedom and constitutionalism penetrated into the government . . . turning the country into constant chaos. That condition paved the way for a radical reaction in the form of the 1921 coup. Now, the condition is identical with then; the same chaos, the same dormancy, and the same suspension" (Ettela'at Mahane, Mehr 1327/October 1948, 3).

Mohammad Reza received a blessing in disguise in the form of an assassination attempt when he was visiting Tehran University in 1949. On February 4, the anniversary of the university's establishment, the shah came to address the students. The would-be assassin, in the guise of a photographer, fired at the shah, injuring him in the face. Using this near miss as an excuse, the shah's men kept the fear of chaos and anarchy alive: they intimated that the disappearance of the shah would throw the country into internal strife and possibly civil war. Although the culprit was a member of the newly formed (1945) radical organization *Fada'iyan*

Islam (Devotees of Islam; Kazemi 1984, 158–176), which was the first religious fundamentalist group that justified terror in Iran, the conservative elements quickly pointed to and condemned a conspiracy of communists, religionists, and national populists as having been behind the
attack.

The shah acted quickly to crush all suspected opposition. Martial law
was declared, newspapers obviously critical of the royal court were closed
down, the Iranian Communist Party was banned, Ayatollah Abolqas-
sem Kashani was deported to Lebanon, and Mohammad Mosaddeq was
confined to his village outside Tehran. The shah, as Abrahamian rightly
observes, "turned the assassination attempt into a royalist coup d'etat"
(Abrahamian 1982a, 250). Despite political opposition and the imposition of martial law, a Constituent Assembly was convened in April and
May 1949. The assembly decided on two important measures. It created
a senate, half of whose members would be appointed by the shah, and it
changed Article 48 of the constitution, making the shah more powerful,
even above the constitution. The new article read: "His Royal Highness
the King can dissolve the houses of the parliament, the National Consultative or the Senate, each separately or both at the same time" (*Ettela'at
Mahane,* 2 Khordad 1328/June 1949, 3). One should mention that these
changes did not yet lead to the complete concentration of power in the
shah's hands. That would come in 1953, when the local and genuine
modernization process was crushed and disrupted and its main voice,
Mohammad Mosaddeq, silenced.

As the shah bid for greater power, the forces of modernization re-
surged. Ideas of constitutionalism once more took center stage. At this
juncture, however, the politics of modernity were tied to the notion of
Iranian independence, which was politically undermined because of the
events of World War II and economically undermined because of the
British involvement with Iranian oil. Both points found expression in
nationalist populism as voiced by Mohammad Mosaddeq, who died
fighting the imposition of modernism. An essay in America's popular
Time magazine, depicting Mosaddeq as the man of the year, summarized accurately what he was all about: "In 1919, horrified by a colonial-
style treaty between Britain and Persia, he hardened his policy into a
simple Persia-for-the-Persians slogan. While the rest of the world went
through Versailles, Manchuria, the Reichstag fire, Spain, Ethiopia, and a
World War, Mosaddeq kept hammering away at his single note. Nobody
in the West heard him" (1951). The slogan "Persia for the Persians" is a
loaded phrase and requires deconstruction.

First, the Persian society that Mosaddeq envisioned was very different from the Persian society that the Pahlavis and their modernist intelligentsia had in mind. Mosaddeq's was a liberal and parliamentary Iran in which tradition, modernity, Islam, and Iran would all come together. He fought arbitrary rule from within the consultative assembly. For example, once he returned to the political scene, he first criticized the Constituent Assembly as illegitimate because of the way it had been convened: "The Constituent Assembly was fake and illegitimate, fake because it did not represent the people, illegitimate because it altered the constitutional laws. In saying this I do not claim that the constitution is sacred and beyond improvement. But I do claim that changes can be made only by the true representatives of the people. . . . If the people wish to change the constitution, they have the right to do so—after all, the constitution belongs to them" (quoted in Abrahamian 1982a, 262). In fact, Iranian parliamentary proceedings show that his opposition to Reza Shah and the way he ascended to power was the result of his concern for the complexity of the modernization process.

For Mosaddeq, the shah had to either play his traditional role as arbiter, patriarch, and head of the patriarchal state, or else sit as a monarch at the head of a parliamentary regime; in either case, he would reign but not rule. Mosaddeq's core perspective on Iran focused on his opposition to the ruling monarch, a stance for which he fought as a member of parliament and which he later used as a reason for nationalizing the Iranian oil industry. He was the last populist leader in Iran before the emergence of Ayatollah Khomeini in 1979.

Just as the first phase of modernization in Iran fell victim to global modernism and "the Age of Empire," Mosaddeq's attempt at reviving Iranian modernization was subject to international entanglement. This time, Iranian modernization was devastated by the age of oil politics. Mosaddeq's return to public life coincided with the coming of World War II and the decentralization of politics in Iran; he was released from "house imprisonment . . . under a general amnesty of prisoners on 22 September 1941" (Diba 1986, 62). He was immediately elected to parliament and once more assumed his old mandate of, first, fighting for constitutionalism and, second, restoring Iranian self-confidence and independence.

The first part of the mandate targeted the centralization of power in the hands of the shah, and the second part targeted foreign concessions. Obviously the shah, who was constantly strengthening the crown against the legislature, did not like Mosaddeq's positions. Despite the shah's constant maneuvering to block Mosaddeq, the forces of modernization were too powerful, so he returned to parliament for the election of the sixteenth Majlis (February 1950–May 1951)—this time as leader of a coalition of the elements of Iranian modernity. The coalition was called the National Front (*Jebheye Melli*), and according to a U.S. State Department report, it included "workers, small shopkeepers, teachers, students, and most government employees below the top political level" (quoted in Diba 1986, 96). It was a middle-class organization whose founding members were lawyers, journalists, businessmen, and professionals. The new party echoed Mosaddeq's double concerns—national constitutionalism and international independence.

The shift of emphasis from domestic to external affairs occurred in June 1950, when the government submitted to parliament a proposal for revising the 1933 agreement between Iran and Britain over oil. Seizing the opportunity, Mosaddeq and his National Front deputies demanded the nationalization of the oil industry instead of the treaty revision. The issue was so politicized that the whole country was mobilized. Prime Minister Ali Razmara was considered the villain, and Ayatollah Kashani, who had now returned to Iran and was the practical leader of the fundamentalist Devotees of Islam organization, called upon sincere Muslims to support Iran and help the "fight against the enemies of Islam" (quoted in Abrahamian 1982a, 265). The campaign was successful: parliament passed the bill for nationalization on March 15, 1951, and the senate ratified it four days later.

Under pressure, the shah appointed Mosaddeq as the new prime minister on April 29, 1951, believing that he would surely fail in the position. Mosaddeq managed to create something resembling a balanced polity, and in the process he alienated local and international forces of modernism. In the atmosphere of the Cold War and the U.S.-Soviet rivalry, the Western powers, which had tolerated the shah's autocratic regime because it was seen as a bulwark against communism, now conspired to eliminate Mosaddeq, who was seen as a communist sympathizer. The coup, planned and carried out by the British and Americans in August 1953, resulted, once again, in the disruption of Iranian modernity and the erection of yet another new state based on the army and foreign elements, which contributed to the fermentation of revolutionary spirit.

The International Context: Regional Modernisms and Imperialism

Reza Shah's rule was part of a broader playing out of modernism across the region as a whole. The modern Middle East emerged from the ruins of a world that had lost its internal cohesion—a world based on the cosmology of Islam, traditional thought, and agrarian production. If the region is extended to include the Indian subcontinent, one is reminded that before modern geographical boundaries were drawn, three gunpowder empires—the Ottomans, Safavids, and Mughals—composed a vast Muslim civilization with internal as well as psychological cohesion (Hodgson 1973, vol. 3). Modernity presented the biggest challenge Muslims had yet faced.

The first consequence was that the internal cohesion and battle of ideas in the Muslim world was replaced with a spectrum of trends and thoughts, resulting in the emerging of a zero-sum battle of worldviews. Soon, a strong sense of nationalism overcame the region, resulting in the abandoning of many age-old responsibilities, such as securing the welfare of various ethnic groups within particular national borders (as was the case in modern Turkey, where the duty to protect Arab and Armenian minorities was abandoned). In theory, the three empires wanted to adopt modern ways, but in practice, India fell to colonialism; the Ottomans made the strategic mistake of siding with Germany in World War I, and their empire was dismantled; and Iran was held hostage by competing interests in the Great Game between Russia and Great Britain. What replaced the three empires was the mirror image of modernism: states more interested in power than either democracy or modernity. We turn now to an analysis of Iran's neighbors.

On the Western side of Iran, the Ottoman Empire had fallen, and a powerful Westernizing group replaced it: nationalist Turkey. At almost the same time a similar effort was underway in Iran, Mustafa Kemal Pasha (Atatürk) (1881–1938) implanted a wholesale program of Westernization and modernism in Turkey. Kemal's plans were the latest in a series of fitful attempts at Westernizing changes. The Ottoman Empire's inability to sustain its position in Europe had led some of the sultans down a path of reform. Sultan Selim III (ruled 1789–1807) realized that partial reform of the army and in a few other technical fields could not prevent the steady decline of the empire; a reappraisal of certain basic institutions was in order. To this end, he consulted a few leading Ottoman officials, and the result was the period of *Nizami Cedid* (New Order), during which the reforms extended to nontechnical areas as well. Modernization of the empire was continued under the plan called Tanzimat ("reorganization") (1839–1878), and the modernizing intellectuals soon called themselves the Young Ottomans (formed in the mid-1860s).

For the early reformers, Ottomanism defined citizenship in such a way that citizens of the empire were equal, irrespective of nation, race, or religion, a conception of citizenship compatible with modernity. By contrast, the Western narrative of modernity demands exclusive rights for the citizens of a particular nation in one state. This was captured in Kemalism. In the new republic, confined to Anatolia and Thrace, the project comprised secularism, nationalism, and wholesale modernism. Turning to the West for inspiration and support, it implemented the following six principles: (1) republicanism, for the realization of the national identity of modern Turkey; (2) nationalism, the independence of Turkish-speaking people; (3) populism, since the Kemalist revolution was also a social revolution, as the old elites gave way to a mass society; (4) secularism, i.e., not just the separation of state and religion, but also the separation of religion from educational, cultural, and legal affairs; (5) statism, the creation of a strong and economically developed state; and (6) reformism, the replacement of traditional institutions with modern ones (Berkez 1964). The new secular bureaucrats changed the alphabet from the Arabic to the Latin, instituted a new dress code, and adopted new ways; even the capital, Istanbul, was considered the capital of a dead empire. Ankara would be the capital of a new state. The similarity between these principles and those implemented by Reza Shah in Iran is striking.

What was problematic about the whole project was that it replaced the modernity process that had begun in the nineteenth century with Europeanization—mimicking the Europeans because for "the Kemalists, being modern meant being like the Europeans" (Sayyid 1997, 67). The abolition of the caliphate by Turkey's grand assembly in 1924 symbolized this attitude and marked a break with the past. The caliphate was an institution that symbolized the power and unity of Islam. It could be compared with the Vatican, which represents a central and universal symbol for most Catholics, even those not practicing all dictates of the religion. The abolition of the caliphate had a paradoxical effect; it both abolished Islam's institutional representation and freed Islam for a resurgence: "The Kemalist, by abolishing the caliphate, disrupted the sedimented relationship between Islam and state authority—a relationship over a thousand years old. Their act of abolition had the effect of reactivating Islam. The master signifier of Islam was no longer fixed to a particular institutional arrangement, which made the task of reinterpreting what its role should be much easier" (63).

Similarly, Hamid Enayat, in his now classic book *Modern Islamic Political Thought* (1982), observes that the abolition of the caliphate not only marked a deep change in Turkey, but was also a turning point in the political thought of the Muslim majority (52). I contend that this was a turning point in all Muslim political thinking. First and foremost, it allowed for an open debate on the nature of Islamic polity, something that hitherto had been settled by the caliphate, and for the minority Shi'as, by the imamate. It made it possible for Muslims to ask what an Islamic state would look like, a completely new area of Islamic discourse. Moreover, the removal of the symbolic institutional presence of Islam from the public sphere forced Islam-minded people to think about the place, function, and significance of their religion.

On the Eastern side of Iran, another modernizing trend was put into place by Amanullah Khan (1892–1960), who emerged in 1919 as the main figure of Afghan independence and a key figure of modernism in Afghanistan. His activities during ten years in office (1919–1929) strikingly resemble what happened in Iran. Initially, Amanullah Khan tried to generate the support of religious scholars in Afghanistan by invoking Islamic symbols—talking about jihad against the British and by establishing himself as a major proponent of pan-Islamism. Indeed, from 1919 to 1928, whatever changes were introduced in Afghanistan took place within the context of the traditional politics of that country. They had such a high degree of sanction that when some younger religious figures voiced opposition to the government and its policies, senior religious leaders issued fatwas "condemning the rebel mollas' [mullahs'] uprising against the government" (Nawid 1999, 119).

After the king and queen's grand tour of Europe, from November 1927 through June 1928, which included a visit to the new Turkish republic in May, however, Amanullah Khan declared that his purpose was to "bring back to my country everything that is best in European civilization, and to show Europe that Afghanistan exists on the map" (quoted in Nawid 1999, 136). Again, modernity came to be identified with Europe, and with it came the notion that it was possible to transplant that experience to non-European regions. A period of sweeping reforms began. In August 1928, the king convened the Grand Gathering (the *Loya-Jerga*) with the hope of attracting general support. The issues that proved sensitive were the unveiling of women and the secularization of many bureaucratic offices in the area of adjudication and education. The latter meant that the ulama would lose many of their traditional governmental functions (145).

To implement these sweeping reforms, the king exercised enormous arbitrary power, providing the ulama with legitimate reasons to oppose them, since "arbitrary use of power by the government had exceeded

45

justification" (151). What made the ulama more suspicious was the implementation of a treaty of cooperation between Afghanistan and Turkey, to
which the king had agreed on his recent trip. Within a year, the king had
alienated everyone so much that he had to abdicate in favor of his older
brother in January 1929. While the failure of Amanullah Khan's effort is
attributed to a revolt brought about by "tribal separation and bellicosity"
(Poullada 1973, 159), the fact remains that the changes in Afghanistan were
as much the product of modernism as were the changes in Iran. Just as the
new forces of modernism in Iran were led by those with little firsthand
knowledge of the modern world, the king of Afghanistan similarly knew
little about the nuances of modernity and its emancipatory mandate (153).

Globally, this period is rightly depicted as "the age of empire." Imperialism, still working, was at its peak. Britain, Russia, and France dominated the region. Iran itself had been divided in 1907 between Russia in
the north and Great Britain in the south. Now, after World War I, Britain
shifted its policy from supporting constitutionalism to looking with favor on a powerful central government in Iran as against the messy constitutional regime.

The Intellectual Context: Religious Reforms

A major consequence of the interaction between internal changes and
external trends was a dynamic intellectual spectrum in Iran. First, there
was the predominance of a modernist intelligentsia. While the process
of Westernization through an imposition of change from above during
Reza Shah's rule focused on imitating Europe, particularly France and
England, the focus changed to Americanization during the reign of his
son. The modernist intelligentsia in both periods supported this wholesale change. Even a respected historian of the time, Abbas Iqbal, stated,
"Today there is no longer the slightest doubt about this fact that European civilization is the source of welfare and progress for humanity. It
is, moreover, a fact that anyone who denies this obvious reality is either
mad or is a sophist" (Iqbal 1326/1937, 1). Westernization was an "obvious
reality," in no need of evaluation or proof.

Thus the modernists of the time advocated complete submission to
the powerful state that Reza Khan had created. They thought the best
strategy to guarantee progress would be complete acceptance of the
West and its ways. They added, however, that the means of achieving
such an aim would be a powerful dictator. For example, in his essay "Social Revolution, the Necessity of the Emergence of a Dictator," Moshfeq

Kazemi stated, "If you want one day to enjoy that freedom which has embraced Europe, produce a knowledgeable dictator (*dikdator-e 'alem*): Yes, a knowledgeable dictator, and an ideal despot who would take the path of evolution many years with each of his steps" (Kazemi 1303/1924, 11). The irony was that when Reza Shah strengthened his position, even the revolutionaries considered him a savior.

Yet a powerful faction remained loyal to modernization, despite the fact that modernism had won the day and the country was quickly moving in a direction that Seyyed Hassan Taqizadeh advocated, becoming "Europeanized in appearance, essence, physical features and spiritual aspects" (Aryanpour 1350/1971, 2:232). The voice of modernization remained active and kept the voice of Iranian moderation alive. The following passage from Kazemzadeh Iranshahr, two years after Reza Khan's coup, is significant: "One point to note is that we recommend moderation and avoidance of any form of extremes. This is neither due to fear nor is it due to imitation, but because we believe this is the right path. We have repeatedly said that Iran neither in its soul, nor in its mind, its appearance or its essence should become like the Franks. At the same time, it should not remain in its present condition. It has to progress and create its own civilization that could be called Iranian" (quoted in Behnam 1375/1996, 120–121).

The most vocal and dynamic voice of modernity found expression in a nationalist populist movement headed by Mosaddeq. At the heart of his views lay the notion of restoring Iranians' self-confidence. As he put it himself, "after fifty years of study and experience I have concluded that only by securing freedom and complete independence can the nation of Iran overcome the countless problems and impediments that it is facing on its path to prosperity and greatness" (quoted in Afshari 1379/2000, 16). The practical way of achieving this, according to Mosaddeq, was free-thinking, which translated into constitutionalism at home and an independent foreign policy abroad. The latter he called the policy of "negative equilibrium," which meant keeping an equal distance from the big powers of the day. Mosaddeq said, "I accepted my responsibility as a member of the parliament only to follow one sacred mission, and that includes, internally, the exercise of the principles of constitutionalism and freedom and, externally, implementing the principle of negative equilibrium" (78).

It is important to note that this was not a project against any person. The Iranian modernity process has been and continues to be for creating self-confidence and progress. It is this type of polity that Mosaddeq yearned for, within the context of Iranian civilization, religion, and nationality: "We have to elevate ourselves to a degree of true independence so as to be moved and motivated only by the interest of Iran, preserving our nationality, religion, and civilization" (quoted in *Mossaddeq va Nehzat Melli Iran* 1357/1978, 5).

The other strong trend at the time was the left, influenced by figures like Jean-Jacques Rousseau (1712–1778) and Claude-Henri de Rouvroy, comte de Saint-Simon (1760–1825). A prominent leftist figure was Sulayman Mirza Eskandari, who led the Iranian Socialist Party (1921–1926). At first, its members allied themselves with the Democrats in parliament, but they gradually came closer to the Iranian Communist Party, whose nucleus group was formed after World War I by Taqi Arani (d. 1937), who was educated in Berlin in the 1920s. Although a medical student, Arani was attracted to Marxist literature. After returning to Iran, he began teaching at the newly established Tehran University and "with former colleagues from Europe, founded a highly theoretical journal named *Donya* (The World)" (Abrahamian 1982a, 157). He was operating in a receptive environment, since many Iranians were ready to hear these "new" ideas.

Iran's political disintegration coincided with the October Revolution in Russia (1917) and the formation of the first Marxist regime. The revolutionary government in Moscow encouraged Marxist tendencies around the world, including in Iran. An Iranian officer and member of the Iranian Communist Party who left the group and is now a prominent historian and author, Enayatollah Reza recounted the reasons for the attraction of Marxist and communist thinking: (1) the "Soviet Union was considered the vanguard of progress and intellectual achievements; (2) compared to condescending Allied officers, the Soviet ones treated us with more respect; (3) the Soviets appeared to be fighting against any stratified society and defending the working class, which was appealing to Iranian intellectuals; and (4) the Soviets' establishment of a dynamic library in downtown Tehran provided progressive books for Iranian intellectuals" (Reza 1992, interview).

Indeed, Marxist and leftist intellectual paradigms became the most prominent ones in Iranian social life until the sixties, when people such as Jalal Al-e Ahmad introduced a rival trend of indigenous discourse. Ironically, the Marxist paradigm contributed a great deal to the emergence of Islamist discourse by excluding other ways of thinking. For a long time, progressive thinking meant ideas that had been sanctioned or supported by the Tudeh Party. To be in any sort of vanguard, one had to be connected to the left. As Iranian scholar Ahmad Ashraf rightly put it,

"Major poets, writers, politically-minded university students, and committed intelligentsia, were among Marxist sympathizers" (1990, 117). The Tudeh Party's influence on Iranian intellectual life received a boost when Fereidun Keshavarz, a party member, assumed the portfolio of minister of education in 1945.

Another intellectual trend that caused an uproar among Islam-minded Iranians was Islamic reformism, which as articulated by Shari'at Sangelaji (1890–1944), Ahmad Kasravi (1890–1946), and Ali Akbar Hakamizadeh (d. 1988), advocated the reformulation of religious thought. Kasravi was assassinated by the radical fundamentalist Iranian group Fada'iyan Islam, and Hakamizadeh left the public life before dying in obscurity in Tehran. A short account of each is in order.

A relative of the traditionalist Sheikh Fazlollah Nuri, Mirza Rezaqoli Sangelaji turned against his relative's position, adopted a reformist posture, and thought that the central message of Islam (monotheism) had been undermined. After his early studies in Iran, he went to Najaf, Iraq, where he proved to be a sharp student. He wrote a book that was so well received that Ayatollah Na'ini gave him the title of Shari'at (Islamic creed); thus he became better known as Shari'at Sangelaji. He returned to Iran, and in 1931 started *Dar at-Tabligh Eslami* (The Abode for Propagation of Islam), an organization for the propagation of Islam. Apparently, his approach to reforming religion was congruent with state policy, so he was encouraged and was granted a plot in downtown Tehran on which to build his center (Richard 1988, 164). He kept his independence, however, because when the minister of court tried "to draw Sangelaji closer into official functions," he refused, and lived by private teaching (163). Sangelaji's integrity and independence may have been the reason for his great popularity—his followers gave him the title of Great Reformer (*Mosleh Kabir*). Also, unlike Kasravi and Hakamizadeh, he avoided direct attacks against clerics and kept his criticism of the religious establishment within the bounds of theological debate, basically relying on Qur'anic citations.

Sangelaji wrote many books, but the most controversial are *Kelid Fahm Qur'an* (The Key to the Understanding of the Qur'an) and *Islam va Raj'at* (Islam and Resurrection). In the former, Sangelaji's main objective was as follows: "I noticed that there are many superstitions, and many delusions and artifices are attributed to religion. I saw that in our society there are false and futile religions in the place of Islam, making it impossible to distinguish between Islam and superstitions . . . I felt obliged to cleanse our religion . . . and show its real face to Muslims" (Sangelaji 1321/1942, 6).

The real lost religion in need of rediscovery was monotheism. Its enemies were associationists and, most importantly, the cult of saints under the rubric of the descendants of the Shiʿi imams (*Imamzadeh*).

Sangelaji criticizes this in his book *Tawhid, Ibaadat, Yektaparasti* (1322/1943; Monotheism, Prayer, and Worshiping the One), and he rhetorically asks how people could follow so many saints when God says he is closer to the people than their jugular veins (Qur'an 50:15–16). According to Sangelaji, to be free from associationism one must go to the source—the Qur'an, through which one reaches perfection. As he puts it, "The Qur'an makes man righteous. Its purpose is to set people on the right path: when they attain this, everything they do will be just and all knowledge they develop will be good" (Sangelaji 1321/1942, 44; also Richard 1988, 168). To understand the Qur'an, one needs some tools and a proper approach, as provided by Sangelaji in his book *The Key,* which is his analytical introduction to the Qur'an. As he writes, "My aim is to show the way to the understanding of the Qur'an because misguided people have closed the path to the understanding of Islam and do not allow anybody to enter this source of monotheism and the ocean of truth" (1321/1942, 8). The two greatest enemies on this path are too much emphasis on the esoteric meaning of passion and the literal following of its injunctions, based on imitation, "that is, the simple repetition of the thoughts and actions of the ancients" (Richard 1988, 168). These two approaches have obscured the true essence of religion. While an accurate and precise criticism, this observation threatened many members of the cleric class, who felt they were being attacked.

At almost the same time, Ahmad Kasravi argued for purifying religion. He was a versatile intellectual, linguist, judge, historian, and proponent of constitutionalism. As he wrote, the works of Iranian intellectuals of the nineteenth century had "shaken me and had flamed the fire inside me" (Kasravi 1355/1976, 47). He became known as a staunch supporter of freedom in Iran and wrote the most authoritative account of the constitutional movement in the country. He devoted his life to promoting modernity. His arguments became more controversial as he went beyond mere religious disputes. Best expressed in *Ma Che Mikhahim* (What We Want), a collection of essays from his monthly journal, *Peyman* (Charter), Kasravi's views threatened both modernist intellectuals and the traditionalist cleric class. He had two types of intellectual adversaries, both of whom were impediments to Iranian modernization. He writes, "These days people are of two categories; one group, in the name of religiosity, insists on its cult worshiping, while a bigger group has abandoned religion altogether and followed European ideas in the name of 'modernity and civilization'" (Kasravi 1358/1979, 76). The most extreme forms of cult worshiping included Shiʿism, Bahaism, Sufism, Europeanism, and secularism. "These five malicious ways were going their own ways, but now they have joined forces . . . destroying all proper ways" (Kasravi 1357/1978, 45). His criticism of Europeanism and secularism is found in all his works, but to refute Shiʿism, Bahaism, and Sufism, he wrote three tracts challenging their belief systems. At the same time, Kasravi felt that the way forward was to be critical, not just by criticizing "the five malicious ways," but by pointing out what can be salvaged from them.

For example, he thought that Shiʿism, Bahaism, and Sufism had not properly understood the teachings of religion. He explains his own position as follows: "We propose 'the path of salvation' by which we mean to live in this world with goodness, pride, and purity and to know the world and its meaning, within the framework of the path of God" (Kasravi 1357/1978, 216). "The first step in this way," he continues, "is to return religion to its true meaning" (110). One should note that religion for him does not mean a body of rituals or a body of rules, but rather "religion in its true sense is to know the world and living in accordance with the rule of reason" (Kasravi 1336/1957, 24). As to Europeanism, the following is self-explanatory:

One could say that Iranians learned from Europeans in the following five areas: (1) constitutional government and the ordering of their lives according to the rule of law, having patriotic attachments, administrative arrangements, military service and things of that sort; (2) new sciences of geography, history, physics, chemistry, astronomy, mathematics, and so forth; (3) spinning, weaving, and the utilization of agricultural machines and other inventions; (4) the "feeling" of Europeanism: an exaggeration of civilization, the uproar of progress, new literary genres, and the like; and (5) materialistic philosophy: the malicious teaching of materialism, treating life as mere struggle, and other radical and useless ideas. Obviously, the first three are good and useful . . . while the last two are bad and costly. (Kasravi 1978, 53)

In some ways, Kasravi was the first Iranian to criticize modernism and Eurocentrism before Al-e Ahmad coined the term "Weststruckness" and made it a genre. Kasravi's thoughts, however, immediately affected the Shiʿi clergy, who felt threatened not only by his writing, but also by the works of his followers and sympathizers, the most controversial being that of Ali Akbar Hakamizadeh, which I will deal with when discussing the young Khomeini, below.

THE VOICES

Reactions by Islam-minded Iranians to these political and intellectual challenges led to the coming of the first generation in the Islamic movement. This generation was apprehensive about how its religion appeared to be on the defensive, and so it gave more emphasis to the religious components of Islam (as religion is understood in the West). The movement included diverse people and groupings and should not be seen as homogeneous; gradually, two important centers emerged. One response was from the voices concentrating in Qom, speaking from within the traditional institutions, displaying a conservative tone, and revolving around the protection and preservation of Islamic tenets. Its members revitalized the Shi'i center there. I refer to this voice as the Islam of Qom. The second response emerged in Tehran from within the context of modern institutions, notably the new institutions of higher learning—more specifically, Tehran University. Its members were prepared to adjust themselves to modern demands; thus they advocated a revival of Islam itself. They felt they had to appeal to the newly emerging Iranian generation within the modern universities. The two cities do not merely signify geographical locations, but represent two distinct intellectual approaches.

The Islam of Qom more or less echoed the more conservative narrative, while that of Tehran echoed the more liberal one. At the same time, both were completely aware of and apprehensive about the challenge of an authoritarian rule that would crush and limit any form of political dissent. Both concentrated their energy on reviving religion in the cultural and economic public spheres.

The Islam of Qom: Ha'eri, Khomeini, and Burujerdi

HA'ERI

Qom had a special visitor in March 1921—Ayatollah Ha'eri Yazdi—who proved decisive for the future of Shi'ism as a religion and for its role in Iranian politics. Qom had been a home for many Shi'is from the early days of Islam, but it gained significance when it became the grave of the eighth Shi'i imam's sister, Hazrat-e Masumeh, who died there in 816 while traveling to see her brother in Mashhad, a city in northeast Iran (Davani 1371/1992, 111).

The shrine to Hazrat-e Masumeh was erected during the reign of the Safavid ruler Shah Abbas I (1571–1629), and the city became an important center of Shi'ism because the "Safavid lavished enormous attention on Qom, the clergies there, and the welfare of its inhabitants" (115). When Mullah Mohsen Fayz established a seminary, naming it Fayziyeh, after himself, Qom gained a new significance. By the late nineteenth century, however, Tehran, Isfahan, and Najaf (in Iraq)—not Qom—had become important centers of Shi'ism. A depiction of the city can be found in a historical account in the journal of Qom seminary: "From the beginning of the fourteenth century [of the Muslim calendar, i.e., the 1920s AD], about eighty years ago, there was destruction everywhere. It was so massive that the living quarters of the most important schools in Qom, namely Fayziyeh, had been turned into storage rooms for the local merchants" ("Tarikhcheye Hozeye 'Elmiye-ye Qom" 1340/1961, 42). The migration of Ha'eri to the city, along with other fortunate coincidences, would change this condition forever. Perhaps Ha'eri could not predict that his action would change Shi'ism and the fate of Shi'i believers for a long time to come. His story, his deeds, and the intellectual trends he supported reveal the political thinking of the Islam of Qom in this period.

Ha'eri was born in Mehrjerd, near the city of Yazd. Following his early education in Yazd, he went to Najaf to study under Ayatollah Muhammad Taqi Shirazi (d. 1920). Apparently, Ha'eri was a very hardworking, intelligent student, and with his modesty and moderation, he soon became his teacher's favorite pupil. He befriended the son of Hajj Aqa Mohsen (d. 1910), one of the politico-economic and social elite of Arak—a city about 200 miles southeast of Tehran. Mohsen's son invited Ha'eri to come with him and reside there (a common practice among traditional scholars and poets) and try to secure the patronage of some local influential family.

Ha'eri began teaching in the "scriptural school" administered by Hajj Aqa Mohsen's family. His arrival coincided with the fervor of the constitutional revolution in Iran. Ha'eri got involved on the side of the constitutionalists and participated in their campaign. The following is an account of his activities by the most authoritative historian of Arak, Ebrahim Dehgan (d. 1987): "In the beginning of the constitutional period, in Arak, as in other Iranian cities, people were attracted to the revolutionary fervor. Everybody was busy establishing secret and semi-secret societies of various kinds. . . . When a notable democrat set up [a political] association, Ha'eri joined this association for a short time and even became its leader" (Dehgan 1331/1953, 19–20).

Two notable groups in Arak did not favor Ha'eri's political activism. One included the more traditional religious people and "the custodians of the school," who were upset and thought any political involvement was unwise and unwarranted (20). The other was his patron, Hajj Aqa Mohsen, who was upset because he did not care for revolutionaries and in fact "was fighting against the Persian Constitutional Revolution of 1905 . . . [and] expected Ha'eri's cooperation" (Hairi 1982, 342). Thus, Hajj Aqa Mohsen "withdrew his financial support," forcing Ha'eri to arrange for the departure of his family and later to leave the city discreetly (Badkobeei 1990, interview).

When he returned to Iraq in 1911, he had become relatively well known as a scholar and master of the principles of jurisprudence (*usule fiqh*). Apparently, he decided to distance himself from politics and public activism. The first sign of this new approach was his decision not to remain in Najaf, a city "also seriously involved in the Persian Revolution [1905]; therefore, he moved to Karbala, where he limited himself to religious activities" (Hairi 1982, 342; *Homayun* no. 2, 4). Two years later, his old friend invited him to return to Arak, possibly because his friend's father had passed away, but also because the revolutionary fervor of constitutionalism had subsided substantially. It was in this period that he emerged as a prominent religious leader, mainly because of his own stature, but also because of a series of fortuitous coincidences.

The first coincidence relates to the departure of the most prominent religious leader of Arak, Aqa Nooreddin, who had joined the parliamentary deputies emigrating from Tehran in protest against the Russian violation of Iranian neutrality in World War I. For doing so, he was labeled a "political mullah," which left a damaging impression on his followers. Many of these followers turned to Ha'eri for guidance, and gradually the latter generated a sizable following.

The second incident relates to the Islamic juridical injunction with regard to cautionary measures (*mavarede ehtiyati*), or issues for which juridical rulings are not explicitly spelled out in the religious books. In these cases, concerned Shi'i should refer to a qualified living clergyman of their own choice. As reported, when the concerned people of Arak consulted with Ayatollah Shirazi in Najaf about what to do or whom to turn to for rulings on cautionary measures, the latter referred them to his former pupil—Ha'eri (Razi 1332/1953, 33). As a result, Ha'eri gained a prominent position in Arak, which continued until his migration to Qom.

Ha'eri's biographers report that during the celebration of the Persian New Year in March 1921, Ha'eri went to Qom, in keeping with the custom of traveling to shrine cities on that day. Once he arrived, "prominent clerics in the city invited him to lead the congregational prayer and later begged him to remain and reside in Qom" (Sadr 1990, interview). They were impressed with this "moderate and soft-spoken man who always wore a sweet smile on his face" (Mehryar 1990, interview). Closer examination of Arak politics reveals that there were other reasons at work that eventually forced Ha'eri to migrate from Arak to Qom. These reasons included the following: he did not like that his patrons increasingly interfered with his school, where he had been promised a free hand; Aqa Nooreddin returned from his self-imposed exile to the south and was able to restore his religious stature, erecting "a newer and a bigger school"; with his old friend now running a rival school, he had little chance of realizing his dream of establishing a strong religious center; and, finally, he believed that, in his words, "a cleric can only flourish next to a possessor of miracle," that is, he should reside next to a shrine (Mehryar 1990, interview).

Ha'eri arrived in Qom determined to establish a strong religious center. He began the task not only of reorganizing the religious schooling in Qom, but also of reconstructing the school itself, whose buildings were in ruin. He was soon able to turn Qom into a lively religious center. First, he invited other prominent scholars to join him, and many of them responded favorably. What precipitated their response was the expansion of secular modernism in all aspects of Iranian life. The religious establishment was affected by the expansion of modern schools, the reorganization of the judicial system, and the politicization and government occupation of all religious endowments. Thus, students of religion welcomed the new place of refuge, and many prominent scholars from Tehran and Mashhad moved to Qom.

An unanticipated and fruitful historical coincidence enhanced Ha'eri's effort greatly—the exile of important Shi'i religious leaders from Iraq in 1923. Following a dispute with King Faisal and the British authorities, which resulted in the issuance of a fatwa against the British, nine prominent Shi'i ulama took refuge in Qom (Akhavi 1980, 28). Although they stayed for less than a year and the Iranian government was able to secure their return to Iraq from the British authorities, the news of their residence in Qom attracted many new students to that city. According to a contemporary witness, "The transfer of the 'Ulama into Iran caused a new revolution. It was reported in all the centers of the provinces, and

TABLE 1.1. RELIGIOUS STUDENTS IN QOM, 1935

School	Chambers	Students
Fayziyeh	91	250
Razawiyeh	24	43
Nasseriyeh	23	22
Haj Seyyed Sadeq	15	18
Dar-as-Shafa	28	42
Haj Mula Sadeq	25	45
Mehdi Qoli Khan	14	20
Others	—	100
City housing	—	200
Total	220	740

Source: *Homayun* no. 3, 3, 8.

very soon many people and new students migrated to Qom. . . . Many also were attracted to Qom from the other parts of the Muslim world, making the city the gathering point for Shi'i scholarship in the whole of the Islamic world" ("Rohaniyat dar Iran," *Homayun* no. 2, 3–4). Some of the new students left when the ulama departed from the city, but many of them remained and continued with their studies in Qom. Also, Ha'eri instituted the office of "tuition" (*shahriye*), that is, a monthly stipend to be paid to every religious student, regardless of age, until he reached religious leadership or died. This also suggests that Ha'eri generated financial resources for students in Qom.

The other reason for Ha'eri's success was his social activities and his strong commitment to public welfare. For example, he is credited with establishing the first public library in Qom (Faiz 1349–1350/1970–1971, 1:681). And during a disastrous flood in June 1934, Ha'eri mobilized the people and generated financial resources to rebuild the flood-stricken areas much sooner and more efficiently than the central government. He established a rationalized system of religious schooling and formalized the stipend paid to religious students from the special Shi'i tax. It is possible that his rationalization of registered students was copied from similar actions at the newly emerging modern institutions in the country. He arranged for new additions to the existing schools and educational institutions (677). As a result, more than a decade following his arrival, the religious centers acquired more than 700 students in their various scriptural schools. Table 1-1 shows the number and the distribution of the students in those schools.

Ha'eri never wrote a treatise expounding his political views. Thus, to portray the political thinking and positions of the Islam of Qom during this period, I looked in two places. First, I will review the positions Ha'eri took with regard to controversial issues of the period. Second, I will present a textual analysis of the journal *Homayun,* published under his auspices for more than a year.

HA'ERI'S POSITIONS ON CONTROVERSIAL ISSUES

I will look at five issues: republicanism in Iran in 1923–1924, the change of dynasty, the Qom incident with the shah's family, the clerical opposition to military service, and the ulama's opposition to the new dress code.

On the first four of these issues, what is notable is Ha'eri's and Qom's silence about the actions of the political establishment. The republicanism episode in 1924 refers to Reza Khan Pahlavi's campaign to gain absolute power by advocating republicanism and attempting to position himself as the first president of a new republic. When opposition grew and it became clear that the parliament would not accept republicanism, Reza Khan quickly turned against it: "Now that the people do not want it, I will give up republicanism" (quoted in Hedayat 1346/1967, 367). To soften the defeat and gain some legitimacy for his new position, Reza Khan traveled to Qom to consult with the religious establishment there.

Upon returning to the capital, Reza Khan published a communiqué that ignored the complex negotiations and debates he had had with parliament. He declared: "After an exchange of views with their holinesses, we finally found it appropriate to recommend that the notion of republicanism be abandoned altogether" (quoted in Maki 1357/1978, 3:14). The religious establishment approved the move and sent to various cities a telegram signed by the major ayatollahs of the day, including Ha'eri. It stated: "Because there have been some views on republicanism, which is approved by the people . . . when the Prime Minister [Reza Khan] came to Qom, we asked him to abolish the said views" (3:15). Qom tacitly approved of the emerging Reza Khan and welcomed the abandonment of republicanism, showing that they too preferred order and security to uncertainty, disorder, and dramatic changes.

The second issue on which Ha'eri's silence speaks concerns Reza Khan's attempt to become king through a change of dynasty. Now that the office of president had been put out of his reach, the only path was to go for kingship. Despite the setback regarding republicanism, he maneuvered to a stronger position by declaring that the perceived corruption of the existing Qajar dynasty was so strong and pervasive that it could easily be dethroned and the opposition removed. His prediction proved accurate, and his rapprochement with Qom worked to his advantage.

A bill to abrogate the kingship of the Qajar and form a Constituent Assembly was passed with little difficulty. A group of modernist intellectuals gathered to formulate a draft for revising certain principles of the constitution, particularly those dealing with the Qajar dynasty—i.e., to make them apply to the Pahlavi family. In those crucial moments, little was heard from Qom or from any religious leader among the traditional "custodians of the religious tradition." Whether Qom's silence should be interpreted as having approved of Tehran or whether it was a response to the fear of autocratic rule is hard to judge. Suffice it to say that Reza Shah was delighted to receive little resistance from Qom.

The third notable silence on Ha'eri's part concerned the Qom incident in 1927. Long before the state officially sanctioned, and sometimes violently enforced, the removal of veils from any Iranian woman who appeared in public, unveiling was exercised within the court, particularly by members of the shah's family. On the eve of the Iranian New Year of 1306 (March 1927), the Iranian first lady and some female members of the court visited the shrine at Qom. While in the shrine, they did not strictly observe Islamic cover, and thus caused a certain Sheikh Muhammad Bafqi (1875–1941) to stir up the crowd against them. Upon hearing the news, Reza Shah personally came to Qom, had the man lashed in public, and exiled him to the city of Rey. Moreover, he forbade henceforth the common practice of taking refuge in any of the shrines, thereby declaring that the sanctity of the shrines could, in fact, be violated by the powers that be.

Ha'eri kept silent about this incident and the reaction of Reza Shah. More than that, he ignored Bafqi's fate, despite the intervention of a close associate who in fact was his confidant, the man "in charge of the distribution of stipends to the religious students in his 'household'"[4] (Faqihi 1990, interview). Ha'eri even "denied having any knowledge of Bafqi and declared that, henceforth, the latter's name should not be mentioned in his presence" (Razi 1332/1953, 46).

Finally, Ha'eri was silent on the issue of military service and the Qom Congress in 1928. The decision to implement an across-the-board, compulsory military-service law, which required all Iranian males to attend military training and service, created distress among members of the religious establishment. Moreover, a bylaw banned religious-minded people from interfering under the pretext of "enjoining the good and forbidding the evil," which, for the religious leaders, meant abandoning their function as the custodians of religious tradition. Aqa Noorollah Isfahani (d. 1928), an activist of the constitutional period, took a strong position against the government two months before his death, allegedly by assassination. He gathered a group of prominent people in Qom and sent invitations to all the religious leaders in the country, inviting them to come and participate in a congress designed to formulate a united policy against Tehran. A high delegation arrived from Tehran to negotiate with the protestors, and a general agreement was worked out to settle the issues of concern. A major participant in the episode reported on the negotiations but made no mention of Ha'eri's role (Hedayat 1346/1967, 375–378). Again Ha'eri practiced noninvolvement.

Ha'eri finally broke his silence when it came to the issue of the dress code and the Goharshad incident of 1935. In June 1935, a bylaw was issued requiring all government employees to wear a special hat, later known as the Pahlavi hat. This was the beginning of an attempt to implement the policy of unveiling women, or *kashfe hijab*, as it came to be known. The previous spring, in a ceremony in Shiraz attended by the minister of education and culture, a group of female singers had appeared onstage and performed without covering their hair. In response to this incident, various religious leaders launched a serious campaign against the new measures, and Hajj Aqa Hossein Qomi, from Mashhad, traveled to Tehran to negotiate with the shah. Upon his arrival, Qomi was placed under house arrest. In July in Mashhad, Muhammad Taqi Bohlul, a peculiar and powerful preacher, delivered a sermon attacking the policy. Military commandos stormed the shrine, and people were killed or injured. It was in response to this incident that Ha'eri sent a mild telegram to Tehran: "Although until now I have not interfered in any [public] affairs, I hear that these days some measures that explicitly contradict the Ja'fari path [the Shi'i school of jurisprudence] and Islamic law have been adopted, which will be hard to tolerate and remain restrained about" (quoted in Razi 1332/1953, 51).

If the custodians of the religious tradition meant to collectively oppose the new changes imposed on Iranian sociopolitical life, this move came too late. By then, the new, modernist elite had reformed a major segment of society and had presented the religious establishment with a fait accompli. All they needed was the normalization of already-existing practices. The test came a few months later, in December 1936.

Reza Shah attended a ceremony at one of the institutes of higher education, and his wife and daughter appeared unveiled. With this presentation, he officially declared the unveiling of women; there was no opposition or protest from Qom.

As far as actual incidents are concerned, the custodians' behavior was no obstacle to the materialization of the secular modernists' goals. Amin Banani, whose work is considered the definitive summation of the period, sees the ideals underlying these changes as threefold: "a complete dedication to the cult of nationalism-statism; a desire to assert this nationalism by a rapid adoption of the material advances of the West; and a breakdown of the traditional power of religion and a growing tendency of secularism" (Banani 1961, 45). However, this defensive posture did not stop the voices of Islam in Qom from formulating a new version of their belief system. Indeed, they continued rebuilding the fortress in Qom, and more interestingly, a revivalist formulation began to emerge. A review of the journal published in Qom may tell us how Islam-minded Iranians in Qom reacted or responded theoretically to the advent of secularism.

HOMAYUN, OCTOBER 1934–JULY 1935

While Ha'eri was absent from politics, he was active in the cultural realm, particularly when it came to defending his understanding of Islam. The main symbol of this attitude came in his support for *Homayun*, a monthly journal published in Qom. Supported by Ha'eri and administered by two religious students, the journal was the voice of the newly emerging Shi'i center. Ali Akbar Hakamizadeh was the founder-editor of *Homayun*, named after local patron Muhammad Homayunpour. The first issue came out in Mehr 1313 (September–October 1934), and the last came out in Tir 1314 (June–July 1935).

In publishing the monthly, Hakamizadeh's main objective was to present Islam "as it has always been" and to target the newly emerging educated Iranians who had stopped listening to their mullahs (*Homayun* no. 1, 2). According to the publisher, the present condition of Islam-minded Iranians was "neither completely European nor completely Muslim," but worse: it was dominated by a powerful instrumental rationality.[5] "When it is beneficial, each person becomes Muslim, crying for Islam, and when it is beneficial to be irreligious, they turn against the creed" (no. 5, 25). Iran had lost its orientation while being constantly pulled toward either traditionalism (not using reason to approach religion) or extreme materialism (not employing reason when adopting modern categories). An author of the journal wrote, "Today the flood of materialism is destroying the world, and soon it will swallow you [Iran] as well" (no. 8, 10). Thus, the editorial board and publisher took it upon themselves to familiarize Iranians with their religion, its demands, Islamic duties, and historical development (Mehrizi-Tabatab'i 1351/1972, 76–79); they also provided a podium for defending Islamic tenets in the face of antagonistic intellectual trends.

The main assumption of the journal was that Muslims had lost their confidence in the face of these challenges. As suggested by the journal's first editorial, "Any nation that has lost its heart to a defeatist posture and fear can never stand up for its rights or defend the assaults of the enemies" (*Homayun* no. 1, 11). What were the challenges that caused such a disheartening condition among Muslims? They included Westernization and modernism; religious reformism, as manifested in the views of Shari'at Sangelaji; and finally, materialism and Marxism, including those views presented by Iranian Marxists in the pages of *Donya*, the official organ of the Iranian Communist Party.

Although the editorial does not refer directly to any of these trends, the implicit references reveal *Homayun*'s target: an attempt to present an updated code of conduct for modern Muslims. Modern Muslims received plenty of criticism from the more conservative people of Qom, but this did not discourage the authors. As the journal's editor said, "The author will not be discouraged by these sorts of mistreatments and has prepared himself for any hardship so as to be able to purify Islam from these pollutions" (no. 8, 8). There was also an enemy from within. According to the journal, the existing condition of Iran could not continue: "Until a few decades ago, Iran was following a path of backwardness and destruction. With the tumult of Westernization, a new path presented itself. Which one should she take: the old path that caused ignorance and perversion or the new one that . . . ends in destruction? We know of a third path, which is the path of reason and humanity (*kherad va mardomi*)—a path guided by reason, supported by God and the people, and its consequences would be welfare and happiness" (no. 8, 13). The last statement set the agenda not just for the journal itself, but also for the second generation of the Islamic movement in Iran.

The second presupposition of the editorial board was that the response to these challenges should come from every member of society, but particularly from the intellectuals. Ignorance was taken to be the root of all of Iran's difficulties. To review the record of one's life is to reveal ignorance, and therefore, "to be awake and aware is everyone's duty, although for the elite it is a bigger responsibility [in any given society], since it is comparable to the head of a household" (no. 10, 4). To battle either traditionalism or modernism, in other words, one must rely on the elite. Both of these vices had to be replaced with virtues, and no one is more successful at doing so than members of the intellectual elite, who are able to guide the people by their words. Thus, "whoever is interested in causing reform among the people should first help enhance the knowledgeable people through talking and writing against, and also silencing and blocking, the ignorant orators and writers" (no. 10, 5). To battle modernism, Westernization, and traditionalism, the authors of *Homayun* followed a two-pronged strategy. Against modernism, reformism, and materialism, they fought by refuting the West. To eliminate traditionalism and superstition—which they viewed as having polluted the purity of religion as the basis of Iranian society—they embarked on presenting a "reasoned, humane," (no. 8, 13) and modern version of Islam, and they encouraged Muslims to take their religion more seriously.

The editorial board was liberal in its approach and invited everyone to participate. For example, Ahmad Kasravi—in those days a religious student at the Razaviye School—contributed an essay that criticized modernism and Westernization while also elaborating on a second theme dealing with modern Islam and its relationship to politics. The journal's criticism of modernism began in the very first issue with a short piece entitled "The Voice of the Heart." The author made an honest confession that he had not seen Europe, "but news agencies report on it daily." He credits Europe for "having achieved major advancements in industry and innovation" (no. 1, 28). Then he wrote, "When ignorant people hear the word "Europe" or hear about life there, enviously they sigh as to why their country cannot join the bandwagon of civilization. Little do they know that this train [Westernization] is heading for destruction. . . . The tumult coming from Europe is empty, with little or no depth" (no. 1, 28–29). Instead, one had to follow neither traditionalism nor modernism, but a third path—that of reason and humanity within the context of one's own culture and society: "Rest assured that we are aware that if a nation desires progress and development, it has to decrease its dependency on other countries and utilize local commodities" (no. 2, 18).

The defense of pure religion and humanism in the face of secularism and traditionalism also began with the first issue. An essay on theology begins: "If one wants to build a strong dwelling, it has to begin with a strong foundation. . . . Similarly, if one wants to have a strong foundation for one's social life, nothing is superior to God and the proper understanding of His nature" (no. 1, 21). This essay does not suggest that one has to create a religious society or a religious polity; rather, it argues that one has to find a proper place for religion in life. After making a prophetic statement that "those who forego their world for the sake of religion, or forego their religion for the sake of the world, are not members of my community," the author concludes, in the next issue: "Religion and the world are two sides of a balance, and they should be equal. This, of course, is a difficult task to perform" (no. 2, 33).[6] The journal proposed that the way forward was to create an interaction between the positive dimensions of the Iranian past and the positive aspects of modernity.

According to the journal's writers, religion is not an abstract notion, nor is its purpose to be served by the people. On the contrary, religion was sent to help man, and it is important because its injunctions are ethically, socially, and hygienically useful. But religion cannot do the job by itself. Religion can and will help, but it should not be treated as a panacea. "The only force that can start all circles of life is the force of human will. . . . Even Islam itself teaches humanity that what is essential is man's action and striving" (no. 7, 18–19).[7]

Religious commandments are here to help and elevate humanity, not to be used as instruments of power. In a long essay on fasting, the practice of not eating during the day but eating excessively at night came under attack. This Islamic injunction, if properly implemented, should contribute to fairness (no. 4, 2–5). Ramadan, the month of fasting, is a month of schooling and of the rebirth of Islamic understanding and solidarity, as a result of which people "have more understanding of God, have gone through ethical exercises, and have acquired virtuous habits" (6). In other words, the authors of the journal believed that what was prevalent among Muslims as religion was nothing more than traditionalism. One author went so far as to say, "I believe if the Prophet himself were to emerge today and tell these people that the religion they practice is not the one he brought them, he would be accused of unbelief, and they would claim that their fathers knew what to pass on to them" (no. 8, 8).

There were many references to governmental and political institutions. In an essay dealing with the place of the king in the polity, the author justified kingship philosophically and in accordance with shariʿa juridical principles. Invoking the founder of Muslim philosophy, Abu Nasr Farabi, the author wrote, "If there are people who oppose kingship and equate it with tyranny and injustice, it is because they . . . do not grasp the philosophy and the foundation of kingship. . . . The position of a king in a given polity is the same as the position of soul in the human body" (no. 3, 9). He then relies on shariʿa and discusses the primary and secondary (*avvaliye va saanaviye*) principles, arguing that it is an obligation in Islamic law to follow those necessary measures that are needed for Muslims' security and welfare and the implementation of the law. Respect for the kingdom is required for security, even if the king is "tyrannical and polytheist (*jaaber-e moshrek*)" (no. 3, 10).

Homayun lasted less than a year, for two main reasons. First, Hakamizadeh wanted quick reforms, which did not correspond with the slower and more prudent approach of Ha'eri. He was attracted to the Islam of Tehran. Apparently, at a weekly meeting in the house of Abassqoli Bazargan (Mehdi Bazargan's father) in Tehran, intellectuals would gather and the participants would exercise much religious tolerance. The more Hakamizadeh was exposed to Tehran's intellectuals, the more he lost interest in Qom, and the more the religious establishment withdrew its support from Hakamizadeh. Also, as the strength of modernism grew, many religious people became more reactionary and conservative. The irony is that neither the voices of modernism nor those of traditionalism could tolerate modernity. As one of the contributors to the journal told me in Qom, "In general, Hawzeh [the religious seminary] turned its back on this journal, and as a result the journal stopped" (Bodala 1990, interview). Second, the more liberal tendencies of the monthly discouraged its patron, causing him to withdraw his financial support, and the journal could not satisfy its financial obligations. For example, Bodala said that it was he who published the last issue, in Tir 1314/June–July 1936, by generating other sources of funds and borrowing.

Ha'eri represented an interesting paradigm, which was at once politically quietist and culturally activist. Whether his approach was due to a tacit agreement between Qom and the authorities in Tehran or to dissimulation or to expediency (*taqiyyeh*), the fact remains: avoidance of "all involvement in politics" (Enayat 1982, 27) became more of the rule than an exception among Shi'is. Generally speaking, this moderate and tolerant approach continued even after Ha'eri's death. This approach, which implied accepting the autocratic order, had important and far-reaching results in the building of Qom, and also in the training of new custodians, such as Ruhollah Musavi Khomeini, Muhammad Kazem Shari'atmadari, and Aqa Murtaza Ha'eri, each of whom became instrumental in preparing the ground for the politicization of the religious establishment and the emergence of the Islamic Revolution in 1979. Before that, however, Qom emerged as the most important Shi'i religious center, under the leadership of Ayatollah Mohammad Hossein Tabataba'i, known as Burujerdi (d. 1961). The latter did for Qom what Murteza

Ansari had done for Najaf before. Just as Najaf had become the center of support of the Constitutional Revolution, Qom became the center of support for the Islamic Revolution.

YOUNG KHOMEINI

Ha'eri died in 1936, assigning the responsibility for guiding the affairs of the Qom religious schools to a group of three clergymen, Ayatollahs Muhammad Hujjat Kuhkamare'i (d. 1952), Sadr ad-Din Sadr (d. 1953), and Muhammad Taqi Khonsari (d. 1951). By then, Qom had achieved a great deal: the religious centers had been revived, particularly in the face of the all-out secularization of Reza Shah's period. The situation continued until 1944, when Burujerdi arrived in Qom and became the new pillar of religious establishment.

The role of the young Khomeini in Qom is significant for at least two reasons. One concerns the years immediately after Ha'eri's death and before Burujerdi's arrival, and the second concerns the period a few years after Ayatollah Isfahani died. The first, coinciding with the departure of the deposed king, paved the way for those segments of the society that had been repressed during the previous two decades to assert themselves. Reza Shah's secularization and personal autocracy had gone too far, and subsequently many of his policies were now relaxed. However, as demonstrated by Khomeini's response to a pamphlet questioning aspects of Shi'ism, the generally cautious practice of the late Ha'eri still dominated the ulama's views.

In the early days of 1943, Ali Akbar Hakamizadeh went to live in Tehran and began cooperating with Kasravi. Before moving, Hakamizadeh used to spend a great deal of time in the city and was exposed to modernizing views (Bodala 1990, interview). As a result, he became a close follower of Kasravi. Soon he wrote a brief article questioning the tenets of Shi'ism, expecting an intellectual debate. Not receiving any response, Hakamizadeh published a longer version of the article in the form of a pamphlet entitled *Asrare Hezarsaleh* (The Secrets of a Thousand Years), refuting and mocking many of the tenets of Shi'ism in Iran. In the last two pages of the pamphlet, Hakamizadeh proposed thirteen questions and invited readers to respond to them.

Qom decided to "formulate a comprehensive response to it" and launched a concentrated campaign to refute the pamphlet.[8] The most notable responses at the time were those written by Muhammad Khalesizadeh and Ruhollah Musavi Khomeini, both recognized religious teachers. Although the former was more prominent at the time, his treatise was rather short (fifty-six pages), and Khomeini's longer, more comprehensive treatise, which thoroughly refuted Hakamizadeh's work, proved more presentable. The leadership in Qom approved Khomeini's treatise and had it published under the title *Kashfe Asrar* (Revealing the Secrets) without the name of the author. It was to be regarded as the position of the custodians of the religious tradition in Qom.

Khomeini's work is organized and modeled after Hakamizadeh's pamphlet—a short tract of thirty-eight pages organized in six chapters: God, Imamate, *Rohaniyat* (the religious establishment), *Hukomat* (government), *Qanun* (the law), and *Hadith* (tradition) (Hakamizadeh 1943). Hakamizadeh's main purpose was to purify religion from traditionalism, which had obscured its real meaning. On the issue of political authority and government, which is most relevant for this discussion of Khomeini, Hakamizadeh made a direct attack against the linear presentation of authority in Shi'ism, whereby the authority of the Prophet was understood to have been transmitted to infallible imams and in their absence to the cleric. He wrote, "Our present religion claims that erecting any government in the absence of the infallible Imam is invalid" (19). Discussing the role of Islamic law in Iran, he then challenged the claim that "the only official laws that command our obedience are those based on the Shari'a" (27). He concedes that humanity is in need of guidance, but claims that "one's faculty of reason" is far superior to all other capacities (29).

Khomeini responded to both challenges. Regarding the general notion that no temporal power is accepted in the absence of an infallible imam, Khomeini claimed that the reason for the former lies in the system of Islamic thought—misunderstood by the author of the pamphlet. He pointed out that the opposition of the ulama relates to malpractice on the part of the men of authority and to the practice of authority itself. Furthermore, he stated that the ulama have no claim to power for themselves and that kingship as a form of government seems to work only when it is occupied by a righteous person.

Despite his defensive posture, however, Khomeini remained firm in claiming absolute authority for Islamic law: "Man has no right to legislation. Whatever laws human beings formulate will be mere academic exercise" (Khomeini 1321/1943, 289). Having no use for the various systems of government, Khomeini was of the conviction that "other than their deceiving appearance, there is no fundamental distinction among constitutional, despotic, dictatorial, democratic . . . and communistic regimes" (289).

On the issue of the clerics' authority, Khomeini remained loyal to the prevalent ideas of Shi'ism—in the absence of an infallible imam, authority belongs to the jurisconsults—but with a qualification. He distinguished between holding office and acting as guardian: "When we say government and guardianship in this period belongs to the jurisconsults, we are not saying that jurisconsult should be king, minister, military officers, or street sweeper" (185). He added, "Government should be based on divine laws so as to guarantee the welfare of the country and that of the people, and this cannot be done without the guidance of the clerics" (222). Similar to al-Ghazali, who preferred an unjust ruler to chaos, Khomeini accepted the existing order, provided it did not contradict the ordinances of Islam: "Although all other forms of kingship other than that of God are contrary to the welfare of the people . . . [the clerics in practice] accept and respect the existing void ones until better ones replace them" (186).

However, there is generally little sign of comprehensive opposition to the regime in Iran, or the presentation of any alternative political order. Thus, while Khomeini was ready to defend the integrity of Islam, he remained within the general tradition of the late Ha'eri, who was culturally active but politically reserved. That tradition was so strong that it continued during the ascendancy of the next religious leader in Qom, namely, Ayatollah Burujerdi.

Young Khomeini's second important role related to his help in promoting Burujerdi to the prominent role of exclusive emulation (marja'iyat). In Shi'ism religious leaders play significant roles as sources of emulation, and at any given time there may be many such "sources." In the twentieth century, only Burujerdi managed to become one; all others recognized him as the sole source. It was reported that in the aftermath of prominent Shi'i leader Ayatollah Abolhasan Isfahani's death, Khomeini actively campaigned for Burujerdi. Some say it was because he hoped to manage affairs in the new leader's office, but if so, he was not successful in the end. Others maintained that his main reason was to keep the power of Shi'i leadership in Qom. Judging that Burujerdi would be the best person to achieve this goal, he organized a campaign letter that was sent to various cities in support of Burujerdi's position. He also visited Toliyat, the government's appointed guardian of the shrine at Qom, and made certain that in the ceremony commemorating Isfahani, Ayatollah Burujerdi would be mentioned as the new leader of Shi'ism. Khomeini acted as the liaison between Burujerdi and the shah (Kazem B——[a close relative of Ha'eri and Isfahani] 2004, interview).

BURUJERDI

Hossein Tabataba'i from the city of Burujerd, hence known as Burujerdi, arrived in Qom on December 30, 1944, and emerged as the new voice of the Islam of Qom. He attracted the support of Shi'is the world over. He strengthened the view that the ulama's main efforts should be exerted on organization, institution building, and the assertion of authority.

Burujerdi was born in 1875 and studied in his hometown before traveling to Isfahan for advanced studies, because "the seminaries were very active at this time there" (Davani 1371/1992, 94). He stayed in Isfahan for nine years and became a solid scholar in jurisprudence, but he was not satisfied with himself, so he traveled to Najaf in 1892. There, he studied with Akhond Mullah Muhammad Kazem Khonsari and Shari'at Isfahani. After a few years, he returned to his hometown for a visit, but when his father died, he stayed home to care for his extended family (101).

By the 1940s, Ayatollah Burujerdi had made a name for himself as a prominent scholar of religious sciences, particularly jurisprudence. In 1944, he was taken to a hospital in Tehran for medical treatment, where Mohammad Reza Shah Pahlavi visited him. The visit brought his name to national attention, since the young shah had a certain degree of legitimacy. At the same time, the people of Qom who wanted to attract Burujerdi extended an invitation to him. He accepted, and the whole city celebrated his arrival.

Ayatollah Sadr ad-Din Sadr invited Burujerdi to teach in his place and even asked him to lead his congregational prayers. Soon, his charisma and leadership qualities proved far superior to those of the existing leadership group. Like Ha'eri, his main concern was the expansion and authority of the religious centers of Qom. Many argue that, like Ha'eri, he had an unspoken understanding with the royal court, as symbolized by the shah's visit to the hospital. Whatever the truth might be, Burujerdi soon became the sole source of emulation, both in Iran and beyond. Other religious centers had no strong leaders, and the two most prominent leaders in Najaf had died.

Burujerdi portrayed himself as apolitical and noninterventionist, but in practice he was actually very political: he made Islam relevant in the public sphere. He might have been apolitical at the micro level—within Iranian politics—but he was very active in promoting Islamic issues globally. He calculatedly positioned himself in relation to important events in Iran and instituted the international proselytizing of Islam from Qom. He encouraged rapprochement between Shi'is and Sunnis, and his contribution to the reassertion of Qom's authority had a remarkable effect on paving the way for an Islamic revival. According to Motahari, Burujerdi's legacy lies in the following areas: his approach to jurisprudence, in that he shifted the emphasis from treating hypothetical questions to addressing practical causes and the motives underlying particular issues; encouraging closer cooperation between Shi'i and Sunni jurisconsults; training and dispatching proselytizers to the other parts of the world; closing the gap between religion and the sciences by encouraging the writing of religious books in a more accessible language and by supporting the establishment of schools; and establishing control over the religious apparatus and regulating the office of the source of emulation (Motahhari 1341/1962, 233–249).

Like Ha'eri's, Burujerdi's modus operandi in the political sphere amounted to quiet accommodation, but he was very active on cultural issues, and, indeed, the five aforementioned areas all fall within the cultural realm. Davani reported Burujerdi's direct expression of his position: "Some people criticize me for not interfering in politics. The reality is that when I was in Najaf, I observed the involvement of Akhund Khorasani and Na'ini in politics and saw the result. Consequently, I became very sensitive about this issue. . . . Since we are not well versed in political issues, I am afraid we will be tricked and stopped from achieving our main objectives" (quoted in Davani 1371/1992, 352).

In his lifetime, Burujerdi faced serious political developments, such as the Constituent Assembly of 1948, the nationalization of the oil industries in 1948–1953, the beginning of land and economic reforms in 1959–1961, and the radicalism of the fundamentalist organization Fada'iyan Islam in the late 1940s. During all these episodes, he remained detached, since "in principle he avoided politics in a serious way" (441–442).

The government was reportedly in direct contact with Burujerdi about constitutional reforms. Many concerned clerics contacted his office, and he responded that the government had assured him there would be no change within the constitution with regard to religious matters; such a guarantee was good enough for him (327–328). Burujerdi's role during the period of oil nationalization is a matter of some controversy, but the actual realities point to his tacit support for the shah against Mosaddeq. Iranian political scientist Shahrough Akhavi confirms Burujerdi's alliance with other conservative clerics in support of the shah (Akhavi 1980, 92). Also, five days after the 1953 coup that toppled Mosaddeq, a telegram from Burujerdi appeared in Tehran's daily paper, *Ettela'at,* congratulating the shah on his safe return to Iran and expressing the hope that his restoration "would correct the past corruptions and lead to the restoration of the greatness of Islam" (3 Shahrivar 1332/ August 25, 1953).

Burujerdi's reaction to the Fada'iyan is indicative of his method for avoiding involvement in politics. The Fada'iyan was a "nonintellectual" and secret organization (Enayat 1982, 94) founded by a charismatic figure, Mujtaba Navvab Safavi (1923–1956), and it was an active political group in Iran from the mid-1940s to the mid-1950s. The organization's main objective was to struggle against irreligiosity (*mobareze ba bidini*), and its immediate and main protagonists were reformist individuals such as Ahmad Kasravi. Soon the organization became a politico-military establishment that not only played an important role at this time, but also became a forerunner of Islamist radicalism. Later Islamist organizations such as the Islamic Nations Party (*Hezb-e Mellal-e Eslami*), which emerged in the 1960s, traced their origins to this organization (Kazemi 1984, 167). As the content of their manifesto, *Ketab-e Rahnemaye Haq* (*The Book of Righteous Guidance;* first published 1329/1950) suggests, they wanted to implement a traditionalist interpretation of Islamic jurisprudence in all aspects of Iranian life (Khosroshahi 1375/1996, 193–331).

The leadership believed that violent means such as assassination and the mobilization of the masses for demonstration were justified and accepted. They succeeded in assassinating historian Ahmad Kasravi in March 1946, Prime Minister Abdolhossein Hazhir in November 1949, and Prime Minister Ali Razmara in March 1951 (Kazemi 1984, 160–165). Ayatollah Burujerdi did not approve of this kind of activism, particularly when the group's daily demonstrations disrupted classes in Qom's religious schools. The relationship came to a deadlock when, in 1949, the Fada'iyan, in an insulting leaflet, attacked Burujerdi for being complacent. The Fayziyeh seminary became a battleground between the supporters and opponents of Burujerdi. Navvab, who lived in Tehran, traveled to Qom, but the ayatollah refused to see him. As Davani put it: "Navvab left Qom with sadness, and henceforth the activism of the Fada'iyan died down in Qom" (Davani 1371/1992, 378).

Burujerdi's active cultural involvement revealed how zealous he was in reviving religious tradition. His involvement in the revision of the *Ressalahs*—manuals of behavior for Shi'i Muslims—is illustrative. The prose of these Persian religious tracts was usually filled with Arabic words and convoluted syntax. A great supporter of clear writing and simple prose, Burujerdi commissioned a group of scholars to revise many of the religious texts, particularly the *Ressalahs*. As Allameh Karbaschi, the man who later established the Alavi High School in Tehran, reported,

"I told his holiness that the manual of acts is filled with complex writings that are hard for people to follow. His holiness commissioned us to revise them under his own auspices" (narrated by one of the scholars, Faqihi 1990, interview). Burujerdi advocated this easy and readable style for other publications from Qom, including the monthly *Maktab-e Islam:* "The writings of a couple of the authors for the journal are difficult to follow. If they are writing for the people, I do not think people can understand these texts, and if they write for themselves, then why do they bother publishing them" (quoted in Davani 1371/1992, 350).

Another example of Burujerdi's cultural involvement came during the anti-Baha'i campaign. Bahaism has grown into a religion with many followers scattered all over the world. It had a modest origin, however, and began with Shi'i cleric Seyyed Muhammad Ali Shirazi (d. 1849) in 1843, when he declared that he was in direct contact with the hidden imam. This was contrary to the established tradition of Shi'ism, according to which there would no longer be any direct contact with the infallible imams after 940. Confrontation with clerics led to his trial and subsequent public execution in 1849. Bahaism developed when an associate of Muhammad Ali named Mirza Hossein Ali Nuri (1817–1892), better known as Baha'ollah (the glory of God), first declared himself the infallible imam and later a new prophet. Even though Bahaism became a world phenomenon, Iran remained its stronghold, and its followers rose to significant political and economic positions during the Pahlavi era.

For reasons that go beyond the scope of this discussion, in May 1955 the followers of the religious establishment physically attacked various Baha'i centers. The attacks began when the government allowed the preacher Sheikh Muhammad Taqi Falsafi free airtime on the radio for his attacks on the Baha'i faith. Subsequently, a wave of anti-Baha'i violence swept the country, including the destruction of the dome of the Baha'i temple in Tehran. The United Nations and the U.S. State Department pressured the shah to stop the attacks. Based on reports in Iranian papers, the religious establishment, including Ayatollah Burujerdi, supported the anti-Baha'i effort. Burujerdi "was urgently pushing for the destruction of Bahaism and the seizure of their assets, which were to be used for the construction of *madrasahs* and mosques. His only reservation was that these steps be taken in an orderly way, without the shedding of blood" (Akhavi 1980, 79). Moreover, he approved of a very active group known as the Hojjati-ye whose raison d'etre was fighting Bahaism. Significantly, this group later became a well-structured organization that assumed power in the newly formed Islamic regime in Iran.

Furthermore, the group enjoyed the backing of prominent religious leaders, such as the present leader, Ayatollah Khamenei, and a member of the Assembly of Experts, Ayatollah Khaz'ali.[9]

Burujerdi's other cultural involvement included supporting private schools and cultural houses for the propagation of religion. He is credited with establishing the mosque and library in Qom, supporting private schools in various cities in Iran, and dispatching preachers to other countries. One of his most revolutionary measures was the establishment of private high schools designed to train students who not only studied secular and Western subjects and the sciences, but were equally committed to Islam and its religious injunctions. This began in 1949, when Burujerdi sent a special request to the Ministry of Education to establish a "prayer room" (*namaz-khaneh*) in existing high schools, which happened first in Fatemi High School (Faqihi 1990, interview). Such a request was novel, considering that Tehran University's mosque was established in the 1960s. The idea of independent high schools came later, with the founding of the *Din va Danesh* (religion and knowledge) high school.

Burujerdi also attempted to establish dialogue with the Sunni centers, notably Al-Azhar University-Seminary, in Cairo. To achieve this goal, he created *Dar-al-Taqrib Beyn al-Mazaheb al-Islamiye* (the house for bringing together Islamic schools). The president of Al-Azhar sent a letter thanking Ayatollah Burujerdi for his support in the effort (Davani 1371/1992, 248). This effort was so successful that even the Iranian government supported it financially. The session of the council of ministers for 6-3-1340 (June 1961), during the premiership of Ali Amini, allocated money for the activities of *Dar-al-Taqrib* (Proceedings of the Council, item 9). Also, the chief mufti of Egypt, Sheikh Mahmud Shltut, later issued a fatwa recognizing Shi'i jurisprudence as the fifth school of law in Islam. Pan-Islamism has had a long history, but the dialogue between Shi'is and Sunnis only began only with Ha'eri, who supported direct contact between the scholars of various Islamic schools of law and jurisprudence. According to the June 1935 issue of *Homayun*, "At the time of this writing, Mirza Abuabdollah Zanjani, who is one of the prominent scholars in Iran, is traveling to Iraq and greater Syria for establishing some form of relations between the Sunnis and the Shi'is" (*Homayun* no. 9, 18).

Finally, Burujerdi's cultural involvement was evident in the multiplication of the number of books and journals published in Qom under his leadership and with the support of his office. According to one of his biographers, during the sixteen years that Burujerdi was the leader of Shi'ism, more than three hundred titles in various fields were published.

"In total," he writes, "the religious seminary of Qom made 346,000 volumes available to the public" (Davani 1371/1992, 137).

In addition, there were many journals that received either tacit or active support from the ayatollah. They included *Maktab-e Islam* (The School of Islam), *Maktab-e Tashyu'* (The School of Shi'ism), *Maktab-e Qur'an* (The School of the Qur'an), and *Maktab-e Anbiya* (The School of the Prophets). The spirit dominating these journals is the same: Muslims are facing the novel and comprehensive challenge of modernity. The first essay in the first issue of *Maktab-e Tashyu'* is entitled "Our Difficulties and Their Causes." It begins: "Suddenly there occurred a transformation in all aspects of life. . . . The flood of Western civilization flowed toward Eastern countries, and Muslim countries faced a new circumstance. The clerical leaders were not against progress and evolution . . . but soon they realized that the new civilization was mixed with some intellectual and moral deviation that threatened the freedom and independence of Muslim nations" (*Maktab-e Tashyu'* 1338/1959, 1:3).

How was one to face this challenge? The solutions the journal offered reflected the strategy advanced by Burujerdi, namely, cultural activism, the revival of religious thought, and moderation and accommodation in politics. "It is necessary today," wrote the authors of *Maktab-e Tashyu'*, "for Muslims to wake up from their benumbing sleep and revive the creed of Islam. To do that, first and foremost, there should be an intellectual transformation" (*Maktab-e Tashyu'* 1338/1959, 1:271). The same spirit dominated the most enduring journal that is still in publication: *Maktab-e Islam*, which first appeared in Bahaman 1337 (February 1958) and continues to this day. While the ayatollah did not commission articles for the journal, he ignored all negative reports, objections, and rumors regarding it. After some issues arrived, he summoned the editors and expressed his full support:

> The Ayatollah said in a happy tone, "Ever since I arrived in Qom and accepted this responsibility, I wanted Qom's religious establishment to publish a journal in a calm and quiet fashion, particularly since I had heard that al-Azhar of Egypt publishes a journal. . . . Now that you have published it just such a way, I will grant you my complete blessing, as long as you follow the same mission." (Davani 1371/1992, 349)

It was due to Burujerdi's prudent approach and his practical modus operandi that by "the year 1957, his general deputyship was confirmed and the religious establishment in Qom became very lively and active" (121).

More importantly, the impact of his politically quiet but culturally active and imaginative approaches encouraged the emergence of a new group of clerics. According to an evaluation in a local weekly a few days after his death, as a result Burujerdi's efforts, "a new generation of clerics and religious students were cultivated, many of whom were intellectuals, prudent, familiar with global politics and new sciences, and could grasp scientific and social developments" (quoted in Davani 1371/1992, 137). At the same time, his quietist approach to politics became the dominant paradigm from the time of his death until the victory of the Islamic revolution in 1979, as evidenced by the actions of such prominent clerics as Mohammad Kazem Shari'atmadari (1904–1985). In the political realm, Shar'atmadari remained loyal to the constitutional form of monarchy until the victory of the revolution. To move forward, he then advocated the creation of a Democratic Republic of Muslims, but faced the opposition and wrath of those filled with revolutionary zeal. Some radical clerics suggested revoking his position of religions leadership (*marja'iyat*).

The Islam of Tehran: Bazargan, Taleqani, and Islamic Groups

YOUNG BAZARGAN AND TALEQANI

The establishment of Tehran University in 1935 had a dual impact. First, it became a part of Reza Shah's modernism, and second, many people made the university an important center of Islamic discourse in Tehran. The most significant voices of the latter trend were Mehdi Bazargan (1907–1995) and Mahmoud Taleqani (1910–1979). There were many others, but these two deserve to be introduced, since they were the most influential in the Islamic discourse in Tehran at this time.[10]

It is ironic that the oldest voice of Islamic discourse in Tehran belonged to a noncleric trained in the hard sciences and educated at Paris, the heart of the secular West. This was Mehdi Bazargan, the son of a well-established merchant, Haj Abbassqoli Tabrizi. In fact, the life his father lived as a serious business professional who was also serious about his religion shaped Mehdi's life. Mehdi became a renowned professor as well as a religionist. The religiosity this father and son displayed was different from that advocated by the traditional clergies. Regular gatherings in Haj Abbassqoli's house were open both to reformists, like Hakamizadeh (Bodala 1990, interview), and to followers of other religions. What was in the air and what was discussed at these gatherings could be considered a liberal approach to Islam and its teachings.

Mehdi completed his early education in Iran, and in 1928 successfully passed the competitive examination to go to France to study. His seven-year stay in Europe significantly affected his life. His first impression of life in Europe remained with him: "The first day in the auditorium of the École Centrale, the head of the school, professor Jean Gillet, a metallurgist and member of the Académie des Sciences, greeted the new students by referring to them as 'dear friends.' We, the young students, were dear for that aged and powerful man" (Bazargan 1356/1977, 61). The mentality displayed by Professor Gillet, Bazargan continues, permeated society as a whole, in the sense that European societies exhibited respect for human integrity, mutual trust, respect for the law, a sense of responsibility, and above all, cooperation.

Unlike his fellow Iranian students, he thought that what had shaped European civilization was a strong sense of religious conviction. As he wrote, "Contrary to what most people think, i.e., contrary to some unaware modernists, religion is not pushed to dark corners of the churches" (Bazargan 1965, 16). Not only did he return successfully, but he returned with "a stronger faith in Islam." He qualified this, however, by adding that his religion was "not the superstitious, individualistic, and ritualistic Islam, but rather the pure, dynamic, and energizing one" (Bazargan 1356/1977, 64).

Bazargan's return to Iran coincided with the establishment of Tehran University, which provided him with his best audience. Like Ha'eri and Burujerdi, Bazargan had a strong conviction that politics and political activism were not the solution and that one should instead concentrate on cultural and educational activities. He later became active in politics, however, and even became the first prime minister of the revolutionary regime. In this and similar cases, Bazargan would claim that he had assumed the post to perform a religious duty (Bazargan 1356/1977, 125). At the same time, Tehran University became the center of an emerging elite that, as a result of the new creed of modernism, was alienated from its local culture. The educated class had so much contempt for native tradition that to display any sense of religiosity or "commitment to Islam took extraordinary courage"; this was so at a time when "in European society to be a Catholic or to attend church to pray constituted a normal act" (Bazargan 1965, 19). He tried to remain religiously committed at a time when secularism was at its peak. Communism and nationalism were the religions of the day in Iran in the first half of the twentieth century.

How could one preserve tradition in the face of aggressive, dominating, and even domineering modernism? And how could one free religion from the grip of traditionalism and superstition? The image Bazargan used is telling and insightful. He compared himself and his generation to a "hinge": "The present generation, to which we . . . belong, is like a 'hinge' in Iranian history. We are the mediators between previous generations, which lived conservatively with no moving ideas, and the future generation, which, God willing, will gain independence and power" (Bazargan 1965, 38). He played this role for almost all his life, first mediating between the newly educated Iranians and the more traditional forces, and later between nationalists and Islam-minded Iranians. He did the same as prime minister, mediating between the revolutionaries and the people.

Bazargan functioned as a hinge in other spheres of his life as well. A voracious reader and prolific writer, he wrote about nearly every subject relating to public life, focusing on three broad categories. First, he tried throughout his life to show that religion and the modern sciences work toward the same goal, revealing the truth about human nature and life on earth. For Bazargan, the most proper hinge is human reason. Second, he wrote in an anthropological mode, presenting human beings as creatures inclined to worship. Owing to natural instinct, humans hierarchically worship "self, fellow human beings, principles, and finally God" (Bazargan 1357/1978, 4). Here, the proper hinge between man and God is freedom. Third, Bazargan worked to show that religion and the public sphere are linked through a proper boundary based on free will and guided by a divine path. Here, I concentrate on this third concern because I feel that Bazargan's role in shaping and advancing Islamic discourse lies in his effort to establish the proper boundary between religion and public affairs. My reason for emphasizing this boundary is based on two challenges facing Bazargan, challenges of which he was fully aware. First, the predominant view at the time was that religion was the cause of Iran's difficulty in facing contemporary life. Second, a traditionalist and conservative narrative of Islam was then prevalent among Islam-minded Iranians. Also, here I discuss Bazargan's career until the 1960s, when polarization and radicalism took over Iranian politics.

Young Bazargan did his utmost to convince his fellow Iranians about the importance of religion in political life. He devoted his first book to the role of religion in Europe. It began as three articles, collectively titled "Religion in Europe," that he wrote for the organ of the newly established *Kanun-e Eslami* (Society of Islam). He claimed that, contrary to common belief, what accounted for the advancement of Europe was that its people had a faithful commitment to religion: "Religion is accepted by most people and particularly by the youth in Europe" (Bazargan 1965, 20). His conclusion was even more telling: "In summary, therefore, religion is prevalent in Europe, and it is pure and orderly" (42). In the end, however, he added, as a devout Muslim, "Their religion is a religion that does not suffice for contemporary humanity" (42). In his estimation, an accurate understanding of Islam would suffice. This accurate understanding was especially necessary, in Bazargan's view, because the internal cohesion of the Muslim world had been shattered: "There was a time, let's say sixty years ago, when an Iranian would be born a Shi'a. . . . He would grow up with this Islamic worldview and would know nothing else. All he needed while he was growing up was to be instructed about religious injunctions (*ahkam*) and how to exercise the derivatives (*foru'*). . . . But now things have changed. From every corner, our imaginary Iranian is bombarded by conflicting and contradictory beliefs and philosophies" (Bazargan 1341/1962, 119).

According to Bazargan, a new reading of Islam would rectify this condition because of the nature of Islam as the last revealed religion. This is a comprehensive yet moderate creed. In fact, Islam advocates the creation of a "middle nation" (Qur'an 11:143). How does one guarantee the moderate position? According to Bazargan, masters of religion and politics should have complete awareness of their respective spheres and functions: "The political profession is specialized and so is the religious one. Not everyone could and should get involved" (Bazargan 1355/1976, 27). This is so because, as a rule, if politics dominates religion, it will lead to the manipulation of religion for political ends. If religion dominates political life, the result will be intolerance, even inquisition.

Bazargan was so concerned with this division that even during Mosaddeq's era, at the peak of the oil-nationalization movement and the revival of democratic politics, he warned existing groups against either too much involvement in politics or too great a preoccupation with religion: "Although formed out of a sense of political responsibility, Islamic associations should avoid any involvement in the political issues of the day. . . . At the same time, political parties, even those that have been founded and established on religious principles, should neither use religion for political ends nor engage in religious proselytizing" (Bazargan 1355/1976, 32–33). Above and beyond these specific comments lies Bazargan's understanding that religion and politics are two faces of the same coin, each of which has specific functions to perform. Religion helps people find answers to broad life questions, such as "Who am I?" and "Why should I choose any given path over another?" Politics, on the other hand, helps them evaluate the means by which to traverse that path. The two forces should stay clear of each other because any interference by one in the realm in the other is detrimental to both. The difficulty is how to recognize and preserve this proper boundary. The next phase of Bazargan's life demonstrated that he experienced both extremes—too much politics and too much religion. Before the revolution, he tried to encourage religious-minded Iranians to get involved in politics, yet after the revolution he was busy doing the opposite, because religious leaders had by then gone too far in using religion for political ends.

The other voice of the Islam of Tehran, Taleqani, seems to have had similar concerns. He too acted as a hinge in mediating between the new generation and the old in matters of economics and politics. Unlike Bazargan, he was a member of the cleric class and remained so until his death; like Bazargan, he challenged the traditional narrative of Islam. Taleqani was born into a religious family in 1910 and obtained his early education from his cleric father, Ayatollah Seyyed Abolhassan Taleqani. He then went to Qom for advanced religious training at Fayziyeh seminary. After completing his studies, he went to Tehran and began teaching at Sepahsalar Seminary. He too was busy with communal and religious activities centered on Hedayat Mosque. He founded the *Kanun-e Eslami* (Society of Islam), at whose meetings he met Bazargan for the first time and immediately found an "affinity in our thinking and a commonality in our views" (Taleqani 1334/1955, 1).

This friendship became a lifelong relationship of civil, religious, social, and political collaboration and activism. Interestingly, though, the challenges and the adversaries that Taleqani encountered were more political and ideological than those faced by Bazargan. For Taleqani, they came in the form of the political despotism of the Pahlavi dynasty and the ideological pressures of the Iranian Marxists. He recounted his adolescent years, in the 1920s, during the peak of Reza Shah's modernism, with the following painful words: "Every morning when my father, who was a prominent member of the clergy and an activist, left the house, we the children and our poor mother would live in fear and anxiety until his return. I spent my childhood years amid such scenes of fear, aggravation, and tension" (Taleqani 1334/1955, 5). Things went from bad to worse in the 1930s, when Reza Shah's policies were fully implemented. His full secularization, which included pressuring the clerics, instituting cultural reforms from above, and, notably, forcibly unveiling women, affected Taleqani greatly. In the same account, he talked about his life as a student: "The days I was busy studying in Qom coincided with the period when the people of this country lived under the severe pressure of tyranny. They would frightfully run away from one another. People's lives, wealth, and dignity, even the turbans of men of religion and the scarves of women, were subject to attack and robbery by the agents of despotism" (5).

When Reza Shah's reign came to an abrupt end in 1941, the new challenge was the burgeoning of leftist ideas, particularly the emergence of the Tudeh Party. In the intellectual life of the country, the party became such a powerful player that even the children of religious families were attracted to it. As Iranian scholar Hamid Dabashi insightfully observed, "One telling example . . . is Jalal Al-e Ahmad, who, despite his religious background, chose to join the Tudeh Party in 1944 rather than seek Taleqani, with whom he even had a family tie, in the Hedayat Mosque" (Dabashi 1993, 223). In Taleqani's diagnosis, there were two reasons for this. First, "the fundamental views of Islam are forgotten by both its followers and the outsiders. Whatever is discussed in [Muslim] books deals with theology and sectarian polemics; there is nothing to be found in them about practical issues" (Taleqani 1334/1955, 3). The second relates to the weakness of the religious grounding of the people, and obviously "those with weak a religious foundation would be attracted to the social methods of others" (3).

Thus, before the polarization of Iranian public sphere in the sixties, he tried to deal with these challenges. He thought a revival of Islamic teaching would do the job, but like Bazargan, he had little hope for the existing narrative of Islam. In his mind, religion had become a tool for "saddling the people with some selfish ruler, finding justification for it in the Qur'an and the traditions, while another group practices silence and conservatism . . . They preoccupy themselves with praying and hoping for the return of the Imam of the Age [the twelfth Shi'i imam]" (Taleqani 1334/1955, 5–6). Thus he thought a revivalist narrative of Islam would be the proper response to this dual challenge.

Taleqani's response to these challenges is found in two works he published in the early 1950s. The first was the tract *Islam and Ownership*, which deals with the challenge of Marxism and the relation between Islam and the economy. The second is an annotated and edited version of Ayatollah Na'ini's 1909 tract, *Tanbih al-Umma va Tanzih al-Mellah*, which defended constitutionalism as a way of limiting despotism; it deals with Islam and politics.

The seventy-two-page *Islam and Ownership* appeared in 1951, at the peak of the intellectual and political activism of the Tudeh Party. What follows is based on an English translation of the fourth edition, which appeared in a much longer form in 1965. The book has two almost independent parts. The first is a review of economic activities pertaining to relations of ownership broadly defined, and the second is an attempt to situate economic relations within the framework of revealed religion. In a way, the first section is a criticism of both centralized (or socialist) and free market (or capitalist) economies.

The main fault Taleqani finds with both systems is that they are divorced from religious precepts. Indeed, all attempts to reform and order human life from Plato to Marx, with Thomas More (1478–1535), John Locke (1623–1704), Denis Diderot (1713–1784), the Mercantilists, the Physiocrats, Adam Smith (1723–1790), Jean-Jacques Rousseau (1712–1778), David Ricardo (1722–1823), Henri de Saint-Simon (1760–1825), Jeremy Bentham (1748–1832), Thomas Robert Malthus (1766–1834), and others in between, suffer from the same shortcoming. This is the reason, according to Taleqani, the West was infected with class struggle and economic imbalance. He takes as a general rule that "any theory or law which does not rely upon the inner self and morality lacks stability and permanence and will not be practiced as it ought to be" (Taleqani 1983, 9). Since Marx is his main adversary, Taleqani devotes one complete chapter (34–71) to his ideas. Despite his critical view and without making any reference to the original source, he tries to present Marxist economic theory as objectively as possible.

Taleqani has two problems with Marxism. First, he thinks that using England as an instance of the "transformation from feudalism to capitalism" does not suffice (46). Furthermore, Marxist theory in practice has produced a new class. According to Taleqani, the Russian Revolution "created a new class in the midst of the revolution, which enjoys unlimited legal privileges and has taken control of the destiny and the affairs of the rest of the people" (67). The main reason is "the absolute negation of private property," just as the main reason for the excesses of capitalism is the "absolute [affirmation of] private ownership" (91). According to Taleqani, Islam avoided the two excesses by proposing that ownership be "relative and limited" (88). Ownership is limited both because absolute ownership belongs to God alone and because ownership of any sort is allowed only within the parameters of Islamic law. For example, "land and natural resources are not the particular property of anyone (either an individual or a society). Only the guardian of the Muslims (that is, the imam or other persons of authority), committed to public welfare, has [the right of] supervision over the earth and its resources" (89). Already, he has gone beyond criticizing both capitalist and Marxist economies to providing a general outline of the Islamic social system and its economy. God is the absolute, but humanity and its dignity also have their proper place: "From the viewpoint of Islam, the desire for wealth and economic relations are connected with modes of thought, innate characteristics, emotions and human instincts" (132). These were ideas that the new generations of Iranians were ready to hear and contemplate.

So far as the challenge of despotism and the relation of Islam and politics are concerned, Taleqani returns for two reasons to the solution that Na'ini had suggested during the Constitutional Revolution. First, he believes that the tract is still a powerful commentary on fighting against despotism, which Taleqani considers an Islamic religious duty. He rhetorically asks, "Isn't the Constitutional [form of] Government a bridle against rampant despotism? Isn't breaking the power of despotism the main objective of the leaders of religions and reforms?" (Taleqani 1955, 14). Second, he presents an alternative system to the existing despotism. He contends that many aspects of constitutionalism are in agreement with the Islamic form of order, since both impose limitations on authority and the power of the ruling elite. He accepts that the tract was written to legitimize the parliamentary form of government, which was established after the Constitutional Revolution of 1905–1911, but he still sees it as a guide for implementing Islamic order: "Although [this tract] has been written to legitimize Constitutionalism, its significance lies more in offering the political and social principles of Islam as well as a blueprint and the overall objectives of Islamic government" (18).

Taleqani's summary of the text and his extensive annotations, almost as long as the main text itself, aim to elaborate on these "overall objectives." More importantly, his editorial comments constitute a systematic appropriation of Na'ini's thought: the annotations representing Taleqani's views and convictions about politics are expressed through a paraphrasing of Na'ini. Another function of the annotations is to make the text more accessible, even to the religious experts, because, as he states in the introduction, "for the clerics and the sources of emulation (*mujtahedin*), this is a well-argued and judicially binding (*ejtehadi*) book, and for the commoners it is a binding (*taqlidi*) tract with regard to social duties" (15).

Na'ini's text is convoluted, filled with Arabic vocabularies, more or less Arabic in its syntax, and short on references. Taleqani's annotations and commentary rectify all that. For example, right at the start, when Na'ini discusses the relation of "the stability of the mundane order (*esteqamat nezam 'alam*)" to the type of nation (*no'-e qom*), it is almost impossible to decipher his meaning. Taleqani rewrites the same idea as follows: "Social stability depends on government, and the more government relies on the beliefs, thoughts and mores of the people, the more will be its power and stability. If a government goes contrary to the type of people [it is supposed to serve], it will not last" (Taleqani's footnote to Na'ini 1334/1955, 6). As in his treatment of the notion of ownership, he emphasizes that the "establishment of government is always based on limited guardianship and control" (50). If government is unlimited, it usurps the authority and sovereignty of God and the people, a principle that Taleqani considers applicable to all forms of government. These limitations of the ruler are far greater in Islamic teachings and law. He also uses pragmatic reasons to defend this principle: "It is evident that the natural foundation of progress and survival is limited and constitutional government ... whereas the more tyrannical and unbridled rulers dominate the more decadent breakdowns, as is the condition of the Muslims today. Thus reduction of despotism is the best means for protecting the integrity of Muslims" (52).

The last part of the book deals with the biggest enemy of limited government, namely, religious despotism. Those who are against limited government attack freedom and equality by interpreting the latter as enemies of religious injunctions. Taleqani writes, "They say that the ultimate reason for Constitutionalism is freedom and equality. The meaning of the first is liberation from religion, and the meaning of the second is sameness of people with regard to religious injunctions and parameters. They conclude that constitutionalism means ignoring religious injunctions and destroying religious ordinances" (72). This, in Taleqani's interpretation, is nothing but the construction of a fallacy for the sake of preserving a privileged position for the clerical class. If the infallible imam were present, he would rule and that would be the ideal solution, but for now, "the only path remaining is to formalize and legalize the election of the people, which also opens a path for the influence of the source of emulation in public affairs, that is, through the people" (86).

Taleqani uses every opportunity to aggrandize and reinforce the role of the people in the public sphere. This was why he supported the popular surge during Mosaddeq's era, despite his known affinity for the radical group Fada'iyan Islam and his first arrest having come from a charge of harboring it. According to Taleqani, despotism can be fought only through democracy supported by a strong legal system. He ends his notes to Na'ini's tract with the following words: "Fighting despotism is possible only through legal limitation" (142). One may question him for insisting on constitutionalism and the rule of law after the 1953 coup, but like Bazargan, he did not think the coup represented a major shift in the polity of Iran. For example, in the later 1950s, when he realized that in fact a major shift had occurred, he and Bazargan founded the National Resistance Movement (*Nehzat-e Moqavemat-e Melli*), which I turn to now.

GROUPS AND INSTITUTIONS

The challenges of the political scene in Tehran in the 1940s and 1950s led to the development of Islam-minded groups as well as individuals. There were many organizations, such as the Society of Islam (*Kanun-e Eslami*), the Engineers Association, and the Muslim Student Associations. The most notable of these were formed in post-coup Iran in response to the new political conditions. The National Resistance Movement (later, the Liberation Movement of Iran), which Bazargan founded, claimed to follow Mosaddeq's path. It kept politics alive among religiously inspired Iranians and provided a breeding ground for the generation that later advocated struggle and revolution. A second group, the Charitable Association of Hojjati-ye Mahdaviye (*Anjoman Kheiriyeye Hojjatiyeye Mahdaviye*), took a more quietist approach, feeling defensive as a result of the advances of Bahaism. In the educational and social institutions it either founded or supported, the organization helped train and nurture many of the later revolutionaries.

THE NATIONAL RESISTANCE MOVEMENT

Within ten days following the coup of August 19, 1953, the National Resistance Movement (NRM) declared its existence. Prominent people of various political persuasions, including members of the National Front under Mosaddeq, gathered to continue his work. The names of the group's publications reveal its views: *Rah-e Mossaddeq* (Mosaddeq's Path), *Maktab-e Mossaddeq* (Mosaddeq's School), and *Nehzat-e Mossaddeq* (Mosaddeq's Movement). One of the main protagonists was Bazargan, who had clearly stated in his writing that political activism was a dangerous path to follow. In his defense before the court on charges of harboring the NRM, he stated that while it was true that he had advocated a division of labor in which everyone did his appropriate duty, he felt that the 1953 coup had made it imperative for everyone to be involved in politics.

True, I have always supported the idea that when, in a country, bakers bake good bread, farmers cultivate good crops, teachers teach well, students study well, ministers perform their duties responsibly, and deputies, journalists, and politicians do their jobs well, the country will develop. . . . When we noticed that freedom has been curtailed and that tyranny has replaced freedom. The country seems to be on fire, so all have to get involved. (Bazargan 1356/1977, 161–163)

The movement's main objective was to keep Mosaddeq's double message of Iranian independence and constitutional democracy alive.

Indeed, members of the National Resistance Movement criticized those who summarized Mosaddeq's efforts as having been concerned only with fighting outside influence and interference: "Those who consider the National Movement of Iran . . . only an anticolonial movement fighting the [Anglo-Iranian] oil company, are wrong" (*Rah-e Mosaddeq* 1364/1985, 2:43). For the members of the movement, Mosaddeq's rise should be seen as "a great development in the history of constitutionalism in Iran" (2:43). Some of these positions glorified Mosaddeq's tenure as prime minister, but some of the views echoed a radical nationalist movement that became paramount in the 1950s in other Third World countries. For example, in evaluating the "Western concern" with the nationalist trend in the Third World, the following view was expressed: "The concern of the West is not just with those powers that emerged [in the Third World], but more so . . . it is worried that the flame of liberation in independence-seeking people might take over in places such as Iraq, Iran, and Afghanistan" (5:247). It is important to note that at this point the members' attitudes toward religion were very much within the traditional paradigm of the individual-centered narrative of religiosity; only later, when the Freedom Movement was born, did the public face of religion become more pronounced.

The National Resistance Movement did not flourish, but, significantly, its position papers and the views expressed in its publications kept its political discourse alive. It also affected many traditional people who had gathered around Bazargan, making them more politically active.

THE HOJJATI-YE ASSOCIATION

In the mid-1950s, a relatively organized Shi'i group formally declared its existence under the official title of the Charitable Association of Hojjati-ye Mahdaviye (*Anjoman Kheiriyeye Hojjatiyeye Mahdaviye*). For many, this group had been known as the Anti-Baha'i Association (*Anjoman*

Zed-e Bahaiyat) because it began with the aim of preserving fundamental Shi'i beliefs in the face of the ideological challenge of Bahaism. What warranted such alarm was the influence of Baha'is within the ranks of Mohammad Reza Shah's machinery of government. To battle the influence of the Baha'is, Hojjati-ye formed itself into a mirror image of Bahaism and formulated a quietist strategy regarding politics and the ruling power of the time; it disagreed with Shi'i groups, such as the Devotees of Islam (Fada'iyan Islam), that advocated armed struggle or political violence. Hojjati-ye wanted to battle Bahaism, though it also aimed to train qualified believers (*momen mosleh*). In the process, it established new schools, penetrated existing ones, and encouraged students to study hard in order to pass the highly competitive entrance exams for good universities.

Hojjati-ye was founded by Sheikh Mahmoud Zakerzadeh Tavalaei (d. 1996), better known as Halabi. A native of Mashhad, he did his early schooling there during a time when religious seminaries emphasized "traditions of the household of the Prophet" and "replaced philosophical approaches and methods" (Khamenei 1365/1986, 27). He shared a room with and became a close friend of another student of the seminary, Seyyed Abbas Alavi (d. 1957), who later played a crucial role in shaping Halabi's career. Alavi moved to Tehran, became attracted to Bahaism, and even became a prominent propagator of that faith. In 1946, Halabi traveled to Tehran to check on his friend, discovering Alavi's espousal of Bahaism and noting the pervasiveness of Bahaism in the "capital of the most prominent Shi'i country." Alavi even wrote a treatise to defend his new religion, "to clarify the existing misunderstanding and to reveal the truth" (Alavi 1328/1950, 2). Halabi responded to this treatise with the urgency of a crusade.

Halabi secured the consent and financial support of the Ayatollah Burujerdi and launched his campaign against the Baha'is (Sabet-Rasekh 1990, interview). He managed to secure permission to spend part of the special Shi'i tax (*Sahm-e Imam*) for the campaign (Baqi 1362/1983, 30). The 1955 anti-Baha'i campaign proved a blessing in disguise. A large group of Halabi's supporters and sympathizers attended the Baha'i gathering at their major center in West Tehran, the "Garden of Tezhe" (now a rebuilt police station), in order to disrupt it. There was a severe clash, in which many people were injured and others arrested. When Halabi intervened with the police to free the detainees, security forces requested a formal identification of the people or group responsible, leading Halabi to declare them all members of the charitable organization called the Charitable Association of Hojjati-ye Mahdaviye.

Because Halabi's association owed its existence to opposing Baha-ism, its organization, activities, and operations, perhaps paradoxically, resembled those of the Baha'is. Two broad areas are worth exploring. First, just as the latter presented their religion as a modern movement that integrated religion with modernity, so did the Hojjati-ye. Second, like the Baha'is, who claimed to be aloof from politics, the members of Hojjati-ye declared themselves to be apolitical also. Further explanation of these two areas is in order. Regarding the first, the preamble of the constitution of Hojjati-ye should be noted:

> A charitable institution is founded for the purposes of scientific and educational activities, and for rendering useful social works in accor-dance with high teaching of Islam and that of the Ja'fari Shi'i school of thought. Its main objective is to cultivate individuals who are skillful, resourceful, and worthy while also being pious and faithful as well as devoted to material and spiritual reform of the society [they live in].

This statement is important because it is at once a criticism of the exist-ing educational order and a vision for the future.

Regarding the tacit criticism of the existing educational system, the assumption was that the modernism of the Pahlavis would produce only skillful, trained individuals with no connection to piety or religiosity; they would be indifferent to religion or even antagonistic toward it. The educated members of the Pahlavi elite had been uprooted from their in-digenous culture to the point that they disliked local norms and values. This shift in culture and values was the beginning of what later came to be called Weststruckness. Islam-minded Iranians, such as members of the Hojjati-ye, instead wanted to cultivate and nurture people who would be both highly trained in the modern sciences and well grounded in their religious tradition and culture. "Skillful and resourceful" indi-viduals are those who have no hesitation in successfully completing their training in Western universities and places of learning. "Pious and faith-ful" people are those who remain steadfast in their local, indigenous tradition.

Concerning the vision of the organization: since the existing edu-cational institutions would not achieve the group's desired objective, new forms of educational institutions were needed, leading to the birth of many semiprivate high schools, the most famous being Alavi High School. When this particular high school was being established, the Hojjati-ye heightened its activity, successfully recruiting new members.

More effective were the organizational functions stipulated in the constitution, which were later implemented for the purpose of educating—or helping with the formal education, acculturation, or socialization—of its members. Article Two of the constitution outlines these as follows:

1. Organizing scientific and religious seminars in various parts of the country, within the context of the public laws;
2. Publishing and disseminating scientific and religious bulletins, within the bounds of the media laws of the country;
3. Establishing classes for the teaching of ethics and Islamic knowledge, within the context of the public laws;
4. Establishing a public library, reading rooms, and a public gymnasium, in accordance with related regulations;
5. Setting up public charities, helping Muslim cultural institutions, and establishing contact with similar international organizations under the supervision of the proper authorities;
6. Educating individuals for scientific, religious, and literary debates in Islamic centers, in accordance with the laws;
7. Establishing cultural institutions, such as high schools and institutes of higher learning, in accordance with the laws;
8. Establishing various medical centers, such as clinics or hospitals, in accordance with the laws.

Two observations are important to note. The first concerns the breadth of the objectives, which helped the growth of Islamic discourse. The aim was not just to criticize the Pahlavi regime, but also to foster an alternative order based on Islamic law. The second observation is that the organizers were careful to emphasize that whatever they planned to achieve would be within the bounds of existing laws and within the rules of the country. To implement these broad objectives, the organizers created an administrative and institutional hierarchy that appeared to consist of six divisions or departments: research, education, guidance, conferences, publications, and foreign relations (*Mahiyat Zed Enqelabi* 1360/1981, 29–33).

The organization became quite active, not just in Tehran, but in all the major cities of the country. Its general policy was to recruit from among the best students in the high schools. The research department would identify them, and the guidance division would go after them. They would review a student's academic achievements and do research on the family's background and social standing. When a prospective candidate was identified, they devised an appropriate and effective mechanism for attracting the person to the organization: "arranging picnics, giving gifts to the best students, setting up prayer sessions for the older people, and arranging ceremonies on religious occasions were among the various ways they attracted new members" ("Gozareshi az Fa'aliyate Anjoman," n.d., 8). Additional proselytizing measures included establishing cultural houses, social clubs, and extracurricular activities at schools. Once in the organization, members would be treated as family and cared for in all respects; a matchmaking division looked for suitable mates and partners for unmarried members, male or female.

As mentioned, the organization, in keeping with its attempt to mirror its main adversary, the Baha'is, portrayed itself as apolitical. In fact, its constitution stated, "In no circumstance does the association get involved in political affairs. Further, it takes no responsibility for the involvement of its members of sympathizers in politics." While it was the official policy of the organization not to get involved in politics, it did not bar its members from doing so. Why did such a position exist? Conspiracy-based explanations (Baqi 1362/1983, 166–177; *Mahiyat Zed Enqelabi* 1360/1981, 18–25) notwithstanding, the following explanations are plausible.

First and foremost, the founder came from a tradition of political quietism that was very powerful within the seminaries. Sheikh Halabi was very close to Haj Mirza Ahmad Kefae'i Khorasani (d. 1986), "who was basically preoccupied with preserving and rebuilding the seminary in Mashhad and was close to the monarchical government" (Mahdavi-Damghani 1990, interview). Second, it was the best strategy for survival at the time. To be apolitical meant to not directly challenge the rule of the Pahlavis, but allowed one to become more active in cultural realms. This was also in accordance with the accepted tradition in Shi'ism, in which no temporal government is legitimate, save that of the infallible imam, but there is no obligation to revolt. In fact, only the infallible imam has the prerogative of initiating violence or war.

The primary reason may relate to the way the association defined its adversaries. For the Hojjati-ye, the challenge Iranian Muslims faced was not Iranian authority, but rather the weakening of religiosity. As one propagator wrote, "No doubt the more technology and knowledge advance . . . [the more they result in] the formation of a society that is eloquent on the surface and materially progressed, but the more it moves away from spirituality and God" (Alavi 1354/1975, 48). The main challenge was not to reform politics, but to train people who were both skillful and devout. The association was successful in achieving this, and, indeed, many of the postrevolutionary elite in Iran were people who took advantage of the educational and cultural support systems that organizations such as the Hojjati-ye produced and supported.

Altogether, the voices of the first generation amounted to a serious cultural assertion of Islamic teaching in the face of the challenge of modernism. Owing to the generation's apologetic tone, its apolitical approach, its dogmatism, and the content of its message, however, it remained defensive, preaching mostly to the converted. It did not capture the imagination of the masses or the intelligentsia. What changed the balance of power in its favor was the further penetration of modernism, the failure of the revival of the constitution by Mohammad Mosaddeq, and the British-American coup that toppled Mosaddeq's nationalist government in 1953. The coup assisted in radicalizing Islamic discourse in Iran.

The groundwork had been laid by Islam-minded Iranians, both in Qom and in Tehran. The soft face of Islam that was displayed in Qom and the cultural and intellectual face displayed in Tehran succeeded, however, in attracting a new generation of Iranian university students to Islam and even presented Islam as a viable alternative to the existing culture of modernism, as propagated by the Pahlavi regime, or the competing Marxist views and challenges presented by the Iranian left. This made it easier for the next generation of the Islamic movement to take the extra step of making Islam an alternative "ideology." The radicalization of Iranian politics and the radicalization of world politics deepened the rift between state and society. And in the 1960s, an intellectual break occurred.

TWO

THE SECOND GENERATION

The Politics of Revolution, 1963–1991

> The mosques are our barracks,
> The domes are our helmets,
> The minarets are our swords,
> And the faithful are our army.

ZIYA GOKALP (1876–1924), "ASKER DUASI"
("THE SOLDIER'S PRAYER"), 1912

In 1971 the shah celebrated the 2,500th anniversary of the monarchical system in Iran. In the same year, Khomeini announced that there was a contradiction between Islam and kingship: "It is reported that the prophet considered the title 'king of kings' (*malak al-muluk*) the most hated phrase" (Khomeini 1361/1982, 2:359). Note that the title "king of kings" was one of the titles of the last Pahlavi king. Moreover, Khomeini claimed that it was the religious duty of the clergy to rise up and fight the Iranian monarch, whereas until then it had generally been an accepted political axiom, even by Khomeini himself, that the shariʿa and kingship composed the two pillars of a Muslim polity. Any pending disagreement between the religious establishment and the political elite was assumed to be anomalous, to stem from clerical opposition to a particular king (Khomeini 1321/1943, 186–187). Khomeini's new position ran contrary to traditional Muslim political thought, the established practice in the seminaries, and even the position he himself had taken before. Why was there such a departure and where did it originate?

In Muslim history, men of politics and religion oversaw the polity. The kings usually acted as the protectors and the patrons of religion, and the clergy contributed to the legitimacy of the former. In the recent history of the Muslim world, however, a completely new development emerged. The kings and other secular rulers abdicated their traditional role and advocated modernism and Westernization, at the perceived cost of diminishing Islamic teachings and institutions. Gradually, the clergy saw this project as detrimental to the cause of Islam. Khomeini's pronouncement on kingship reflected this concern and can be considered a paradigm shift whereby Islam became an ideology of struggle and a political program for presenting an alternative framework of governance. Ironically, however, "although firmly opposed to the West, most of this type of 'fundamentalism' often incorporates certain nineteenth- and twentieth-century European political thought, including the very notion of revolution. It politicizes Islam, not in the traditional sense, but in a way that is an innovation in Islamic history" (Nasr 2003, 181). The present chapter captures the thought of those people who adhere to this form of understanding Islam.

CONTEXT

Commenting on French society, Victor Hugo wrote, "If the soul is left in darkness, sins will be committed. The guilty one is not he who commits the sin, but the one who causes the darkness" (*Les Miserables,* Chapter 4). The darkness that covered Iran in the early 1960s was caused by a sin committed by both state and society. Both replaced ambivalence and ambiguity with polarity, each claiming to know the truth and each forcing the other side to accept and follow it. The state presented what it later termed "the great civilization," and society presented a vague notion of a "return to the self." Revolutionaries' utopian theories alone could not steer the masses, however. Internally, the polity created by the proponents of modernism alienated the masses and pushed them toward ready-made ideologies. Internationally, the state in Iran did not act as a guardian of Persian interests, but openly declared itself the gendarme of American interests in the Persian Gulf and in the region as a whole. The 1967 war between the Arabs and Israel changed the politics of the region entirely, rendering a return to Islam the only legitimate way of seeing the world for many. And yet the Iranian ruling elite closed their eyes to this change. State and society reached their final breaking point when Third World radicalism made it possible for new voices to find legitimacy.

The Internal Context: From the Coup to the Revolution

The break between state and society resulting from the 1953 coup against Mosaddeq proved detrimental. The following encounter between Prime

Minister Fazlollah Zahedi, who toppled Mosaddeq, and Mehdi Bazargan is revealing. Before the coup, Bazargan had headed the water utility of Tehran. After the coup, he remained in his post but kept his loyalty to Mosaddeq and his political activism. The new prime minister reminded Bazargan to be loyal to the new ruling elite. When Bazargan objected, claiming that a change in the executive branch should make little difference to his political affiliation, the new prime minister reinforced the idea that "the country has changed" (Bazargan 1356/1977, 148).

What was this change all about? The main development was a regression toward a state that did not rely on an indigenous elite, a shift that had begun in the 1940s, with the young shah. Instead, the state was based on the army, represented by General Zahedi, and on foreigners, represented by the United States. The United States was receiving 40 percent of Iranian oil under a renewed 1954 agreement. The prime minister was right in claiming that the country had changed: the coup set the tone for a new Iranian way of life and for a new dimension in American relations with Iran. In Iran, the tendency to imitate Europe was replaced by an imitation of America. One of the most notable consequences of this change related to the shah's credibility after the coup. Since "it was generally believed that the United States had saved his throne, the Shah lost his legitimacy. From then on, he was tainted as an American puppet, a label that stuck to him throughout his life" (M. Milani 1994, 76). The other most significant consequence related to the middle class, which, instead of supporting the shah's reforms, turned against him because "the foreign-orchestrated coup seemed to have touched the very sensitive pride-nerve of some middle class Iranians who perceived the monarch as America's Shah" (76).

Among the shah's supporters, a new class of businessmen, interested only in making money, replaced the middle class. One such example was Habibollah Sabet Pasal, who secured a near monopoly over durable consumer goods with his son Firuz, a graduate of Harvard Business School. They began their massive operation in the late 1950s, and they established the first Iranian television station in 1958. Firuz had written a thesis at Harvard on adapting television for Iran, an enterprise that coincided with the shah's plan for Westernization, or pseudomodernization. The Pahlavis, both the father and especially the son, "literally created the Iranian Pepsi generation, importing soft drinks, cars, and television. Through his Firuz Trading Company, Sabet virtually controlled the domestic consumer durable market, holding the franchises for Electrolux, Kelvinator, Westinghouse, General Electric, Volkswagen, General Tires, and Pepsi-Cola" (Sreberny-Mohammadi and Mohammadi 1994, 61).

TABLE 2.1. IRAN'S DEPENDENCE ON OIL REVENUE, 1954–1976

Revenue	1954	1955	1960	1965	1970	1971	1973	1974	1975	1976
Oil and gas	11	37	42	54	49	60	67	86	80	76
Direct taxes	5	5	8	10	15	12	12	5	10	11
Indirect taxes	35	28	25	23	26	20	17	6	7	9

Note: Numbers indicate percentage of the total budget.
Source: Najmabadi 1987, 215.

Iran's power structure also changed. The 1958 Constituent Assembly had granted the shah unlimited power, which he began to utilize in the early sixties, when he launched his "enlightened autocracy" and "reform from above" programs. Some openly referred to the program as President Kennedy's design to dominate Iran. In reality, this program asserted a single authority, masked with the appearance of a sophisticated modern state and achieved through a council of ministers headed by Amir Abbas Hoveida (1919–1979), who was prime minister from 1965 to 1978. Highly trained, Hoveida was "a true intellectual, a man of cosmopolitan flair, a liberal at heart" (A. Milani 2000, x). The shah's reforms changed the political landscape of Iran because they destroyed its social structure, enabled the emergence of the "Pepsi Generation," paved the way for the American presence, polarized Iranian society, and encouraged a zero-sum battle of worldviews. By the mid-sixties, Iranian society had become a dependent entity.

As a consequence, Iran's "backward" but self-sufficient economy regressed, and even became dependent. Iran's heavy reliance on oil only worsened the situation. Economically, it had become a rentier state and a satellite entity of the United States, and oil had become the most important source of rent. Table 2.1 captures the change in Iran's economic condition. Henceforth, revenue depended on outside players, and external rent sustained the economy, which lacked a strongly productive domestic sector. As a result, few people shared in this wealth, and most were involved in its distribution or utilization.

Since chance and reward, or proximity to the center of power, replaced the mechanism of work and reward, and since citizenship was replaced by a clientele mentality, the state apparatus grew, especially the part managing its earned revenue, and allocation replaced production. For economic purposes, "we may define allocation states as all those states whose revenue derives predominantly (more than 40 percent) from oil or other foreign sources and whose expenditure is a substantial share of GDP" (Luciani 1987, 70). Big government, corruption, and giant bureaucracies became the norm. A reliance on imports and low productivity ruled the economy, and the progression from agriculture to industrialization to a service economy lost its meaning as secondary rent-seekers with little attachment to the locality of their life or work were emphasized.

Because of the reform policies and Americanization, double fault lines divided Iran, politically and morally. Politically, modernism won the day. One proponent of this trend called it Pahlavism, referring to the ruling dynasty: "Pahlavism is a school of thought that takes [Iranian] society by detour from feudalism to a stage higher than social democracy or a parliamentary [system]. Pahlavism is a school that at the moment takes the nation to a bright future from darkness in unimagined haste" (Honarmand 1351/1972, 50–51). The shah himself referred to his reforms as the "great civilization" (*tamadon-e bozorg*), or "the creation of a country in which welfare is available to everyone. . . . where one would enjoy social insurance from birth to death, study, get a job, work, retire, and in the end die in peace" (Pahlavi n.d., 7:6264). The reforms were to create a consumer society with some degree of a social safety net, but in practice they turned Iran to dependent entity. The state wanted more and more of this dependency, while society wanted something else.

Then there was the moral fault line. A new, corrupt group of Iranians took charge, and the state's dominant attitude became one of disdain for everything Iranian. For them, as Abbas Milani insightfully observed, Persia had become "synonymous with all that was abject, deceitful, and retrograde, and they distanced themselves from the very culture they were born into and now felt superior to" (A. Milani 1996, 128). They admired everything non-Iranian. The irony was that society's perception was the reverse. The outsiders were seen as a group from which to remain distant. The following statistics are significant: "A 1963 West German poll showed that 33 percent of young Iranians saw America as 'aggressive' (compared with only 19 percent who so labelled the USSR); 85 percent believed that the American aid worked 'to make the rich richer'; and only 8 percent thought American aid 'improves the standard of living of many.' Fifty percent thought the U.S. 'was too much on the side of having things remain as they are'" (Rubin 1980, 113). Clearly, there were two worlds emerging in Iran: the world of modernism, which became the dominant paradigm of the state, and the world of modernity, which was alive in society.

The years 1963–1965 were years of confrontation between state and society. The shah, who had initiated his police state through the Americanization ushered in by his reform program in 1960, decided to identify political dissidents. He announced a referendum for his reforms in January 1963. The fault line was drawn: Khomeini became the most vocal and radical opposition leader to incite demonstrations against the reforms. In June 1963 there was a clash resulting in many killed and many others jailed or exiled, including Khomeini. The fight against the government gave birth to a new kind of thinking and vocabulary that justified revolution and violence. For example, in its June–July 1969 issue, the popular dissident publication *Iran-e Azad* (Free Iran) summarized the effects of 1963 as follows:

> The Uprising of June (15 Khordad) is one of the most important
> events in Iranian history and one of the bloodiest in contemporary
> Iranian history. It has forced us to draw the following three conclu-
> sions: first, that the clerical leaders have a crucial role to play in the
> struggle against the Shah and against imperialism; second, that the
> progressive secular forces must work with the religious ones against
> the tyrannical regime; and third, that the unarmed struggle—however
> popular and widespread—cannot possibly succeed against such a blood-
> thirsty regime. The only way to bring down the detestable regime is
> through a concerted armed struggle. (quoted in Abrahamian 1982a, 85)

This 1969 hindsight accurately marks the 1963 uprising as the beginning of a shift in Iranian politics. The government of the new prime minister, Amir Asadollah Alam, had either executed or imprisoned the leaders of 1963 and had portrayed the riots as an opposition to "progress and modernization." Khomeini and other religious leaders were either put on trial or released conditionally. So by 1964, having tightened his grip on the country, the shah felt confident enough to fully implement his idea of Westernizing Iran. What sealed the fate of this shift was an assassination attempt on the life of the shah in April 1965.

The would-be assassin was shot on the spot, but the incident provided an excuse for the regime to arrest the remaining members of the opposition. In a sense, both sides—the ruling regime and the opposition—resorted to political violence. The leaders of the contemporary political parties, the National Front, the Freedom Movement of Iran, the Third Wave, the Nation of Iran Party, and the Islamic Nation Party, were arrested and put on trial before the anniversary of the 1953 coup in August

1965. By 1967, the regime had won the battle, and the country was on its way to full-fledged Americanization. Iran was to resemble the sala model, as developed by an American scholar of public administration, Fred Riggs. On the surface, everything appeared rational, modern, and bureaucratic, and the country was developed with dams, electric plants, factories, assembly lines, and so forth, but in reality, the system was despotic, autocratic, and nepotistic (Riggs 1964). The country was becoming "a theatre of the absurd" (Al-e Ahmad 1364/1986, 229, letter dated October 9, 1968).

This theatre of absurdity best manifested itself in the early 1970s, when the shah, promising Iranians that their country would surpass West Germany, inaugurated his great civilization. It was in this period that the shah made the industrialization and modernization of the Iranian economy, based on oil revenue, his government's first priority. It was also in this period that the United States became increasingly embroiled in Iranian politics and was identified more closely with the shah's policies. This in turn made Iran more dependent and increased U.S. involvement with the country's internal affairs. During this process, the shah established his power and authority by suppressing all opposition critical of his authoritarian rule; from having witnessed the potential challenges that the opposition could pose to stability in Iran, the United States supported the shah's efforts to consolidate his position.

One cannot dismiss the wealth generated in Iran in the aftermath of the shah's reforms. There were more goods to buy and there was more money to spend. A personal example exemplifies this change: When I left Iran in 1975, I had one cousin who owned "the nationally produced" car, the Paykan, but when I returned for vacation in the summer of 1977, my extended family owned more than twenty cars, some of which, in my village, travelled on dirt roads. But this wealth could not make up for Iran's sense of lost identity or lost balance. Indeed, Fouad Ajami's comment about the Arab world applies to Iran's "great civilization" as well: "Wealth has only underlined a painful gap between what a society can buy and what it can be, between the vast means available to buy into things and the limited capacity to create a somewhat autonomous public project, a liveable public order" (Ajami 1981, 21). The great civilization that the shah had promised was at best a welfare state and at worst a consumer society. In the end, he did not deliver either.

While other developing countries in similar circumstances relied on manufacturing exports to pay for a portion of their imports, Iran continued to depend almost solely on its oil, and consequently was heading for financial disaster. In 1972, the government was confronted with an accumulated budget deficit amounting to $2.6 billion, all of it financed by long-term loans. Furthermore, although the government was investing heavily in industry and the military, it was neglecting the agricultural sector. Relative stagnation in that area, together with the migration of villagers and small farmers to prosperous cities, increased the demand for food and drained the country's foreign reserves. During this time, many influential individuals became increasingly corrupt—the shah's family in particular.

The shah's family members used their power either to gain quick and easy profits or to bypass all trade and banking regulations for their own benefit. These benefits gave them greater power. It was in this atmosphere of profiteering that the shah embarked on his large-scale modernist program through the Fifth Development Plan. Under the Fifth Plan, the regime expected agriculture to grow by 4.6 percent, manufacturing by 15.5 percent, and services by 15.3 percent. To promote this growth, he contracted with several foreign companies; as a result, the number of foreign nationals living in the country rose, leading to serious political and economic impacts. The country became more dependent on Western governments. By 1977, the Fifth Plan had failed to accomplish many of its objectives and had totally failed to expand agriculture. The dependency of the country's foreign-exchange rate on oil revenue made the economy and the stability of the government vulnerable. Prices and the cost of living increased sharply, especially consumer prices, which shot up by 15 percent between 1975 and 1977. To battle these difficulties, the shah initiated more projects, but they only exacerbated the failing condition.

The final collapse came when the two artificial bases of the Westernizing state, namely, the army and the shah's foreign supporters, withdrew their backing, and in so doing rendered the state disposable. The state failed because it was now artificial, words became play, and theory and practice lost their constructive tension. Tocqueville's depiction of French statesmen before the revolution might just as well explain the tragedy of those in power in Iran: "Even the politicians' phraseology was borrowed largely from the books they read," but in Iran the books they read were not local or indigenous; because of this, "One group [the politicians] shaped the course of public affairs, the other [the writers on politics] that of public opinion" (Tocqueville 1955, 146). Such artificiality alienated almost everyone. Politically, citizenship and civil society shrank, since oil revenue had made "no taxation, no representation" the prevalent rule of political discourse. Society became depoliticized, and power relations, repressive.

Loyalty, instead of being a result of "reward, punishment and respect," as in Max Weber's formulation, was maintained through fear and suspicion. The Iranian secret police (the SAVAK [Sazeman-e Ettelaat va Amniyat-e Keshvar, or the Organization for Intelligence and National Security], created in 1957) had become the agent of this police state by the 1970s.

Although the crisis seemed obvious, it took a long time for the shah and the people around him to realize they were in its midst. The first sign was a demonstration in support of Khomeini on January 8, 1978, in reaction to the publication of a short article in the daily *Ettela'at,* which defamed Khomeini and called the opposition to the shah an alliance of "red and black" reactionaries (Rajaee 1983, 33). When government forces attacked the demonstrators, particularly those in Qom, some people were killed. Using the occasion, Khomeini delivered a long sermon, blaming the shah for the bloodshed. More importantly, he accused the shah's father of having been a lackey of the British and the shah himself of being one for the Americans. This view had enormous prevalence among those opposed to the shah in the 1960s and 1970s. The Pahlavis rarely represented Iranian interests but instead acted as agents of the outside powers in the region. Note, for example, the following statement made in the name of the Qom seminary in the summer of 1972: "This is the nature of the Pahlavi court that in the past committed any kind of terror and crime to preserve British interests, and now it works as a mercenary for Israel and America and does not hesitate to commit any terror and crime" (quoted in *Payam Mojahed* 1 (4): 7). The sermon was distributed on cassette tapes all over Iran, inaugurating the first political revolution of the information age.

Jimmy Carter's election in 1976 as U.S. president gave a great boost to Islam-minded Iranian activists and to other dissidents. His emphasis on human rights marked a change in the U.S. policy of unlimited support for the shah. Carter promised a new U.S. attitude toward the rest of the world. He indicated that henceforth human rights would be a cornerstone of American foreign policy, and he designated every ambassador as his personal human-rights representative. As a result, events quickly turned in Iran, starting in mid-June 1978, when a particularly huge anti-government demonstration occurred in Qom. The demonstration was not taken seriously, however, and by July, demonstrations that appeared to be harmless were growing in strength and frequency with every passing day. Army desertions began, and Khomeini's leaflets (*e'lamiyeh*) appeared, calling for the formation of revolutionary committees (*komiteh*), which meant making the mosques places for political activism.

On August 13, a bomb exploded in a Tehran restaurant that was a regular hangout for Americans. A week later, a blaze started in a crowded cinema in the oil town of Abadan, and 430 people burned to death. Because of this, Abadan saw fierce antigovernment rioting, which included attacks on public buildings and shouts of "Death to the shah!" There was an attempt to liberalize the regime, and Ja'afar Sherif Emami was appointed new prime minister. The son of a cleric, Emami was a politician of the old school and one of the last of the middleweight politicians; he was clever, devious, and ambitious, and though he was for a time associated with Mosaddeq's National Front, his long years in charge of the Pahlavi Foundation had made him as closely committed to the regime as anyone. He had already served as prime minister in 1960 and had been president of the Senate. Yet these credentials were of little value; a week after Emami's installation, in August 1978, Tehran witnessed its biggest demonstration yet. An estimated 100,000 marched through the streets, demanding the shah's deposition, the installation of an Islamic republic, and Khomeini's return from exile. As days passed, the demonstrations grew bigger and spread to other cities. Khomeini's leaflets continued to pour into the country, challenging the army, not with threats of force, but by offering to talk with the soldiers. On December 29 the shah appointed yet another prime minister, the more nationalist Shapour Bakhtiar—a change that did nothing to improve the situation.

Now Khomeini warned against any compromises along the path to revolution. As the revolutionaries became more confident, the shah became more compromising. He ordered the members of the royal family to transfer their fortunes to the Pahlavi Foundation and to prepare to leave the country. The shah remained in Tehran until January 16, 1979. In the meantime, the new prime minister, Bakhtiar, remained confident, believing he had the loyalty of the army and the people. The situation inside Iran became even more confused. On February 1, the revolution took the final step toward victory with Khomeini's triumphant return from Paris. The streets were packed with well-wishers crying with joy, waiting for their leader to arrive. The end to Bakhtiar's rule closed one major chapter in Iranian history and opened another: the formation of the Islamic Republic.

The International Context: The Cold War and the Polarized World

The Cold War (1945–1989) was the most significant framework shaping world politics in the second half of the twentieth century. The views and practices of statesmen and politicians were shaped by it, as were their ways of understanding politics. The Cold War peaked with Stalin's successive invasions of Eastern Europe and began dying down in the early 1970s. In 1970, the German chancellor, Willie Brandt, reflected easing tensions when he travelled to East Germany in March, to Moscow in August, and to Poland in December, but tensions really cooled down when President Richard Nixon travelled to Moscow in May 1972 and signed the SALT (Strategic Arms Limitation Talks) agreement with Leonid Brezhnev. The relationship between the two power blocs turned from one of deterrence to détente, making regional disputes local by removing the shadow of superpower competition. However, while the Cold War was at its peak, the world looked different: bipolar, Manichean, and intransigent.

In the aftermath of World War II, a double movement occurred around the world. On one side was "the age of economic modernism," resulting from the expanding market economy and "the great transformation" of economic life: no longer embedded in politics and culture, the economy became the motive for which everything else was done (Polanyi 2001). On the other side, and possibly in reaction to the first, there emerged a trend toward authenticity, usually referred to as "the return to the self." Both trends, interestingly, were universal, purporting to cover the whole of humanity. In the Third World, these trends took the form of either liberation movements or religious fundamentalism, and in the West, they swept both the leftists and the conservative elements.

The left had sympathy for the liberation movements, later subsumed under postcolonial and postmodern approaches; on the right, the tendency manifested as religious rethinking. Both sides influenced Islamic discourse in Iran. Just as the decades around 1900 were the age of constitutionalism and parliamentary government, the post–World War II period, particularly the 1960s, was the age of a return to authenticity. Regionally, pan-Arabism overtook secularization and Westernization. One movement for self-determination gave rise to Ba'thism (renaissance), a blend of Arab nationalism and Arab socialism, which took hold in Syria and Iraq. Globally, the decolonization and liberation movements, including the nonaligned movement, were very powerful even when the Cold War was at its peak.

As far as the Muslim world was concerned, the Cold War led to the militarization of the region, particularly with the escalation of the Arab-Israeli conflict. Over the course of six days in June 1967, the Israeli Air Force destroyed the Egyptian Air Force and the Israeli army beat back attacks from Jordanian and Syrian forces, changing the face of the region. Israeli occupation of most of Palestine, the Sinai, and the Golan Heights led to the impression that secular regimes had failed in their most fundamental duty—providing security—thus discrediting all secular ideologies and giving impetus to Islam-minded Arabs. In the aftermath of the attack, Egypt accepted massive military aid from the Soviet Union. In 1973, Egypt and Syria, joined by Jordan and Iraq, again attacked Israel, in what became known as the Yom Kippur War, the Ramadan War, or the October War. The United States, in turn, got involved in the politics of the region by persuading Israel to accept a UN-negotiated cease-fire. America's role made it the target of criticism, since it was seen as the source of the problems in the region.

Further shoring up the cause of Islamic fundamentalism was a global resurgence of religion. The Second Ecumenical Council of the Vatican (Vatican II) met from October 1962 to December 1965 to work at *aggiornamento*—updating and renewing Christianity, making it an active player in the public life of the Christian world—or, as Father Luigi Giussani termed it, Christianizing the modernity process (Kepel 1994, 66). The documents generated by the council encouraged both a sociopolitical presence for religion and a dialogue between religions. For example, the declaration on religious freedom, *Dignitatis Humanae,* guaranteed the rights of individuals and communities to social and civil freedom on issues related to religion: "The human person has a right to religious freedom. . . . This right of the human person to religious freedom is to be recognized in the constitutional law whereby society is governed and thus it is to become a civil right" (Abbott 1966, 679).

At the same time, there emerged a resurgence of religion in other faith traditions: The Vishva Hindu Parishad (the World Hindu Council) was founded in 1964 on the birthday of Lord Krishna to revive Hinduism (Marty and Appleby 1992, 536–557). A few years later, the followers of Rabbi Zavi Yekuda Kook (d. 1982) founded the Gush Emunim (the Bloc of the Faithful), which argues against the legal concept of the state of Israel in favor of the biblical concept of the land of Israel (*Eretz Yisrael*), ruled by the *Halakah* (Jewish law). For the Muslim world, this trend toward religious rethinking took a very sharp turn in 1967, when, as mentioned, the Arabs suffered a disastrous defeat by Israel and lost enormous territories. Many faulted secular ideologies and propagated a return to Islam. In Iran, religion became a political issue and spurred an intellectual debate in 1963–1964, in the aftermath of Ayatollah Burujerdi's death.

The Intellectual Context: The West as the Enemy

The condition of political polarization in Iran directly corresponded to polarization in the intellectual realm. The break between state and society was becoming obvious. The state was quickly moving toward modernism and imitating America, which society cast as a disease.

We have already encountered Kasravi's criticism of the West, but it became part of a powerful discourse in post–World War II Iran. Of the many critics of the West, the more prominent included Fakhreddin Shademan (1907–1967), Nassereddin Sahabzamani, Ahmad Fardid (1912–1994), Mehdi Bahar (b. 1920), and Jalal Al-e Ahmad (1923–1969), who collectively shaped the debate.[1] I concentrate on the last two, because Bahar influenced the political discourse on America and Al-e Ahmad helped change the intellectual discourse. Al-e Ahmad's work, the most read and possibly most debated essay in modern Iran, is entitled *Gharbzadegi* (Weststruckness); Bahar's book *Miraskhar-e Este'mar* (The Inheritor of Colonialism) likewise caused long debate. Both works are still in print and have gone through many printings. Both authors had sympathy for the Iranian communists and were part of the leftist clique that was so dominant at the time.

In the preface, I mentioned my introduction to Al-e Ahmad's work. I literally lost sleep over it. *Gharbzadegi* offers a particular analysis of Westernization, which the author himself, in a 1965 Harvard Summer Seminar, equated with the "Occidentalization" of non-Western societies (Al-e Ahmad 1364/1986, 141, from his letter dated August 3, 1965). Al-e Ahmad was a versatile man. Novelist, essayist, social critic, self-taught anthropologist, and political activist, he was born into a religious family and began as a student of religion but was soon attracted to the Iranian Communist Party (the Tudeh), which he joined in 1948. The coup of 1953 was decisive for him: he broke with the left and became one of the first postcolonial thinkers to pay attention to the unequal relations between East and West (Vahdat 2002, 114).

Al-e Ahmad was then attracted to the circle of a colorful and idiosyncratic Heideggerian philosophy professor named Seyyed Ahmad Fardid (1912–1994), who was extremely concerned with the fate Iran faced with an aggressive Europe with its "creed" of modernity. When Al-e Ahmad heard about the notion of Weststruckness, he appropriated it and, as Fardid told this author in 1982, changed the meaning. In November 1961, Al-e Ahmad submitted *Gharbzadegi* to the Commission on the Goals of the Iranian Ministry of Education, but after waiting fruitlessly to hear from it, he published part of the book the following year in the journal *Ketab-e Mah.* The full text was finally published in September–October 1962, only to be banned immediately.

For Fardid, the West had become hubristic because of its nontheistic and egocentric worldview and philosophy. Because such a philosophy, according to Fardid, had originated in ancient Greece, he invented the word *dysiplexia,* from the Greek words *dysis,* meaning "the West," and *plexia,* meaning "to be struck by" (Gheissari 1998, 177–180; Vahdat 2002, 114). Since the clearest manifestation of the contemporary West is modern technology, Al-e Ahmad concentrated his argument on it. In his introductory chapter, in which he "outlines the sickness," he identifies Weststruckness as "the token of the machine" and lists three main features of it:

> *Weststruckness* is the characteristic of a period in our history when we have not yet obtained the machine and do not understand the mysteries of its configuration and structure;
>
> *Weststruckness* is the characteristic of a period in our history when we have not become familiar with the prerequisites of machine making, that is, new sciences and "technology";
>
> *Weststruckness* is the characteristic of a period in our history when we are compelled by the pressure of the market, economy, and oil trade to acquire and use machines. (Al-e Ahmad 1375/1996, 35)

For Al-e Ahmad, these characteristics would not change unless Iranians understood the philosophy behind what had made the West what it was: "The fact is that as long as we have not grasped the essence, the foundation, and the philosophy of Western civilization and only imitate the West in appearance, including the use of its machines, we appear like the ass going about in the lion's skin" (28). He concludes, "As long as we are consumers, and until we build the machine ourselves, we will remain *Weststruck* (29). In subsequent pages, he traces the roots of "this period" in Iranian history and concludes that Iranians have lost their sense of history and orientation (39–54).

Al-e Ahmad diagnosed the cause of Iranians' disorientation as their ignorance of modernity. His solution was to master the machine and grasp the logic of new mechanisms and techniques. Despite his reminders of the schism between the industrial West and the agrarian East, for him the gap was bridgeable, and there was no serious contradiction between the two. Others saw it differently though. For example, Mehdi

Bahar published *Miraskhar-e Este'mar* (The Inheritor of Colonialism) two years after Al-e Ahmad's *Gharbzadegi*, and in it he emphasized the intellectual gap between the two worlds as well as the structural and power inequalities. By the time of the 1979 revolution, the book had gone through sixteen printings, more than one a year.[2]

Bahar's book opens with the following: "World War II turned the foundation of the political and economic relations between the industrialized and developed countries with those of backward and nonindustrialized countries from the relation of open colonialism into something else" (Bahar 1344/1965, 1). The author identifies the present condition of Iran and suggests a possible solution. In his view, Iran was caught in the web of "imperialism" (357); the book deals with what the jargon of these days has labelled neocolonialism, indirect colonialism, economic colonialism, and dependency.[3] According to Bahar, history moves as a result of competition between economic interests. The world of his time centered on competition between the dollar and the pound sterling over the commodity of oil. The new oil consortium dominated post-Mosaddeq Iran. Before continuing, I should mention that Bahar teeters on the edge of conspiracy theory: "In recent centuries, the West has tried to explain the poverty of Third Worlders by attributing it to their laziness and ignorance. *It even invented Nazism and Fascism as theories of inferior and superior races in order to justify the economic disparities among nations*" (40; emphasis added). He obviously had sympathy for the Soviet bloc, stemming from his connection to the Iranian Communist Party (Tudeh) and to the preferences for leftist politics among intellectuals in post–World War II Iran, which lasted until the revolution in 1979.

This new face of imperialism, according to Bahar, was the United States, whose capital and financial strength made it a major global political player in the aftermath of World War II. Bahar's premise was that the old colonialism relied on specified territories, which he called "hunting fields," over which the colonizing power exerted exclusive authority. This was the reason for direct rule over the colony and for appointing the administrative elite from the mother country. Neocolonialism needed an "open door" because "monopolies and specified territories were blocking penetration by U.S. economic and financial interest" (2). On the surface, the political dependence of the colonized areas had eased, but the great powers' economic domination remained intact.

Likewise, the nature of competition on the global scene had changed. Political and military struggle for mastery of the world had given way to the struggle of the capitalist and socialist systems of the Third World to resist those economic systems, whereas the forces of "economic and colonial imperialism" worked at "preserving the status quo" (40). To verify his framework, Bahar looked first at Africa, concentrating on the Congo and the faith of its leader at the time, Patrice Lumumba (1925–1961) (11–42). He then looked at Latin America and the encouragement of "single commodity" economies by American financial monopolies (70–84); the Far East, including India (84–125); and an account of how the oil cartels came about (167–239), concluding, "Obviously [Iranians'] nation and country have been reduced from a powerful country and a civilized nation to a dependent territory" (239). To see the real cause of this condition, he turns to a "look at the record of colonialism" (240–357) before concentrating on how Iran fell "into the trap of the West." The remainder of the book (358–649) is a history of Iran from the beginning of the Qajar dynasty (1796) until 1954, when, according to the author, American oil companies gained ascendancy in Iran. He adds that this could not have occurred without the changes that took place in the West itself. He spends over a hundred pages explaining how new companies and trusts, particularly oil companies, became dominant and how economic liberalism in America evolved into "the despotism of American trusts" in all areas, such as industry (General Motors and Chrysler), oil (Gulf, Texaco, and others), finance (Bank of America, Chase Manhattan, Chemical, and Morgan Guaranty), and even insurance (Prudential and Equitable) (146–157).

Bahar's book is a penetrating portrait of the world as an arena of conflict between "us" and "them"—a view that was becoming fashionable in Iran. Al-e Ahmad's intellectual depiction of the West as a disease and not a place of refuge, along with Bahar's political depiction of the West as Satan, gradually came to dominate intellectual discourse.

While these cases capture the mood of the new revolutionary spirit in Iran, they may not capture its pervasiveness. The politicization of art, poetry, literature, and intellectual activities was enormously valued, and the catchword became "committed" (mota'ahed), that is, concerned with social and political justice. In fact, commitment was more than a buzz-word or fad; it became the criterion for social responsibility. A combination of Franz Fanon's idea of revolutionary struggle and Karl Marx's notion of praxis, commitment defined the renaissance person in the Iranian context. The enlightened soul was not one who was free from superstitions and guided by science and progress, but one who engaged in action, rebellion, and martyrdom, particularly if directed against the West (Nabavi 2003, 70–80). Nothing captured this spirit more than an observation by Ali Asghar Haj Seyyed Javadi, a leading intellectual of the day, about the Cultural Revolution in China:

> I do not know the nature of what is taking place in Communist China by the name of the Cultural Revolution. However, at the same time, I cannot believe the news [broadcast] by Western news agencies and reflected in the evening papers. The reason for this disbelief is the fact that I feel that we too are in need of a cultural and moral revolution . . . If, in Communist China, the Cultural Revolution, too, has meant that all signs of Western imperialist attitudes as well as of the former bourgeoisie have been purged, then in our view, it is praiseworthy. (quoted in Nabavi 2003, 87)

Note the clear confession of the author that his judgment about the Cultural Revolution is not based on any research or knowledge, but since it aimed at purging "all signs of Western imperialist attitudes as well as of the former bourgeoisie," it should be praised.

Nothing could have paved the way for the coming of political Islam better than this elevated anti-Western sentiment. However, while the atmosphere fostered strong opposition to the existing order, the debate among Islam-minded Iranians made a more positive contribution, since they talked about alternatives to the status quo and formulated discourses to replace that of modernism and Westernization. An important text, *Bahsi darbareye Marja'iyat va Rohaniyat* (A Discussion of Religious Authority and the Clergies; 1341/1962), is worth discussing here.[4] Two main features of the book stand out. First, the content superficially avoids any overt references to the politics of the day. The timing for the presentation of the issue of religious leadership and the popularity of the book had broad political implications. Second, the contributors, some of whom later became prominent members of the revolutionary council in 1979, addressed fundamental issues in Shi'i political thought, marking a new beginning.

Three contributors in particular are important to recognize. The first is Mohammad Hossein Tabataba'i, who contributed two essays, one entitled "Guardianship and Leadership," which deals with the core question of authority, and the other, "Ijtihad," which deals with the right of the clerical class to exercise political leadership. On the notion of guardianship and authority, he avoids jurisprudence altogether, looking at it from the angle of "the social philosophy of Islam and not through juridical (*fiqhi*) discussion" (*Bahsi darbareye* 1341/1962, 74). His reasoning was that "the sphere of guardianship relates to necessary affairs and . . . is a natural phenomenon" (75). Since, according to the word of God (Qur'an 30:30), Islam is a natural religion, Islam's social philosophy does not contradict the claim that guardianship is a natural phenomenon (*Bahsi darbareye* 1963, 76–78). He then concludes, "No society in any circumstances can be free from the need for guardianship" (93).

How Tabataba'i reconciles this unavoidable necessity with the traditional theory of the imamate in Shi'ism is interesting. For him, one has to read the traditional narrative as pertaining to two aspects: the office and the person who occupies it. The fact that the ideal imam is not present now does not negate the office, because that would be to deny nature (96). Second best for him, after the infallible imam, is "the person who is supreme in religious righteousness, sane judgment, and awareness of the situation who would be appointed" as the leader (97)—an idea not far from Khomeini's theory of "the guardianship of the jurisconsult," which lies at the heart of the political system in postrevolutionary Iran.

Tabataba'i strengthens his argument in "Ijtihad," declaring the exercise of independent reasoning to be a natural phenomenon. The exercise of such a faculty is the source of religious injunctions, since "the trajectory of independent reasoning (*ijtihad*) and following (*taqlid*) constitutes one of the fundamentals of the execution of human life. Each member of humanity, based on his very nature, traverses the path of his life either by *ijtihad* in areas he is able to or by *taqlid* where he does not have the ability" (17). Since not all Muslims can exercise independent reasoning, it is natural that some of those with the knowledge and intellectual disposition to derive religious injunctions by independent reasoning emerge as leaders. Those without this disposition should emulate those who possess it. It is a general rule that whoever enters into social existence must assume the role of one or the other (20). This line of reasoning is different from the quietist attitude of the first generation, which limited itself to defending the faith.

The second major contributor is Morteza Motahhari, who deals with the same ideas and the notion of ijtihad in two essays. In the first, "Ijtihad in Islam," he compares this notion in Shi'ism and Sunnism and then reaffirms in detail the Usuli school of ijtihad, which allows for a more independent role for the clergy. For him, the legitimate notion of ijtihad is one that avoids the extremes of the Sunni version, which allows for independent reasoning based on one's own opinion (*ijtihad be ra'y*), and the version of the Shi'i Akhbari (literally, "reporting") school of thought, which reduces the clergy's intellectual exercise to a sincere reporting of the imams' traditions. The first leads to innovation in religion, while the second leads to traditionalism and stone-headedness (37–43). Now, it takes serious thinking to exercise imagination: "the challenge of ijtihad lies in adapting the general injunctions with new issues and changing circumstances. A true mujtahid [one who exercises ijtihad] discovers the secret to meeting this challenge" (58). The implementation requires that the persons who assume this role are knowledgeable about religious principles, and, more importantly, that they enjoy personal confidence and independence. This is the topic of Motahhari's second contribution, which deals with clerical organization and structure. For Motahhari, there are contradictory trends in the system. On the one hand, the clergy's dependence on the special religious tax coming from the people compromises its independence (168); on the other hand, there is no regulation of who can be considered a cleric and who cannot (175). Neither of these trends is conducive to independent reasoning; thus, he invites the "leaders of the religion to launch deep reforms" and take over the leadership of "our awakening nation" so that they can play the role of true leaders rather than that of indirect followers (197).

While Tabataba'i and Motahhari are vague on the clerics' role in politics, the third contributor, Mehdi Bazargan, in his essay "The People's Expectations of the Religious Authorities," is revolutionary in that he advocates direct political involvement by the clergy. He begins with the premise that since Islam is a comprehensive way of life, the clergy must actively participate in all aspects of life. This, he continues, has been the tradition among the Shi'as: "Shi'ism stood for truth and justice," making the religious leadership in Shi'ism "both the source of authority (*marja'*), and the place of refuge (*malja'*)" in the face of tyranny (113–114). He advocates the restoration of such a dual function now that Iran is under an undesirable ruler and the Shi'as are under ideological bombardment. On the political front, he reminds readers that Iranians live in "a state where the government has usurped everything from the people. Power, wealth, culture, adjudication, education, propagation, media, and urban affairs are all under its control. Even the election of the [parliamentary] representatives, the true right of the people, is taken away from them" (115). As for ideological challenges to Shi'ism, there is not only state propaganda, but also, and even more detrimental, the prevalence of Marxist thinking among the youth. The way he expresses this is rather insightful: "In the past, the Iranians were born Shi'as . . . and they would know nothing else. . . . Nowadays, however, things have changed. Young and old, men and women, are subject to irreligious and doubtful temptations from various sources" (119). The latter statement echoes the doubt and animosity toward nonindigenous trends expressed in the writings of Al-e Ahmad and Bahar, with an additional dimension: Islam was being cast as an alternative way of thinking and acting. This became much more explicit in the works of the second generation.

THE VOICES

It was an intentional irony to begin this chapter with lines from the Turkish poet Ziya Gokalp, a prominent enthusiast of Mustafa Kemal Atatürk, in order to capture the essence of a religious revolution in Iran. The lines nicely capture what happened to Islam-minded Iranians in the 1960s and 1970s. Beginning in 1961, the year of Ayatollah Burujerdi's death, there was a paradigm shift among Iranians on the relations between religion and politics. Various Iranian groups and notable individuals marked their opposition to the state, and the religious establishment reevaluated its own position. Internal and external events paved the way for the emergence of what I term here the second generation in the development of Islamic discourse in Iran. This generation of Muslim activists gained enough confidence to consider replacing the plans of the modernizing group with their own. It was also in this year that the Shi'is reformulated their views. A series of internal, regional, and international events provided them with the impetus to achieve that purpose as well as a "breathing space" in which to accomplish it.

What helped an Islamic project to emerge was the predominance of the new generation. While the first generation had been under the influence of the guardians of tradition, the revolutionaries now set the tone. It took a significant amount of time for this Islamic discourse to replace the Westernization model with a "return to the self," which, for Al-e Ahmad, was "the most necessary step out of the contemporary nihilism, chaos, and anarchism in which Iran found itself" (Al-e Ahmad 1375/1996, 75, from an interview given in April 1964). This necessary step was to turn Islam into an ideology, without which no revolution would have been possible.

As in other classical traditions—including the ancient Greek, Hindu, Confucian, and others—cosmology within traditional Islam was based on the assumption of an orderly universe in which a person's primary aim was to discover his or her place in that order. The individual was central, and justice was defined as living according to the demands of one's nature. Those who engaged in revolutionary activities, understood in the modern sense, were branded as violators of accepted norms and transgressors against the nature of things. In other words, as the creation of a new order, revolution is a consequence of modernity and modern thinking, and this applies to revolutions among Muslims as well, even if they deny it. Both the Islam of Qom and that of Tehran experienced this shift, each in its own fashion. First and foremost, Islam—an ethical system comprised of faith, rituals, obligations, responsibilities, and a continuous search for the meaning of God's intention—was gradually transformed into an ideology that claimed to have already discovered God's plan, which was manifested in its practical program. Soon the Islamic discourse in Iran acquired orators, ideologists, and even its own press.

Islamic discourse focused on three main ideas: articulation of the other (in this case, demonization of the shah and his supporters, mainly, the West); romanticization of the past (idealization of Islamic heroes and ideologization of Islamic precepts); and formulation of an alternative imagined community against modernity and, particularly, Westernization (that is, drawing a distinction between modernization and Westernization on the one hand and the use of all modern applied knowledge on the other). As has been noted, the intellectual debate in the country had already focused on the first objective. The image of the West was being transformed from one characterized by progress, science, and imagination to one marked by disease, decadence, and problems. The Islam of Tehran succeeded in achieving the objective of romanticizing Iran's past identity, while the Islam of Qom presented the alternative future.

The Islam of Qom: Khomeini and Associated Groups

Who was the voice of the Islamic discourse in Qom at this stage? Right after Burujerdi's death, the government sent a telegram of commiseration to the residing religious leader in Najaf, Muhsin al-Hakim (d. 1970), with the hope of initiating his succession to Burujerdi, but the overture did not have desirable results. There were qualified candidates residing in Qom, Tehran, Tabriz, and Mashhad. An article appearing in the weekly *Khandaniha* less than a year after Burujerdi's death listed eight qualified candidates "who can assume the position of the source of emulation (*marja'iyat*) . . . and one of whom may be selected." They were ranked according to their scholarly prominence, with "his eminence Ayatollah Hajj Aqa Ruhollah Khomeini who teaches in Qom Seminary and has more than 400 students" appearing at the top of the list (1962, 8–9).[5]

Later, he proved to be the voice that vociferously challenged the regime in Iran and initiated a new shift in the political thinking in Shi'ism with his notion of the guardianship of the jurisconsult (*velayat-e faqih*).

KHOMEINI

Khomeini was at the heart of the new theory of an Islamic state. Born in 1902, Khomeini was the last child in a family from the small town of Khomein. His older brother Murtaza was his first teacher and taught him Arabic grammar and logic (Pasandideh 1990, interview). He attended seminary in Arak, where Ha'eri ran the school. When Ha'eri moved to Qom in 1921, Khomeini followed him. From early on he was interested in a mystical understanding of Islam; thus, he began studying the works of Mullah Muhsin Fayz (d. 1680) under the tutorship of Mirza Muhammad Ali Shahabadi (d. 1950), who greatly influenced his antagonism toward the West (Ebrahimi-Dinani 2004, interview).

After Burujerdi's death, Khomeini felt his turn had come to assume leadership. He followed the tradition of the Prophet of Islam by combining religious scholarship with political action: "My brother Moses was blind in the right eye [only attending to this world], and my brother Jesus was blind in the left eye [concerned only with the other world]; I, on the other hand, have two eyes" (quoted in Khomeini 1367/1989, 243). He defined his leadership as being opposed to the existing order of modernism and advocating an Islam-based polity, whose final shape he had not yet decided on. I earlier discussed his emphasis on the dominance of divine law in a Muslim society, but he was prepared to tolerate and to live with the institution of kingship. However, things were now changing, and Khomeini altered his views accordingly.

The government's economic reforms of the early 1960s provided ample opportunity for Khomeini to reinforce his opposition to the existing order. As a response to the 1963 reform program of modernism, he summoned meetings of his colleagues in Qom, sent individual and joint telegrams in protest, and issued a strongly worded declaration denouncing the shah and his plans, but none of this made the government change its plans (Davani 1360/1981, 3:40–52). Reforms proceeded, and a referendum to secure the people's support for them was held on January 26; the government crushed any opposition. Yet neither side showed any willingness to compromise. On March 23, government forces gave Khomeini his greatest ammunition when they attacked the Fayziyeh seminary in Qom, killing at least one student and beating and arresting several others. The showdown had begun.

The government's strategy for breaking the ranks of the clerical establishment failed. When the emissary of the government went to contact the more moderate clerics, Khomeini openly attacked any form of compromise, including positions of silence that could be considered compromise: "Woe to this silent Najaf, woe to this silent Qom" (quoted in Moin 2000, 99). On June 3, 1963, Khomeini delivered a speech at the Fayziyeh, warning the shah that if he did not change his policies, the day would come when the people would celebrate his departure from the country. Khomeini warned the shah about his entourage's weak loyalty, which was prophetic, considering how in 1978 they all abandoned him in a moment of danger and crisis: "You don't know whether the situation will change one day or whether those who surround you will remain your friends. They are the friends of the dollar. They have no religion, no loyalty. They have hung all the responsibility around your neck. O miserable man!" (quoted on 104).[6] The government could not tolerate any more; Khomeini was arrested early in the morning on June 5, imprisoned, and later put under house arrest in Tehran until April 7, 1964.

Upon his release, Khomeini returned to Qom temporarily. When the government forced a bill through the parliament extending diplomatic immunity to American military personnel, Khomeini resumed his criticism, this time with a new target: the "foreign devil." His shrewd exploitation of the shah's American link and his playing on the notion of Iranian sovereignty struck a chord with many Iranians and reminded them of the images of Amir Kabir, Modarres, and Mosaddeq—the heroes of Iranian independence. Khomeini had become an Iranian leader that the Pahlavis could no longer tolerate. On November 4, 1964, commandos again surrounded Khomeini's house in Qom, arrested him, and took him directly to the airport in Tehran for immediate banishment to a life of exile in a Turkish intelligence officer's home.

His stay in Turkey was an opportunity to experience modern secular life. The Turkish intelligence officer showed him things he would not otherwise have been exposed to: beaches, travel, sightseeing, and living with a modern nuclear family. He also learned Turkish and saw firsthand many issues that comparable religious leaders would never have seen. One of his biographers claims that the inclusion of many new ideas in his books on jurisprudence "must have been inspired by his journey to Turkey and contact with a world which was unfamiliar to him" (Moin 2000, 138). On September 5, 1965, Khomeini left Turkey for Najaf in Iraq, where he remained until 1978, when he went to Paris before returning to Iran in 1979.

For reasons that are still unclear, in 1978 the Iranian authorities made an agreement with Iraq to deport Khomeini. Although Khomeini had obtained a visa to go to Kuwait, upon realizing that the visa holder Ruhollah Mustafavi was the famous Khomeini, the Kuwaiti authorities refused him at the border (Rajaee 1983, 33). For Khomeini, this was a blessing in disguise, because he then went to France. Upon his arrival in Paris on October 12, 1978, Khomeini became a media celebrity. He was afforded complete access to television and radio, and the first media revolution was born. The quick unfolding of events inside Iran shortened Khomeini's stay. After the shah was forced into exile on January 16, 1979, Khomeini triumphantly returned to Iran two weeks later. The clock started ticking for the instantiation of a polity based on a blueprint that Khomeini had designed in 1970.

Khomeini seized every opportunity to shape the new political order that emerged from the revolution. Seeing himself in the traditional role of a great arbiter and thinking that he might steer events from Qom, he moved there from Tehran on February 29, turning Qom into a second capital. But after he came to Tehran on January 23, 1980, for medical treatment, he resided in north Tehran until his death on June 3, 1989. He died of natural causes at the peak of his power. Tehran had not seen such an outpouring of overwhelming and spontaneous grief for a long time. The presence of an estimated nine million mourners was so intense that the body ultimately had to be transported by helicopter to its place of burial. This completed the birth of the Islamic state—now it had its own shrine.

Khomeini's personality and views appealed to Iranians because he spoke to their anxiety. This is difficult for many people to comprehend, since the public image they have of him is that of a man obsessed with power: irrefragable, uncompromising, anachronistic, traditionalist, and parochial. That image blurs Khomeini's real character; indeed, this image might be called Khomeinism. However, there is truth to the fact that Khomeini was interested in power. How is this contradiction explained? Ironically, both within the ranks of the clergy in Iran and within the opposition, it was believed that Khomeini changed after tasting power in Iran. He endorsed freedom and pluralism while in Paris (1978) and became an autocrat after he felt secure in a position of power in Tehran, particularly after 1982.

A satirical short story written by the late Iranian historian and writer Ali Akbar Sa'idi Sirjani depicts that conversion. The story focuses on a mystic who revolted against a ruling family and who, with the collaboration of outsiders, liberated a woman named Lady Power (*Qodrat*

Khanom), the daughter of a non-Muslim family, from her home. While some said the daughter should be returned to her parents, apostles of the mystic, who were more opportunistic than he was, argued against this return on the grounds that if the parents had deserved her, they should have protected her. Resolution came when Lady Power was entrusted to a respectable bazargan (a Persian word meaning "merchant" and also the last name of the first prime minister of the new regime) in the city. The merchant's reluctant acceptance and his constant complaints about the difficulty of the task (which resonated with Bazargan's behavior during the few months when he was in power, from February to November 1979), in addition to the apostles' lobbying, led to the transfer of Lady Power to the mystic's headquarters. This occurred even though many argued that no women had ever entered the sacred domain. When the mystic saw the beauty of Lady Power, he fell in love with her, wanting her absolutely for himself. No one knows the end of the story, because, at this juncture, the magazine that used to run the story was banned, and the author never finished. The implication was that Khomeini remained a mystic and a pious leader for as long as he was without power. After tasting power, he became its victim, more and more consumed by the desire for it.

A recent biography of Khomeini generally argues the same point. According to the author, "While in Paris, Khomeini had assured a Western journalist that 'an Islamic republic is a democratic state in the true sense of the word.'" After the ayatollah's return to Iran, "vote-rigging, violence against undesirable candidates and dissemination of false information were all used to produce an Assembly overwhelmingly dominated by clergy loyal to Khomeini and a handful of laymen who followed 'the Imam's line'" (Moin 2000, 218–219). A cleric who is also very perceptive about the evolution of the Iranian polity attributed Khomeini's preoccupation with power to the changing condition of the state. According to him, Khomeini was an autocrat from 1982, when he made the decision to continue the war with Iraq until the end, and extreme measures became necessary. Khomeini even formalized his power under the notion of "absolute guardianship." After the war, he became the voice of the Iranian middle class, issuing fatwas allowing music, chess, and even women singing with an orchestra (Mohammad M-J 1990, interview). In an interview with me, a prominent ayatollah confirmed this change in Khomeini, but dated it much earlier. According to him, there was a change in Khomeini's scholarship, in his approach, and in his ethics. "In his scholarship, he began with philosophy and mysticism, but turned to law and jurisprudence; in his approach, he belonged to the group of 'compromisers' (*salah nist*), but suddenly became revolutionary; and in his ethics, he was against violence, but turned radical" (Sadr 1990, interview).[7] Finally, the first president of the revolutionary regime, Abolhassan Bani Sadr, who now lives in exile, claimed that Khomeini had always wanted to establish the despotic power of the clerical class, but his impulses were moderated by other Iranian revolutionaries in Paris, who would prepare Khomeini's responses to the media, which he simply "repeated verbatim" (Bani Sadr 1360/1981, 9–10). Upon returning to Iran, he fell back on the "strong movement of favouring the dictatorship of the mullahs" (14).

Research on Khomeini's past shows that he had intellectual sophistication, alert timing, and a clear idea of what he was after. His comments on wanting to be the future king of Iran, as well as many other indicators, show us his determination. From early on, he was conscious of the role he wished to play in Iran's future. The more modernism dominated Iran, the more determined Khomeini became. It is reported that he trained seminary students for important future positions, saying, "You have to shoulder great responsibility in later life" (quoted in Moin 2000, 148). When he decided to get married, he was careful to choose a bride from a prominent family. In fact, his former friends said that Khomeini's first claim to fame in Qom came from his marriage to a woman from the prominent house of Ayatollah Saqafi from Tehran (Bodala 1990, interview). It seems that Khomeini saw a means of rising through the ranks of the clerical class in a modernized fashion rather than through the old practices common among the clergy at the time.

Khomeini was aware that the traditional, feudal leadership no longer bore the desired fruit. He targeted younger clerics and university students, particularly those living outside Iran. As his biographer noted, "Khomeini was extremely sensitive about keeping in touch with these [Iranian students abroad]" (Moin 2000, 150). Since neither of these groups cared for old-style leader-follower patterns, he forbade his students to follow him into the street, a common sign of respect and reverence among the older generation. At the same time, he was very conscious of his public status and image. Khomeini knew how the hierarchy of the Shi'i clerics functioned, so he never violated any of its protocols. For example, as long as Burujerdi was alive, Khomeini remained silent, even if he disagreed with him, out of deference (67). His famous three-decade silence about mysticism and philosophy is another indication that he did not intend to antagonize the ranks. The best example of his image consciousness came out of his exile in Turkey in 1965. Ali, the Turkish intelligence officer who hosted Khomeini, recounted how, despite the fact that Khomeini was later very close to Ali's wife and daughter, he objected to their presence and their lack of head covering (*hijab*) the first night he arrived at their house—an Iranian colonel, who certainly would report on Khomeini's response, was accompanying him. Analyzing this episode, Ali concluded, "Khomeini's whole life was based on image [and] I believe this was part of his image. It was part of his cunning. Later we noticed that he was very careful to preserve an image, and did everything to conform to that image. If the Iranian colonel had not been there, I think he would not have reacted to my daughter the way he did" (quoted on 133). In fact, Ali became so close to Khomeini that he would call him father.

This reveals only one facet of Khomeini's paradoxical character. One Khomeini was the man of ambiguity and sophistication, a soul preoccupied with poetry, philosophy, and mysticism; he spoke in the language of Plato, Mulla Sadra, and other sophisticated scholars. The second Khomeini was the populist man of moral clarity who spoke the language of power and communicated with the masses in the language of Lenin, Stalin, and Castro. One example of this paradox manifested after Khomeini's death, when a book of his poetry was published. Many Iranians claimed that this was an attempt to put a soft face on a "power-hungry despot." I have no doubts about the authenticity of the work. Khomeini had been writing poetry for years, but this was not the image he wanted to project. Also, the contemporary Iranian poet Nader Naderpour (1929–2000) was reported as saying that he had spent many hours exchanging poems with Khomeini in the early 1960s: "For four hours we recited poetry. Every single line I recited from any poet, he recited the next" (quoted in Moin 2000, 316).[8]

On one level, Khomeini was an arbiter and guardian of modern Iranians desiring identity and self-respect, though he considered himself a humble servant of the people. On another level, he was the most important spokesman of revolutionary and political Islam at the end of the twentieth century. He represented what his followers perceived to be the truth of religion, and his whims became law. In this capacity, Khomeini was also the voice of traditionalism and Islamism; he easily navigated the sophisticated clerical system of Shi'ism, a hierarchy determined by a labyrinth of ranks, titles, and rituals. In this capacity, he represented the truth of revolution and religion and became the embodiment of an oriental despot. In what follows, I deal with these two features of Khomeini's character, one appealing to the elites, and the second to the masses.

The Khomeini of the elite was a humble scholar who combined philosophy, mysticism, and jurisprudence to traverse the path of devotion to God; the central idea here relates to Khomeini's theory of man as a soul devoted to God. Such a person would be unaware of all worldly events, including the great political, economic, social, and cultural forces he had unleashed. For example, upon his victorious return from a long exile, when asked how he felt about this return home, knowing that he had destroyed both the present regime and the monarchy in Iran forever, he responded, "Nothing!" Or this account by a high-ranking official: "While the council of ministers was reporting about the condition of the country, the war, the economy and all other difficulties, Khomeini appeared to me as a driver going down a sharp hill in a car with no brakes and no steering wheel, yet laid back, his hands behind his head, as though nothing were the matter. Then he began talking about God in the most esoteric language and wishing us a good day" (Hossein K-A 1987, interview). In his approach to God's revelation and intention, he clearly states that the essence of God's will lies beyond the reach of any human capacity: "The Qur'an is not a book that someone can interpret comprehensively and exhaustively, for its sciences are unique and ultimately beyond our understanding" (Khomeini 1980, 365).

It is important to contextualize this statement in his works in order to grasp my distinction between the two Khomeinis. This statement is taken from his lectures on the first chapter of the Qur'an. A few months after his triumphant return to Iran, Khomeini began delivering these lectures on Iranian television. He was now the supreme leader of the revolution and, in theory, the most powerful man in Iran. In these lectures, his interpretation was basically mystical and philosophical. He even began with an implicit criticism of groups who used the Qur'an for political purposes and tried "to impose their own objectives and ideas upon both the Qur'an and the Sunna" (366). Yet the clerical establishment could not tolerate the lectures beyond the first few, so they sent him a message, with which he complied, to stop.

To grasp Khomeini's essence, one must concentrate on his philosophy. He was a disciple of the seventeenth-century Iranian philosopher Mulla Sadra, the last great Muslim philosopher and the founder of transcendental theosophy. Khomeini combined the four disciplines of *fiqh* (jurisprudence), *'erfan* (mysticism), *akhlaq* (ethics), and *falsafe* (philosophy) by applying the idea of "four journeys," as argued by Mulla Sadra in his magnum opus *The Transcendent Theosophy Concerning the Four Intellectual Journeys of the Soul*, to the idea of the "perfect man," which he studied in the works of Ibn Arabi (1165–1214).

For Mulla Sadra, an individual seeker of truth completed his quest through a four-stage journey. The first stage was to elevate oneself from "the masses (*khalq*) to the truth (*haq*)." The second was "to immerse oneself in the truth and comprehend the various dimensions of it." The third was "a journey of return from the truth to the masses." The final journey involved "immersing [oneself] in the masses but armed with the truth" (Nasr 1996, 643–662). The journey was completed when the seeker acted as a contributing member of humanity. This philosophy resonates with Plato's allegory of the cave, in which man is drawn to the light but is responsible for returning to the cave and living as an example for others. Khomeini did exactly that and was able to attract a following.

Khomeini thought the highest form of intellectual exercise was contemplating God's attributes. In his mind, God was the beginning, end, appearance, and essence. Whatever exists, including each person, is nothing but a sign from and of God: "We imagine that we have some independence, that we are something in and of ourselves. It is not so . . . It is by the means of God's manifestation that the whole world has acquired existence" (Khomeini 1980, 370). If God is all there is, and whatever appears is simply his manifestation, then humanity is part of a bigger scheme of things, which is orderly and good. In other words, everything on earth emanates from God. The destiny of humanity dictates a harmonious life with the natural order of things.

In Platonic fashion, Khomeini advocated that one should discover one's place within the natural order. Since people are incapable of achieving this on their own, they need outside assistance. While Plato considered the source of this aid to be human reason and philosophy, Khomeini considered God to be the source, through the medium of prophecies. As a devout Muslim, Khomeini explained his theory within the main articles of Islamic faith: monotheism, prophecy, and the Day of Judgment: "All religions have been revealed to reorient man. Man has been the subject of prophetic missions. All Prophets from Adam [the first messenger, according to Islam] to the last one [Muhammad, the Prophet of Islam] were concerned with man. They did not think about any other thing, because the essence of all existence is man" (quoted in Rajaee 1983, 36).

Humanity's need for orientation relates to two factors. First, humanity in its essence is endowed with the potential either to follow the right path, in harmony with nature, or to set a path contrary to it. What was the basis for such a claim? Here again, Khomeini's anthropology echoes the story of the creation in Islam, whereby God made the first human "from dust" and then "breathed into him His spirit" (Qur'an 32:7, 9). The second factor relates to how Islam considers the role of Satan in the life of humans on earth. According to Islamic cosmological doctrine, after the creation of the first being, God asked all the angels, including Satan, to prostrate themselves before his new creation. Satan refused because he considered only God to be worthy of prostration. God angrily forced Satan out of his presence. Satan then asked for permission to tempt humanity in order to prove them unworthy of reverence. God agreed. We read in the Qur'an that Satan says: "My Lord: Because Thou send me astray, I verily shall adorn the path of error for them in the earth, and shall mislead them every one, save such of them as are Thy perfectly devoted followers" (Qur'an 15: 39–40).

The last phrase in the passage points to an important window into Khomeini's thought. He accepts the dual dimension of human nature, yet he does not think that people are condemned to this duality forever: "Man . . . is a mystery, a mystery within mystery. All we see of man is this outward appearance, which is entirely animal and maybe even inferior to other animals. Man, however, is an animal endowed with aptitude of becoming human and attaining perfection, even absolute perfection; of becoming what is now inconceivable of him and transcending existence" (quoted in Rajaee 1983, 37).

What are the factors that make man "even inferior to other animals," and what are the factors that make possible "even absolute perfection?" Khomeini's answer is understandable at one level and surprising at another: he blames internal forces at work within man's nature. For him, man has a tripartite soul composed of reason, spirit, and passion. The last provokes desires for mundane pleasures and worldly gain; thus, a person's greatest enemy is his or her internal desires and individual self-centeredness. For Khomeini, "all the disasters that afflict man derive from the love of self" (quoted in Rajaee 1983, 39). Indeed, in an important lecture in 1972 on this topic, he referred to self-love as "the struggle against the passionate soul or the supreme jihad." In other words, he affirmed the prophetic saying that the greater aspect of the holy struggle (jihad) is the one launched against the demands of sensual desires and internal temptations. According to the tradition, as narrated by Nasr, "The Prophet said to his companions after a major battle in which the very existence of the early Islamic community was at stake, 'Verily ye have returned from the lesser jihad to the greater jihad.' And when one of the companions asked what the greater jihad was, he answered, 'to battle against your passionate souls (nafs)'" (Nasr 2003, 97).

But how can humanity carry on the greater jihad? According to Khomeini, God has bestowed within people's spirits the desire for perfection and the power of reasoning to materialize this desire. "Reaching perfection," Khomeini writes, "is the true desire of man because the nature of man is [the same as] 'the nature of God' [Qur'an 30:30]. And because man's nature is by essence perfect, he will constantly search for truth and perfection" (quoted in Rajaee 1983, 41). The desire to elevate is natural and self-motivated except when disrupted by the forces of evil. To invoke Plato's parable again, Khomeini claimed that humanity lives in an in-between state wherein the forces of passion push it toward failure and the forces of spirit and reason encourage it toward a higher life and stature. The greatest aids on this path are mysticism and philosophy, two disciplines dear to Khomeini's heart. In his letter of January 4, 1989, to Mikhail Gorbachev, the then general secretary of the Soviet Union's Communist Party, Khomeini invited him to study Muslim mystics and philosophers.

For the "Khomeini of the elite," the main purpose of all revelations has been to elevate humanity to its highest possible stature, and Islam is no exception. According to Khomeini, "Islam has a thesis. It is to make a complete human being out of man. It has come to upgrade man from his current status. . . . Islam and other religions have come to help this undeveloped man, with all his aspects, to grow and develop" (quoted in Rajaee 1983, 47). What makes this passage so significant is that similar assertions with regard to revelations or the raison d'etre of humanity are not cited from Khomeini's scholarly, obscure, mystical, or philosophical tracts, but from speeches he delivered in Paris in his last days of exile, at the peak of the revolutionary confrontation between state and society in Iran. Even in the crucial moments of mundane chaos, he did not forget or underestimate philosophical or mystical discussions. The opposite of this stance manifested in the "Khomeini of the masses," who appealed to passion and the will to power.

The son of Mirza Muhammad Ali Shahabadi (d. 1950), Khomeini's mysticism teacher, said his father believed one must talk to the people in a way that they understand. Khomeini's speeches, writings, and leadership style show that he took that advice to heart. In fact, the apparent simplicity of his prose has given rise to the speculation that Khomeini forgot the flowery syntax of the Persian language during his long exile. However, Khomeini's linguistic spareness may have rather been a conscious effort to be understood by the masses and to simplify the religious discourse that began with Burujerdi. Additionally, communing and communicating with the masses constituted the last journey required by Khomeini's transcendental philosophy, "immersing [oneself] in the masses but armed with the truth."

What helped Khomeini most in his dealings with the masses was being a natural master of timing and language. He knew when to talk and when to use the enormous power of silence. He communicated with and behaved toward his fellow men in the light of the truth as he understood it. In his version of the truth, an ideal leader has absolute authority over the life and property of the people at large. While the Khomeini of the elite clearly stated that God's message was beyond human grasp, with the masses he suggested that there are those who can grasp God's wishes, wills, and commands. He presented this conviction in the theory of "the guardianship of the jurisconsult."

Why did Khomeini talk about guardianship and not government? In the Islamic theory of politics, only God has sovereignty, which he delegated to the prophets, whose main job was to act as guardians of God's words on earth. In Shi'ism, this duty was delegated to the infallible imams, the last of whom are present, though they remain absent from day-to-day affairs. In the absence of direct access to these infallible leaders, the third-best thing, after the prophets and the imams, in Khomeini's theory, was the rule of Muslim scholars. For the qualifications of those who could assume this role, he turned to Islamic jurisprudence. His approach stemmed from his absolute devotion to God, from the belief that God's will was best manifested in the juridical narrative of Islam (*Islam-e Feqahati*), and from his serious concern for implementing God's injunctions and commandments. In other words, as a revolutionary, Khomeini's alternative order was the politics of shari'a, guarded by the absolute authority of the jurisconsult. This became the accepted paradigm, and was incorporated in Articles 5 and 107 of the constitution. The latter is worth reporting: "During the Occultation of the Guardian of the Age (*Vali-e Asr*) [the twelfth Shi'i Imam] (may God hasten his reappearance), the guardianship and leadership of the community devolve upon the righteous and pious Jurisconsult (*faqih*), who is fully aware of the circumstances of his age."

The idea had its root in a series of lectures Khomeini delivered in Najaf between January 20 and February 6, 1970, on the theory and implementation of an Islamic government. In them, Khomeini entered into the revolutionary discourse of the day, a competition to capture the minds of youth. The left presented a Marxist alternative to the existing monarchy, but more alarming to Khomeini were the so-called "Islamist-

Marxists," the People's Mojahedin, who presented a Marxist narrative of Islam. In fact, Ali Davani, a contemporary historian and member of the clergy who devoted his life to the study of Islamic discourse, said that Khomeini's lectures were a response to the claim that Iranian youth were infected with un-Islamic views. In the 1960s, a group of activist clerics, whose members became prominent leaders of the revolution, had sent a report to Najaf about the rapid progress of Marxist ideas among Muslim youth, alarming Khomeini (Rajaee 1983, 22). In response, Khomeini delivered a series of easily understandable lectures intended for those unfamiliar with Islamic discourse and the nuances of Islamic jurisprudence.

He called for a revolution, justifying it as follows: "So, courageous sons of Islam, stand up! Address the people bravely; tell the truth about our situation to *the masses in simple language . . . and turn the people . . . our simple-hearted workers and peasants, and our alert students into dedicated warriors* [mujahids]" (Khomeini 1980, 132; emphasis added). Who were they to fight? According to this Khomeini, the ayatollah of the masses, the enemy was not within man but without—the larger world. The war would have to be a total war because the world had turned against Islam: "The imperialists, the oppressive and treacherous rulers, the Jews, the Christians, and the materialists are all attempting to distort the truth of Islam and lead the Muslims astray" (127). Further, he presented his theory of government, an alternative to the existing monarchy, because "Islam proclaims monarchy and hereditary succession wrong and invalid" (31).

What did Khomeini consider a valid form of authority? A shariʿa-based order: "Islamic government may therefore be defined as the rule of the divine law over men" (356). No special status or preference need be shown for any particular form of government within Islamic injunctions and juridical principles. All supporters of Islamic government, including Khomeini, invoke the following verse when asserting political authority: "O ye who believe! Obey God, obey His Prophet and those who are in authority amongst you" (Qur'an 4:59). Regarding this authority, most Muslims developed the notion of the caliphate; the minority Shiʿis developed the notion of the imamate, stipulating that formation of government was the prerogative of an imam designated by God.

Since Khomeini argued for the rule of the jurisconsults, in some ways his theory represented an innovation in the history of Shiʿi political thought. Khomeini declared that henceforth it would be possible for any jurisconsult, rather than an infallible imam, to take charge, provided that he was capable and, more importantly, righteous and well versed in Shiʿi law: "In addition to general requirements such as intelligence and managerial ability (*tadbir*), there are two essential qualifications: knowledge of the law (*'elm be qanun*) and righteousness (*edalat*)" (quoted in Rajaee 1983, 65–66). It is common to translate the Arabic word *edala* and the Persian word *edalat* as "justice," but "righteousness" is closer in meaning to Khomeini's understanding. In fact, Muslims, Greeks, Indians, and Persians traditionally understood justice to mean living within the natural and divine order of things. "Righteousness" is defined in the *Oxford English Dictionary* as the "conformity of life or conduct to the requirement of the divine or moral order." Khomeini followed this approach, and when he considered *edala* as a quality, he meant a condition of absolute observance of the principles of shari'a, Islamic law, and complete compliance with divine ordinances.

Why did Khomeini's discourse become the dominant view in the wake of the revolution? One can posit at least two explanations. On the one hand, it appealed to the masses of indigenous Iranians, who could relate to the vocabulary, syntax, and cultural context of Khomeini's vernacular. On the other hand, the leaders of the Islam of Tehran were unable to develop a positive appeal for their plan. They were extremely successful, however, in generating opposition to the ancien regime and exciting people about an Islamic imagined community; but when it came to practical plans and collective action, they failed to communicate effectively with the people. Indeed, the Islam of Tehran, particularly Shari'ati's version, in which Islam was portrayed as an ideology of power, paved the way for the predominance of the jurisconsults in Iranian politics. We now consider the organizational support that propagated Khomeini's ideas.

GROUPS ASSOCIATED WITH KHOMEINI: MO'TALEFE AND ROHANIYAT-E MOBAREZ

The most notable organization that voiced the Islam of Qom in this period was a group called *Hey'atha-ye Mo'talefe-ye Eslami* (the Coalesced Islamic Societies), which functioned under the guidance and organizational supervision of the clerics. Indeed, it later served as the core of *Jame'eye Rohaniyat-e Mobarez-e Tehran* (the Society of the Combatant Clergies of Tehran), the important conservative wing of the clerical class in the Islamic Republic. The institutional headquarters of both groups, Mo'talefe and Rohaniyat-e Mobarez, were in Tehran, but both propagated the Islam of Qom, particularly Khomeini's views.

Three different Islamic societies came together to form Mo'talefe in April 1963. The notion of society (*hay'at*) here refers to semiformal gatherings of Islam-minded Iranians, usually sponsored by well-established

merchants and meeting in no specific location, which made them difficult for the authorities to penetrate. The elite of the Islamic Republic was
rooted in these societies. Some societies had connections with particular
mosques, others did not. The core of the Mo'talefe was formed from the
Isfahani society and from groups connected with the Amin al-Dawleh
and Shaikh Ali mosques. In March 1963, "Khomeini in Qom introduced
and connected them to one another" (Badamchian and Banaei 1362/1983,
35). This connection was soon expanded into a sophisticated underground
network guided by the Council of Clergies (*Shura-ye Rohaniyat*), composed of Khomeini's prominent and loyal friends, such as Mohammad
Beheshti and Morteza Motahhari. One of the founders, Badamchian,
recalled that this gathering of societies was intended to create part of
a new "Islamic *umma* (community), ready to revolt whenever its imam
[Khomeini] would ask it of them. . . . The reason the founders wanted it
was that the imam of the *umma* [Khomeini] declared the necessity for
its creation" (161). The groups agreed on a commitment to the following
three principles: "Islam, particularly Shi'ism; the *marja'iyat* (authority)
of Ayatollah Khomeini; and the necessity of struggle, in contradistinc-
tion to the accepted notion that Muslims should not get involved in
politics" (173).

A council of clergies was needed to ensure that the new group moved
in line with religious precepts. As one of the organization's founders said,
"Brothers in the *Mo'talefe* who considered their move an ideological one
based on the leadership of the imam of the *umma* [Khomeini] felt that
if they wanted to advance based on the revelation and the words of the
Prophet, they had to have a council comprised of the jurists among their
management" (quoted in Badamchian and Banaei 1362/1983, 181). While
it was the duty of this council to set the ideological direction of the society, time and again the organization made it clear that its own main duty
was to propagate Khomeini's understanding of Islam and politics, and
the council echoed the same concern.

The Mo'talefe distributed Khomeini's messages and propagated
his ideas through its two short-lived publications, *Be'sat* (Birth) and
Enteqam (Punishment) (284–285 and 301).[9] *Be'sat,* named after the birth
of Islam, aimed to revive "the prophecy and . . . the dynamism of the
Islamic life. For now, it is published occasionally, and its first issue is
out on the anniversary of the appointment of the prophecy [in Islam]"
(quoted in Hojjati Kermani 1368/1989, 13). The name of the second publication was taken from the Qur'an 3:3: "Surely those who disbelieve in the
communications of God, they shall have a severe chastisement. God is

Mighty and the Lord of Punishment." The last phrase of this verse was used for the title, with the word "punishment" enlarged. The publication identified two objectives: revenge against those who go against Islam and the reestablishment of Islam in contemporary Iran.

Reestablishment, according to the Mo'talefe, would happen only if Iranians followed the demands of Khomeini, who was depicted in *Be'sat* as follows: "The people of Iran consider Ayatollah Khomeini the symbol of freedom, free-spiritedness, and sacrifice for the preservation of people's rights and the integrity of the sacred principles of Islam" (quoted in Badamchian and Banaei 1362/1983, 294). Another theme in *Be'sat* was the encouragement of religious and ideological forms of struggle. As, for example, a regular piece entitled "Maktab-e Mobarez" (the Ideology of Struggle) put it: "Now, we continue our struggle in its new form, and it will last until the final victory . . . because it is the path of God, the path of Islam and that of the Qur'an. It is an ideology that Muhammad (peace be upon him) and Ali (greeting to him) and other leaders began, and in our time our great source of emulation, his Excellency the Great Ayatollah Khomeini continues" (quoted in Hojjati Kermani 1368/1989, 56).

Casting the struggle as a religious war between right and wrong was a recurrent theme in *Be'sat*. It was treated as superior to any other form of struggle—economic, political, or social. It could go on forever, justified by the claim that God does not necessarily want victory now and that the reward for those who fight is eternal. As reported in the seventh issue of the Journal's first volume: "The advantage of a religious movement is that there is no defeat, damage, or loss. It is a battle in which loss is the same as victory [owing to God's rewards]" (quoted on 98). At the same time, there was enormous ideological preparation for a possible victory. What kind of government would be appropriate for the future? The idea of an "Islamic government," or a shari'a-based government (*hokumat-e shar'i*), was discussed and elaborated in detail; educational measures, the establishment of the government, and the administration of preparatory classes were outlined in impressive and enormous detail (Badamchian and Banaei 1362/1983, 312–319).

By the late 1970s, politics in Iran had changed. In 1977, the clerical council of the Mo'talefe created a new organization, the *Jame'eye Rohaniyat-e Mobarez-e Tehran* (the Society of the Combatant Clergies of Tehran). Not only was this the most important mechanism for mobilizing mass support for Khomeini, but it also became "the most powerful religious-political organization in the Islamic Republic" (Moslem 2002, 50) from 1979 until the 1997 presidential election. Here, we are concerned with the ideas of the group before the revolution, those that set the agenda for the Mo'talefe.

The views of one of the most prominent members of the group, Mohammad Hossein Beheshti (assassinated in 1980), are also worth noting. Like most of the religious elite, Beheshti confirmed the views of Khomeini, particularly his ideas on the guardianship of the jurisconsult (for a summary, see Badamchian and Banaei 1362/1983, 321–340). Had he not been assassinated, he would have been Khomeini's successor. He was instrumental in legitimizing the new revolutionary position of the clergy among the people. As he wrote in a collection of essays on the future leadership in Shi'ism: "If the government is not Islamic and does not commit itself to Islamic laws . . . Muslims are obliged to force it to do so, and if that is not successful, they should create organizations to help them do so" (*Bahsi darbareye* 1341/1962, 148). He affirmed the traditional position in Shi'ism that legitimate authority belongs only to the infallible imams, who are designated by God, but he also argued that issues related to worldly affairs could, with certain qualifications, be delegated to the people: "During the occultation of the Twelfth Imam, and in the absence of government by his knowledge and righteousness, those prerogatives that were not specific to imamate could be assumed by anyone qualified to implement them" (142). Beheshti and the members of the Mo'talefe argued for the same principles that Khomeini later advocated.

The same line of reasoning was expressed by other organizations, such as the *Hezb Mellal-e Eslami* (Islamic Nations Party), whose declared objective, in a publication called *Khalq* (Nation), was to create an "Islamic Government" in a "republican" form, and which advocated struggle, assassination, and terror (*Keyhan*, Bahaman 1344/February 1966, 3).

The Islam of Tehran: Motahhari, Shari'ati, and Associated Groups

While Iran's modernism depicted the West as a mecca of progress and advancement, and Iran as a secular polity, the opposition propagated the exact opposite view: the West was to be avoided, and Iran was a Muslim state. There were many Iranian writers and thinkers whose works proved influential in the 1960s and 1970s, including Bazargan, Yadollah Sahabi, and Taleqani. Most relevant to the discussion here were Morteza Motahhari (1920–1979) and Ali Shari'ati (1933–1977). These figures became the central intellectual pillars of what can be called "the Islamic ideological alternative." Their works are still reprinted and are still best sellers, despite their authors having been dead for over two decades. At the same time, many Islam-based educational and cultural institutions developed to echo and promote the alternative discourse to modernism and Americanism.

MOTAHHARI

In some ways, it may seem surprising to treat Motahhari as a contributor to the politicization and ideologization of Islam. An interesting intellectual, he concentrated on philosophy and the harmony between science and religion (see, for example, Rajaee 1993b, 110–111). At the same time, he played a major role in making Islam relevant to the lives of the younger Iranians who were becoming active in the political life of the country. However, he went beyond the prevalent defensive posture of simply responding to the country's problems. He wanted to create out of Islam a system that could compete with other ways of organizing a polity: "Islam can resist and survive in the face of atheistic and nonatheistic systems only after it has become a philosophy of life dominating the society and is not limited to the corner of mosques and temples" (Motahhari 1382/2003, 93). This was the task Motahhari set for himself, and in that capacity he became a primary architect of Islamic ideology in the twentieth century, ensuring his reputation as a radical man. Indeed, in the summer of 2004 the conservative elements in Iran celebrated him as the voice of Islamic ideology.

Motahhari was born in 1919 in Fariman, near Mashhad, a major center of Shi'i pilgrimage in Iran. He began his early schooling in Mashhad, but because of his interest in philosophical inquiry, he left for Qom to study with Mohammad Hossein Tabataba'i and Khomeini in the 1940s. In his works, Motahhari mentions that he was keenly interested in the philosophical approach to Islam from early on: "Doubt is the beginning of certainty, questions are the preface to reaching [understanding] and anxiety is the beginning of serenity" (Motahhari 1357/1978, 7). As he put it in an autobiographical note: "I recall how from the beginning of my studies in Mashhad . . . the philosophers, the mystics, and the theologians, even though I was not familiar with their ideas, impressed me more than other men of knowledge and scholars. My reasons were that I thought of them alone as heroes on the stage of thought" (quoted in *Seyri dar* 1382/2003, 36). But he did not ignore other branches of Islamic studies. He "finished his course of juridical studies in Qom" (Dabashi 1993, 149), then followed up with theology, ethics, and philosophy in Tehran.

The move to Tehran provided him with a different kind of challenge. He discovered that his main antagonist was the Iranian left, which dominated intellectual discourse at the universities. He began teaching at the university, as part of the theology faculty, in 1955. He felt he had to be the voice of Islam now that it was faced with a contemporary adversary: "The main objective in all my writings is to address the dilemmas and respond to the questions that Muslims face in our time" (Motahhari 1357/1978, 8). In cooperation with like-minded persons, he founded a more modern institution of Islamic learning: a "Monthly Religious Society," whose organ, *Goftarha-ye Mah* (Monthly Discourses), was widely distributed.[10] Motahhari was involved in the June 1963 uprising, arrested for it, and briefly jailed. Afterward, he decided to concentrate on the intellectual domain. Motahhari's most significant podium came with the establishment of Hosseiniye-ye Ershad, in 1965, when he finally succeeded in attracting university students to Islam. In all three arenas, the university, traditional institutions, and the new hosseiniyes, Motahhari was effective and successful.

The new hosseiniyes were significant—their very being represented change and revolution. Traditionally, they were simple community centers created to honor Imam Hossein, the third Shi'i leader—hence their name—but the new ones were equipped with modern facilities: sound systems; theatres; furniture, in place of sitting on the floor; youth centers; libraries; social clubs; and educational centers. They hosted regular religious meetings, instead of sporadic special-occasion meetings.

Motahhari authored over fifty books, which dealt with theology and philosophy as well as practical issues such as sexual ethics, usury, and insurance. In these works, he managed to construct an imagined community of Islam that appealed to Iranians of diverse intellectual and political persuasions.

The revolution of 1979 included all people and groups, and part of this success was due to Motahhari. Not surprisingly, immediately after Motahhari's death, Khomeini described him as "the intellectual infrastructure of the Islamic Republic" (*Seyri dar* 2003, 20). Khomeini referred to Motahhari that way for two reasons. First, in the early days of the revolution, his house functioned as "the central command of the revolution inside the country, [the place of] its coordination with the leadership of the imam [Khomeini]" (Rafsanjani, quoted on 119). Khomeini appointed him to "form the revolutionary council," and before he returned to Iran from Paris, he informed Motahhari about the decision and suggested that he (Khomeini) reside at Alavi High School (124, 126, 132). More importantly, Motahhari succeeded in constructing an image of an Iranian state with no contradictions among its pre-Islamic national heritage, its clergy, and modernity.

Two themes in Motahhari's work have left the biggest marks. The first concerns the relationship between Islam and Iran, which Motahhari addressed in a three-part 750-page book entitled *Khadamat-e Motaqabel-e Islam va Iran* (The Mutual Contributions of Islam and Iran). The second topic relates to the question of women's rights and the Muslim women's dress code. He addressed these concerns in two books. The first, *Mas'ale-ye Hejab* (The Question of Women's Coverings), was popular when it was originally delivered as a series of lectures to the Islamic Society of Physicians and is among today's best-sellers in Iran; the second was *Nezam-e Hoquq-e Zan dar Islam* (The System of Women's Rights in Islam).

Khadamat-e Motaqabel deals with the triad of Islam, Iran, and nationalism. For Motahhari, this was not an academic exercise but, rather, "real and relevant to the fate, strategies, manners, and future of a polity and society we call Iran today" (Motahhari 1372/1994, 18). It had been assumed that nationalism was contrary to Islam, and by the same token, that those concerned with Islam failed to serve the national interest of the modern Iranian polity. Motahhari argued against such a dichotomy: "Nationalism should not be condemned categorically, and when it conveys positive qualities, it leads to solidarity, good relations, and common welfare among those we live with. It is neither irrational nor is it contrary to Islam" (62). Indeed, Iranian solidarity indirectly helps Islam because those ventures are intertwined: "The more I study this matter [the relation of Islam and Iran], the more I am convinced that the commonality between Islam and Iran is a source of pride for both of them" (15). For Motahhari, pre-Islamic Iran was an important human achievement. His opinion was significant because the pre-Islamic world had been traditionally branded "the age of ignorance" (*jahiliya*), whereas Motahhari paid special respect to Iran's human and secular heritage: "This is an obvious fact . . . pre-Islamic Iran had an illuminating civilization that became a part of the essence of Muslim civilization" (282).

There were two reasons for celebrating pan-Iranism and ancient Iran at this time. First, to downplay the Islamic aspects of Iranian identity by emphasizing pure Aryan greatness; second, to fight the pan-Arabism that had become prevalent in the Muslim world in the aftermath of the 1952 Egyptian revolution and the emergence of Gamal Abdel Nasser (d. 1970). Local papers in Iran referred to Nasser's campaign to call the age-old Persian Gulf the "Arab Gulf" as the "second Arab invasion." Motahhari wanted to change the argument altogether and show how Iranians' welcoming of Islam had little to do with Arabism then or now, but was due to the notion of social justice in Islam. Iranians asked for justice in the century when Islam came, and they ask for it now: "If Islam had not come to Iran, Christianity would have taken over what had remained of Zoroastrianism" (177).

As testimony that Iranians had welcomed Islam and made it part of their identity, Motahhari cited a long list of prominent Iranian-Muslim scholars who had advanced Muslim civilization in all fields of human knowledge and achievement. This acceptance was significant because, as he writes, "One can force a nation to obedience, but one cannot force it to be dynamic, enthusiastic, and faithful. The domain of force is rather limited, and all human masterpieces have been created only with love and faith" (384). This analysis is an important reference point for understanding Iranian society's relationship to religion at this time. Motahhari's attempt at establishing harmony between Iran and Islam offered Iranian youth a glimpse of an imagined balanced community and attracted them to Islamic discourse.

The second theme of Motahhari's major works deals with women's rights. This issue proved more significant than the coming of Islam to Iran because the women's movements emerging at the time became a subject of Islamic discourse. In his book dealing with women's coverings, Motahhari presented a narrative that ran contrary to those of both the modernists and the traditionalists. In Motahhari's view, the former confused liberation with promiscuity, while the latter confused the confinement of women with chastity. For example, regarding the dress code for women, he approved of covering, but argued against those who used it as an excuse to "imprison women at home" as well as those who proposed its elimination altogether. Both extremes ran contrary to the Muslim notion of boundaries and limits, which is the literal meaning of "hijab." "Imprisoning women in the house" in the name of keeping them covered undermined their basic human rights, yet encouraging women to display their bodies would lead to their becoming sex objects. Respecting boundaries should be considered a civilizational principle "for this observation, that any sexual pleasure belongs to the private world of the family, freeing the social sphere from sensuality" (Motahhari 1376/1997, 184–185). The recognition of boundaries applied to women's covering as well as to their rights and responsibilities.

In his book on the rights of women, Motahhari concentrated on the relation between the two sexes. He stated the obvious, that men and women are not the same: "From an Islamic point of view, men and women are both human, thus they enjoy equal human rights. . . . Because one is male and the other female, they are dissimilar in many ways and the world does not look the same for them. Creation and nature have made them differently, thus it is imperative that they have different rights and obligations" (Motahhari 1382/2003, 122). He concluded that men and women should not be treated equally. This idea was appealing to many traditional male Muslims and also to modern female Muslims who could be branded "essentialist feminists" within the broader women's movement. Interestingly, these ideas made it possible for a modern Iranian to be Muslim, Iranian, and traditional simultaneously. This was one of the successes of the contemporary Islamic movement, and in fact, for Motahhari, the success of the Islamic movement lay in "convincing the people that they have an ideology and an independent one" (Motahhari n.d., 36).

SHARI'ATI

More radical than Motahhari was the mystical figure Ali Shari'ati (1933–1977), whose poetic prose was sharper than a sword. Shari'ati was influenced by the writings of many modern critical and revolutionary minds, but most of all from those of Franz Fanon. Shari'ati translated his book *The Wretched of the Earth* into Persian; it enormously influenced a generation of Iranians. Fanon was a renowned analyst of the colonial situation, effectively guiding people out of apathy, indifference, and defeat to oppose colonial thinking and intransigence. He provided the best analysis of revolutionary violence and one of the best critiques of the insufficiency of nationalism. Shari'ati aimed to assume such a role among Iranians.

To achieve this objective, he first had to fight the existing quietist attitude so prevalent among Muslims, particularly Iranians. In this, he was not alone; even moderate people such as Bazargan were encouraging the religious establishment to take an active role. But he alone was expected to change the paradigm among Islam-minded Iranians. An example of their traditional passivity was reflected in the view among Shi'is that "one must endure the tyranny and injustice of existing governments" (Black 2001, 42). According to Iranian scholar and professor Hamid Enayat, who pictured the condition so well, "With the increasing tendency of the Shi'is to [adopt] a passive form of *taqiyyah* [the precautionary concealment of one's religion] and acquiescence in the established order, the concept of the martyrdom of Husayn as vicarious atonement prevailed over its interpretation as a militant assertion of the Shi'i cause" (Enayat 1982, 183).

Shari'ati received additional help to change this quietist attitude. The most notable revisionist approach appeared in a book published in 1968, entitled *Shahid Javid* (The Immortal Martyr), wherein Imam Hossein is depicted as a calculating revolutionary who "took all the precautions that a responsible political leader should take" before embarking on his "well-planned attempt to overthrow" the Umayyad ruler Yazid (Najafabadi 1349/1970, 330–339). The main story: Imam Hossein, a grandson of the Prophet, did not approve of the caliphate of the Umayyads. Upon the death of Muawiyya (caliph from 661 to 680 and father of Yazid), Hossein set out to challenge Yazid's claim to be caliph. During a military confrontation with Yazid's forces at Karbala (in Iraq) in 680, Hossein and around seventy of his followers were killed. This event, marked annually by Shi'is around the world, is traditionally interpreted as representing the martyrdom of innocence before injustice, and Hossein's death is taken to be redemptive for Muslims (Ayoub 1978).

Najafabadi boldly claimed that neither Imam Hossein's opposition to the new caliph nor his death was for anybody's redemption and that he had not been ordained to die a martyr. Instead, he had objectively and rationally planned to assume the power of the newly appointed caliph. Upon the death of Yazid's father and in the wake of the promising political circumstances in Kuffa, he embarked on this revolution. But given the suppression of Hossein's followers in Kuffa and how badly outnumbered Hossein and his followers were during the battle, the tragic end was inevitable (Enayat 1982, 193–194). The operationalization and in some ways secularization of the event in Karbala made Hossein a symbol of political resistance and revolutionary planning, a model of extreme significance during the revolution. The book's argument let to a heated debate and the mysterious death of a clergy member in the spring of 1976 in Isfahan. The victim's "alleged murderers were said to be advocates of the author's [Najafabadi's] thesis" (191).[11] The improvident and divinely ordained act of Imam Hossein became a failed revolutionary attempt, its collapse explainable by objective and rational causes. Shari'ati approved of Najafabadi's thesis without ever mentioning the author's name or the book's title (Shari'ati 1357/1979, 19:149–150).

For Shari'ati, Imam Hossein's martyrdom constituted a common occurrence in human history in the perennial struggle between truth and falsehood, between "crime and martyrdom" (*jenayat va shahadat*): selfish people and tyrannical rulers commit the first, and conscious and responsible ones embody the second. It began with the division between Cain and Abel, then Moses and pharaoh, Muhammad and the Quraish,

Ali and Muawiyyah, Hossein and Yazid, and later, other Hosseins and other Yazids (19:17). Indeed, one of Shari'ati's major presuppositions about life on earth was that it is a permanent and constant struggle between justice and tyranny. The struggle began when Adam gave "his divine dimension to Abel and gave the Satanic one to Cain. Then, Abel died young at the hand of Cain. Those who live on earth are all descendents of Cain, unjust, and killers" (13:4). This was a recurrent theme: "As I have delineated in my lecture on the philosophy of history in my [work] *Islamology,* the first cause of all aberration in history is the emergence of . . . the Cainian system and . . . I do not understand any other cause" (19:98).

Here is the irony about Shari'ati. The conclusion to Shari'ati's line of reasoning dictates that one must live with injustice because, in an Augustinian way, we are all sinful and thus condemned to commit injustice. Yet he thought it possible to create a revolution and advocated the training of souls who, despite their unjust inheritance, can act like Abel. It was his job to provide a model for such behavior, and Imam Hossein presented Shari'ati with such a model. For example, there is an invocation depicting Imam Hossein as the inheritor of previous holy men, but Shari'ati interpreted it to mean "to inherit all revolutions from Adam to his time" (19:98). Yet Hossein was more than an inheritor; he played a paradigmatic role in "the vanguard of this glorious human struggle" (*Hossein, the Inheritor of Adam,* audio CD by Shari'ati, in author's possession). Shari'ati depicted Imam Hossein as the Ernesto Che Guevara (1928–1967) of Islam.[12]

How did Shari'ati argue his case? Like most Muslim thinkers, he was preoccupied with reasons for Muslims' backwardness. His diagnosis of the problem is interesting and unique. The first distinction to note is that he did not blame outsiders or the despotic regimes in Muslim societies for Muslims' ills, as did most of the other thinkers. Instead, he blamed Muslims themselves: "In our cultural and Islamic intellectual backwardness and being marginalized, we have to blame ourselves. As the great [Imam] Ali puts it, 'In order for injustices to occur, two sides are needed: those who commit the oppression and those who accept it'" (6:10–11). While he blamed both sides of the dichotomy, he placed more responsibility on those who accept tyranny. In his mind, outside enemies have always existed and will exist in the future. One must fight against weaknesses that facilitate penetration by outsiders: "No doubt outside elements and the hand of foreigners cannot be denied in our backward condition, but when has Islam been without enemies? . . . We should avoid freeing ourselves from our responsibility for our dismal condition by fighting outside enemies and incriminating them in order to exonerate our friends. Instead, we should remind ourselves that if the enemy has been able to exacerbate our decadence, it is our weakness that has facilitated it" (20:394).

He spends abundant energy delineating the meaning of self-responsibility. However, there are two impediments to realizing it: first, political and intellectual inaction and a quietist attitude; second, turning Islam into a creed of the status quo. Shari'ati wanted to remedy these by making Muslims responsible, self-conscious, and dynamic human beings. He believed this to be possible through a process he called "the return to the self" (*bazgasht be khish*). His main task was, thus, to elaborate on the ideal version of what it means to be human and on how Islam can be turned into an ideology. The two are related in that the ideal version of humanity helps explicate the ideology: "The ideal types display the ideology with their being and their lives, and that is far more valuable than a thousand books, lectures, sermons, or even scientific discoveries" (2:13).

What, then, was Shari'ati's notion of the ideal person and responsible citizen? Here, we look to his anthropology, best presented in *Ensan va Islam* (Man and Islam), a collection of six lectures delivered at the Petroleum College of Abadan. Immediately, one should be reminded that Shari'ati spoke as a Muslim, so his definition of man or his discussion of any other related topic was based on the Islamic worldview as he narrated it.[13] Not only is his definition of man true because he confessed to it himself (Shari'ati n.d., 32–33), and not only is it true because all his thinking makes sense within his Islamic worldview, but his definition is true because the Qur'anic story of Adam and the fate of his two sons served as the basis for his philosophy of history.

Shari'ati saw history as a struggle between two forces—good and bad—a struggle that began with the fight between Cain and Abel. The main cause was Cain's loss of genuine belief: "Cain . . . brushes aside his belief in God, and sacrifices [the sacred] for personal gain. . . . More so, Abel's religiosity is such that he utilizes religion for personal gain" (39–40). Thus, one finds the beginning of Shari'ati's anthropology in the story of creation according to the Qur'an, which states, "We created man in the best make, then we rendered him the lowest of the low" (Qur'an 95:4–5). For Shari'ati, the verse showed that "in his potential, man is an extraordinary phenomenon, but in actuality he is earthly, material, and biological . . . [and] can ascend to a position high above any material standing in the world" (Shari'ati 1357/1979, 5:135–136). God has both provided the means by which man can make the journey and set the goal. God provided the means by revealing the secret of life to humanity: "He taught

Adam all the names" (Qur'an 2:21). More importantly, God offered "the trust" to man (Qur'an 33:72), which, according to Shari'ati, meant that "man's free will . . . [is] the only virtue that distinguishes him from other creatures on earth and enables him to act even contrary to his own instinct. No other animals or even plants can act contrary to their natural instinct" (Shari'ati n.d., 11). Humans require this free will because God wants them to act as his vicegerents on earth. God stated clearly, "I am going to place in the earth a vicegerent" (Qur'an 2:30). This verse is very significant for Shari'ati in that "this sets man's destiny on the earth. . . . He has to act as God's agent." According to Shari'ati, this exceeds the status granted to humanity by modernity: "Even European humanism, even that of the post-Renaissance, has not granted such a high status to man" (Shari'ati n.d., 7).

In summary, man can potentially elevate himself to nearness to God, but in actuality, this will happen only if he wills it to be so. This led Shari'ati to distinguish between "hominid" (*bashar*) and "human" (*ensan*). The first relates to a generic creature, including all members of humanity, while the second refers to the unique individuality of each person, provided that, according to Shari'ati, the human quality of free will is materialized:

> A hominid is always natural, and remains always the same. His main features have not changed since the time of the early apes, which appeared on the earth fifty thousand years ago. His weapons have changed, his clothing has changed, his food has altered, but generically it is the same as before. . . . In contrast, a human is one who does not exist on his own. He has to evolve and to become, and this is a permanent becoming. . . . One can imagine three qualities for it. The human who has to become is self-conscious, able to choose, and able to create. (Shari'ati n.d., 101–105)

Shari'ati sought the creation of this type of human for his ideal society, and he felt that only they could rid Muslim societies of their backwardness.

All his writings revolve around this objective, and he was quite aware that it was not an easy task. A hominid aspiring to become a human faces many impediments. Shari'ati deals with four of them, which he calls "the four prisons of man": "The first prison is the forces of nature, which shape us according to their own laws. . . . The second is history, that is, the continuation of past events that influence our identity. The third is society. The Iranian social system, its class relations, economy, and evolution affect me. The fourth prison is the jail of the self, which confines 'I' in the free human" (Shari'ati 1357/1979, 8:151). On another occasion, he called the first three "biologism," "historicism," and "sociologism" (Shari'ati n.d., 117). Man can break free from these three with the aid of science and scholarship: "From the first jail, the prison of nature, man will enhance his self-consciousness, will, and creativity through an understanding of nature. From the second jail—that is, historicism—man gains freedom by grasping the philosophy of history. From the third jail, sociologism, again man gains freedom by knowing and constructing [a desired] social system" (128–129).

Shari'ati also dealt with the last jail—the self—and considered this the worst of the four; because it is an inseparable part of one's very existence, it is the jail against which man most often struggles in vain. Humans are unable to avoid self-alienation, primarily because recognizing the need to free oneself from alienation is difficult, as is solving the conundrum. Any great philosopher of history can free man from the determinism of history, but is rarely able to free his own soul from the entanglement of the self (132). Shari'ati did not think psychology would help man's soul, because logical knowledge and rationality are of no help. The soul requires a different measure, which he calls love: "I am not talking about love as understood in mysticism (sufiyaneh) or Gnosticism ('arefaneh), for they are also jails of a different kind. I am talking about an extraordinary force, beyond utilitarian and instrumental rationality, that is human essence, that in the depth of our nature causes a revolt against our very being" (133). This category does not mean reckoning with costs and benefits, damages and interests, or gain and pain.

In Shari'ati's understanding of love, one may incur cost, damage, and pain without the slightest expectation of any return. As he understands it, love is a force that provokes selflessness and sacrifice for the sake of the other: "Love refers to a force that invites me to sacrifice all my interests, benefits, and even my life, whatever my life is based on, for the sake of others and for the ideals that I stand for, even if it means my life would be sacrificed [for them]" (134). According to Shari'ati, neither scholarship, nor science, nor philosophy can deliver this; love requires prophecy. Since the age of prophecy is over, because Muhammad, the Prophet of Islam, is considered the last of the prophets, humanity is on its own.

Shari'ati further claimed, "The end of prophecy means that from now on . . . humanity is able to continue without revelation on his own" (Shari'ati 1347/1969, 69). At the same time, he felt that humanity required intellectuals who would show and tell others how they should live. He identified them with ideologues and even demagogues. Thus, in the end, what distinguishes the ideal human being from either generic homos or knowledgeable and artful humans is the ability to rebel and swim against the current. Shari'ati echoed Marx's conviction that a person's job is not to explain the world, but to change it. Thus, life is a permanent revolution in which one "sacrifices everything for one's objective without expecting any rewards . . . [and] gives one's life so that another may survive" (Shari'ati n.d., 136). Indeed, for Shari'ati, martyrdom, which he in fact considered a panacea, was central: "Martyrdom is a call for all seasons and all generations. If you can cause death (*bemiran*), do so, and if you cannot, then die (*bemir*). . . . Our nation, our future's history, and the heart of our time need you and your blood" (quoted in *Payam Mojahed* 2 [October 16, 1973]). It is also important to note in what type of publication this message was reproduced: *Payam Mojahed* was a monthly published by Iranian students abroad who were voicing their views on Islam-minded revolutionaries.

The responsible and conscious soul who was to live in this state of permanent revolution required a revolutionary doctrine and philosophy. Thus Shari'ati moved on to the next phase, namely, the presentation of a new version of Islam, one that could facilitate individual and social revolution. Of course, he claimed that Islam had always been revolutionary, but like a man trapped in a certain prison, Islam had to be freed from the forces that were suppressing its revolutionary spirit. He had begum this effort many years before he became known as a Muslim activist. For example, among the first courses he taught at the university in 1966 was one called *Islam-Shenassi* (Islamology) (Rahnema 2000, 176). Even the title is important to note: Islam was in need of a modern investigation, tone that resembled contemporary studies of society (sociology), crime (criminology), and human thought and behavior (psychology). At the heart of Shari'ati's thought was an understanding of Islam as an ideology.

For Shari'ati, Islam had degenerated from an ideology into a hereditary and customary rite (Shari'ati 1357/1979, 7:72), and it became his lifelong mission to present an Islam independent of history, tradition, or any institutional forms. He first discussed the clerical institution in Shi'ism: "Islam ended any form of mediation between man and the divine, and made the relation a direct one, thus there is no formal spiritual class in Islam" (7:32). He later labelled this the thesis of "Islam without the clergy" (*Islam menha-ye Akhond*), about which his colleague and later competitor Morteza Motahhari had this to say: "I am opposed to any form of antagonism toward the institution of the clergy, and I consider the thesis 'Islam without the clergy' to be a colonialist idea" (quoted from a letter in *Seyri dar* 1382/2003, 270). But this kind of accusation did not deter Shariʿati. He targeted an audience other than the traditional clerical establishment—the Iranian youth, who were becoming politicized and were looking for an "authentic" voice: "To start an authentic struggle, one has to depend on the people, in particular the youth and the intellectual generation, for once they become true believers, they will sacrifice everything for their beliefs" (Shariʿati, quoted in Rahnema 2000, 280).

To free Islam from tradition, Shariʿati made a distinction between Alavi and Safavi Shiʿism. The former is named after Imam Ali, who was designated the first leader of Shiʿism, while the latter was taken from Safavid rule in Iran (1501–1736). In fact, Shariʿati devoted an entire volume to this distinction. From the start, he referred to his own version of Islam as "red Shiʿism and the creed of martyrdom," whereas Safavi, or dominant, Shiʿism was "the black Shiʿism and the creed of mourning" (Shariʿati 1357/1979, 9:4). Similar only in appearance, they are contradictory in meaning and content. Both versions adhere to various tenets of Shiʿism, but attribute different meanings to them. The first is a creed of opposition, revolution, activism, responsibility, commitment, and movement. The second is a creed of acceptance, the status quo, quietism, and institutionalization. Table 2.2 captures these distinctions. The third column of the table represents the characteristics of Shiʿism during the rule of the Safavids, and, tragically for Shariʿati, they have become permanent features, propagated by most Shiʿa clergies, who present it as Islam's true spirit and the authentic version of religious tradition.

In Shariʿati's estimation, the Safavids successfully turned "religion against religion": "The Safavids turned Shiʿism from an underground ideology of struggle into [the means of rule in] the halls of power. . . . A minister of religious affairs travelled to Eastern Europe and learned the rituals of the church and turned Shiʿism into a creed of mourning" (9:169–170). This, in his mind, was an innovation. In Islam there should be scholars and intellectuals but not guardians and custodians of religious affairs. To fight the Ottomans, the Safavids needed an institutionalized Islam that would strengthen ethnic identity and historical tradition in Iran, just as the Ottomans had turned Islam into an ethnic Turkish narrative. In both places, Islam has become an institution instead of a "movement" (*harekat*).

According to Shariʿati, there is a natural tendency for any movement to degenerate into an institution. A movement is driven by ideals and

TABLE 2.2. SHARI'ATI'S NOTIONS OF ALAVI AND SAFAVI SHI'ISM

Concept	Alavi Shi'ism	Safavi Shi'ism
Vesayat (recommendation)	Recommendation of the Prophet for qualified persons	Appointed, hereditary government based on race
Imamat (leadership)	Pure and revolutionary elevated human leadership	Twelve "superhuman" leaders who are to be worshipped
Esmat (infallibility)	Belief in righteous leaders and government by the people	Attributable only to nonearthly creatures; affirmation of unjust rulers
Vellayat (guardianship)	Love for the just rule of Ali, which is needed for humanity	Love Ali and feel no responsibility
Ijtihad (independent reasoning)	Source of religious movement and the permanent revolution	Source of permanency and means of suppressing any new thinking
Taqlid (emulation)	Rational relation of commoners and religious scholars	Blindly following the clergies
Adl (justice)	Belief that God is just and that the world functions justly	Part of God's plan that will make sense only in the afterlife
Entezar (waiting)	Practical and psychological preparation for reform and revolution	Belief in submitting to the status quo and legitimizing tyranny
Ghaybat (occultation [of the Twelfth Imam, i.e., the current age])	Time when people are responsible for determining their own fate	Tine of irresponsibility and the petrifying of all Islamic ordinances

Source: Shari'ati 1357/1979, 9:258–262.

goals, whereas an institution is a repository of solidified ideals in need of conservation. One has to avoid succumbing to the latter at all costs. The danger of this line of thinking is that the tension between ends and means is destroyed, and thus the end appears to justify the means. For example, when Shari'ati wrote that "to achieve the aims that the movement has established, everything and everyone become means" (9:30–31), he did the same thing he accused the Safavids of doing. Most political Muslims today acknowledge that the end justifies the means, but Shari'ati was oblivious of this problem.

In an important lecture entitled "How to Be," Shari'ati talked about Islam as a wave, a calling, and a social mission (*resalat-e ejtema'i*). He even interpreted "nation" in verse 143 of Chapter 2 of the Qur'an, in which God says, "And thus We have made you a medium nation," to mean "a group that is involved in the heart of time . . . and the battles of intellectual and social interactions and forces" (2:16). This was quite different from most previous interpretations, which had suggested that the term meant either "a just nation" or a nation "in the middle of Christians and Jews." And for him, "the heart of time" referred to the age of man's struggle for justice: "Time in our philosophy of history begins with struggle and ends with struggle (from Abel to the Imam of the Age [the Mahdi in Shi'ism]). . . . [And] our philosophy of history is based on the contradiction between good and evil and the struggle of the two poles 'oppressor-oppressed,' 'God-Satan,' 'monotheism-associationism,' and 'tyranny-equity'" (2:223). His version of Islam would make possible the implementation of this struggle. It was "a calling, a mission, a commitment, a responsibility, and a struggle for the people." It would lead to "equity, justice, welfare, and the elevation of humanity" by means of the "government of consensus, consultation, and covenant" (7:70–71). This version corresponded to the human needs of love, freedom, and equality, or, as he put it, the triad of "God, freedom, and equality" (2:61).

Liberalism had successfully guaranteed freedom but not equality. Socialism had guaranteed equality but not freedom, and both had ignored God. Shari'ati felt that his version of Islam provided the best remedy because it guaranteed all three (2:87–90). As for the best way to implement his version, Shari'ati emphasized the notion of struggle, or jihad, which, he insisted, "has been forgotten and left in the pages of history books" (6:12).[14] Indeed, he suggested that jihad constitutes the most sacred dimension of Islam. He claimed that the Prophet had said, "Every religion has a sacred dimension and that of mine is struggle" (2:10). It is this sacred dimension that needs to be revived. As discussed, Shari'ati felt that Shi'i leaders such Ali and Hossein were the best models to follow because not only did they embody the three dimensions of freedom, equality, and love, but their lives were also examples of struggle and jihad.

The irony of Shari'ati's effort is that although he was fighting clericalism in Islam, he paved the way for the clergies to participate in the public sphere. One of his works, *Ummat and Immat* (The Community and Leadership) (26:461–634), did the most damage. Mehdi Bazargan commented that more than any other work, this one helped consolidate Khomeini's position as the leader of the movement (Bazargan 1988, interview). In this pamphlet, Shari'ati forcefully argued for the necessity of a leader if there were to be a revolution. Although he also argued in support of the compatibility of democracy and Islam, he did not advocate this for Muslims or particularly for Iran (26:599–600). Instead, he wanted a guided society of faithful followers who obeyed a "committed revolutionary leadership." Shari'ati's idealism led him to believe that such a leader would have only the best interest of the people in mind, so he would "direct" them toward a society in which notions of "*shura* [consultation], *ijma'* [consensus], and *bay'ah* [oath or contract of allegiance to the ruler]" would materialize. These, according to Shari'ati, "are the same as democracy, an Islamic principle explicitly mentioned in the Qur'an" (26:631). In practice, traditional religious leaders both assumed leadership of the revolution and occupied centers of power.

The tragedy of Shari'ati lay in his attempt to revive self-reliance. His imagined community of Islamic solidarity placed absolute dependence on the traditional institutions of Islam, as depicted in Khomeini's notion of the jurisconsult guardianship. His imagined community was so innovative and yet so uprooted from local traditions that it was easily attacked from all sides. The following depiction captures the paradoxical fate of Shari'ati: "He failed . . . to provide the bridge between Islam and the basically secular thought not only of the West but also of the Persian ruling elite. By falsifying the outside world, he reinforced isolation and increased the possibilities for political demagoguery rather than knowledgeable self-reliance" (Fischer 1980, 167).

ASSOCIATED GROUPS

Both Shari'ati's and Motahhari's work influenced Islamic discourse by stimulating the creation of institutions and movements that attracted a younger generation to Islam, a process that has been referred to as "re-Islamization from below" (Kepel 1994, 33–35) and that occurred in the Islamic world as a whole. In Iran, this process took two forms: the establishment of various private schools and high schools focused on both religious and secular training, and the formation of private Islamic banking, literally, a "treasury for lending in the path of God" (*sanduq-e qarz al-hassaneh*). No wonder the first bank of its kind, established by Mohammad Beheshti (later a powerful leader in the revolution), was called *Din va Danesh* (Religion and Knowledge). *Din va Danesh* also referred to theorizing about a practical plan for the formation of an Islamic state. In Tehran, the most prominent institutions dedicated to this type of planning included the Freedom Movement of Iran, the People's Mujahedin of Iran, the Hosseiniye-ye Ershad, and Alavi High School.

An influential, though not revolutionary, organization was the Freedom Movement of Iran. Its members were mostly from the middle class and were aware of what was going on in the world. They knew about the Cuban and Algerian revolutions and the Vietnam War. While some members' political beliefs had been formed before the 1963 uprising in Iran, this episode created an idealized version of the politics of resistance and revolution among the youth.

At the heart of the Freedom Movement was Bazargan, one of its founders.[15] The respite from oppression during 1959–1961 opened the Iranian political scene to the widespread development of political organizations, and in 1961, Bazargan established *Nehzat-e Azadi-ye Iran* (the Freedom Movement of Iran). The Freedom Movement was to follow exactly the same objectives as the National Resistance Movement: "The establishment of the Freedom Movement of Iran and the formation of our ideals and views resulted from the national events and composed a part of the evolutionary national trend" (Bazargan 1356/1977, 112). It was to follow the path of the nationalist movement headed by Mosaddeq, but emphasize the religious aspect of Iranian nationalism. In the opening session of the organization, Bazargan declared the following regarding this new group's identity:

> We are Muslim, Iranian, and followers of Mosaddeq. Our Islam does not mean performing the rituals [of religion], but rather [utilizing it] as a progressive ideology of struggle to satisfy the material and spiritual needs of society. . . . We are Iranian not in a chauvinistic fashion, but rather . . . patriotic in a [realistic way of] recognizing our shortcomings and appreciating the virtues and the strength of others. . . . We are the followers of Mosaddeq and consider him a sincere and great servant of Iran and the East. (quoted in *Bistomin Salgarde* 1362/1983, 31)

The key phrase in the passage is "progressive ideology of struggle," which, when used to describe Islam, distinguished this new organization from others.

Bazargan expressed it this way: "I do not say that others were not Muslims, or even are unfriendly to Islam. I contend that for them Islam was not a social and political ideology, whereas for us, it was the foundation of our thought and the cause of as well as the engine behind our political and social activism" (Bazargan 1977, 207). Politically, the main objective of the group included the promotion of constitutional democracy, one in which freedom and people's active participation were respected and protected. For example, Article One of the constitution of the organization called for "the establishment of the rule of law" and "the government of the people over themselves" (Nehzat-e Azadi 1364/1985, 1:44). Article Two stipulated the predominance of ethical rules based on Islam, and Article Three advocated the socialization and political education of the people so that they could participate in the public sphere.

Although the organization devoted its activities to the promotion of freedom and the politics of constitutionalism, its delivery of welfare services and its cultural activism paved the way for the clergies' coming to power. The organization promoted a more active role for the clerics in the public sphere, but more importantly, it advocated Islam as one of the major components of contemporary Iranian identity (Barzin 1374/1996, 154–166). In many ways, the border between Islam and the clergies was not clear; on many occasions the clergy was treated as synonymous with Islam. As Islam increasingly appeared more appealing compared to the existing secular ideologies, the more active members within the Freedom Movement helped socialize Islam for the emerging generation of Muslim activists.

In short, the Freedom Movement sought changes in the regime, but not by destroying it altogether. In the tradition of Mosaddeq, the movement aimed to make the regime more responsible within the constitution. After the 1963 uprising, however, some younger members of the organization could not tolerate the moderate, incremental approach it had adopted. After the uprising, three members established a discussion group to consider the future course of action. They became the nucleus of a radical organization called the People's Mojahedin of Iran, which promoted armed struggle as the only way to fight the shah, believing that the question was no longer "whether, but when and how, we should take up arms" (quoted in Abrahamian 1982b, 85). For this radical organization, the need for taking up arms was recognized by all who opposed the shah's regime. All attempts at reform and accommodation had failed, as attested to by the 1963 uprising.

For the founders of the People's Mojahedin, the struggle was a way of being; as with Shari'ati, the "movement" was to be the rule. According to the founders, the struggle was three-pronged—"an ideological struggle, an organizational struggle, and an armed struggle" (quoted in Abrahamian 1982b, 86). The founders—Mohammad Hanifnezhad (1938–1972), Said Mohsen (1939–1972), and Ali-Asghar Badizadegan (1940–1972)—were modern both in their educational training and in the sources of their intellectual outlook. University friends studying engineering at Tehran University, they had begun their activism with a series of intensive studies of the Qur'an and the *Nahj al-Balagha* (Imam Ali's sermons, sayings, and letters) as well as a new review of Iranian history in light of the modern theories of revolution and liberation. Marx, Lenin, Liu Shaoqui (the Chinese leader who wrote on revolutionary ethics), Che Guevara, Franz Fanon, and some others who wrote on the Latin American liberation movements were popular with them. They paid close attention to the works of Amar Ouzegan, the ideological guide of the National Liberation Front (FLN) in Algeria. These were of particular importance because Ouzegan, "a former communist turned nationalist," argued for the same ideas that the Mujahedin wanted to implement in Iran. The Mojahedin "argued that Islam was a revolutionary, socialistic creed and that the only way to fight imperialism was to resort to the armed struggle and appeal to the religious sentiment of the masses" (Abrahamian 1982b, 89). Religion was important and significant, but only as a tool of struggle. In some ways they agreed with Marx that "religion . . . is the opium of the people," but parted with him in that they felt the people needed it. It is not surprising that "the group soon adopted Ouzegan's work as its main handbook" (89).

The message of the People's Mojahedin was clear: they wanted to create a communist utopia legitimated by Islam. In the process, they affirmed monotheism and prophecy, the most important principles of Islam. They acknowledged God as the creator of the world, but felt that he had deterministically set into motion the law of historical evolution. Of all human scientific inquiries, only Marxism has grasped the essence of this miracle. That was why in 1980 the Mojahedin declared in defense of their ideological position that "scientific Marxism was compatible with true Islam" (quoted on 93). The prophets were sent regularly to help the masses in their struggle for the good life, which is possible by living in a "monotheistic system" (*nezam-e tawhidi*), defined as "a classless society free of poverty, corruption, war, injustice, inequality and oppression" (93).

In the Mojahedin's interpretation, religious texts were not meant to explain or even interpret the world, but to change it. In a two-volume work entitled *Chguneh Qur'an Betamuzim* (How Does One Learn the Qur'an?),

TABLE 2.3. THE REVOLUTIONARY INTERPRETATION OF ISLAMIC
NOTIONS BY THE PEOPLE'S MUJAHEDIN

Notion	As seen by tradition	As seen by the Mujahedin
Tawhid	Monotheism	Egalitarianism
Adl	Righteousness	Justice
Prophecy	Reminder of the covenant	Agent of change
Imam	Hojjat (evidence of God)	Charismatic leader
Jihad	Exertion	Struggle
Ijtihad	Independent reasoning	Revolutionary promulgation
Mo'men	Believer	Fighter for justice
Mostazafin	Meek masses	Oppressed nation

Source: Adapted from the Mojahedin's published works.

the group criticized the long-lived tradition of Qur'anic interpretation and suggested that the science of *tafsir* (interpretation) should be made into a process for revealing the revolutionary content of the sacred text and for helping formulate a plan of action. Moreover, the Mojahedin interpreted other notions and concepts of Islam in light of a revolutionary epistemology. Table 2.3 provides a general map of their interpretation.

While both the Freedom Movement and the Mojahedin played major roles in the coming of the Islamic Revolution, both were banned from participating in the new regime: their understanding of Islam ran contrary to the traditionalist understanding of Islam that dominated Iran. The beliefs of the Freedom Movement were too liberal, and those of the Mojahedin were too radical. The Freedom Movement played a more significant role than the Mojahedin in paving the way for the Islamic revolutionaries because its prominent members formed the provisional government right after the revolution, but the group was not radical enough for the revolutionary spirit of the Islamic movement, so it was banned. The Mojahedin, on the other hand, was very significant in the last days of the old regime, but it experienced more challenges because it quickly became the opposition, and its members were punished and exiled. Just as the shah had branded its members Islamic Marxists, the Islamic Republic considered their views impure and eclectic. The following describes how Khomeini characterized them when they were banned: "When I was in Najaf, they [the Mojahedin's representatives] came to fool me too. Some say they stayed about twenty-five days. . . . I listened to what they had to say. They referred to the Qur'an and the *Nahj al-Balagha* a great deal. . . . I concluded that they want to destroy us by using the Qur'an and the *Nahj al-Balagha*" (sermons in *Ettela'at,* June 26, 1980, 10).

Most influential in the preparation of the revolution were cultural and religious institutions such as the unique amphibian institution called Hosseiniye-ye Ershad and the Alavi High School. I refer to the hosseiniyes as an amphibian institution because it was neither a traditional religious institution nor a completely modern one, but both at the same time. It was traditional in that it was established to uphold Islamic tradition, yet it was modern because it was a complex of mosques, lecture halls, and theatres equipped with the latest technological amenities. Also, it was neither a mosque nor a hosseiniye in the traditional sense of either institution. Hosseiniyes were religious meeting places usually set up temporarily during the month of Muharam (the first month of the lunar calendar) to commemorate the Imam Hossein's martyrdom in 680, while this new one was to be permanent. Ershad was the archetype and the most important.

Established in 1957 and still in operation, Ershad is an important religious and cultural icon. The structure is a beautiful building located in a wealthy neighborhood of northern Tehran. The architecture is a mixture of traditional Islamic art and modern techniques. This particular hosseiniye "was to be a place where Iranians were to be guided toward fundamental change in the affairs of society" (Chehabi 1990, 202). The official name of the institution—*Mo'assesseye Khairiyeye Ta'limati, 'Elmi, va Dini-ye Hosseiniye-ye Ershad* (The Charitable, Educational, Scientific, and Religious Institute of Hosseiniye-ye Ershad)—and its program of activities, however, put more emphasis on the propagation of Islam to the new generation of Iranians.

The founders may have had Plato's Academy in mind, a place where people would experience paideia, a conversion in their soul. This conversion was to be achieved through regular lectures, "research on Islam," publications, the "study of socioreligious trends," regular pedagogical classes on religious and faith-related matters, help in the creation of formal education institutions from kindergartens to high schools, and the formation of "circles for debates and questions and answers" on faith-related issues, particularly for the youth (*Seyri dar* 2003, 245–247). It is also important to note that, compared to mosques, hosseiniyes are the more popular and populist centers of religious gathering and are therefore less under the control of the clerical establishment. Ershad became the podium from which Shari'ati propagated his ideological version of

Islam and a center for the exchange of ideas, the recruitment of possible revolutionary activists, and planning. Many of the people who were attracted to this new institution were students of the new private schools, especially Alavi High School.

The founders of the school were Ali Asghar Karbaschi and Reza Ruzbeh (1921–1973). Karbaschi, an associate of Burujerdi, was responsible for revising the traditional Manual of Acts (*Resaleye 'Amaliye*), a book of guidance that any Shi'i leader is supposed to prepare for his followers to use when performing religious duties. The difficult syntax of the traditional manuals led Ayatollah Burujerdi to commission this revision. Karbaschi did such a good job of it that he earned the title of Allameh (the most erudite), and he became better known as Allameh Karbaschi. He moved to Tehran in the early 1950s and is reported to have said, "Instead of waiting for students to come to the mosques, we should take religion to the schools" (Sarza'im 1381/2002, 12). Ruzbeh was a high school teacher in the city of Zanjan, where he met Karbaschi and befriended him immediately. Ruzbeh had been a top student, well trained in modern physics, and an employee of the Ministry of Education. The two found common ground in their aim of establishing a modern school that would turn out well-educated, strongly religious students. It was to be a school at which academic pursuits were to be taken seriously, but religious socialization and acculturation were to be taken even more seriously. It succeeded in both objectives.

Academically, it became the best high school in the capital, competing with existing schools such as Alborz High School (established by the Americans in 1873), at the time the breeding ground for the elite class (Musavi-Makoei 1376/1998, 12–14). The top members of the political elite of the Islamic Republic are graduates of Alavi. The founders named the school Alavi, from the name of Imam Ali—the founder and first leader of Shi'ism—to emphasize their commitment to the Prophet's household. In actual practice, though, the approach was highly modern and pluralistic. One researcher has identified six narratives of religion in the school: ethical, scientific, social, theological, ideological, and political (Sarza'im 1381/2002, 18). Having to fight a common enemy, namely, the Pahlavis' modernism, forced the various religious narratives to tolerate one another and even to converge. This proved to be the case not only for the students of the new high school, but also for the seminary students who would spend their summer holidays there learning about modern sciences. Many of the future top leaders of the Islamic Republic completed this training. At the same time, there was absolute loyalty to the tenets of Islam and a common conviction that one could master modern technology without accepting the values accompanying it.

The school was organized around three main objectives. First and most prevalent was the view that one could be modern without having to compromise one's cultural and religious values. Second was a strong loyalty to the basic tenets of Shiʿism, and particularly the notion of the Mahdi (the messianic figure of the Twelfth Shiʿi Imam). Alavi High School "was in essence a response to the concern that when the Imam returns, measures should be taken to prepare for his coming" (Sarzaʿim 1381/2002, 23). More importantly, a teacher of the school and close associate of Karbaschi mentioned that "he founded the school on the presupposition that soon the government would be in the hands of Islam-minded Iranians, so there needed to be technocrats with virtuous predispositions" (Faqihi 1992, interview). The third feature was the school's elitism. Not everybody was considered worthy of being entrusted with knowledge and righteousness, which is why almost all these types of schools have instituted a selection process and restrictive entrance qualifications. As one official explained, "There are limits to our capacities and resources, so we have to make sure that students are worthy of receiving this valuable resource" (quoted in Sarzaʿim 2002, 40).

Soon the wealthy and politically active families became interested in these schools. Since the life of a dissident could be disruptive, schools such as Alavi provided a secure environment for the children of political activists. The school also organized many extracurricular sports and social activities so that the students would become a well-connected and organized network. Today, for example, the graduates of Alavi and similar private schools help one another enormously. In fact, in postrevolutionary Iran, these schools are branded sarcastically as "the schools of the future ministers." But whether its graduates have joined the government or worked in the private sector, they are highly successful and influential. The most notable name among the graduates of Alavi is Abdolkarim Soroush, who also taught there.

Alavi High School, in combination with the aforementioned institutions and groups, made the biggest contribution to the training of future revolutionaries. Furthermore, they provided organizational facilities for networking and communication in the face of the growing power of the police state and the notorious SAVAK.

Both the voices of Tehran and those of Qom turned Islamic discourse into revolutionary radicalism. Indeed, the revolutionary zeal of the second generation attracted the support of many Iranians who were taken with the movements of nativism, liberation, and anti-imperialism. It was unfortunate that the revolutionaries truly believed that brotherhood, as well as their theory of the Islamic revolution, state, and government, would create such a harmonious body politic that everyone, even the secular and the nonbelievers, would welcome the new order. The case of Sadeq Qotbzadeh is a good example. He was an active member of the political dissidents abroad, became one of the close associates of Khomeini in Paris, returned to Iran with him, and soon rose to the rank of minister of foreign affairs in the revolutionary government. When Khomeini arrived in Tehran in February 1979, Qotbzadeh was one of the last to leave the plane. At the terminal entrance, he was asked what would be the fate of secular Iranians who did not accept the Islamic Republic. He responded that, upon experiencing the Islamic regime, they would embrace it.

Iranians who were supposed to implement the grand theories of the second generation found themselves facing enormous challenges. Internally, at least three important challenges did not allow Iranian modernization to return to its natural course and form a balanced polity. One challenge was the legacy of the Pahlavis' pseudomodernization, which militated against any form of authenticity and any inclusive approach. In the words of Iranian political scientist Asghar Schirazi, "the political legacy of the shah's regime is evident in systems of values such as the primacy of politics, particularism, absolute authoritarianism and gigantism" (Schirazi 1993, 76). An all-embracing politics, exclusivity, the arbitrary power of the rulers, and the setting of unobtainable goals contributed to the strength of the revolutionaries.

In the second challenge, the battle of ideas against the unholy alliance of internal pseudomodernization and external Americocentrism, which had resulted in the emergence of a relatively monolithic voice of the opposition against the former regime, dispersed into competing groups that did not share the same intellectual framework (*mavazin*) and game rules (*qava'ed*). Thus the earlier unity of approaches and strategies in the battle of ideas became a bloody zero-sum battle of worldviews. The struggle for power, terror, and assassination replaced the civility by which the revolution itself had been won. By autumn of 1982, the juridical Islam (*Eslam-e fiqahati*) had become victorious and eliminated all secular or those who did not follow the juridical version of Islam. Mir Hossein Mussavi became prime minister for a decade, until finally his position was removed from the polity altogether.

Third, a by-product of the second trend was the emergence of Islamist politics, which proved to be as particularistic and absolute as that of the Pahlavis. The Islamists established what the revered late professor of philosophy and staunch Heideggerian, Seyyed Ahmad Fardid, termed "vertical democracy" (Fardid 1983, interview). The authoritarian, absolutist, ideological, and in some sense militaristic system of the Islamists permitted one sort of politics (or pseudopolitics) only—a politics of supplication to the high authorities. There was little chance for what political philosophers term "horizontal voices" (Elshtain 1993, 133) to find self-expression.

It soon became clear that revolutionary zealots had little tolerance for souls not committed to Khomeini's theory, including Qotbzadeh himself, who was hanged. In other words, the Jacobin political dimension had stricken from Islamic discourse any depth, making the whole movement of restoring Islam susceptible to adventurism, opportunism, and radicalism. This became even clearer in subsequent decades, when Islamic ideology became directly linked with power and political interest, and even became a tool for radicalism and political violence. I will turn to this reductionism next.

THREE

THE THIRD GENERATION

The Politics of Islamism, 1989–1997

*Any religion that considers itself, or any religious leader who perceives
himself, to be an agent of God entrusted with the responsibility
of establishing His sovereignty on earth and over the people . . .
through ignoring the worldly needs of man and his human rights will
inevitably cause slavery and violence.*

MEHDI BAZARGAN, *SHOURA-YE ENQELAB WA DOULAT-E
MOWAQAT* (THE REVOLUTIONARY COUNCIL AND THE
PROVISIONAL GOVERNMENT), 1983

"The Spirit of God joined the celestial domain": that was
how Iranian radio broke the news of Khomeini's death on
Sunday, June 3, 1989. The announcer eloquently played with
words: Khomeini's first name, "Ruhollah," means "the Spirit of God."
Dealing with Khomeini's death proved much more challenging than had
been originally assumed. His successor was decided on smoothly, and
the transfer of power was easy, but the institutionalization of the Islamic
Republic in the post-Khomeini era proved much more difficult and was
still unfolding in 2006, at the time of this writing.

While there was enormous sadness over the loss, many had considered Khomeini the engine of political Islam. They thought his death
would end extremism and revolutionary politics. This idea was further
strengthened when the new president, Ali Akbar Hashemi Rafsanjani
(in power 1989–1997) promised to open Iran to the West and normalize
the birth of "the second republic," as some called his tenure (Ehteshami
1995, 27–44). The period of elation lasted only three years. The unfolding of events indicated that Khomeini's death signified only a departure
from rule by a patriarchal arbiter rather than an end to the revolution.
The present chapter captures the emergence of the third generation of Islamic discourse, a radical group that may be termed Islamists. They saw

Khomeini as a radical and a great enemy of the West, and they wanted to continue in his tradition.

Khomeini died of abdominal cancer and heart problems. His death was natural and ordinary, yet very significant historically. He was the only Iranian leader in quite some time to die of natural causes while in power. King Nasir al-Din Shah died by an assassin's bullet; Muhammad Ali Shah, Ahmad Shah, Reza Shah, and Mohammad Reza Shah died powerless and homeless somewhere outside of Iran. In the twentieth century, only Mosaddeq died a natural death (in 1967), but even his occurred under house arrest, and no one was allowed to mourn publicly for him. Khomeini's case was different. Following his death, people mourned fiercely, freely, and to the point of madness. An ocean of human flesh striving to be near his coffin did not allow for a normal burial. The century's suppressed feelings were now pouring out. The government acceded to this unforeseen and unprecedented event. Despite the Islamic injunction that corpses should be buried immediately, Khomeini's was displayed inside a glass freezer for three days while the public paid its respects. Even then, when finally the body was to be returned to the earth, it was impossible for the funeral procession to break through the dense sea of spectators and mourners, so the corpse was carried by helicopter, at the cost of ten lives and 10,000 injuries. Only a heavy container placed on the grave by a crane saved the body from being torn to bits by lamenting devotees. I observed Khomeini's shrine being erected in a flash. From hour to hour, the construction changed significantly as bulldozers, trucks, and heavy machinery worked in the midst of crowding pilgrims.

Khomeini's death tested the survival of the polity he left behind. Amazingly, just after the news of his death was broadcast, the government hastily announced that all activities had to halt. When widespread compliance was observed, things relaxed. That day I was to attend a meeting at the Institute of Political and International Studies, located in the northernmost section of the city, in the vicinity of Khomeini's residence. All meetings were cancelled, mine included. Out of curiosity, I drove toward the institute, but when I neared the neighborhood, the crowd had halted all traffic, and the roads were closed. As the day wore on and masses of people poured toward Khomeini's residence, the government's confidence was restored. For many, he had been responsible for continuing the war and promoting revolutionary zeal. His death was supposed to bring calm, but instead it opened the way for a new form of radicalism, one that became vocal in the 1990s, and gained control in 2005, and continues to haunt Iranian politics. Those who thought Khomeini symbolized revolutionary zeal were taken aback by his death because, contrary to their expectation, his death unleashed the power of the third generation of Islam-minded Iranians.

This generation considers revolution a universal phenomenon against disbelief, a movement that should continue until there is an end to "decadence and corruption." Who is in this group? I had seen some of them on various occasions after I arrived in Iran in 1986, but the first time I observed them closely was in the summer of 1988, when Khomeini "drank the cup of poison," as he described accepting UN Resolution 498, which ended the Iran-Iraq War. The day the resolution was accepted, I was in the Headquarters for War Propagation. When Iranian radio broke the news, absolute silence dominated the room. The message from Khomeini was long, but the reaction of the people, mostly armed, was astonishing to me. As they listened to the message, tears poured from their cheeks, yet their silent, stony faces displayed contemplation, resolution, resentment, and anger. Many of them were writing on scraps of paper in front of them. I looked at the papers and saw that their writing expressed inner anxiety. Here are the writings I noted: "You are my spirit Khomeini"; "I will die for you at any moment"; "I am your devotee always"; "Your revolution continues until the return of the Mahdi"; "Long live Khomeini"; "You are the spirit of God"; and similar phrases of praise and sympathy. Taking the "cup of poison" meant more than accepting the UN resolution; it unleashed the mobilized population's enormous energy, which had been building up during the previous decade. As long as he was alive, Khomeini was able to manage, control, and quiet them, owing to his charisma, stature, and revolutionary reputation. Now that he was gone, revolutionary chaos began.

THE CONTEXT

Khomeini succeeded in forcing the Westerners out and branding the Pahlavi dynasty as an agent of foreign influence, but the regime he created was in need of guarding. Although the traditional state gained control of the new polity in the aftermath of the revolution, the forces of Iranian modernization had their own victory. The revolution had revived the politics of modernization, which had been diverted and pushed aside by the Pahlavis' modernism. The Islamic Republic came to life with an inherent contradiction that only Khomeini's presence kept from exploding into the open: quietly, two states took shape side by side in Iran, even within the constitution. The jurisconsult (or, leader), the Council of Guardians, the Assembly of Experts, the traditional clergy, and some segments of the new parliament composed the traditional narrative of Islam, while segments of the three branches of government, the new intelligentsia, reforming members of the clergy, women, students, and most of the media represented the new narrative of Islam and the state.

The unfolding of this dual state was not straightforward. One factor delaying and complicating the process was the towering figure of Khomeini. As long as he was alive and at the peak of his power, his personal charisma set the bounds within which the political game was played. And Khomeini himself played a paradoxical role in these counterbalanced trends. He was enormously loyal to the forces of the traditional state, yet he wanted to modernize it in order to make it relevant to the contemporary world, and so he helped the survival of the modernizing forces. Another factor was the Iran-Iraq War (1980–1989), which postponed the postrevolutionary state-building altogether. The end of the war and Khomeini's death provoked a serious discussion about the nature of the regime, the place of religion in the public sphere, modernity and tradition, foreign capital, the extent of freedom, and the moderation or radicalism of the political system. The discussion took place against a background of two parallel developments. One was the strengthening of economic development, construction, and modernization, this last symbolized by the publication *Yadvareye Fajr* (Memory of the Dawn). Subtitled "on the occasion of the tenth anniversary of the revolution," the publication promoted self-reflection and looked critically at both the revolution and the presidency of Rafsanjani, which became known as "the administration for construction" (*dolat-e sazandegi*). The other development was the return of war veterans, prisoners of war, and the more devoted revolutionaries from the "battleground of right and wrong" and the war "of Islam versus disbelief" to the mainstream.

Ironically, the constitutional revision of 1989, designed to make the state more efficient and practical, strengthened both of these trends; it simultaneously stipulated a more efficient state and absolute rule for the jurisconsult. As the context within Iran became more sophisticated and less manageable, the external world changed radically. The fairly stable world of bipolarity ended along with the Cold War, globalization set in, and the region went up in flames when Iraq invaded Kuwait, bringing the American military to Iran's border. The intellectual climate in Iran also changed, becoming darker as the ascendancy of radical Islamists led to the mass killing of intellectuals, yet at the same time ushered in a new discourse on democracy and reform.

The Internal Context: The Ascendancy of the Radical Right

Factions, parties, political trends, and policy preferences are natural in all polities, but the proponents of the Islamic revolution took pride in their "unity of outlook," cohesion, and collaboration. Factionalism was already underway when they took over the country, but grew particularly during the last years of Khomeini's life and after the dissolution of the umbrella organization, the Islamic Republic Party, on June 1, 1987. Soon the main organizational group of the party, the Society of the Combatant Clergies of Tehran (*Jame'eye Rohaniyat-e Mobarez-e Tehran*), gave birth to the Assembly of the Combatant Clerics of Tehran (*Majma'e Rohaniyun-e Mobarez-e Tehran*). Khomeini granted permission in March 1988 for the formation of the new organization, which identified social justice as the main principle of Islamic teachings and disagreed with the previous organization's insistence on the need for private property and capitalism. Now that the revolution was aging, practical issues and policies were gaining priority over revolutionary zeal; elections for the Third Parliament, in 1988, drew candidates holding either of these two positions. On the surface, pragmatism was gaining ascendancy, and zealous revolutionaries seemingly were no longer tolerated. The coming to power of the new president promised an opening to the West and provided more opportunities for moderation.

The new president elected in 1989 was Ali Akbar Bahramani, better known as Hashemi Rafsanjani. Born in 1934 near Kerman, southeastern Iran, to a family of farmers, he had been part of the Islamic movement from his early youth. At the age of fourteen he went to study in Qom, where he chose to study with Khomeini and remained loyal to him until his death. Rafsanjani also had good business sense: he got into the construction industry and acquired an enormous amount of property, which generated considerable wealth. Along with Khomeini, he was involved in politics, and political trouble, in the 1960s; he was repeatedly imprisoned for his allegiance to Khomeini and his campaigns against the Pahlavi regime during the 1960s and 1970s. In the new Islamic Republic, by contrast, Rafsanjani's fortunes kept rising. He began as a member of the Council of the Revolution and became first deputy minister of the interior and then minister of the interior. A founding member of the

Islamic Republic Party, he was elected to Parliament, becoming its speaker for the two terms that he served as a deputy (1980–1989).

When appointed one of Tehran's Friday prayer leaders by Khomeini in 1981, Rafsanjani found an important nationwide forum for his views. In October 1981 he was appointed the leader's representative to the High Council of Security, and in July 1983 he was appointed vice president of the Assembly of Experts, a post he still holds as of 2006. He was even appointed acting commander in chief of the armed forces in 1988–1989. In 1989, Rafsanjani was elected president, securing nearly 95 percent of the vote. He characterized his government as "neither left nor right and in some sense both left and right—in short, a moderate government" (quoted in Rahmani 1382/2004, 68). He casts himself as a moderate pragmatist and claims that these qualities are at the heart of Islamic teachings. Islam warns against either indulgence or asceticism. As he states, "Islam came to the world with realism, moderation, and pragmatism. Whether in Mecca [where Islam was born] or Medina [where the Islamic community was formed], this was the modus operandi of the Prophet and the imams" (quoted on 74).

Rafsanjani's public life has had conflicting results. He took many moderate positions in the 1980s, such as normalizing relations with the United Kingdom in 1990, despite the crisis over Salman Rushdie's controversial novel *The Satanic Verses* and Khomeini's fatwa against the author. He sought to revive Iran's badly flagging economy on free-market principles and moved to improve relations with the West. It was in this spirit that he launched what he called "the Great Islamic Civilization, or the project of Iran 1400 [2021 CE]." It was a plan to make Iran a society with moderate wealth and good international standing. To achieve this, he referred to his administration as one of construction and work. Although he himself was moderate by all accounts, his religious and political convictions bent toward pragmatic conservatism. Privatization, economic adjustment, construction, the ordering of public welfare, and rebuilding were introduced into the politics of the Islamic Republic. One side effect was an invasion of consumer goods and services. Another effect was a restricted factionalism.

The main feature of this factionalism was that only those who accepted the supremacy of the guardianship of the jurisconsults were allowed to participate in the political process. Ibrahim Yazdi, leader of the Freedom Movement, refused to accept this condition during the presidential election of 1989, guaranteeing his own disqualification. The powerful Council of Guardians, responsible for the enforcement of this rule, disqualified

Yazdi and 223 other candidates from participating in the 1993 presidential election, and this ideological enforcement continues to this date.

In President Rafsanjani's first term, the lines of political demarcation sharpened. By the election of the Fourth Parliament, in 1992, at least four recognizable political factions had emerged in Iran. All professed an Islamic identity and displayed "practical commitment" (*eltezam-e amali*) to the principles of the constitution. I would categorize them as follows: the traditional right (*rast-e sonnati*), the modern right (*rast-e modern*), the left (*chap*), and the radical right (*rast-e efrati*).[1] Each is a coalition comprised of smaller groups, each publishes its own newspaper, and each is supported by a host of prominent politicians and religious leaders.

The traditional right is composed of the Society of the Combatant Clergies of Tehran (*Jame'eye Rohaniyat-e Mobarez-e Tehran*), the powerful Society of the Teachers of Qom Seminary (*Jame'eye Modarressin Hozeye 'Elmiyeye Qom*), and various merchant and guild groups, all united under the umbrella organization the Coalescing Islamic Societies (*Hey'atha-ye Mo'talefe-ye Eslami*). The newspapers *Ressalat, Farda*, and *Shoma* reflect its views. The traditional right relies on the support of the head of Imam Sadeq University, Mohammad Reza Mahdavi Kani, Ahmad Tavakoli, Habibollah Asgaroladi, the head of the judicial branch (the Shahrudi), ex–foreign minister Ali Akbar Velayati, and the traditional merchant class (the bazaar). During the controversial 2004 parliamentary election, it helped create the Coalition of the Islamic Iran Developers (*E'telaf-e Abadgaran Iran-e Eslami*).

In the early 1990s, the modern right, which had been in close collaboration with the traditional right for many years, began to form its own faction. In the January 1996 parliamentary election, a group of technocrats and officials formed a group called the Servants of Construction (*Kargozaran-e Sazandegi*), which attracted many educated Iranians and was declared a political party headed by Gholamhossein Karbaschi in the summer of 1998. In addition to the Kargozaran Party, the modern right enjoyed the support of other powerful groups, such as the House of Workers (*Khane-ye Karegar*), as well as of many close associates of former president Rafsanjani. Its views are reflected in the popular morning paper *Hamshahri*; the dailies *Akhbar, Kar va Karegar,* and *Iran;* and the English-language daily *Iran News.* The former head of the central bank, the late Mohsen Nurbakhsh, the then-MP Fa'ezeh Rafsanjani, and the new Iranian middle class supported this group.

The left included such prominent subgroups as the Office of Strengthening Unity between the Universities and the Seminaries (*Daftar-e*

Tahkim-e Vahdat-e Hoze va Daneshgah), the Organization of the Mujahedins of the Islamic Revolution (*Sazeman-e Mojaheddin-e Enqelab-e Eslami,* created right after the revolution), the Society of Islamic University Teachers (*Anjoman-e Eslami-ye Modarressin-e Daneshgahah*), and the Assembly of the Combatant Clerics of Tehran (*Majma'e Rohaniyun-e Mobarez-e Tehran,* created on March 20, 1988, by Mehdi Karrubi and Muhammad Mussavi Khoe'iniha). These subgroups later united under the name of the Front for Participation in Islamic Iran (*Jebheye Mosharekat-e Iran-e Eslami*), supported President Khatami, and became the voice of reform until 2004. The popular paper *Salam* and the biweekly *Asr-e Ma* reflect their views; the short-lived *Jame'e* (Society), the newly founded *Khordad,*[2] and many others that would emerge but were soon banned expressed sympathy for their positions. They enjoyed the support of former prime minister Mir Hossein Mussavi; former minister and chief negotiator of the hostage crisis Behzad Nabavi; editor in chief of *Asr-e Ma* Mohammad Salamati; Ali Akbar Mohtashami; and the aforementioned Karrubi, as well as the new intelligentsia.

While the first three groups are known relatively thoroughly, the radical right seems to be an unknown quantity. It is a new faction, mainly composed of Revolutionary Guards, young students, and remnants of the Mobilization Forces (*Basiji*) of the Iran-Iraq War. While the more mature Revolutionary Guards were incorporated into the state apparatus, particularly in the Ministry of Jihad for Construction, and are the main state contractors, the Mobilization Forces have returned to their studies and have become more politically active. The recently formed Association for the Defense of the Values of the Islamic Revolution (*Jam'iyat-e Defa' az Arzeshha-ye Enqelab-e Eslami*), whose offices are temporarily closed for financial reasons, founded by former intelligence minister Hojjatoleslam Mohammad Mohammadi Reyshahri, was the radical right's most important group. Another vocal faction of this group is the Helpers of Hizbollah (*Ansar-e Hizbollah*), whose main functions included organizing street demonstrations and disrupting liberal gatherings. The newspapers *Arzeshha, Keyhan, Lesarat al-Hossein, Shalamche,* and the monthly *Sobh* reflect their views. Ayatollah Ahmad Janati, Ahmad Pournejati, Massud Dehnamaki, Mehdi Nassiri, the aforementioned Reyshahri, and Hossein Allahkaram support the views of this group. Table 3.1 maps the political landscape of the Islamic movement in Iran's contemporary context.

Rafsanjani came to power with some support from all four factions, but soon he alienated both the left and the radical right. For the left, his emphasis on economic development undermined social justice, while the radical right saw the same program as detrimental to revolutionary values. The radical right was also upset when Rafsanjani appointed Mohammad Khatami, with his tolerant policy toward print media, as minister of Islamic guidance (1989–1992), seeing the move as helping the left not only voice its concerns, but also position itself within the governing system. Some of my students with liberal and leftist tendencies worked for the Ministry of Islamic Guidance and asked me to apply for a license to publish newspapers or magazines; they said they were trying to secure as many licenses as possible for future use. Since I had no intention of getting involved in politics, I refused. But they secured many licenses, which proved prudent; in the 1990s, when attacks against reformist media became the rule, as soon as one publication was banned, another would be published.

Also for the radical right, Rafsanjani's economic policies of privatization and adjustment meant the return of the capitalists. The young revolutionary Iranians, mostly uneducated and unskilled, who had rushed to the battlefields in the war against Iraq now, in the postwar era of "construction and foreign investment," found themselves on the margins of society. All over Tehran, fancy new, neon-lit billboards advertised cell phones, consumer goods such as imported cars and appliances, and even bananas. Returnees from the war front used them as canvases for graffiti declaring the greatness of God or the magnanimity of the revolution. War-veteran students would ask me whether bananas were more important than God, since there was so much advertising for them. I explained how the fruit companies hired designers and architects to create the most appealing advertisements possible, not realizing that the students lacked the resources to purchase the produce. As a result of special privileges granted by the government, war veterans entered the universities, took over existing newspapers or established new ones, and infiltrated into the world of radio, television, and the cinema. They brought with them the mentality of war, seeing society as a battleground—a zero-sum game of right and wrong—and having few inhibitions about using violence to eliminate their adversaries.

Soon Rafsanjani gave in, and by 1992 the perceived liberal members of Rafsanjani's cabinet had been sacked. The most prominent was Khatami, who had been perceived as too tolerant toward what the Islamists considered unacceptable in an Islamic society and polity, and so was replaced by a traditionalist and radical minister, Mustafa Mir-Salim. A perceptive

TABLE 3.1. THE POLITICAL LANDSCAPE OF FACTIONAL POLITICS IN IRAN, 1995

	Left	Modern right	Traditional right	Radical right
Religion	Ideology	Personal conviction	Ideology-jurisprudence	Ideology
New ideas	Conditional innovation	Contemporary use of religion	Insistence on traditional jurisprudence	Prerogative of jurists
Intellectual heritage	Marx, Shari'ati	Dynamic jurisprudence (Mutahari)	Jurisprudence	Traditional jurisprudence, radical Islamism
Intelligentsia	Engineers, doctors	Graduates of private Islamic schools	Hawzeh Seminary, Imam Sadeq University	Militant students
Media	*Salam, Asr-e Ma, Khordad*	*Iran, Akhbar, Kar va Karegar, Hamshahri, Iran News*	*Ressalat, Farda, Shoma*	*Arzhshha, Shalamche, Keyhan, Lesarat al-Hossein, Sobh, Mashreq*
Groups	MEI (Front for Participation in Islamic Iran), RM (Assembly of the Combatant Clerics of Tehran), DaftarTV (Office of	Islamic technocrats, Hojjatiye, Kargozaran Party, House of Workers	RMT (Association of the Combatant Clergy of Tehran), JMH (Association of the Teachers of Qom Seminary)	JDAE (Association for the Defense of the Values of the Islamic Revolution), Ansar-e Hizbollah, Revolutionary

	Strengthening Unity between the Universities and the Seminaries), Khaneh Kargar		HMI (Coalesced Islamic Societies)	Guards, Mobilization Forces
Known leaders	Khoe'iniha, Nabavi, Salamati, Khatami, Mohtashami	Fa'ezeh Rafsanjani, Karbaschi	Kani, Sobhani	Janati, Pournejati, Dehnamaki, Nassiri, Allahkaram, Rey Shahri
State	Corporate	Capitalist welfare	Customary, shar'ia	Traditional populist
Government	Guided democracy	Rule of the bureaucrats	Rule of the jurists	Totalitarian under rule of the jurists
Society	Revolutionary	Modern/religious	Religious	Religious/guarded
Economy	Mixed	Moderate privatization	Privatization	Islamic corporatism
Culture	Open	Guided openness	Controlled	Controlled
Women	Modern	Modern/Islamist	Traditional	Traditional
Globalization	Dichotomous (us-them)	To be used	Use for proselytization	Dichotomous
Praxis	Militant	Moderate	Accommodating	Militant

Source: Adapted by the author from various sources, particularly *Asr-e Ma* 2 (14): 6.

local poet, who does not want his name revealed, had this to say about the change:

> Alas, today the people of art, collectively
> Have been inflicted with a disaster, very great it is
> Has befallen on the creators of arts and creative works
> A sickness, known as MS, Mir-Salim it is.

Khatami was not the only victim; others included Abdollah Nuri, the minister of the interior, and Mostafa Moein-Najafabadi, the minister of higher education and culture. Nuri had been one of Khomeini's staunchest supporters before the revolution and had continued with him after Khomeini rose to power.

During Khomeini's rule, Nuri had headed a committee that purged many dissident employees of the state radio and television agencies. He had been Khomeini's representative in the Ministry of Jihad for Construction and, until August 1989, his representative in the Revolutionary Guard Corps during the Iran-Iraq War. As Rafsanjani's minister of the interior, Nuri was also chair of the National Security Council from 1989 through 1993, a position to which he was reinstated after Khatami's election as president in 1997. Mostafa Moein-Najafabadi, a pediatric physician, had been Khomeini's representative on the Supreme Council of Cultural Revolution from 1983 to 1989; he was also the reformist candidate for president in the 2005 election. As Rafsanjani's minister of higher education and culture, he helped the war veterans' entry into the universities enormously by reserving almost one-third of the available places at public universities for the Revolutionary Guards or for relatives of the martyrs. The people who replaced Nuri and Moein-Najafabadi provide good indicators of why they were purged. In short, despite their revolutionary and even radical credentials, Khatami, Nuri, and Moein-Najafabadi had to be eliminated because they tolerated freedom of thought (*azad fekhri*) and nonconformists (*degarandishan*).

Mohammad Ali Besharati Jahromi, who is close to the conservative camp and served as deputy to Foreign Minister Ali Akbar Velayati for a long time, became the new minister of the interior, and Muhammad Reza Hashemi-Golpayegani became the minister of higher education and culture. Hashemi-Golpayegani imposed tougher restrictions on those working in the universities, and in fact reportedly said in 1995 that if Ferdowsi (the greatest Iranian national poet) were to try to teach at a university, he would have a hard time being accepted because he had written about monarchs and monarchy:

> Q: With your standards in this ministry, would Ferdowsi be able to obtain a university position?
> A: . . . with today's criteria, I doubt it. In our present framework, praising kings is not accepted. Despite all his good qualities, since this feature exists in Ferdowsi's works, it is possible that his practice of praising may cause difficulties for him. (*Ruz-e Haftom* 3 (712): 2)

Others were also fired. Notably, in the change of management at Iranian Radio and Television, Ali Larijani, a former Revolutionary Guard, replaced Rafsanjani's brother. This change was in line with the three aforementioned, and the new management was eager to open the broadcast media to members of the radical right. As I will discuss further, Larijani allowed the airing of programs whose main objective was to discredit Iranian intellectuals, particularly those who disagreed with the radical right's reading of Islam. In fact, the notion of nonconformity entered into Iran's political language for the first time, and those accused of it were either treated as criminals or mysteriously eliminated. Any form of dissent was characterized as undermining to the regime. In a candid conversation with former president Rafsanjani, his "insider critics" from the radical newspaper *Keyhan* laid the following charge against him:

> Our criticisms of the cultural policies of your government relate to the officials who neglected a destructive and degenerative trend that crept into the system after the war. It utilized the print media, art, and literature for a comprehensive assault against the integrity of the values derived from the revolution. . . . We targeted the world of books, media, and publications. . . . We were concerned with the success of the policy of "attracting and absorbing" the Iranian compatriots [Iranians who had been sidelined by the revolution]. (Rahmani 1382/2004, 109)

The speaker is specifically referring to the publication of some articles by Ali Akbar Sa'idi Sirjani (who mysteriously died in jail in 1994), the publication of the books of Taqi Modaressi (an Iranian American writer and the late husband of American novelist Anne Tyler), and the publication of the works of Bahram Beyzaei (the Iranian director and filmmaker).

What made the radical right become so prominent? First, Rafsanjani gave into its pressure without foreseeing that war veterans and members of the mobilized forces—two powerful components of the radical right—now wanted their part of the spoils of the revolution. The political administration of the country, instead of being entrusted to members of the Iranian middle class, both from within the country and returning from the diaspora, was taken over by the radical right. Privatization became merely an excuse for distributing economic privilege to war veterans. Second, no longer was the grand arbiter Ayatollah Khomeini alive to preserve the political balance, as he had done so successfully for ten years. His successor, Seyyed Ali Khamenei, behaved more like a ruler than an arbiter, and he sympathized with the radical right in all his decisions and positions. Third, the left, which had become the voice of reform and democratization, had few actual resources with which to resist its own elimination. It relied on the traditional Iranian middle class, the media, and intellectuals. Fourth, and more importantly, the radical right, driven by its own ideology, was ready and willing to inflict terror and violence on any individual or group that got in its way. Its members were ready to kill—their victims included former friends and foes alike—and they did so to preserve their position. Changes in the intelligence apparatus proved helpful to them; as was later revealed, the mass killing of dissidents and intellectuals in the 1990s was directly linked to the Intelligence Ministry. Finally, civil society in Iran was not very strong, nor did it enjoy the international support that came later, when the 1998 student movement became the voice of democracy and democratization. The forces of radicalism were so entrenched from about the mid-1990s that eight years of a reformist administration (1997–2005) did not succeed in effecting deep reform.

The International Context: The Fall of the Soviet Union and the Iraq-Kuwait Crisis

Internationally, the androlepsia against sixty-six American diplomats in Tehran from November 4, 1979, to January 20, 1981, unnecessarily intensified antagonism between Iran and the United States, resulting in America breaking off its relations with Iran and imposing an oil embargo that shadowed Iranian foreign policy.[3] The real or perceived fear of the revolution and its export led to the formation of regional and international alliances for containing it. The Iraqi invasion of Iran on September 20, 1980, drained Iran of its human and financial resources for almost a decade. The eight-year war took priority over everything else. Every other impulse was subordinated to winning the war, and all other considerations, including the problems of agriculture, industry, labor, justice, education, welfare, and recreation, were delayed and deferred (Schirazi 1993, 82). The complexity of the war notwithstanding (see Rajaee 1993a), in Iran it was seen as an "invasion" or as an "imposed" and "aggressive" war.

The reality was not as dark, however, because the international context unfolded paradoxically. The revolution of 1979 destroyed the balance in the Middle East in favor of forces that were antagonistic toward Western interests. This shift produced a special urge in the West to punish Iran, resulting not only in policies that imposed sanctions against Iran, but also in an American policy of dual containment toward Iraq and Iran. This was ironic: in the aftermath of the Iraqi invasion of Kuwait and the American invasion of Iraq in 1990–1991, the American invasion of Afghanistan in 2001, and the invasion of Iraq in 2003, Iran remained neutral and even helped America when opportunities presented themselves, as they did during the Iraq-Kuwait crisis of 1990–1991.

It is important to note that hardening American attitudes encouraged the emergence of the third generation of Islam-minded Iranians. America took an adversarial position beginning in 1979, when American diplomats were taken hostage, but this stance became acute with the policy of dual containment, which began on May 18, 1993, when Martin Indyk, special assistant to the president for Near East and South Asian affairs at the National Security Council, delivered a speech to the Washington Institute for Near East Policy, a conservative think tank Indyk helped found. Among other things, he said that the United States would no longer play the game of balancing Iran against Iraq. This was the policy that had kept the war going for eight years. According to Indyk, the relations of the United States with Egypt, Israel, Saudi Arabia, Turkey, and now the (Persian) Gulf Cooperation Council (composed of Saudi Arabia, Kuwait, Bahrain, Qatar, the United Arab Emirates, and Oman) accorded Washington enormous strength to "counter both the Iraqi and Iranian regimes" (copy of speech in author's possession). His logic was that any focus on Iraq would change the balance in the region in favor of Iran.

He then suggested that the United States would "not need to depend on one to counter the other." Indyk pointed out that although the United States intended to preserve the territorial integrity of Iraq, it also aimed "to establish clearly and unequivocally that the current regime in Iraq is a criminal regime, beyond the pale of international society and, in our judgment, irredeemable"—leaving little doubt that a regime change in Baghdad was the ultimate goal of American policy. To justify containing

Iran, the country was accused of pursuing the following unacceptable policies: "supporting international terrorism, pursuing the creation of weapons of mass destruction," and "opposing the peace process in the Middle East." Based on these positions, the United States firmed up and maintained unilateral sanctions against Iran starting in 1995 and continuing to the present. Ironically, the policy of dual containment failed to secure American interests in the region, entangled the United States in the politics of Islamic radicalism, made it an occupying power in the Muslim world in both Afghanistan and Iraq, and helped the ascendancy of the third generation by providing them with the best excuse to remind Rafsanjani that the West could not be trusted.

The Anti-Intellectual Context: "The Western Cultural Onslaught"

This duality of us versus them was reflected in the cultural milieu as well. In December 1995, the then minister of foreign affairs, Ali Akbar Velayati, delivered a lecture on the position of Iran in the world. During the question-and-answer period, he was asked "whether 'the question of Dr. Soroush' would cause a problem for Iran at the global level." Soroush's name had become synonymous with Islamic reform and the liberal narrative of Islam in Iran by this time. Velayati's response was too radical and somewhat shocking. He characterized Soroush's activities as "antagonistic toward the nation," as "weakening the foundations of national independence and cohesion as well as damaging the stature of the government," and as "definitely impacting our foreign situation" (*Keyhan,* 5 Dey 1374/February 24, 1996, 2). He then went beyond the call of duty and compared Soroush to the historian Ahmad Kasravi, who had been assassinated by radicals in 1946 for his reformist religious views. The implication was grave, and this attack came against a person who had spent his public career promoting Islamic discourse and upholding the cause of Islam. Soroush's response to Velayati's allegations insightfully captured the intellectual condition of the time: "If 'the question of Soroush' has become an international issue, it is because his condition epitomizes the insecure condition of the people of the pen in this country" (*Salam,* 12 Dey 1374/January 2, 1996, 2). What was he referring to?

The case of Soroush symbolized the intellectual and cultural condition of Iran at that time. Politically, the third generation had gained actual ascendancy, and men of swords took over the intellectual, cultural, and societal spheres and spaces. As they themselves said, they had finished their "smaller jihad" (fighting external enemies, that is, the war with

Iraq), and now the era of "the greater jihad" (fighting against internal temptation) had come. But they confused fighting man's internal temptation with quashing dissent within the country. Why was there such an emphasis on this now? Members of the third generation apparently considered Rafsanjani's shift of emphasis from revolution to "construction, consumption, and ideas of personal freedom" to be both a degeneration of the revolution and a diversion from it. In their minds, the most obvious sign came when sixteen top bureaucrats, calling themselves agents of construction (*kargozarane sazandegi*), made a public declaration in the 1990s, emphasizing that priority should be given to development over religion. The radicals underlined the following statement from the declaration and drew an interesting conclusion from it:

> We the executives and servants the regime are of the belief that from the First to the Fourth Parliament [1980–1996], a sufficient number of representatives have devoted themselves to strengthening the values of the revolution and the regime. . . . Now the time has come to utilize our skill and efficiency to face those challenges arising from the lack of development, to strengthen our economic policies, to improve the social structure, to gain the people's confidence . . . and to increase the trust of the people toward our service-oriented polity. (*Ettela'at,* 28 Dey 1374/January 18, 1996, 2)

While the statement simply echoed the economic policies of Rafsanjani's regime, the radicals considered it a declaration of the end of the Islamic revolution because of the assertion that there had by now been enough emphasis on Islamic values: "It is evident that this statement invalidates and pushes back the main path of the revolution, which was originally intended to establish religious values and continue with them. . . . In short, it amounts to the death of the revolution as well as of Islamic values" (*Lesarat al-Hossein,* 21 Bahman 1374/February 10, 1996, 8).[4]

Soon a phrase was proposed to describe the intellectual condition of the day: "*Tahajom Farhangi Gharb*" (Western cultural onslaught). Ironically, the warning against liberal tendencies began not with radical Islamists, but with thirty-five highly trained Muslim university professors who wrote a letter to the leaders of the revolution on June 27, 1991. They suggested that Rafsanjani's administration had begun with the promise of moderation and the opening of Iran to the world, but had permitted the Western cultural invasion of Iran, as indicated by the broadcasting of selected Western programs on Iranian television. The letter began by attacking some of those programs, which, they claimed, propagate "disloyalty to tradition, family and social mores . . . , promote ideas of anthropocentrism and the denial of the nonmaterial world, and, more significantly, mock [revolutionary] struggle and ideologies" (*Keyhan*, 6 Tir 1370/June 27, 1991, 18). The authors also criticized such notions as "one world culture," "the global village," and the New World Order, which had been discussed among Iranian intellectuals in the wake of the Soviet Union's fall and the coming of globalization. According to the letter, these were new forms of Western camouflage for the preservation and extension of its domination.

The professors went on to say that since the West had not been able to tame the revolution through military means, that is, through "the imposed war of Iraq against Iran (1980–1988)," it had "resorted to [exporting] cultural degeneration. Not only are we observing slovenly and unrestrained behavior and apathy among the people about Islamic values, but more importantly we see that people are justifying and formulating theories for the slovenliness and apathy." They ended their letter by promising to give their lives for the preservation of Islamic values: "If I do not sacrifice my life for the dear beloved, what other use do I have for the jewel of my life?" A dark time was in the making, and the justification for it was the Western cultural onslaught. What did it all mean? The answer may be found in the sermons of the country's spiritual leader, Ayatollah Seyyed Ali Khamenei.

By Khamenei's account, "cultural assault" was another Western strategy designed to "uproot and destroy our national culture" (Khamenei 1375/1996, 20). In his mind, it was not an imaginary idea, but a real phenomenon with a long and sophisticated history. "We have to believe that we are subject to the cultural assault of our enemies," he writes (4), and that it was part of "a hundred-year history of assault against Islam" (8). The assault was based on the assumption that Western culture is superior and that "for the Europeans, their culture should become the dominant culture, accepted by everyone, and whatever they consider base, the people of the world should agree" (150). There had been a change, however, because the Islamic revolution had awakened Muslims and because the cultural assault of the West against Iran was twofold: "Suddenly the Islamic revolution threatened and undermined the very existence and the value system of the West and the capitalist world" (11). This threat intensified the antagonism that had existed for centuries between the West and Iran, though it should be noted that "the cultural assault against our nation specifically began from the time of Reza Khan [the first Pahlavi king]" (102).

To fight this continuous threat required first and foremost the realization that it was real and could be defended against only through comprehensive mobilization and, most importantly, the revival of the spirit of
revolution and struggle. There had to be permanent readiness to defend
"the venerable Islamic Republic. Groups of the faithful, mobilized forces,
and Hizbollah fighters should act in such a way throughout the country
that America, the Zionists, and the rest of the enemies of the Islamic Republic lose any hope of [dominating us]" (232).

Revolutions, in which state and society confront each other and all
members of the society are mobilized and politicized to participate in the
public sphere, are usually exceptions in human history. And when nor-
malcy returns to the polity, general economic activity and the division
of labor again become the rule. The third generation in the Islamic discourse disregarded this norm. Instead, it advocated permanent revolution and expected the constant presence of the masses in politics. In fact,
politics became the business of everyone, commoners and elite. Thus,
more than half of Khamenei's 1996 book, *Farhang va Tahajom-e Farhangi*
(Culture and Cultural Assault), is devoted to how revolutionary Iranians
could resist Western cultural assault. Those he addressed included the
masses, students, officials, Revolutionary Guards, seminary students, the
clerical class, artists, writers, poets, and media types (171–435).

Khamenei talked about the arts in a way that resonated with the
issue of commitment that was so prevalent in the second generation.
Ideas such as aesthetics or art for art's sake were alien to Khamenei and
his supporters: "The criterion for art is the degree to which it affects society. . . . What is real and fundamental (*asl*) in poetry and other forms
of art is the degree to which they influence [life]" (322). Commitment,
praxis, and action should dominate every step of the way for anyone
who lives in an Islamic society, a society made of activists, a society in a
permanent state of revolution and in constant conflict and struggle with
others. As Khamenei reminded students, "Do not think that the revolution has ended. It continues" (358); it is "not a struggle of today, or one
day, two days, one year or two years. It is the struggle of generations"
(361). He instructed teachers to train the new generation to be "people
who can preserve the revolution, even though it appears to be a difficult
task" (406). This was a recurring theme in Khamenei's thought: all mobilization and revolutionary activities should aim to promote and uphold Islamic principles, so schools must concentrate on educating "our
children as Muslims in their beliefs, training, morals, and also in the
area of practical obedience" (402).

To help this process, the third generation indirectly defined the terms and framework of a discourse that closed the public sphere and made life increasingly difficult for the Iranian intelligentsia and the middle class. Quietly, intellectuals were taken to the security agencies and forced to confess to imagined or actual crimes against the regime. In closed societies, political humor best captures the situation. The following is a story shared in confidential quarters in Iran: In a competition between the intelligence agencies of Iran, Israel, and the United States, each was assigned to find a rabbit that had been left in an area of thick woods. The American agents set the woods on fire and forced the rabbit out in less than four hours. The Israeli agents did not disturb the woods, because they used a special chemical gas and captured the rabbit in two hours. The Iranian agents did not touch the woods at all and came to the judges twenty minutes after the assignment had begun, claiming to have captured the rabbit. When they were asked where the rabbit was, the agents pointed to a pickup truck, in which a big bear was sitting. The judges pointed out that there was no rabbit in the truck, just a bear. The Iranian agents responded by telling the judges to ask the beast. When asked, it said, "I was a bear until twenty minutes ago, but the revolutionary brothers 'convinced' me that I have been a rabbit all along and did not know it, so I 'confess' that I am a rabbit."

More radically, the third generation carried out a policy of killing or imprisoning nonconformist citizens, a policy formulated and executed by the Iranian Ministry of Intelligence and Security in the mid-1990s. The result was a massive emigration of the Iranian intelligentsia and the death of nearly 100 people connected with art, letters, and literature before the campaign ended with the reforms of the late 1990s. The first such case occurred in 1992, when cartoonist Manouchehr Karimzadeh was accused of insulting the memory of Khomeini and sentenced to a lengthy prison term. The murders of the intelligentsia became known in Iran as "chain killings." A group calling itself the Devotees of Pure Muhammadan Islam claimed that it would complete an assassination after a judicial panel declared someone "corrupt on earth." They delivered on their claim first in March 1994, when Hossein Barazandeh-Lagha, an independent Islamic scholar critical of the government, was murdered in Mashhad.

The killings continued. In November 1994, the writer, historian, and critic Ali Akbar Sa'idi Sirjani was found dead of mysterious causes. In October 1995, Ahmad Mir-Allai, a member of the editorial board of the cultural magazine *Zendehroud,* was found dead in the street in Isfahan. In March 1997 the body of publisher Ebrahim Zalzadeh was discovered in Tehran. The peak of the killings came in the fall of 1998: Darioush and Parvaneh Forouhar were murdered in their Tehran home on Sunday, November 22; translator and writer Majid Sharif was found dead on November 24; Pirouz Davani was executed on November 28; and Mohammad-Jafar Pouyandeh and Mohammad Mokhtari, writer and poet, were both murdered on December 9.

The anti-intellectualism subsided when the main culprit in the murder cases, Said Emami (better known in the intelligence quarter as Islami) was arrested, and when President Khatami promised to punish the people responsible for the atrocities. The defensive and reactionary attitude toward the intellectual world of Iran continued with a "legal ban" on the publication of the more independent and critical newspapers.

THE VOICES

What narrative of Islam could justify such dark times and discourse? The promise of heaven on earth proved much harder to deliver than the revolutionaries originally thought. The insightful observation of French scholar Fernand Braudel in 1963 seems prophetic and relevant for this discussion: "Today, the liberation of Islam is very nearly complete. But it is one thing to secure independence, and quite another to keep pace with the rest of the world and look clearly towards the future. That is much more difficult" (Braudel 1994, 93).

Rather than take up the difficult challenge Braudel described, radical Islamists took the easier path of suppressing all human impulses for living in the contemporary world. Some features of their ideas may be characterized as follows:

1. While the main promise of modernity is human liberation and the encouragement of questioning, the Islamists promote an active prohibition against any form of questioning.
2. While pluralism requires accommodation and inclusiveness, the Islamists see the main feature of the human condition as a friend-enemy divide. A crude sense of "us" and "them" constitutes the core of their ideology, with paranoia and a strategy of revenge and punishment as its consequences.
3. While human interaction leads to accidental and historical schisms that can be overcome, the Islamists feel that ideological divisions are a permanent feature. They speak of "ideological living" (*zistan-e*

eideologic) (Maddadpour in Fardid 1381/2002, 497), insisting on a ritual-istic, juridical understanding of religious tenets. Nuance and ambiguity belong to those who have gone astray and either are in need of guidance or should be eliminated for their own good.

4. While modern and even tradition-based thinking is based on reason, the Islamists trust instrumental rationality only as a Machiavellian way of mastering the others.

Who are the people or institutions that propagate such a narrative? We turn to the two major centers of religiosity: Qom and Tehran.

The Islam of Qom: Mesbah Yazdi and the Haqqani School

On February 29, 1979, Khomeini returned to Qom after many years of exile, turning that city in a way into a second capital of Iran. Although his stay there lasted less than a year, it gave an enormous boost to the politicized clerics and directly connected Qom to power. Religious institutions in Iran have always been great centers of influence, over both the people and the political elite. Now there was a big shift. Most of the clerics had joined the establishment, at the price of weakening their influence. Most religious schools participated in the political process and gave up the quietist approach of the second generation, yet many of them remained aloof from political activism.

Like any other religious order, the Shi'i one in Qom is diverse and has many voices. There are people such as Abdolkarim Mussavi Ardabili, who rose to prominence in the judicial system but now resides in Qom, pursuing scholarship and the traditional dissemination of Islam. One group, however, the most vociferous supporters of the official line, lends its ideological and religious support to the radical right in Qom. I concentrate on this group, which is associated with the notorious Haqqani School and with the name of Ayatollah Mohammad Taqi Mesbah Yazdi.

MESBAH YAZDI

As his name suggests, Mesbah Yazdi comes from Yazd, where he was born in 1934. He traveled to Qom to study, and in the 1950s joined the ranks of Khomeini's students. He also studied the philosophy of Avicenna and Mulla Sadra with Mohammad Hossein Tabataba'i. During Khomeini's period of opposition to the shah, Mesbah Yazdi was more interested in ideological discussions. Thus, in collaboration with the late Mohammad Beheshti, Ahmad Janati, and Ali Quddusi, Mesbah Yazdi has been active in the teaching and dissemination of Islamic tenets. He has published many works, most of them dealing with the social and political implications of Islamic teachings. He began lecturing at *Mo'assesseye Rah-e Haqq,* an affiliate of Haqqani School, where he also delivered many lectures.

One of Mesbah Yazdi's more influential publications is *Pasdari az Sangarha-ye Eidiologic* (Guarding the Ideological Trenches), a treatise arguing for Islam's superiority to Marxism. He served on the board of directors of the Rah-e Haqq institute for ten years, then founded the Imam Baqir educational complex, a partly publicly funded enterprise that enjoys the financial support of the richest foundation in the world, *Bonyad-e Mostazafan va Janbazan* (the Foundation of the Oppressed and Disabled). Finally, he advanced to the position he holds at present (2006): director of *Mo'assesseye Amuzeshi va Pazhuheshi Khomeini* (Educational and Research Institution of Khomeini), located in Qom.

At the same time, Mesbah Yazdi has been active in the political life of the country since the revolution. Since 1990 he has been an elected member of the *Majlis-e Khebregan-e Rahbari* (Assembly of Experts for Leadership). He has authored numerous works on Islamic and comparative philosophy, theology, ethics, and Qur'anic exegesis. All along, he has been the voice of conservatism and the most vociferous spokesman for a combination of traditionalism and Islamism. For example, he is on record as having praised the Fada'iyan Islam and its leader Navvab Safavi (the first Muslim group to use assassination in modern Iran, it took pride in killing historian and intellectual Ahmad Kasravi), and he encouraged the elimination of the enemies of the Islamic Republic. Moreover, after reformist Mohammad Khatami was elected president on a platform emphasizing political development and pluralism, Mesbah Yazdi condemned the reforms altogether: "What is being termed as reform today is in fact corrupt. What is being promoted in the name of reforms and the path of the prophets is in fact in total conflict with the objectives of the prophets and the masters" (*Resalat,* March 29, 2001). He described President Khatami as "a betrayer of the Islamic revolution," and in one meeting he reportedly encouraged militants to eliminate notable pro-democracy figures, the most obvious being Abdollah Nuri, minister of the interior.

Similarly, on November 16, 2002, during the peak of the reform movement for democratization, he spoke about the role of the prophets. The central theme was that pluralism has little to do with revelation: "The prophets of God did not believe in pluralism. They believed that only one idea was the right one" (IRNA news agency). He was critical of President Khatami's talk of "independence, freedom, and progress" (*esteqlal, azadi, va pishraft*), accusing him of either ignoring or undermining the original slogans of the revolution: "independence, freedom, and the Islamic Republic." Mesbah Yazdi also supported the murder of intellectuals. It is strongly believed that he issued the fatwa permitting the chain killings. Supporters of Khatami accused Mesbah Yazdi of being "the ideologue of violence" who provided the religious justification for attacks on figures accused of undermining the Islamic system. This applied to everyone—both secular and religious—including the active members of the revolution.

Many believe that Mesbah Yazdi's inflammatory sermons provided rhetorical cover and encouragement for extremists already prone to violence. In fact, they claim that he encouraged the assassination attempt on Saeed Hajjarian in March 2000 (this is discussed in the next chapter) by condemning the reform movement and, two days before the attempt, threatening that its proponents "would be dealt with." His argument was that state violence is justified and legitimate when carried out for the defense of Islam. Mesbah Yazdi branded the people who were killed or murdered as *nasebi* (enemies of Imam Ali and his household), who deserved to die. When the reformist newspaper *Neshat* denounced any form of the death penalty and pointedly criticized Mesbah Yazdi, Khamenei spoke in Mesbah Yazdi's support, revering him as "a learned scholar, well versed in Islam," while accusing the journalists of "misleading the public" (*Neshat*, August 10, 1997).

Why does Khamenei revere Mesbah Yazdi, and in what narrative of Islam is he well versed? The answer is obvious: Mesbah Yazdi propagates the official version of Islam that is dominant in Iran. The official ideology of the Islamic Republic of Iran is Khomeini's theory of "the absolute guardianship of the jurisconsult." While some people brand Khomeini's theory as an innovation imposed on Iranians by the zeal of the revolution and because of the charisma of Khomeini himself, Mesbah Yazdi considers it the very idea of politics in Shi'ism: "With the exception of one or two contemporary jurists, the rest of the [Shi'i] jurists accept that during the occultation [of the Twelfth Imam], it is the qualified jurist who can and should assume the position of the ruler" (Mesbah Yazdi 1381/2002, 64). Historically, of course, the reverse was true: all jurists agreed that only the infallible imams were the rightful successors to the Prophet of Islam, and very few explicitly assigned such a lofty position to ordinary jurists. Even Khomeini's theory should be understood within the context of philosophy and mysticism.

174

The Khomeini of the elite was frightened of the two forces that Mesbah Yazdi embodies and fosters, namely, traditionalism and Islamism. Khomeini referred to the first as "being stone-headed" (*motahajer budan*)—that is, freezing the past and casting it as the only guide to the future—and branded the second radicalism (*tondravi*), which he associated with youth, particularly the "Islamic Marxists." After Khomeini's death, it seems that an unholy alliance of the two became dominant, and Mesbah Yazdi echoed both accurately.

The irony is that Mesbah Yazdi has studied philosophy, but he takes a utilitarian and instrumental approach to it. For him, a human activity is peculiarly and exclusively human "when the activity is linked to reason" (Mesbah Yazdi 1360/1981, 5–7). But reason does not mean human wonder about the mysteries and nuances of life, but, rather, thought put at the service of realizing the centrality of God, because "God is the creator of the totality of the world and all its interconnections" (380). Mesbah Yazdi uses his educational and philosophical training to propagate such a narrative. What is the logic of this argument? How does he explain the absolute authority of the jurist? And why is it that any means, including violence, is justified to implement his version of Islam?

Mesbah Yazdi builds his discussion of the guardianship of the jurisconsult on two presuppositions that he calls "fundamental issues" (Mesbah Yazdi 1381/2002, 66). The first is a warning to not prejudice real understanding with what is fashionable. According to him, democracy and freedom today constitute a fashionable trend, one that has become an accepted paradigm, and even religions are presented in the light of democracy. Indirectly, he is criticizing the reform movement in Iran. He accuses liberal-minded and freedom-conscious Muslims in Iran of putting forward *ejtihad-e be ra'y* (legal ruling based on one's own opinion) (66). The second is a reminder that the real source of any religion is the text and revelation, not the way in which religious adherents have presented it: "To grasp what Islam wants, one has to go the text of the Qur'an and the real leaders of the religion, not to the sayings and actions of Muslims" (69). He then begins his main argument.

The very first principle is that God is the cause of all existence and the world, including humanity: "He is the real owner of whatever exists on earth; 'whatever is in the heavens and whatever is in the earth is God's' [Qur'an 4:131]" (70). The implication is that man has no authority whatsoever over anything, including his own body. The fact that God is the real owner means that all authority belongs to him. What about human reason? It helps people realize that they cannot have something that does not belong to them, unless there is permission. Any exercise of authority runs contrary to the very principle of God being the absolute creator, possessor, and authority. Right from the start, it appears that Mesbah Yazdi treats Islam as a very closed system, and one should be reminded of the maxim that in a closed system, "nothing is permitted unless noted," as opposed to an open system, in which "everything is allowed unless noted." Who can tell humanity what is permitted?

As Mesbah Yazdi argues, "Based on the evidence at hand, this right is granted to the Prophet of Islam and then following him come the infallible imams" (71). Here he invokes two verses from the Qur'an: "The prophet has greater claim on the faithful than they have on themselves" (33:6), and "O you who believe! Obey God, obey the Apostles and those in authority among you" (4:59). It is of course considered ostensible in Shi'ism that those in authority are none other than the infallible imams, all twelve of them, the last one being in occultation. The next step is to consider who should assume their post, since there is no apparently infallible imam to lead the Shi'a community. As mentioned before, Mesbah Yazdi echoes Khomeini's theory and considers such a position of authority to be reserved exclusively for a qualified jurisconsult. It is a generic designation, insofar as any qualified person could be the ruler: "Based on proven evidence during the occultation of the imam, such a right is granted to the qualified jurist . . . but there is no evidence that the people or the lay members of society enjoy such a right" (71). So what is the role of the people in this theory?

Here Mesbah Yazdi distinguishes between legitimacy (*mashru'iyat*), that is, the source of authority, and acceptance of the rule (*maqbuliyat*), or the means for rule implementation (51–54). For Mesbah Yazdi, authority stems from God, since he is the author and possessor of all existence; people have a small role to play. People cannot grant or dispossess privilege from "those in authority among you"; only God can do that: "As in the time of the Prophet and the Imams, during the period of occultation, the people have no role to play in granting legitimacy [in designating the ruler or justifying the rule]" (73). He explains that the position of the jurisconsult is based on reason (*aql*) and is transmitted as tradition (*naql*).

Reason dictates that government is a necessity and helps us realize that, in the absence of an ideal, one should strive for the closest approximation thereof. The closest we can get to the rule of the infallible imam is "the coming together of knowledge of Islamic injunctions [jurisprudence]; . . . righteousness; and skillfulness in managing society" (85). Reason also helps us realize that God, the possessor of all authority, still requires the implementation of these injunctions, even in the absence of infallible imams. To implement them, the qualified jurist takes the exact position of the ruler in the absence of the imams (94–96).

As for transmitted traditions, Mesbah Yazdi narrates the same two traditions that Khomeini invoked in his treatise. The first is "a tradition, known among the jurists as the *Toqih Sharif* (The Exalted Stamp) . . . which reports the response of the Twelfth Imam" to a certain Muslim for guidance on problems he might face in "newly occurring circumstances" (97). The imam reportedly said, "In case of newly occurring circumstances, you should turn [for guidance] to those who relate our traditions, for they are my proof to you, as I am God's proof" (97–98; Khomeini 1980, 84–85). Both Mesbah Yazdi and Khomeini go on in detail to prove that the "newly occurring circumstances" refer to social and political issues, since it was an already established practice, even in the lifetime of imams, to refer questions and issues of a personal nature to the jurists.

The second tradition is known by the name of its reporter, "Umar ibn Hanzala," a known narrator of Shi'i traditions. When he inquired whether it was permissible for Muslims to refer their disputes over debt and inheritance to temporal rulers, the Sixth Imam responded as follows: "They must seek one of you who narrates our traditions, who is versed in what is permissible and what is forbidden, who is well acquainted with our laws and ordinances, and accept him as judge or arbiter, for I appoint him as judge over you" (quoted in Khomeini 1980, 93). This tradition has been quoted frequently in defense of the authority of the jurists in Shi'ism, and even Khomeini cited the passage—"I appoint him as judge over you"—whereas Mesbah Yazdi cites it as "I appoint him as ruler over you" (Mesbah Yazdi 1381/2002, 103).

Based on reason and tradition, Mesbah Yazdi concludes that jurists are the rightful possessors of the privilege to rule and do need support from the people. He equates the rule of the jurist with that of God, so government of the Islamic Republic of Iran is the government of God, since, in the end, the jurists "represent God and the Imam of the Age and are designated by them" (104). Politics and government are elevated to a sacred exercise, making any argument against the policies difficult and any dissension impossible: "Disobeying the rule of the jurist and not accepting his ordinances is a grave injustice and constitutes a sin that God will not forgive" (101).

This belief represents a regression of almost a century to when, during the constitutional revolution, the traditionalists opposed any role for the people. In other words, Mesbah Yazdi, by insisting on the traditionalist approach to politics in Shi'ism, echoes an idea that was stated "in various ways at the peak of constitutionalism. As a way of opposing 'the disgusting notion of freedom,' the late Sheikh Fazlollah Nuri argued against allowing any grocer or shopkeeper to sit as a lawmaker" (Hajjarian 1379/2000, 642). Like Nuri during the Constitutional Movement, Mesbah Yazdi grants a minimal role to the people. When there is the possibility of establishing an Islamic society, people can accept or reject the Islamic system. Once they have accepted it, their only recourse is obedience. Iranians exercised that right in 1979 and overwhelmingly endorsed the Islamic Republic. Now, as Mesbah Yazdi puts it, "Islam cannot accept that a group of people congregate and decide to initiate laws for themselves" (*Ettela'at*, 10 Mehr 1372/October 1, 1993). When the reform movement in the late 1990s advocated democratization, he warned them in a similar fashion: "Be careful that you are not fooled. Accepting Islam as the dominant rule in society contradicts completely the acceptance of democracy in legislation" (*Iran*, 30 Tir 1377/July 20, 1998).

Who decides the content of legislation? According to Mesbah Yazdi, Islamic jurisprudence contains all the answers; one must simply invoke its principles. He reiterates the cliché among Muslims that "Islam has ordinances for humanity from birth to death and the Qur'an contains all the answers." Islamic jurisprudence should thus be revived in its totality, even if some of its rules have lost relevance. According to Mesbah Yazdi, Islam itself has solutions for these ordinances. Consider slavery. In 1993 he said, "Islam has devised solutions and strategies for ending slavery, but this does not mean that slavery is condemned in Islam. If, in a legitimate war, Muslims gain dominance over unbelievers and take them captives, in the hand of the victorious Muslims they are considered slaves and the ordinances of slavery apply to them" (*Ettela'at*, 10 Mehr 1372/October 1, 1993). In other words, Islam is a totality; it is sacred; and once accepted, it must be implemented. The Islamic Republic of Iran now represents this belief, and any opposition to it will not be tolerated. Mesbah Yazdi believes it is his mission to fight to preserve the Islamic Republic, even if, as he said in one of his sermons, it requires "a million martyrs" (reported in the *Guardian*, June 11, 2001). To kill or to die for the implementation of "God's commands" constitutes the highest status one can achieve, and sometimes it is a necessity. As he said explicitly in June 1999, "If implementing Islamic objectives would not be possible except by violent means, then that becomes a necessity" (cited in Ganji 1379/2000a, 239).

In his reiteration of Khomeini's theory, Mesbah Yazdi has simply justified the existing power of the clergy. Khomeini initiated the theory, and his charismatic position guaranteed that it was institutionalized both with the constitution and in actual practice. Institutions such as the Assembly of Experts, the Council of Guardians, and the position of leadership guaranteed the survival and the continuation of the system. After Khomeini's death, the Assembly of Experts selected the new leadership. In turn, the leader appointed the clerical members of the Council of Guardians, appointed overseers for the election of the members of the Assembly of Experts, and barred people he considered undesirable from participating in the process. According to Mesbah Yazdi, these actions created a philosophical circle wherein "the guardian jurisconsult legitimizes the Council of Guardians, and that in turn legitimizes the Assembly of Experts, and that in turn legitimizes the guardian jurisconsult" (Mesbah Yazdi 1381/2002, 142). The Council of Guardians, whose members are more or less appointed by the leader, must approve the qualifications of those who want to join the Assembly of Experts. For example, in the 1994 election of the Assembly of Experts, many clerics, including Muhammad Mussavi Khoe'iniha (a leftist clergy member) and Sadeq Khalkhali (the chief judge of the revolutionary court, better known as the hanging judge) were disqualified. Mesbah Yazdi's narrative became the dominant ideology of the Haqqani School and other institutions.

THE HAQQANI SCHOOL

Most people first heard about the Haqqani School in 1989, after Ayatollah Khomeini issued his fatwa on the life of British writer Salman Rushdie. A group calling itself the Students of Haqqani School in Qom declared that it would be willing to carry out the death sentence. The name of the school became synonymous with the politics of the radical right from the mid-1990s onward. Many of its graduates occupy important positions, and Ali-Akbar Fallahian-e Khuzestani, a controversial minister of intelligence and a presidential contender in the June 2001 election, attended the school.

Founded in 1964, the school was named after one of its conservative benefactors—a merchant named Haqqani-Zanjani. Some active clerics, later turned prominent revolutionaries, joined the faculty and even served on the school's board of directors. For a long time the most challenging adversaries of the school were the Marxist Iranians, so the school concentrated on cultural interactions and polemics. This explains why most of its early publications aimed at refuting Marxism and developing a comparative account of Islam and Marxism. Also, it tried to establish a network with like-minded Muslim institutions, most notably Mo'assesseye Rah-e Haqq, headed by Mesbah Yazdi, and the organization behind the monthly *Maktab-e Islam,* a center headed by Ayatollah Nasser Makarem-Shirazi.

The 1979 revolution offered the biggest boost to the Haqqani School. Ironically, while Khomeini was alive, his style of arbitration did not allow any particular group to dominate the political scene. In fact, to maintain a balance, he tacitly supported the left by allowing them to remain in power. For example, Mir Hossein Mussavi was prime minister for the first decade of the revolution. Khomeini's death made Haqqani and its supporters more powerful. When Ayatollah Muhammad Yazdi became head of the judiciary, a host of Haqqani graduates joined this branch of the government (Ganji 1379/2000b). Furthermore, they took over the Ministry of Intelligence and Security, the Islamic Propagation Organization, the Revolutionary Guards Corps, the Revolutionary Courts system, the Special Court for the Clergy, and the ironically titled Jury of the Media Court, which is responsible for the suppression of newspapers and journals.

The members of Haqqani School support one another. It is commonly held that they behave like chain links: if any link is touched, the whole chain moves in protest. Since the early 1990s, the prominent members of the judiciary who believe in "the rule by law" rather than "the rule of law" have come from Haqqani. They include Mohseni-Ejei, Razini, Hosseinian, Ramandi, Sadeqi, and Mobasheri. To be fair, the school has also turned out some fine minds with liberal tendencies. One example is Ayatollah Yusuf Sane'i (b. 1927), who has been part of the school since 1975 and is a voice of reform. Today, in 2006, the graduates of Haqqani are the most powerful group in the key centers of power in Tehran, including the judiciary and the Ministry of Intelligence.

The Islam of Tehran: Fardid and Davari

In postrevolutionary Iran, the hostage minds, particularly those who opposed the West, saw Iran as "the mother of territories" (*Um al-Qora*) for fighting against injustices. Thus its members began formulating a philosophy of opposition that would appeal to younger Iranians. For example, in politics, America was to be cast as "the Great Satan," and the West totalized as "demonic essence." Those who became central to the emerging radical right were the oral philosopher Seyyed Ahmad Fardid and a professor of philosophy at Tehran University, Reza Davari. Others followed them and wrote for publications such as the monthlies *Mashreq* and *Sobh* and Tehran's daily *Keyhan*. It should be mentioned that both Fardid and Davari are sophisticated intellectuals with two faces: philosophers concerned with lofty ideas and human decency who are nonetheless perceived to have Heideggerian minds, with similar implications. Just as Heidegger was considered the intellectual force behind Nazism, these philosophers are considered the minds behind the extremism and radicalism of the Islamic Republic.

SEYYED AHMAD FARDID

I first met Fardid in the early 1980s and discussed many issues with him. At the time I could not guess that the revolution would have an even more radical phase than that which had already been shown. Fardid became a public philosopher and influenced many among the revolution's devotees. For example, one of his followers was the late Murteza Avini, a very popular figure among the war veterans. A writer, he published a monthly dealing with art and media, particularly cinema.

Fardid was highly regarded, and upon his death, his home was turned into a foundation. He was known as an oral philosopher because he "refused to write" (Maddadpour in Fardid 1382/2002, 506), and as his critic Daryush Ashuri put it, "Writing was hard for him . . . but [he] enormously liked lecturing" (Ashuri 1383/2004, 3). Ashuri, who bitterly criticized Fardid, claimed that he wrote for posterity, "so that future generations would not laugh at us, saying what a foolish generation that could not distinguish between hallucination and philosophical discourse" (52). The fact remains that, hallucination or not, Fardid's ideas have become the legitimizing source for many of the violent actions of the radical right in Iran.

To discuss Fardid here, I rely on the recent publication of his 1979 lectures at Tehran University. The book was edited by a loyal student and follower who transcribed the lecture tapes and gave them a very idiosyncratic, ambitious, and, I think, accurate title: *Didar-e Farahi va Fotuhaat-e Aakhar-e Zamaan* (The Divine Encounter and Illuminations at the End of Time). One might read the text as conveying Fardid's aim to explore the possibility of encountering the divine light in an age of materialism. But from a distance, it seems to be the result of a paranoid mind filled with hatred, conspiracy, and vengeance, with no appreciation for anyone except Heidegger.

But who was Fardid? Ahmad Mahini Yazdi, better known as Seyyed Ahmad Fardid, was born in 1910 and died in 1994. He was a professor of philosophy at Tehran University until the mid-1970s, but he became controversial because of his idiosyncratic philosophy, oriented toward "Eastern spirituality," as Ashuri calls it (Ashuri 1383/2004, 7–9). Fardid was a passionate and in some ways genuine intellectual who allowed his passions to rule. He was a loner with a naive conviction that he could save humanity from its present historicist condition and allow it to reach its true destiny. His dismissive attitude toward fellow intellectuals, Iranian or otherwise, could be unnerving.

Fardid explicitly criticized and even condemned philosophers for distancing humanity from the divine. Indeed, he considered Socrates the first to initiate this process (Fardid 1382/2002, 363), which has continued to the present. He even condemned some Muslim philosophers as *zendiq* (unbelievers), including the founder of Muslim philosophy, Abu Nasr Farabi (334) to the last great Muslim philosopher, Mulla Sadra (367). He considered them all infected with Greek thought, which in turn had turned away from the divine by emphasizing human reason. Contemporary Iranian thinkers and intellectuals were doubly at fault because they followed the contemporary West, itself under the spell of Greek thought and dominated by the notion of anthropocentrism, which has equated man with God. Why did Fardid make such a claim, and what was he after?

Here is how he described his destiny: "My wish is to be free from the modern cave, which is filled with self-founded nihilism, enchantment by earthly gods (*taghutzadegi*), and historicism. This is my ideal, and wherever I see a lack of angered fists and the prevalence of compromise, I will be disappointed . . . because to possess and insist on a position is the right move" (149). Obviously he was unhappy with the status quo, which he equated with *Gharbzadegi* (Weststruckness). In fact, his most significant contribution to Iran's intellectual discourse was this notion. Though Al-e Ahmad made the concept popular, Fardid claimed that the former had misunderstood his notion, presenting a journalistic and vulgarized version of it. In Fardid's analysis, East and West do not pertain to geographical designations and have little relation to material progress, advancement, and mastery of the machine. The East involves *dawn* while the West involves *dusk*. The first connotes the coming of light, enlightenment, truth, and discovery, while the second refers to the end, degeneration, and decadence. Humanity is divided along these lines.

This split goes back to ancient Greece (339). The whole of Greek philosophy and what the world holds as the great human achievements constitute a form of Weststruckness. The greatest form of darkness resulted from humanity's turning away from the heavens and the source of light in the earth, relying instead on human reason as the highest and most exalted good. The totality of the post-Renaissance world has fallen completely; the exception was Heidegger, who diagnosed the problem. In the midst of this total darkness, there occurred a revolution in Iran that inaugurated an Islamic regime devoted to the divine plan. This naive hope explained his support for the Islamic revolution: "The totality of Western history is void. Humanity has to strive to elevate itself. Elevation has come to us under the leadership of Khomeini" (392). According to Fardid, Heidegger was the only Western philosopher who understood the world and the only philosopher whose insights were congruent with the principles of the Islamic Republic. These two figures, Khomeini and Heidegger, helped Fardid argue his position. But what was this position?

First and foremost, Fardid believed that human life on earth could be divided into epochs, each marked by "a name" (*esm*) that found "presence" (*hozur*) and manifestation. In fact, history is made of cycles, and "in each cycle a reality manifests itself in humanity and history" (42). At a far distance and at the beginning was the era of the unseen, when there was God and nothing else. Then came God's creation of humanity and his teaching of all names: "And He taught Adam all the names" (Qur'an 2:31). This era coincided with the age of Hellenism and Greek philosophy. In this era the "name" amounted to "rebellion against the Gods, and humanity considered the manifestation of truth" (310). The next era included the Middle Ages and the arrival of Islam, when the essence of God manifested itself again, but modernity arrived with "demonic man as its truth" (311). Fardid spent a lot of time on this era because he considered modernity his biggest adversary and defeating it his biggest challenge. In this era, all categories—manifest and hidden, objectivity and subjectivity, essence and appearance, and finally "actuality and reality[—]united and became what I call '*khodbonyadi*'" (self-foundation). The name for our contemporary epoch is humanism, which Fardid understood as the declaration of man as God. Modern selves, modern times, and modern ways are all characterized by self-foundation, with little concern for humanity or the common good: "The Universal Declaration of Human Rights has no sign of humanity in it . . . brotherhood, equality, freedom of *nafs amare* [concupiscence and sensuality], and leveling of everybody into nobody" (78). Iran was no exception. It became part of this world in recent centuries, particularly since the constitutional revolution of 1905.

This last assertion is of course contrary to my thesis. That revolution was the peak of Iranian modernization and held the possibility of uniting modernity with Islam, whereas for Fardid, that revolution took Iranians away from God: "Weststruckness has dominated us for a hundred years. . . . The youth are looking for the God of the yesteryears and that of the future. They are looking for the God of the Qur'an, while the nihilistic and self-founded history of the contemporary world has put down deep roots among us" (103). Instead, they are promised democracy and democratization. What did he think of democracy and the rule of law? Like Plato, he opposed these because they inhibit an encounter with the divine: "Democracy means the asceticism of taking refuge in Satan" (53). He criticized modern Muslims who defend the congruity of Islam and democracy, maintaining that "in no way could democracy converge with the Qur'an . . . . Democracy belongs to the Greek, and the Greek man is the embodiment of *taghut* [rebellion against God]" (79). The final epoch, which is called humanism, coincides with the "struggle between the oppressed and the oppressors . . . and end[s] with the relinking of humanity and the divine" (311); hence the necessity of a revolution.

Fardid espoused the radical position of advocating a continuous revolutionary condition: "I believe in permanent revolution, and today I am very frightened that the revolution may be undermined and the bourgeoisie take over" (37). Was it to be a permanent revolution for the sake of revolution, or was it for an exalted objective? For the Platonic Fardid, it was the latter. It was to put an end to Weststruckness and to allow "real heart-consciousness" to set in (75). The revolution that Fardid sought will occur when humanity "in its totality embodies a different 'name' [than that of modern humanism], and that 'name' is the name of God's grace (*lotf*)" (80). "The real revolution," he said, "means elevation from ephemeral times to existence and from existence to eternal time, and finally from eternal time to God's grace" (197).

There could be no toleration for dissent in such a context. Slight aberrations from the official line should be dealt with. This is what he meant when he said that the Islamic Republic is a "vertical democracy" in which everything is granted from above (Fardid 1982, interview). His lack of tolerance for a plurality of thought, to which I have already referred, was another indicator. He accused the founder of Islamic philosophy of being an unbeliever, but more relevant to the evolution of the Shi'i discourse was his depiction of the major work of Khaje Nassir Tusi, *The Nassirian Ethics*. Khaje Nassir, a thirteenth-century philosopher, was a major figure in Shi'ism, yet Fardid branded his work as unbelief: "*The Nassirian*

Ethics is a work of unbelief and is dominated by the quadruple virtues of the Greeks, none of which is found in [Islamic] jurisprudence" (Fardid 1381/2002, 413).

If Khaje Nassir was not puritanical enough, it was no wonder that contemporary Iranian intellectuals, secular or nonsecular, came under attack (see, for example, 371–375, 386–390, and 405–407). Those who did not think like Fardid or follow his line of thinking were *taghuti* (rebellious against the truth) or *taghutzadeh* (involved with the rebellion against the truth): "Whoever is not concerned with the epoch of names, I would call *taghutzadeh* . . . that is, negligent in the remembrance of names and the manifestation of the names of God" (18). Not surprisingly, the radical right began intimidating, threatening, and terrorizing Iranian intellectuals by airing programs called *Hoviyat* (Identity) and *Cheraq* (Light) on Iranian television. In the 1990s, the intellectuals who came under attack were also those whom Fardid had criticized in his work. Fardid's ideas remain strong within the conservative discourse and have thrived more explicitly through a student who continues teaching philosophy at the same university.

DAVARI

Reza Davari Ardakani (b. 1933) also came from the Yazd region. After high school, he joined the Ministry of Education and became a teacher, only to be laid off after the 1953 coup as a result of his sympathy for the nationalist movement. He then attended Tehran University, where he pursued a PhD in philosophy and wrote a dissertation on al-Farabi, and where he later joined the faculty and still teaches. I first met Davari in 1986, when, as the chair of the department, he invited me to teach a course called "Philosophy of Politics." From then on, I saw him sporadically, many times in seminars and conferences. I found him sincere and genuinely interested in philosophical inquiry, but like Fardid, he has a public image that is revolutionary and radical. Since the revolution, he has been part of the cultural establishment of the Islamic Republic: a member of the Headquarters for Cultural Revolution; an editor of the journal *Name-ye Farhang* (Journal of Culture), published by the Ministry of Culture and Islamic Guidance; and, at present, head of the Academy of Sciences of the Islamic Republic of Iran. His philosophical dimension aside, he was a close associate of Fardid, and confesses that he was "saved" by him "from Durkheimian positivism and sociologism" (quoted in Vahdat 2002, 186).

Davari had taken a critical stance toward the West long before the revolution, but the new Islamic regime provided broader possibilities for encouraging his way of thinking. Davari agrees with his teacher that Weststruckness lies at the heart of Iran's problems. He thinks there is a structural inequality between the two worlds, but does not believe its nature is economic and political. He also agrees with Khomeini that spirituality is wanting everywhere, particularly in the West, contending that "politically the East and the West may struggle and contradict each other, but they have the same roots." He even claims that "Russia before the revolution of October [1917] was more distinct from the West" (Davari 1373/1994, 82), whereas what emerged in the postrevolutionary era was an extension of the West. But he plans to study the phenomenon much more deeply.

Davari holds that it is impossible to eradicate the Western appetite for domination either by defeating the empire or by injecting spirituality into its life: "Political and military domination is nothing new in human history" (Davari 1357/1978, 85). But Western domination is unique in its comprehensiveness. Thus "it is no surprise that the relation between Western civilization and non-Western nations is that of economic, political and military subjugation" (83). What makes the subjugation of Iran so deep is not that Iranians are fascinated by machines, but that they are the embodiment of "the disease of modern science, technology, and industry" (Davari 1373/1994, xix). Davari thinks Weststruckness has deeper roots.

What is different in the new relation between East and West is that the inequality is total: "The West has tried to capture and make everything on the earth its own. . . . More than military, economic and political domination, it has made a mockery of the traditional thought of the other nations, presenting them as nonsensical so that the path would be paved for them to [take the West as the model and] imitate it" (Davari 1978, 85). One should ask the "right" question, which, according to Davari, is "what made this possible?": "The West succeeded in colonizing other nations because it possessed a corresponding philosophy of dominating humanity and the world. In other words, domination, colonialism and imperialism are endemic in—are in 'the essence' of—modern Western philosophy; the West did not become politically and economically powerful all of a sudden" (85). But what, then, is the West?

Davari and his followers begin with the presupposition that there is no distinction between the West and modernity. They are identical. That explains why, for Davari, the West is much more than a geographical region or even a political bloc. It is a phenomenon that now exists in many parts of the world: "Historically, it is a way of thinking and acting . . . and has a presence in all philosophies, ideologies, policies, and literatures of modern European history. . . . In short, [at one level] the West is the dusk and the demise of the celestial truth, [and at another level] it is the rise of a human [being] who considers himself the beginning, the end, and the center of the universe (*dayereye madar*). It is everything, and its final perfection is to possess everything, the celestial world included" (Davari 1373/1994, 73). Davari has devoted most of his works to elaborating on the consequences of such a definition. What then is "the essence of the West?" What kind of relations can one have with such a phenomenon and what has historically been Iran's relation to it? What are the institutional implications of such an understanding?

Davari agrees that the modern West is based on and operates according to subjectivity, and by implication is based on the autonomous self. He does not agree that subjectivity should be associated with such virtues as self-respect, rights, freedom, responsible individuality, mutual respect and responsibility, and social accountability. Instead, he reads it as revolt, subversion, looseness, heedlessness, egoism, and hubris. He wrote a controversial essay entitled "*Johar va Mahiyat-e Gharb*" (The Essence and Substance of the West), kindling a heated debate with the contemporary Muslim thinker and reformer Abdolkarim Soroush. He begins his essay with the following words: "Subjectivity (*nafsaniyat*) is usually used in opposition to religiosity and spirituality, and it conveys the sense of following the demands of the senses and passions (*ahvaye nafs*)."[5] He continues, claiming that the desires of the senses "constitute the axis of the Western thought" (Davari 1373/1994, 65).

The rest of the essay elaborates on the meaning and consequences of this statement. He enumerates them as follows:

1. Subjectivity entails independence from the divine. This does not reduce the greatness of the modern West and its rationality: "Westerners enjoy reason. Rationality exists in the West today not less than in other historical epochs. There may be even more rationality today, except it is of a kind that does not go beyond sensuality, and it is utilized for verification and domination only" (66).

2. The faculty and virtue of reason are situated in this world only because modern man needs nothing but his own mundane rationality. In the West, Davari writes, "with the exception of [Soren] Kierkegaard and [Max] Scheler, who were marginal in the foundation and establishment of the West anyway, no other philosopher has felt the need to talk about human follies; instead, they all admire and verify man's potential powers. . . . In other words, man is at the center of the universe" (68).

3. Philosophy then turns from the question of what to the question of how. In other words, method becomes central to all inquiries, removing man from any quest for the ultimate. All aspects of life in the West are thus unholy, and "Western man is the embodiment of passion and subjectivity" (69).

4. Subjectivity makes sense in the world of here and now, and since the latter deals with tangible stuff, "the new thinking does not relate to the heart, and modern man's trajectory is bound to and ends with man himself. He has taken it upon himself to conquer space and time and leave his mark on everything" (70).

5. Corollary to these features is the following conclusion: "Each historical epoch revolves around an axiom. The pivot of modern history is subjectivity. And in a world in which subjectivity rules, religiosity and the worship of God has no place" (71).

Davari's essay led to a heated debate about the West and what it meant (Boroujerdi 1996, 158–165; Vahdat 2002, 187–211). Davari was accused of essentializing and totalizing the West. In his own defense, he wrote the following:

> When I said the West amounts to sensuality and subjectivity (*nafsaniyat*), I did not use the latter concept in its metaphysical or ethical connotation. . . . I meant to say that in the West the "rational animal" has been replaced by an "animal that utilizes rationality." In the case of a rational animal, animalism is the material substance and rationality is the essence, whereas in the case of an animal that utilizes rationality, logos and reason are the matter and animalism becomes the essence. The pivotal principle is that the life of man on earth, along with everything else, is reduced to a means for satisfying that essence. (Davari 1373/1994, 160)

Davari does not dismiss the West as contrary or antagonistic to truth or God. For him, the modern world is not a world where there is animosity against religion; it is a world where religion has been declared irrelevant within the public realm: "Western societies do not oppose religion, but they are based on the principle that religion should be pushed aside. Note that a conscious intention has set such a path" (23). He maintains that in the West itself there were major philosophers who understood this reality about "the essence of the West," and that they could help us realize the deep and dark dimension of it, could remind some of us of the depth of our entanglement in the "prison of the West." The most notable, according to Davari, was Martin Heidegger, whose "thought in the Western tradition could be categorized as 'preparatory thought' (*tafakor amadegar*). He is one of those who can show us the inner essence of the West" (155).

Davari goes further. He discusses the most important political manifestation of modernity in the West, namely, nationalism. In his book on nationalism, Davari explicitly states, "Nationalism is an imperative of the West, and wherever it appears, the West will follow" (Davari 1364/1985, 105). At the heart of nationalism remains the notion that if a particular group of people desires to live independently, it is natural, legitimate, and rightful. These rights extend to the "exercise of power, the creation of laws and social norms, and the supervision and control of social relations and transactions, free from any outside authority" (22). What is the source of nationalism? According to Davari, nationalism is the direct result of the idea of subjectivity. He believes "the spirit of independence appeared in political, civic, social, and economic domains shortly after man considered himself the center of the universe and the source of knowledge, power, and will" (22). Like non-Westerners who try to become modern, non-Western forms of nationalism end up half-baked and not genuine. These forms of nationalism rest on "a weak foundation" because they do not grow from the same intellectual root as that of the West (24). There are nationalists who have fought imperialist powers, but they either were defeated or else become autocratic (25).

Finally, regarding the relationship between Iran and the West, Davari thinks that Iran has been badly affected by modernity: "Modernity is a tree that was planted in the West and has spread everywhere. For many years we have been living under one of the dying and faded branches of this tree and its dried shadow, which is still hanging over our heads" (quoted in Boroujerdi 1996, 159–160). For Davari, this is not a normative position; rather, It is a factual account of both the nature of the West and the fate of Iran. According to Davari, the revolution has made Iranians aware of this relationship and empowered them: "People are not afraid of death anymore" (Davari 1364/1985, 125). This awareness has made it possible for them to rectify the situation: "Although . . . the shadow of this branch [modernity and the West] has still not yet totally disappeared from over our heads" (quoted in Boroujerdi 1996, 160), Iranians should have no fear because when "a nation turns to the truth, God will turn toward it" (Davari 1364/1985, 126). This divine fortune is, of course, the Islamic revolution, which has introduced new ways of thinking and behaving. It can remind people of their forgotten origin of unity with the divine. In Davari's mind, "The Islamic revolution must . . . summon a return to the beginning and a renewal of the covenant. This renewal . . . requires us [Iranians] to break the covenant that we acquiesced in regarding Westoxication [Weststruckness]. . . . [We] take refuge in God and ask Him for assistance in our renewed covenant, a covenant that is the future of mankind" (quoted in Vahdat 2002, 192).

The outlook presented by Mesbah Yazdi in Qom and Fardid and Davari in Tehran created a mentality that I call "hostage minds," and has helped the emergence of groups such as Hezbollah, the *Ansar-e Hezbollah* (Helpers of Hezbollah), and *Goruhaye Feshar* (Pressure Groups), which have penetrated all branches of government. They see themselves on the side of right and the rest of the world on the side of wrong. This is why the world has been against "the greatest event in contemporary human history" (Zarshenas 1373/1995, 5)—that is, the Islamic revolution, the only modern revolution that has resisted "implementing the political and social features of modern civilization" and is not following "the Satanic approaches of humanism and the Renaissance" (5). To preserve this revolution, all means are legitimized and accepted—elimination, assassination, the silencing of intellectuals, the closing of newspapers, and the burning of bookstores. When the bookstore *Morgh-e Amin* was burned down, one of the organs of the radical right group, *Sobh,* described it as a good thing and reported on a Hezbollah group that celebrated the event as having said, "We have gathered here to inform you that Hezbollah insists on its principles and takes pride in being fundamentalist. Hezbollah considers the enemy a permanent conspirator and faithfully insists on the validity of conspiracy theory" (*Sobh* 21, 14 Sharivar 1374/September 1995, 3).

Ironically, although these groups are antagonistic toward modernity, their convictions and behaviors resemble the major features of modernism. Table 3.2 puts their views in perspective and captures my narrative of the message of Islam and modernity, as well as the message of their degenerate forms—Islamism and modernism. I contend that the people and groups analyzed here think of both Islam and modernity as ideologies rather than as sophisticated bodies of thought and tradition. Both Islamism and modernism suffer from the intellectual poverty common to all ideologies. Fazlur Rahman's observation is to the point: "The greatest weakness of neo-revivalism, and the greatest disservice it has done to Islam, is an almost total lack of positive effective Islamic thinking and scholarship within its ranks, its intellectual bankruptcy, and its substitution of cliché mongering for serious intellectual endeavor" (Rahman 1982, 137).

TABLE 3.2. FUNCTIONAL COMPARISON OF ISLAM, ISLAMISM,
MODERNITY, AND MODERNISM

	Islam	Islamism	Modernity	Modernism
Paradigm	Faith	Tradition	Freedom	Power
Audience	Humanity	Exclusive group	Individual	State
Means	Conversion	Obedience	Reason	Rationality
End	Salvation	Homogenization	Emancipation	Gain

The society that these Islamists promise or have partly created in Iran is a peculiar one. First and foremost, the division between state and society is complete and total. "We" are the state and "they" are society, though the boundary may be more artificial than real. Such a generalization is allowable because those who make up the state pretend to be in one camp, whereas society members claim to be in another. The following anecdote may clarify this division. In 1994, I delivered a one-day seminar on development and nation building to a group of middle managers at the headquarters of Iranian Radio and Television. I argued that development is a national project that requires everyone to participate, just as a successful family involves all of its members. In the afternoon session, when many of "us" (members of the state apparatus) had not yet returned from lunch, a lady made the following comment: "I could never feel as though I were part of this family that you are talking about, because everyday I am accused of being either a terrorist or a thief." When I asked for clarification, she added, "Both my car and my person are searched in the morning because I might be carrying explosives for a possible terrorist activity, and searched again in the afternoon because I might be stealing something from the organization."

Second, pervasive duality has become the rule. The revolutionaries, particularly the Islamists, promised a puritan lifestyle of religiosity and commitment to an elevated life of the soul, yet they delivered a feigned life of what Iranian anthropologist Fatemeh Givechian calls "playing religion"—and ironically, they made it standard for all citizens. This includes those in high political and economic positions, even within the state. Officials compete among themselves to pretend to ever-greater religious commitment in order to protect their privileged positions.

However, maintaining this constant duality is exhausting and takes up an enormous energy that could be used to produce a dynamic and meaningful life. By making public life a vaudevillian drama, the

Islamists have turned most of the country's creative minds into foot soldiers of revolutionism and totalitarianism, or into isolated souls living either as passive spectators or as disdained second-class citizens preferring to live a degraded life outside of Iran. At the same time, just as modernism under the repressive Pahlavis did not succeed in undermining the process of genuine modernization, traditionalism and Islamism also are failing in many ways. A new wave of liberation and emancipation has grown from within and outside the camp of the Islamists. A new generation of Islam-minded Iranians able to rise above the game of "playing religion" has come to the fore. They have disenchanted themselves from the spells of traditional religious narratives. They dare to question the very basic tenets of the revolution, or even its religious foundation—Islam itself. This group constitutes the fourth generation of Islamic discourse in Iran, to which I will turn in the next chapter.

FOUR

THE FOURTH GENERATION

The Politics of Restoration, 1997–2005

Failing to reform traditional autocratic thinking, preventing the formation of an epistemology that strengthens democratic political structures, and emphasizing the preservation of traditional political structures—these are among the sources for generating violence in contemporary Muslim societies.

SHABESTARI, *NAQDI BAR QARA'AT RASMI AZ DIN: BOHRANYA, CHALESHHA, RAHHALHA* (A CRITIQUE OF THE OFFICIAL READING OF RELIGION: CRISIS, CHALLENGE, AND SOLUTIONS), 1381/2002

In late 1987, an official at the Institute for Political and International Studies, a think tank, asked me to help organize a conference on the ongoing Iran-Iraq War. When I agreed, I was invited to a meeting with a group of Iranian officials who were different from any I had encountered in various revolutionary institutions or in the public sphere. They were sophisticated and well versed in the intricacies of the international system. They knew that politics entails the art of give-and-take, and for them, accommodation and compromise were not dirty words, as they were for other revolutionaries. These people represented a new generation and a particular class. Interestingly, when the meetings dragged on until the time for daily prayers, the same sophisticated officials excused themselves for the ritual act of ablution and then lined up for the required prayers. I felt a holy aura replace the worldly, mundane, and secular atmosphere as these same protagonists displayed an enormous degree of religiosity. The paradox of the saint-merchant, the combination of idealism and realism, echoed in my head. This was very different from the stereotypes of "hostage takers," "the hanging judge," radicals, or violent extremists. For these people, there was a sophisticated relationship between religion and politics. Who were they, and where were they when the shah fell?

Some of them were very young during the revolution, and others were drunk on revolution, radicalism, and Islamism at that time. As they matured, they lost their revolutionary zeal, and those born years after the revolution grew up in a different world, one of globalization and interconnection. The youth who created "the epic of June 1997" for political reforms and who marched with student demonstrators make up this generation, which includes journalists and writers such as Abbas Abdi, Saeed Hajjarian, Akbar Ganji; educators such as Hashem Aghajari, Alireza Alavitabar, and Mohsen Kadivar; and politicians such as Mohammad Khatami and Mostafa Moein, who have suffered at the hands of Islamists.

No evidence, however, is more telling than the career and films of the celebrated Iranian filmmaker Mohsen Makhmalbaf (b. 1957). Born into a poor family from Tehran, Makhmalbaf was a classic recruit for the revolutionaries. After dropping out of school to join a militant group, he was arrested in 1974 for attempting to steal a policeman's gun, only to be shot and jailed until he was freed in the aftermath of the revolution. His 1996 film *Nun va Goldoon* (known in English as either *Bread and Flower* or *A Moment of Innocence*) not only captures this event, but also portrays the aforementioned generational metamorphosis. Revolutionary, activist, and extremist, young Makhmalbaf is helped by his relative's girlfriend, who is supposed to ask the policeman trivial questions to keep him occupied while Makhmalbaf stabs him and steals his gun. To help the girl gain confidence, she is instructed to go to the policeman a few times before the event is to occur. This makes the policeman think she likes him, and he prepares to offer her a small flower the next time around. Twenty years later, the matured revolutionary places an ad in the paper to recruit actors for his movie *Salaam Cinema* (1995). The old wounded policeman responds to the ad. In *Bread and Flower,* both the victim and the assailant are provided the chance to tell their sides of the story. The policeman hopes to relive his innocent first love, while Makhmalbaf tries to recapture the event, restating his current position that freedom and democracy are categories one must learn and live by, not categories to be implanted by a revolution. In the process, the policeman realizes that the girl was an accomplice, becomes enraged, and instructs the actor portraying his younger self (who is from the new Iranian generation) to use a real gun. The director wants the actor portraying his own younger self to reenact out the actual event and use the knife, hidden under the large Iranian flat bread. At the moment of truth, neither actor commits violence; instead, one offers the flower to the girl and the other offers the bread, hence the title of the movie.

While this film offers a symbolic version of the change among some members of the revolutionary generation in Iran, the election of President Khatami in the summer of 1997 was an example in reality. Dialogue and accommodation were to replace violence and revolutionary zeal. In a lecture on November 2, 1998, Khatami said, "The meaning of dialogue among civilizations is to sit together and, while relying on our commonalties, discuss our differences and use them for our evolution and progress." He proposed that the year 2001 be labeled "the year of dialogue between civilizations"—a title unanimously endorsed by the General Assembly of the United Nations on Wednesday, November 4, 1998. Ironically, November 4, 1979, was the day that Iranian revolutionary students, calling themselves "the followers of the line of the imam [Khomeini]," took American diplomats in Tehran hostage, violating diplomatic immunity, the most important rule of international law. Whether it was a coincidence that such a proposal was considered and approved on the day the American embassy was seized is incidental. What is important is the symbolic significance of confrontation being replaced by dialogue on the same day. What are the views of the fourth generation, which embraced this shift?

THE CONTEXT

The presidential election of June 1997 brought the left faction back to center stage, but it also did much more. The election marked a new phase in Islamic discourse. The new president, Mohammad Khatami, came to power as a result of an interesting alliance among the left, the modern right, and, most importantly, Iranian civil society, which had been expanding through the use of some of the products of globalization. Internally, the growth of civil society, a concern with material welfare, and a preoccupation with a complex, updated Iranian identity demanded a kind of politics different from the simple revolutionary posture of "us and them." Internationally, democratization, globalization, and the war against terrorism changed the inwardly focused politics of the developed world into a politics of global concern for ethics and human rights. Khatami came to power when the international context was conducive to the voices of moderation, dialogue, and tolerance. Intellectually, post-

Khomeini and post–Iran-Iraq War, serious debates were possible regarding the nature and place of religion in the public sphere.

The Internal Context: The Politics of Restoration

Iran's political condition in the 1990s was characterized by awe and shock. From 1982 to 1989, the left, as defined in the previous chapter, held positions of power, with Khomeini's blessing. Following Khomeini's death, an alliance of the modern right and the traditional right ruled, yet the implications of their governance were paradoxical. For one thing, this time, which saw the chain killings of intellectuals and the mass emigration of the Iranian middle class, marked one of the darkest periods of the Islamic revolution. However, such severe repression paved the way for the emergence of reform politics and the democratization of Iran's political language, discourse, and agenda. Under former president Rafsanjani (1989–1997), the modern right advocated economic development and practiced a neoliberal economics of reconstruction and adjustment. When Khatami served as the minister of Islamic guidance and culture, some degree of cultural openness and debate was encouraged, but this was disrupted when Khatami was removed as minister in 1992.

In the late 1990s, the left and Iranian civil society found each other and formed an unspoken alliance. The best example came from Khatami's interview with the influential magazine *Zanan* (Women) when he was a presidential candidate. At the same time, *Zanan* reported that the candidate for the conservative camp, Nateq Nuri, had refused an interview, an act that portrayed him as unfriendly to women's causes (*Zanan*, 34 Urdibehesht 1376/April 1997). The radical right's monthly *Sobh* described the interview with Khatami as "time wasted on insignificant issues" (*Sobh*, Khordad 1376/May 1997, 11). Iran watchers believed that this incident alone guaranteed women's votes for Khatami.

Some scholars of Iranian affairs have termed the period from 1997 to 2005 the era of lost hope for reforming the Islamic Republic and bringing it into line with international norms. The degree of lamentation and elegy for reform among commentators was amazing, but Saeed Hajjarian (one of the main proponents of democratization in Iran) made a much more insightful comment on what happened. At a youth summer camp hosted by the Participation Front Party, he said, "Reform is dead, long live reform." He made this comment more than a year before the parliamentary election of 2004, which brought a conservative majority to power. What did he mean by this statement? When one means of reform fails, another must be tried. As he said, "Look, we have the following options: (1) reform is dead, long live revolution [let's revert to revolutionary zeal]; (2) reform is dead, long live apathy and passivity; (3) reform is dead, long live reform of a different kind; (4) reform is dead, long live submission [to repression]; and (5) reform is dead, long live the hidden hand [American intervention]. Obviously, among the five alternatives, I prefer long live reform" (*Emruz*, 27 Tir 1383/July 20, 2004).

The new reform to which Hajjarian was referring did not mean turning away from religion, but rather making religion and modernity relevant. I should note that contemporary Iranian society in the postwar and post-Khomeini era is becoming interested in the modern form of secularity, just as Iranian society in the late nineteenth and early twentieth centuries did. As I suggested, this process began with the revolution of 1979, but war, revolutionary zeal, and traditionalism postponed it for more than a decade. The war caused an alliance of traditionalism and revolutionary zeal that gave rise to a culture of duality: right versus wrong, piety versus irreverence, and sacred versus profane. I remember teaching in Tehran and having difficulties with people who accused me of trying to water down the revolution by suggesting that moderation and compromise were the main components of political life; those people later turned up in the vanguard of the reform movement.

The postwar and post-Khomeini era, however, gave rise to a different discourse. Significantly, it was proved to many protagonists of the revolution that under the banner of "political Islam," one can only struggle, revolt, and fight wars; to create order, a different narrative of Islam was needed and with it, inevitably, a new kind of "religious intellectual." This development has been criticized as a turning away from religious symbols and toward the material world. As was shown in the previous chapter, the Islamists presuppose a sharp divide between the religious and the secular, a divide that both logic and history refute. If anything, the religious and secular domains have had to cooperate in all civilizational contexts. No civilizational milieu can afford either to isolate one from the other or to mix the institutions that deal with the two realms. The new protagonists of the Islamic discourse, the members of the fourth generation, seem to be quite aware of this nuanced relationship between the profane and the sacred. As I will show, it is not surprising that the voices of this phase are staunch supporters of religious and secular discourses simultaneously. After all, the age-old tradition in Islam that "the world is the cultivating ground for the hereafter" suggests that the path to salvation is to be found on earth.

The fourth generation held power from 1997 to 2005. The parliamentary election of February 20, 2004, and the presidential election of 2005 appear to have been setbacks for this coalition, but reforms continue nevertheless. Both votes, parliamentary and presidential, proved this. Voters favored the conservatives for Parliament, but by only a very slight margin, signalling that they did not completely share the conservatives' vision of society. Despite constant pleas for voters to turn out, they objected to the various institutions of the government being sympathetic to the conservatives, and so they took measures to help their favorite candidates. These institutions include the Expediency Council, the Council of Guardians, the Supreme Council for Culture, and the head of the judiciary. According to the recent report of Ambeyi Ligabo, the UN special rapporteur on the right to freedom of opinion and expression, these groups exercise "institutional locks on governmental, parliamentary, and judicial processes" (Ligabo 2004, 23–24). As a result, out of 8,200 hopefuls who registered as candidates, only 4,446 competed for 289 seats (for one, representing the earthquake-stricken city of Bam, no election was held). A new coalition took the majority of the seats in Parliament, with 50.57 percent of the votes. The coalition calls itself *Abadgaran Iran-e Islami* (the Developers of Islamic Iran). It has secured the support of conservative clerics, radical student organizations, radical groups of war veterans, and many traditional and radical associations.

This victory makes more sense if it is contextualized within the factional politics of Iran. Despite a formal ban on the activities of all political parties, postwar and post-Khomeini Iran experienced fierce factional politics. The reform movement of the mid-1990s made this factionalism even more intense. Figure 4.1 captures the political factions in Iran today. Those represented on the left side of the figure put forth a narrative of Islam that justifies repression and extremism, while those on the right side represent "a humanist and rational" understanding of it (Ganji 1379/2000b, 194–195). The former sees politics as a war wherein one side must be eliminated. The pages of the daily *Keyhan,* for example, propagate such an understanding of politics. As editor Hossein Shari'atmadari wrote: "In political science, the arena for competition between two rivals is compared with a one-lane road on which both sides are driving toward each other. Because there is no space for them to pass, one must be eliminated. Men of politics believe that the winner is the one who is not afraid to crash, and would even throw away the steering wheel to demonstrate that he has no intention of giving way" (22 Tir 1378/July 12,

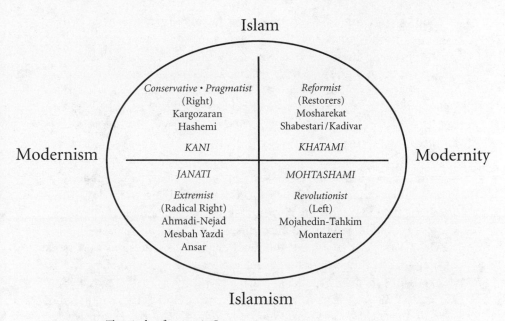

FIGURE 4.1. The circle of power in Iran

1999). These four groups have dominated Iranian politics since Khomeini's death. The election of the Fifth Parliament (1996) proved significant. While it brought to power an interesting coalition of moderate conservatives and reformers, it also allowed for the emergence of the radical right. Thus a double process has unfolded since that election.

As far as its bearing on the reform movement and democratization, political participation has increased enormously. One can refer to the burgeoning of civil-society organizations, women's movements, and environmental activism as examples, but most notable is what Iranian scholar Mehrdad Mashayekhi accurately called "the revival of the student movement," which has made the universities in Iran once more the most important centers of dissent (Mashayekhi 2001, 283–313). As has been the tradition, the voice of dissent began at Tehran University; in July 1999, students demonstrated against a restrictive press bill and the closure of the daily *Salam*. The situation worsened when the police aided and abetted the sometimes fatal attacks on students by Ansar-e Hizbollah vigilante thugs. For six days students confronted the police and antiriot forces, and those clashes, along with subsequent demonstrations in other cities, led to the arrest of "1,500 students and young activists" (284). The situation deteriorated further when the Islamic Revolutionary Guards Corps threatened to take matters into its own hands; there were mass arrests, televised confessions, and eventually a judicial whitewash.

The forces of repression received encouragement when a letter from the Supreme Leader Ayatollah Ali Khamenei was read in the Parliament, instructing the representatives not to debate new press laws in August 2000. Soon, (on April 23–24, 2001) fourteen proreform papers were banned. But the saga continued, more papers were published, and the people found alternative means of expression. For example, when, on November 6, 2002, university professor Hashem Aghajari was sentenced to lashes, imprisonment, and death for a speech made the previous June attacking the monolithic official understanding of Islam, public reaction led to the reduction of his sentence and, in July 2004, his release.

The politics of the left and the reformers led to enormous openness in society regarding politics, culture, society, and foreign policy. It was then possible to openly challenge the very legitimacy of the regime.[1] The most extreme example was the vociferous works of Akbar Ganji, who became the most controversial figure among the reformers and whose works became best-sellers. In his books, he advocated absolute openness in politics and revealed many of the behind-the-scenes dealings and alliances made by what he called "autocrats" (*eqtedargarayan*) in Iran (Ganji 1379/2000a and 1379/2000b). He got into trouble for challenging the powerful Rafsanjani and served a long prison sentence before he was freed, but even from inside the notorious Evin Prison, he declared that an Islamic republican government was no longer possible. He smuggled out his *Manifest-e Humherikhani* (Manifesto of Republicanism), which was widely distributed across the Internet. This is an important indicator because Ganji was an official in the Ministry of Islamic Guidance and Culture before becoming a journalist. He then helped disseminate Soroush's ideas, founded the journal *Rah-e No* (The New Way, published for more than two years), and became one of Iran's most powerful voices of reform and political development. In the end, he parted ways with the reformers by declaring the impossibility of creating an Islamic republic.

According to Ganji, "republic" and "Islamic" are contradictory terms because, first and foremost, republicanism begins with the understanding that it is impossible to perfect human beings. As he writes, in a republican frame of mind, "not only is man incomplete, but all humans are completely earthly and thus susceptible to error" (Ganji 1381/2002, 6). At the same time, republican systems "are based on human rights . . . and republican regimes are proper for the 'rights-bound man' (*ensan-e moheq*), whereas absolutist states are proper for the 'duty-bound man' (*ensan-e mokalaf*)" (6). The notion of the "rights-bound man" entails free will and the availability of choices for members of society, including the choice to accept or refuse belief and faith—an idea that even the proponents of liberal Islam do not approve of or tolerate (17). Second, the republican idea is based on the equality of citizens, regardless of ideological considerations, social status, or profession (12, 14, 16). While it is possible to combine Islam and democratic dispositions in the abstract and in theory, within the framework of the Islamic Republic's constitution, "there is no possibility for establishing a democratic regime" because the society is based on and recognizes a hierarchical order of citizens, with supremacy accorded to the religious establishment (20). In short, in a society in which one person "is free" while all others are "subjects," true democracy is impossible (31).

Is it possible to have a secular republic in Iran? Ganji treats this question in the rest of his manifesto. Based on historical evolution in Iran, demographic changes in the country, and the failure of the economic, cultural, and social policies of the past twenty years, both the volition and the potential exist for the implementation of a republican regime (37–40). Ganji claims that he has written this manifesto "for the new generation" (41), though I doubt the new generation is ready to abandon religion altogether. My biggest problem with Ganji's manifesto is that he is as extreme as his radical opponents. He also sees the world in terms of "us" and "them," with no middle ground for compromise: "The project of rationality is an all-or-nothing. It is not for the defense or support of a particular position but rather for the evaluation and analysis of any" (27). This position is too rigid and idealistic and removes his ideas from the context of an Islamic discourse. However, his presentation indicates how serious the debate about the place of religion in politics has become in Iran. There is no longer a vertical relation between men of power and revolution and the members of society at large; the marketplace of ideas and debate has been turned into public property.

Another factor that has made the idea of reform an almost irreversible process may be termed "the changing demands and expectations" of the very same people who, in their leader's words, "had not revolted for a reduction in the price of watermelon" (Khomeini 1361/1982, 9:469). The mid-twentieth-century global concern for the future and the pressures of daily life hit the revolutionary corps and members of the Islamic movement hard. University degrees, higher education, technical skills, and a welfare-state orientation found their way into the psyche of the revolutionaries, who were now beginning to reach their thirties and even to experience midlife crises. The presence of a large number of young people in Iran and the growing women's movement accelerated this change and played a significant role in setting the political agenda for the fourth generation. The new revolutionary government had encouraged rapid population growth. After the population increased dramatically in the 1980s (an average annual increase of 3.6 percent for the years 1979–1988), however, this policy was reversed, and there was a significant reduction in the rate of population growth in the 1990s (to 1.5 percent annually from 1989 to 1998). Iran's population explosion—the population almost doubled between 1979 and 2001—has placed great demands on the economy. This pressure is evident in the infrastructure (with shortages of electricity, oil, water, and housing), education, health, and the workforce. Creating gainful employment for the country's youth has been and will continue to be the major challenge for Iran in the first decade of the twenty-first century and beyond.

Related to this development is the quality of population growth. While those familiar with Iran may argue that the population has always been young, there have nevertheless been qualitative changes. It is true that the proportion of youth in the population has not changed. People thirty years and younger constituted 65.6 percent of Iran's population in 1946, and in 1996 the percentage was 67.9 percent (Abdi and Gudarzi 1378/1999, 11). Though the quantitative difference has not been significant, qualitatively this population is now more educated, urbanized, politically conscious, and modernized, either because of or despite the Islamic Republic, and, more importantly, it is preoccupied with such notions as quality of life, satisfaction, social mobility, and economic and political participation (153–225). These youth are urbanized, interested in the politics of accommodation, and willing to express demands for gender equality, democracy, accountability, and participation.

There is enormous pressure on the state to observe due process in judicial proceedings. The case of Iranian Canadian freelance photographer Zahra Kazemi, who died while in custody, dragged on mainly because of pressure from certain elements in the Iranian government and civil society, though international pressure helped as well. On June 23, 2003, Kazemi was detained while taking photographs outside Evin Prison. She was killed while being interrogated by the local police, the judiciary, and the intelligence ministry, but officials claimed she died of a stroke. Had this case occurred ten years earlier, the story would have ended. In 2003, however, Khatami ordered an investigation, which revealed she had died not from stroke but as a result of a "brain hemorrhage caused by a beating." The reformers pointed a finger at Saeed Mortazavi, a prominent judge in the judiciary, and a parliamentary investigation reported that Mortazavi had both played a role and engaged in a cover-up. Iranian activist lawyers, aided by an international outcry over the murder, intensified their campaign. The judiciary in turned charged a Ministry of Intelligence official, who was acquitted by the court on July 24, 2004, and the matter was declared closed. But the saga continued because an alliance of Iranian civil society and reformers within the state continued to ask for justice. The reformist president and Kazemi's team of activist lawyers, headed by Nobel laureate Shirin Ebadi, called for a new trial.

The International Context: Globalization and Postmodernity

Along with these internal developments, there was enormous change externally in the 1990s, both quantitative and qualitative, generally related to the condition of globalization. What does globalization mean? The following e-mail I recently received may provide some clues:

> Q: What is the height of globalization?
> A: Princess Diana's death.
> Q: How so?
> A: An English princess with an Egyptian boyfriend crashes in a French tunnel, driving a German car with a Dutch engine driven by a Belgian who was high on Scottish whiskey, followed closely by Italian Paparazzi on Japanese motorcycles, treated by an American doctor, using Brazilian medicines. And this [e-mail] is sent to you by an American, using Bill Gates' technology, which he got from the Japanese. And you are probably reading this on one of the IBM clones that use Philippine-made chips and Korean-made monitors [that were] assembled by Bangladesh workers in a Singapore plant, transported by Lorries driven by Indians hijacked by Indonesians and finally sold to you by a Chinese salesman in a store owned by a Jewish guy!

The passage conveys a feature that I call the world of "one civilization, many cultures." It is a new civilization of technological communication and information processing, wherein there is a possibility of expressing the multiplicity of human cultures.

This in turn has given rise to plurality and multiculturalism, something modern processes and the industrial revolution did not provide.

Like all civilizational processes, technology allows for "opportunities and presents dangers. It helps us to discover the unknown by opening new horizons. But it also threatens to shake the foundations of our known world. It is up to humanity to act responsively and proactively" (Rajaee 2000, 131). The indiscriminate empowerment that technology has caused is unprecedented in human history. The tragic events of September 11, 2001, for example, would not have been possible without globalization, but just as globalization has enabled international terrorism, it has connected all parts of the world, facilitating global debate and creating new arenas for civil interaction. As far as this discussion is concerned, the most important consequence of these developments is the disruption of the Eurocentric system and the delegitimization of its foundations. Many conscious thinkers have questioned the one-dimensional nature of the dominant system, but now it has become self-evident. The postcolonial postindustrial postmodern poststructural post–Cold War world has had to accept the horizontal voices—something that could not even have been imagined a few decades earlier. The politics of "us and them" have been replaced with the global politics of earth-ship and the inclusion of humanity as a whole.

Regarding regional politics, on both sides of Iran the political conditions have become volatile. In Afghanistan, Muslim warriors backed by Western powers defeated the Soviet Union, quickly making that country a hotbed of Muslim radicalism and militancy. But when the Western alliance destroyed that regime, even the radical leader and head of the Organization for the Propagation of Islam in Iran at the time, Ahmad Janati, referred to the Taliban as fundamentalists. On the eastern side of Iran, the Iraqi invasion of Kuwait led to an American presence in the region, which had contradictory results. The U.S. presence helped moderate many elements, but it also aggravated the more radical forces into asserting "the Satanic nature of the West and its allies."

The Intellectual Context: Democratization and Civil Society

Iran's 1996 parliamentary election and 1997 presidential election were committed to reform and democratization, but they did not occur in a vacuum. In a way, both the reformist Parliament and the liberal president should be considered the voices that had demanded reform a decade earlier. The enormous intellectual dynamism of the 1990s led to complicated and paradoxical results. Such issues as the meaning and purpose of economic development, environmentalism, women's rights, children's rights, freedom of the press, and political participation were just some of the issues that preoccupied concerned minds and covered the pages of popular journals and magazines such as *Farhang va Tose'e* (Culture and Development), *Iran Farda* (Tomorrow's Iran), and *Zanan* (Women) as well as journals that were directly published by government agencies, such as *Keyhan-e Farhangi* (Cultural Weekly, published by the *Keyhan* newspaper) and *Name-ye Farhang* (The Journal of Culture). Here I am more concerned with the intellectual trends that influenced Islamic discourse and informed ideas than with Islamic vocabulary and cosmology. Many publications could be mentioned here, such as the daily *Salam,* which continued until 1999 and became the voice of Iranian civil society, as well as *Hamshahri, Iran, Bayan, Payam Daneshjju, Asr-e Ma,* and *Kiyan.* No other issue preoccupied Islam-minded Iranians more than the question of the meaning of Islam in the contemporary world, and no journal's content was more important than that of the newly published *Kiyan.*

When the conservative wave hit in the early 1990s, the dynamic young group that published *Keyhan-e Farhangi* was sacked. They were not discouraged, however, and moved on to found *Kiyan* as a forum for discussing religious reforms. The journal had a fruitful life for a decade before being banned in 2001. In its active existence, it covered all aspects of intellectual life and allowed for diverse views, including some from outside Iran. But what is most relevant here is the notion of religious pluralism, one of the main preoccupations of the fourth generation in Islamic discourse. While the official line in the Islamic Republic has maintained that there is one way to understand and implement religious precepts—the voice of the guardianship jurisconsult, epitomized in the slogan *Marg bar Zed-e Velayat-e Faqih* (Death to those who are against the guardianship of the jurisconsult)—*Kiyan* advocated religious tolerance and pluralism. In every issue, there was some sort of discussion about this question, but here I will say a few words about one issue dedicated to "religion, tolerance and violence" (volume 8, number 45, February–March 1999). It aired the views of not only Abdolkarim Soroush, Mohsen Kadivar, Mohammad Shabestari, Saeed Hajjarian, Emadoddin Baqi, Alireza Alavitabar, Dariush Shayegan, and Baha'odin Khoramshahi, but also of many dissidents, including Ayatollah Montazeri, Hassan Yusefi Eshkevari, Mehrangiz Kar, and Abdolali Bazargan from Iran; Mohammad Ali Katouzian, Mohammad Reza Nikfar, and Farhad Khosrokhavar from Europe; and Seyyed Hossein Nasr and Hamid Dabashi from the United States.

The main message was that there are two types of discourse, one based on dialogue (*mokaleme*), associated with language and communication, and the other based on conflict (*monaze'e*), associated with violence and strife. What kinds of discourse do religions encourage? The crux of the answer is that "logically, no reading of religion necessarily leads to violence, but some narratives may pave the way for it" (95). Do the authors mean to say that the more fundamentalist narratives pave the way for violence? The answer appears to be yes, but it is interesting that another contributor dismisses this assertion: "Logically there is no inevitability between absolutism and the infliction of violence. People can hold that the truth is with them and yet avoid violence. And if you ask how this can be possible, my answer lies in accepting 'the right of others to be wrong.' Even divine religions recognize this right. . . . And historically there were many who believed that they had the truth and yet did not exercise violence" (112). In short, the prevalence of violence has causes other than religion, and those narratives that advocate violence have been influenced by structural and historical causes. To deal with their ontological crises and existential predicaments, the people of subjugated regions have developed a mentality that may be called a "hostage mind": a state of constant paranoia in which the world is seen in terms of absolute right and wrong. This mindset turns their indigenous cultural forces into ideologies, and this in turn encourages confrontation and violence. As one contributor, Hajjarian, put it, "The text has no voice of its own; it is indeed the context that brings the text to life" (103).

While *Kiyan* voiced the more abstract ideas and the higher intellectual discourse, there were other publications that related the intellectual debates to political and practical measures. One was an influential bi-weekly called *Asr-e Ma* (Our Time, began publication in 1994), which identified itself in its first issue as a sociopolitical publication with the aim of promoting "political participation" and enhancing people's right "to determine their own fate," since these rights constitute "the most significant foundation of any free, progressive, and developed society" (27 Mehr 1373/October 1994, 1). To ensure that they remained loyal citizens and affirmed the principles of the revolution, the contributors constantly reiterated the main features of Islamic discourse, yet interpreted them within the context of liberal and democratic attitudes. Criticizing the libertarian economic policies of the Rafsanjani's presidency, they argued that one cannot follow liberal measures in economics while practicing Stalinism in culture and politics. In their minds, only people's participation can guarantee the continuation and moral authority of an

Islamic system. But they distinguish between mobilization and participation, arguing that there are fascist regimes that mobilize the people,
but that does not mean "people take part in any decision-making process" (23 Azar 1373/December 1994, 5).

Interestingly, in a discussion in the same issue about "religious leadership and political authority," they argue that "having religious leadership and political authority combined in the theory of 'the guardianship
of the jurisconsult' represents an ideal type that has happened only
during the life of the Prophet (may peace be upon him) and the imams
(blessings to them) and would be possible again only at the end of time"
(4). While accepting the theoretical validity of Khomeini's theory, they
wanted to postpone its implementation to an indefinite future. For this
publication, the ultimate and ideal regime amounted to an Islamic Republic that could truly combine both Islam and republicanism: "In other
words, republicanism should be conditioned with a narrative of Islam
that accepts the legitimacy of the will and the vote of the people either
directly in the laws or indirectly through associations and councils" (16
Farvardin 1374/April 1995, 6).

THE VOICES

Who is in this new generation? Many groups and a host of individuals
come to mind: names such as Ayatollah Yusuf Sane'i, Abdollah Nuri,
Hadi Khamenei, former hostage-taker Abbas Abdi, Mohsen Mirdamadi,
Monireh Gorji, and Masoumeh Ebtekar; such educators as Hashem
Aghajari, Elaheh Koolaee, Alireza Alavitabar, Ayatollah Mustafa Mo-
haqeqdamad, and Yusef Eshkavari, to cite just a few. In another context
I have called them "the Islamic yuppies" (Rajaee 1999, 217–231) because
their aptitudes, ideals, and praxis display an amphibious nature: they are
at home with Islamic vocabularies, mores, and traditions when they find
themselves in a traditional Muslim context, such as a mosque, a hosseiniye, or a traditional ceremony; when they find themselves in a modern milieu, however, they are at home with the intricacies and mores of
modernity and even postmodernity. They recognize and appreciate the
achievements of modernity just as they appreciate the intrinsic values of
their religious tradition. They do not reduce modernity to the applied
sciences and technology, nor do they reduce Islam to an ideology of
power. There has been a major paradigm shift in their minds about the
role of the intellectual.

Makhmalbaf's depiction of intellectuals in Iran is very telling and relevant here, and it effectively summarizes the views of the fourth generation. According to him, there are two kinds of intellectuals: "One is Mirza Reza Kermani, who took arms and killed Naseredin Shah [in 1896] without thinking what would be the consequence. This has been the most powerful trend in Iran. . . . The other intellectual type is Amir Kabir, who established *Dar al-Fonun* [School], a place for thinking. He was concerned with institutionalizing the foundation of democracy, unlike Kermani, who unintentionally paved the way for fascism. . . . With guns one can only fight where there remains no place for any form of dialogue" (quoted in Golmakani 1377/1999, 195).

This new generation is opting for dialogue over guns. It displays enormous confidence and actively presents its narratives of both modernity and religion, completely aware of the challenges involved in making tradition relevant in a globalized world. Furthermore, it appreciates modern achievements and strives to blend religion and modernity in order to formulate a new paradigm for the future of the Muslim world. For example, one of the voices, Mohsen Kadivar, openly states the following: "I want to remain Muslim and live as a participant in the globalized world. [To do that], I feel I have a right to present a contemporary narrative of Islam and [the legacy] of the Prophet" (2004, interview). As has been the practice thus far, I will look at some of the major voices in the Islam of Qom and the Islam of Tehran.

The Islam of Qom: Montazeri and Kadivar

There is an assumption that Qom is a bastion of religious and cultural conservatism. The revolutionary spirit of the third generation proved true to the original and literal sense of the word "revolution" in that it wanted society to revert to an understanding of the nature of power and authority based on traditional Islamic political thought. While the notion of post-Islamism in Qom thus appears to be a contradiction in terms, in reality the situation in Qom is much more ironic and paradoxical. It is important to note that in the February 2004 parliamentary elections, Qom's level of participation decreased by close to 16 percent from the time of the election of the Sixth Parliament, four years earlier, when the reformers gained an absolute majority. Moreover, the most powerful internal voice of dissent—that of Ayatollah Hossein-Ali Montazeri—comes from Qom. Here I concentrate on him and one of his students, Mohsen Kadivar.

HOSSEIN-ALI MONTAZERI NAJAF-ABADI

Montazeri is now considered the highest-ranking religious dissident in Iran. He was under house arrest in Qom for five years (1997–2003) for calling into question Khamenei's authority. Montazeri considers the members of the clergy class to be grand patriarchs, so their main job should always be guardianship and supervision. In many ways, he echoes traditional ideas about leaders acting as arbiters rather than rulers. This ran contrary to the views of Khamenei, who considered the jurist to be the absolute ruler. So the authorities dealt with Montazeri indirectly: approving attacks on his residence by Ansar-e Hizbollah mobs and then formally restricting his movements.

However, it was not always so: Montazeri was once Khomeini's right-hand man, one of the old revolutionaries in the Islamic movement. He was responsible for framing the position of the guardianship jurisconsult within the Iranian constitution (Montazeri 2004, interview). He was Khomeini's designated successor, and in fact, the Assembly of Experts chose him for the position within the stipulation of Article 107 in November 1985. He is an enlightened soul, and in some ways modern, but a firm believer in the traditional and juridical narrative of Islam.[2] To be fair, while Montazeri believes that it is possible to have the rule of the jurist, he thinks the position should be limited and accountable, and thus he objected to some of Khomeini's policies, leading him to resign from his post as successor in March 1989.[3]

Hossein-Ali Montazeri Najaf-Abadi was born in 1922 in Najafabad, near Isfahan. His father was a farmer who also acted as the spiritual and religious leader of the neighborhood (Izadi 1359/1980, 25). He began his early studies with his father, but at the age of eight traveled to Isfahan to continue his schooling. He later traveled to Burujerd to study with Ayatollah Burujerdi, and then took up residence in Qom (30). Montazeri there discovered Khomeini and remained loyal to him until the end, even lobbying for Khomeini's leadership of the Shi'i community, particularly after Burujerdi died, in 1961, and very openly after Hakim died, in 1970 (40). He was arrested many times for his opposition to the shah's regime and was either jailed or exiled to various Iranian cities, the first time in 1963 and the last in 1975, when he was imprisoned for a ten-year term. He was freed in October 1978 as a result of mounting international pressure and the revolutionary atmosphere (106). After the revolution, he was elected a member of the Assembly of Experts, which was formulating the new constitution, and was even elected head of the assembly. In 1980 he was appointed leader of the Friday prayers in Tehran (143). His

loyalty for Khomeini was returned when the latter declared him his deputy as early as 1970 (see Khomeini's letter on 41). Their relations turned
sour in the last days of Khomeini's life, resulting in Montazeri's resigna-
tion and turning him into a political dissident to this day.

As I have noted, Montazeri is responsible for incorporating the notion
of the rule of the jurist into the present constitution of Iran. I repeat this
point because he is out of favor with the clerical establishment precisely
for opposing the absolute rule of the same jurist. How could he be condemned for opposing something that he himself is responsible for incorporating into the constitution? It became a bigger puzzle when I met
Montazeri in May 2004. He was very friendly and free from any of the
self-righteous attitudes associated with those who consider themselves
the possessors of the "truth of religion." I noticed how modern he was in
his personal traits, how respectful of individual rights, how free-spirited,
how open to debate, and how ready to listen. But in his approach to Islam,
he has remained loyal to the country's juridical narrative, and thus he
approves of the rule of jurist, but insists on its moderate implementation,
conditioned by its accountability to the people's welfare. For Khomeini
and his followers (as was shown in the case of Mesbah Yazdi), the jurist
is directly appointed by God through the Prophet and the imams, while
for Montazeri, he should be elected. In other words, for the more authoritative narrative of Islam in Iran, the rule of the clergy is summarized as
"the absolute and appointed guardianship of the jurisconsult" (*Velayat-e
Entesabi-ye Montasab-e Faqih*). His authority is absolute, people have
little to do with his selection, and he must be from the clerical establishment. Montazeri accepts the general theory that the leader of an Islamic
state must be a member of the clergy, but he does not accept either that
his authority is absolute or that his appointment is predetermined.

To select the ruler, Montazeri opts for election by the people from
among a multiplicity of qualified jurists. First, he refuses the interpretation given to the traditions of the infallible imams by people like Mesbah
Yazdi. The most famous is the tradition known as *Maqbule-ye Hanzaleh,*
according to which people should refer their questions and problems to
the jurists, now that the infallible imams are not present in the world. As
shown in the previous chapters, starting with Khomeini, this tradition
was invoked to justify the political authority of the jurists. Once one at-
tains the qualifications of a jurist, he has automatically obtained authority over the life and possessions of all Muslims. For Montazeri, this is not
so. The position the tradition permits is that of a judge. He refers to the
precedent of historical Shi'ism, in which this tradition was invoked to

establish the legal and judicial authority of the jurists with no reference to any broad political authority: "The authority of the jurists is not a new issue that contemporary religious scholars have introduced" (Montazeri 1379/2000, 22). What is new is that its application to actual situations has been broadened to justify the political dominance of the clerical class. Montazeri corrects this broadened scope, arguing that even if "the appearance of a tradition implies designation, it is necessary to interpret it as a mere 'declaration of qualification' (*bayan-e salahiyat*) of the ruler and not the actual designation of [any person to] the position, because the latter happens only with the consent of the people" (234).

This analysis is rather nuanced. When Montazeri accepts that the position of authority and rule belongs to Muslim jurists, he remains in the traditionalist camp. He reasons along the same lines as other jurists, i.e., that society requires leadership. Muslim law has not neglected this important dimension. The Prophet and the infallible imams served as early leaders. They in turn did not neglect the ongoing good of the community, so they listed the qualifications of the person who is potentially to assume that role. Montazeri invokes a variety of traditions to prove this position (248–250). Two broad consequences follow from this line of reasoning.

First, for the proponents of jurists' absolute authority, the nature of leadership is a religious issue, and the designation of a leader happens through a religious edict issued by the divine; in Montazeri's theory, the actual implementation of political authority is tantamount to a binding contract. He turns the political theory of Shi'ism into that of the caliphate, as developed by Sunni jurists, who maintain that the question of leadership is a contractual matter between the ruler and the ruled. For them, the position is one of deputyship of the Prophet, and the person who strives to assume that responsibility must enjoy certain qualifications; most importantly, he should gain the support of the community. The difference is that in the Islamic Republic, the jurists would act as the deputies of the imams. Like the caliphs, according to Montazeri, the jurists must secure their position with the consent of the people. In this way, the government would reflect a religious treaty between the people and the sovereign.

Montazeri devotes the second volume of his six-volume work on Islamic government to the notion of leadership and the various dimensions of its contract. Chapters 4 through 11 contain a detailed discussion of the qualifications of the jurists (33–140). They are as follows: wisdom and common sense, faith and religiosity, righteousness, scholarship and jurisprudence, statesmanship, good habits, being of the male gender, and purity of birth. They are similar to the qualifications of the caliph as outlined by Al-Mawardi, the founder of the Sunni theory of the caliphate. Also, they reflect the traditional way of understanding politics, whereby politics was basically preoccupied with and responded to the question of "who should rule" rather than the modern question of "how to rule."

Montazeri concentrates on the first question, dealing not only with the qualifications of the ruler but also with the process by which such a ruler should be instituted. He suggests that there are only two ways to do this. One, designation, turns the state into a theocracy. In it, authority is vertically assigned to the person appointed by God and then through his deputies. The other way is a consequence of the belief that "the Islamic community in general possesses supremacy, power, and real sovereignty, while 'the will of the people who loose and bind' [the elite] embody the supremacy of the community" (190). Theoretically, the people decide who should rule. According to Montazeri, the preferable alternative is to combine the two positions, particularly at this juncture in human history, when there is no direct access to the divine.

In other words, Montazeri assigns an important role to the people, an act that could be categorized as democratic, but he recognizes and advocates roles conditionally. In the final analysis, people have the authority to decide who the ruler will be, though they are required to choose from among qualified jurists (202). People can choose the best from a group of good candidates, but they cannot decide on the nature of the good. Only God and his infallible representatives can do so: "The imams (may peace be upon them) have recommended the jurists for assuming this role [of leadership], so the community may not choose others" (202).

Montazeri devotes Chapter 3 of his volume (213–281) to the reasons why the imams recommended that the ruler be chosen from among the jurists. Ironically, the traditions of the Prophet and the imams and the verses of the Qur'an that he invokes to prove the legitimacy of the jurists as candidates are the same as those invoked by the authoritative narrative of Islam to establish their right to rule. Montazeri interprets the same traditions differently: "To conclude [that the traditions and verses imply] the automatic appointment and installment of the jurist as the leader is not accurate . . . but to read these texts in order to establish that the jurists are the most qualified (*aslahiyat*) and that they have priority over others for assuming the position [of leadership] is quite accurate" (280–281).

The second consequence of Montazeri's contractual vision of government is that the agreement becomes invalid if and when the rulers fail to live up to their qualifications: "The members of the community impart the responsibility of guardianship to someone by volition, but they remain accountable for its protection and proper implementation. . . . In case the elected ruler lacks the leadership qualities or does not perform his duties properly . . . they will discharge him from the position of authority" (204). In other words, only the rulers' qualifications are decided a priori; all other terms and conditions of the contract, such as the duration of tenure and the extent of power, are to be outlined in a binding constitution.

Thus, the resulting government would not have absolute authority. And since people are the final source of all decisions, the democratic feature is guaranteed. Montazeri outlines many reasons for such a claim in Chapter 4 (283–304), the most important being that God has granted man the power of reason so that he can choose the best path (284). On the same page, he invokes the following verse to maintain that man is endowed with the rational ability to choose: "Offer the news . . . and those who listen would follow the best of it" (Qur'an 39:17–18). This implies that man has the ability to know the difference between better and worse choices and to exercise the will to choose one way or another. Second, to affirm that no political decision should be taken without the active participation of the people, Montazeri invokes the famous Qur'anic verse "in affairs take councils among you" (42:38) as well as the prophetic traditions relating to consultation (286–292). Third, he suggests that a number of Qur'anic verses clearly appoint man as God's successor (*khalifa*) on earth (2:30, 11:61, 29:55, 27:62, 35:39, and 38:26), without specifying any particular person to be sovereign over another (292–295). Once again, it is the people who decide how much power the ruler should possess and for what purpose that power should be wielded, provided the procedure is followed within the guidelines of Islamic jurisprudence. Thus, Montazeri's ideal polity is democratic insofar as the people actively participate in choosing the leader, and it is Muslim in its foundation and guiding principles. Nevertheless, Montazeri remained loyal to Khomeini's theory, which, according to him, began with the hope of combining theocracy with democracy, though it regularly favored the first over the second.

If one claims that this is a contradiction because Islam and republicanism cannot be combined, one might easily fall into essentializing both; however, criticizing Montazeri's position for being too idealistic is justified. Indeed, when I questioned Montazeri about the possibility of abuse and about how to guarantee the functionality of his system, he placed the responsibility of oversight on the clerical establishment itself, based on the following tradition from Imam Ali: "The clergy rule over the rulers and the rulers rule over the people." In other words, the religious establishment would and should act as guardian, but when I asked, "Who guards the guardians?" he dismissed the question by claiming that a true Muslim cannot undermine respect for human rights and dignity, implying that those who rule Iran today are not good Muslims. When I pressed him further for practical ways for guaranteeing the working of "Islam and democracy," he suggested two mechanisms. First, the leader should be assigned a limited term, and second, political parties and the media should play an active role (2004, interview). In many ways, Montazeri displays good intentions, but he remains loyal to the traditional understanding of Islam, failing to take the leap to a postmodern reading of his religion. He has contributed to that process, however, through his most influential student in Iran today, Mohsen Kadivar.

MOHSEN KADIVAR

Kadivar was born in 1959 into an enlightened family in the small town of Fassa, near Shiraz, in the southwestern province of Fars. His father was a law school graduate, and his mother was a high school teacher. As Kadivar told me with special emphasis, they "had a newspaper subscription" when he was growing up (2004, interview). He also mentioned that he had inherited his father's rationalism, concern with freedom, and religiosity, though this inheritance was indirect—people like Bazargan and Taleqani had influenced his father enormously. Although he did his undergraduate studies in electrical engineering and electronics, he joined a seminary in Shiraz in 1980 and later the clerical establishment, despite initial disapproval from his family. "My father did not agree with me joining the clerical establishment," he told me. "But when I was thrown in jail, he came to visit me all the way from Fassa, despite being frail and elderly, only to tell me that now he understood what I had been up to."

In 1981, Kadivar moved to Qom, where he studied jurisprudence, philosophy, theology, mysticism, and Qur'anic interpretation for seventeen years (Rudi-Kadivar 1379/2000, 19). While he enjoyed the lectures and seminars of many contemporary masters, he became Montazeri's special student. He attained the highest status of religious learning and received permission from him to exercise independent reasoning (*ijtihad*) in 1997. Meanwhile, Kadivar also attended the University of Tarbiyat-e Moddares, changing his field of studies from electronics to humanities and obtaining a PhD in philosophy in 1999. Concomitantly, he was lecturing on jurisprudence, philosophy, logic, and Qur'anic interpretation at Qom Seminary as well as at Imam Sadeq, Mofid, and Shahid Beheshti universities. Kadivar considers his field of studies and scholarship to be multidisciplinary and has diversified into such areas as Islamic political thought and public law in Islam. He is currently a faculty member of the Department of Philosophy at the University of Tarbiyat-e Moddares.

Kadivar is a public intellectual, publishing many articles and academic papers in various Iranian journals. He has also published more than a dozen books; the first, entitled *Nazareye-haye Dolat dar Fiqh-e Shi'a* (Theories of State in Shi'i Jurisprudence), appeared in 1998. Kadivar was arrested and jailed in 1978 before the revolution, and again in 1999, when the *Dadgah-e Vizhe-ye Rohaniyat* (Special Court for the Clergy) sentenced him to eighteen months for asserting that Islam and democracy could reinforce each other. A taboo breaker unafraid to challenge prevailing traditionalist views, Kadivar has become a vocal advocate of reconciling Islamic traditions and modern democracy. He says, "We cannot use the prevalent historicist interpretation of religion in the modern world" (Kadivar 1378/1999, 20). Although many Muslim intellectuals in positions like his choose to don civilian attire, he continues to wear his clerical robes in order to show that it is possible to be a Muslim, even a "professional one," and a democrat at the same time. How does he propose to show the congruency of Islam and democracy?

As far as his views and practices, in addition to following his teacher's approaches, Kadivar claims he has tried to combine "the schools Ayatollahs Burujerdi, Abolqasem Khoei [d. 1992], and Muhammad Baqir Sadr [d. 1980]" (21–22).[4] He tries to be pragmatic like Burujerdi, concerned with education like Khoei, and innovative like Sadr. At the same time, he goes beyond all of them. Two main features of his works are readily identifiable. The first is a rereading of the views and works of previous Muslim thinkers. The second is the formulation of a new paradigm for the "Islamic Republic," which he thinks is potentially the best system for Iran today. To achieve the latter, he first presents a critique of the existing traditional narrative of *ijtihad* (independent reasoning), then formulates his own narrative of a religious regime.

For his first objective, Kadivar reviewed the ideas of some prominent Islam-minded Iranians in two of his works on Islamic political thought. His main objective is to show that it is possible to have a "religious government" in modern times (8), but he is quick to point out that "religious government" does not necessarily mean "a shari'a-based regime." Here he wants to show two things. One is that, in Islam, governance is expressed by the notion of guardianship (*velayat*), which means holding authority in combination with friendship (21). This is how the notion is employed in the two main sources of Islamic teachings: the Qur'an and the tradition (59–98). It is not a relationship built around the dichotomies of ruler and ruled, master and subject, or superior and inferior. A polity is a family, and the leader is a responsible head. Second, nowhere in any of the sources is this leadership position granted to anyone, particularly to the jurists as their special privilege (99). This is contrary to the position of the ruling elite in the Islamic Republic, who insist on designating the jurist for the position.

In fact, regarding the question of who is responsible for guardianship, Kadivar identifies two powerful trends in Shi'i political thought. One insists on divine legitimacy, for which he identifies four theocratic types, as follows:

1. The oldest is the "appointed mandate of the jurisconsult" in matters of religion, along with the monarchic mandate of a Muslim ruler (*Saltanat-e Mashrou'eh*) in secular matters. This type is associated with such prominent Shi'i scholars as Mohammad Baqer Majlesi (d. 1699), Mirza Aboolqasem ibn Hassan Gilani-ye Qomi (d.1815), Seyed Jafar Kashfi (d.1850), Sheikh Fazlollah Nuri, and Ayatollah Abdolkarim Ha'eri Yazdi (Kadivar 1380/2001, 64–79).

2. The second type is the "general appointed mandate of jurisconsults" (*Velayat-e Entesabi-ye Ammeh*), which he associates with the views of Molla Ahmad Naraqi, Sheikh Mohammad Hassan Najafi (Saheb Javaher), and Ayatollahs Burujerdi, Golpayegani, and Khomeini (before the revolution) (81–96).

3. The third type still insists on the rule of the jurist, but makes it a collective enterprise. Kadivar calls this "the general appointed mandate of the Council of the 'Sources of Imitation'" (*Velayat-e Entesabi-ye Ammeh-ye Shora-ye Marje'eh Taghlid*), which was advocated by Ayatollahs Abdollah Javadi Amoli, Mohammad Beheshti, and Seyyed Hassan Taheri Khorram Abadi (97–106).

4. The fourth and last type introduces the idea of the "absolute appointed mandate of the jurisconsult" (*Velayat-e Entesabi-ye Motlaqe-ye Faqih*), which the founder of the Islamic Republic, Ayatollah Khomeini, proposed. This represented a shift in Khomeini's ideas: he no longer tolerated the secular rule of the monarch and considered the government to be the embodiment of "the practical philosophy of jurisprudence in all aspects of human life" (quoted on 110).

Kadivar then deals with the second trend regarding the responsibility for guardianship, which attributes legitimacy to a combination of divine and popular sources. This trend could be categorized under five headings:

1. The "constitutional state" (with the permission and supervision of jurisconsults) (*Dowlat-e Mashrouteh*), as argued by Sheikh Esma'il Mahllati and the proconstitutionalists Ayatollahs Abdollah Mazandarani, Mohammad Tabataba'i, Mohammad Kazem Khorasani, and Mirza Hossein Na'ini (116–123).

2. The popular state, first discussed by the Iraqi cleric Muhammad Baqir Sadr, who suggested the notion of "popular stewardship with clerical oversight" (that is, *Khelafat-e Mardom ba Nezarat-e Marjaiat*) (127–140). Kadivar puts more emphasis on supervising the clerics who "nominate" the head of the executive branch (139).

3. The "elective limited mandate of jurisprudents" (*Velayat-e Entekhabi-ye Moqayadeh-ye Faqih*), which Kadivar's teacher Ayatollah Montazeri has propagated, but which has also been discussed by Ayatollah Motahhari (148–154).

4. The fourth is the "Islamic elective state" (*Dowlat-e Entekhabi-ye Eslami*), which Ayatollah Muhammad Baqir Sadr developed when he changed his mind and insisted on popular participation, although the judicial branch was to remain the special function of the jurists. There are also Lebanese scholars and jurists (Ayatollah Javad Moghniye and Mohammad Mehdi Shamseddin) who advocate this form of polity (167–174).

5. Finally, there is the "collective government by proxy" (*Vekalat-e Malekan-e Shakhsi-ye Mosha*), as suggested by philosopher and scholar Ayatollah Mehdi Ha'eri Yazdi, who further added that government "belong[s] to the area of practical reason" and must be performed with the "absolute supervision of the people" (183).

Kadivar treats all nine views with reverence and draws two conclusions from them: first, discussion about government is an open-ended field in Shi'i political thought; and second, the current jurists are all wanting or inappropriate for the present juncture in Iranian history. Of course, he finds some precedent for his own democratic reading of Islam among the second category of states, particularly in Montazeri's notion of a "limited and elected guardianship of the jurists," in Sadr's notion of "an elected Islamic government," and in Ha'eri Yazdi's "absolute accountability" of the government to the people (159–186). On a different occasion, he deals with the views of Mirza Hossein Na'ini, whose work *Tanbih al-Umma va Tanzih al-Mellah* is seen as the most significant religious statement in support of the constitutional movement (1905–1911) and parliamentary monarchy. Kadivar thinks, however, that more attention should be paid to these views because ignoring them has caused Iranians to fall either for a singular narrative of Shi'i thought or for the view that "people like Khorasani [a major religious leader of the late nineteenth and early twentieth centuries] have only criticized [the existing order]—namely, despotism by religion (*estebdad-e mashru'e*)" (Kadivar 1382/2003, 2).

In Kadivar's reading, Khorasani was doing much more. The latter's view can be summarized as follows: there are two types of regimes, shari'a-based and non-shari'a-based, and the latter can potentially be either just or tyrannical; shari'a-based regimes are possible only with the presence of an infallible imam; and during the occultation of the imams, in the contemporary history of Shi'ism, it is impossible to form a shari'a-based regime. This notion constitutes an intrinsic part of Imami Shi'ism (7). But life does not stop because the infallible imams are not present, so what happens to politics? Kadivar spends a great deal of time showing that in Khorasani's view, in the absence of the infallible leaders, it is the people who rule, because now everyone enjoys equal and similar rights. The jurists cannot lay claim to any special status in the polity (11–18). On this point, according to Kadivar, Khorasani not only disagreed with Nuri, who opposed the constitutional revolution, but also went beyond the aforementioned Na'ini, who approved of the constitutional regime only as a secondary alternative. For Khorasani, the people were the masters of politics, and the jurists should remain in the field of legal studies and affairs (20–23).

What is Kadivar's own paradigm? First and foremost, he believes a religious government would be ideal. The form it should take is the one that the revolution achieved in Iran, that is, an "Islamic Republic," which, he contends, is "appropriate and efficient for our time" (quoted in Rudi-Kadivar 1379/2000, 112). But is he talking about the actual ruling regime in Iran? Obviously not, or else how could he be a dissident reformer? Thus, the first pillar of his own paradigm is his opposition to the rule of jurist as an Islamic form of polity. In his book *Hokumat-e Vallae'i* (Government as Guardianship), he details his criticism of such a reading of Islamic political thought. The following is his final verdict on the prevailing notion of the "absolute authority of the jurists":

> The result of the discussion is that the principle of *velayat-e faqih* is neither obvious nor rationally necessary. It is neither required by religion

nor dictated by the denomination (*mazhab*); that is, it is not a part of Imami Shi'i jurisprudence, not among the Shi'i religious principles, and not a doctrinal issue. By a near consensus of Shi'i jurists, it is part of the jurisprudential minor hypothesis, and its validation requires proofs from the four Islamic sources (the Qur'an, traditions, consensus, and reason). (Kadivar 1378/1999, 237)

Of course, he has already shown that such proofs are not available. Clearly, this conclusion is contrary to Khomeini's assertion that "the principle of *velayat-e faqih*" is one of the "primary principles" of Islam, for the preservation of which even such solid pillars of religion as daily prayer or performance of pilgrimage to Mecca could be temporarily stopped. Kadivar is not intimidated by this claim. Thus, in the last part of his book, he considers whether reason can support the rule of the jurists, and comes to a similar conclusion, arguing that in any religious government, whereas the presence of revelation and jurisprudence are legitimate, to give the same status to jurists is illogical: "The appointed guardianship of the jurist lacks any credible rational evidence" (390–391). As to the practical difficulties of the "absolute authority of the jurist," he devotes an entire book, *Hokumat-e Entesabi* (Government by Appointment), to delineating the practical consequences, disappointments, and disenchantments brought about by government based on divine mandate (Kadivar 1379/2000b).

But with what does Kadivar want to replace the existing narrative of Islamic government? He elaborates on this idea in most of his subsequent works. One recent volume containing about eighty of his articles and interviews, appropriately called *Daghdaghe-ye Hokumat-e Dini* (Preoccupations with Religious Government), reveals what he is after. He distinguishes between two narratives of religious government. The first claims that all aspects of governance, including the identity of the ruler, the extent of his power, and the areas of its functions, are delineated in religious texts: "People do not play any role in the legitimacy of such a government" (Kadivar 1379/2000a, 264). Government is in the hands of those who know better than the people themselves what is good for them. The second narrative proposes that religious government has two pillars, one is God's consent—no decisions should be taken that contradict God's master plan—and the second relates to people's satisfaction, or their will and demands. "Religious government, therefore, refers to rational governance implemented within the parameters of religious edicts" (264) and functions in the service of the people. The last phrase is critical because in this narrative, "if a government is not accepted by the people, even if its laws are in congruence with the shari'a, it lacks legitimacy" (264). Thus religious government could be called religious democracy or a theo-democracy.

In many ways, Kadivar wants to preserve Islam and its prominent role in the public sphere, but he differs from his fellow clergy members by thinking that economic, political, and social interactions, contingency, and practical reason—not permanent abstract principles—should rule in the realm of the mundane. Religiosity belongs to a deeper level: "For people to become religious means they would become God-fearing . . . and the penetration of religious consciousness, and not simply observe the rituals and appearances" (615). This is contrary to what the ruling elite in Iran offer as Islam. They insist on a series of legal principles found in juridical manuals [resaleh], "as though they [the manuals] embodied contemporary Islam" (592). If religion is limited to jurisprudence, its moral and ethical dimension is undermined (cited in Rudi-Kadivar 1379/2000, 135). The Islamic injunctions "appear absolute when formulated, but if they do not hold when tested against the criteria then they are annulled" (Kadivar 2004, interview).

When asked about his understanding of the criteria, Kadivar revealed the revolutionary nature of his ideas. For him, there are three criteria: "fairness (edalat); reasonability (oqalaaei), similar to common sense; and efficiency (karamadi), that is, compared with other solutions, they are workable and superior" (Kadivar 2004, interview). He considers his contribution to be "surgically" changing some of the main components of the social and contractual aspects of Islamic jurisprudence (Kadivar 2004, interview). What do these criteria amount to? Fairness in politics means recognizing the role of people in the polity, treating them not as instruments to be wielded, as in a nonliberal democracy, but as meaningful participants in the life of the society. It is the people who decide what is fair, rational, and efficient. Kadivar thus spends a lot of time discussing freedom, civil society, media, and civil discourse rather than violence and terror (Kadivar 1379/2000a, 256–284, 419–434, and 784–794, for example). This is why he actively participated in the reform movement and supported President Khatami.

In short, he is prepared to allow people of authority to be nonclerical, and thus his ideal government breaks away from the official formula of the Islamic Republic, which emphasizes the centrality of the jurist. For him, the ideal government is "a legally elected authority for a short time and with a limited mandate" (Aameriyat-e Entekhabi-ye Moqayade-ye

Qanuni). What makes it different from a Western form of limited government is that it operates within the bounds of contemporary Iranian identity, which is simultaneously religious, native, modern, and progressive.

The Islam of Tehran: Shabestari, Soroush, and Hajjarian

The death of democratic-minded Muslims such as Bazargan did not diminish the voice of liberal Islam in Tehran; in fact, it marked the coming of a new generation. The new generation enjoys greater legitimacy than Bazargan's because its members participated in the revolution, lost lives in the war, endured the postrevolutionary hardships, and strengthened the nascent Islamic regime. Many names come to mind, but here I concentrate on Mohammad Mojtahed Shabestari, Abdolkarim Soroush, and Saeed Hajjarian. My selection is significant because Shabestari is a cleric who has decided to confront contemporary challenges; Soroush is in the middle, a noncleric and an Islam-minded intellectual at the heart of the controversial debate over the authority of the religious establishment in the postrevolutionary Iranian public sphere; Hajjarian, the youngest, is a political activist and a practical actor in the revolution and in policy-making circles. They believe they must respond to the challenges of modernity and globalization. In the process, they have confronted three types of adversaries. The first are those who see tradition as sacred in its totality—it must be obeyed uncritically and not be rethought. Second are those Muslims who have turned Islam into an ideology of revolution and terror. And third are those who feel that Muslims should submit absolutely to the demands of the globalized world and embrace the demands of capitalism and a free-market economy. The three adversaries could be termed traditionalists, Islamists, and modernists, respectively. However, the three men discussed here propose a renewed narrative of Islam that critically accommodates both Islam and the demands of modernity.

MOHAMMAD MOJTAHED SHABESTARI

Shabestari is a cleric who teaches in the Department of Theology at Tehran University. He has had a long career as an Islam-minded Iranian who has tried to revive Islamic teaching. He comes from a prominent clerical family in Tabriz, where he was born in 1936. Shabestari studied theology in Qom for a long time and studied philosophy at modern universities as well. In 1970 he became director of the Islamic center in Hamburg, where he studied German and English and, more importantly, immersed himself in Christian theology. He returned to Iran in

1979, and after a short involvement in politics, decided to work and act as a scholar and public intellectual. Presently, Shabestari has become one of the prominent voices challenging the "official version of Islam," which became dominant in postrevolutionary Iran and retains substantial power today. He claims that there is no one version or reading of any religion, as the preface to one to his books, *Naqdi bar Qara'at Rasmi az Din: Bohranya, Chaleshha, Rahhalha* (A Critique of the Official Reading of Religion: Crisis, Challenges, and Solutions), states: "Indeed, any religious expression amounts to a reading of a religious text, and the fact is that the latter can be understood and interpreted in various ways" (Shabestari 1381/2002, 7).

The first part of the book includes three essays dealing with the issues of religion and development, the rational reading of religion, and the official reading of religion. The first essay opens with this controversial sentence: "The official reading of religion in our society is in crisis" (8). Shabestari identifies two causes for this crisis. The first is "the irrational and erroneous position that claims that Islam as a religion is a comprehensive political, economic, and legal system based on jurisprudence; that [this system] is applicable to all times; and that it requires Muslims to live by it in all aspects of their lives and at all times. The second is an emphasis on this erroneous claim that the duty of the government among Muslims is only to implement the ordinances of Islam" (11). Instead, Shabestari invites Muslims to see the reality of their lives in the face of modernity. For him, the main features of modernity can be explained as follows: human will and volition constitute the foundation; the new empirical and social sciences are dominant; industry shapes the modes of production; there is long-term planning; the main discourses involve a plurality of ideas and universal participation; objective rules and regulations are at work; the state acts as a manager of scientific rules; there is a new meaning of justice; there is compatibility between religion and development; and, finally, contrary to traditional ways, results are never predictable (15–18).

At the heart of this sophisticated process lies freedom; thus at the heart of Shabestari's theology is the notion of freedom. He believes it is freedom that allows for any dialectic between tradition and modernity. Indeed, to grasp the internal logic of Shabestari's thoughts, one must concentrate on his understanding of freedom. How is the term to be defined and understood? For Shabestari, it appears that freedom means manifestation of the autonomous self, so one must enjoy "freedom from, freedom to, and freedom for." "Freedom from" requires removing all forces, whether inside or outside of the agent-actor, that might impede his or her way of exercising volition. "Freedom to" applies to the realm wherein the agent-actor can display volition, that is, "the realm of action." And the final form of freedom allows for the "securing of one's objective, which is nothing more than the preservation of freedom of action" (27). These distinctions may appear repetitious and tautological, but they are another way of saying that freedom is both an end and a means and constitutes the very reason for humane life on earth: "The reality of being human is 'to be free always.' To live as a human means to live freely. A human being comprises the essence of freedom and its very manifestation" (Shabestari 1378/2000, 33). By this definition alone, Shabestari embraces the most significant element of modernity and globalization, namely, the free, autonomous self.

To show the centrality of the notion of freedom, Shabestari then investigates the relation of freedom to faith—both in the reading of any sacred text and in political thinking based on religious tradition. The relation of freedom and faith is significant because, for Shabestari, the essence of religion is faith, and religiosity makes sense in what he calls "religious experience," which is different from a collective movement or even a religious revival. He refers to the last two as "political movements" with religious coloring (122–124). Religions usually manifest themselves in the world either as faith or as beliefs and rituals. According to Shabestari, only through faith can one experience the presence of the divine, while the other two are servants and facilitators of such proximity: "Religion means presence, [while] beliefs, rituals, ethics, and ordinances of religion are but servants to this presence. Their value depends on the role they play in facilitating that presence" (Shabestari 1381/2002, 334). The ultimate manifestation of such a presence comes when, through faith, one loses oneself in God, free from the four earthly "jails of history, society, language, and one's body," an experience described best, according to Shabestari, in the Bible (Matthew 10:39), where it is stated that if one loses oneself, one gains God (Shabestari 1378/2000, 38). In a way, faith is a conscious choice, and remains so only as long as it is in constant logical dialogue with other human experiences. For a religious mind, no conscious effort toward progress happens without society's "serious criticism of religion, religiosity, and the dominant tradition," provided that there is no limitation or "red light" on the path of criticism and rethinking (Shabestari 1377/1998, 202–203).

Grappling with any divine text or religious tradition, like finding unity with God, occurs through human experience. Here is the logic of

Shabestari's argument. Any religious thinking is shaped by three elements, which in turn are related to how we as humans experience ourselves, how we experience the world, and how we understand or experience revelation: "A Muslim can approach and experience revelation only with the help of a particular understanding and experience of himself and the world. It is by a combination of these that any religious thought is formulated" (Shabestari 1381/2002, 161). No one can claim to understand the true intent of a text because one is always reading the text with a particular pretext. In other words, any religious expression is a human phenomenon and cannot be presented as something divine or sacred. This challenges the traditionalist approach, which claims to know absolutely the truth about religious teachings. It also paves the way for religious pluralism and for forms of cultural, social, legal, and political plurality and toleration.

Shabestari then returns to the relationship between freedom and religion. For him, freedom is ingrained in religion, which explains why any religious history exhibits a variety of religious interpretations. In other words, there should not be a single interpretation of religion: "Freedom of religion is related to religion itself and does not mean that a person has the freedom to choose any particular religion. Religion has to be free, whereas the personal freedom to chose a religion is a social right that in turn is part of the principle of 'human rights'" (335).

If freedom is the essence of the human condition, and the text is always subject to a context, and the narrative of the subject of the text is that of whoever experiences religion, then what is the function of the text? Here, like his coreligionists, whether conservative, liberal, or radical, Shabestari holds that values come from the divine and are reflected in the text. Man cannot establish or construct values. Whether regarding revelation or the traditions of the Prophet and his household, the main function of the text is to initiate and establish values. The clergy distinguishes between values and countervalues and sets the boundaries. For example, when it comes to governance, the Qur'an is concerned not with the form but with the final objective of governance. The following passage clearly conveys what Shabestari expects of religion:

In the Qur'an there is no affirmation of the forms or the systems of government, but the emphasis is on the justness of the government. It seems that the Qur'an considers the determination of the methods and forms of government to have a status below that of revelation and religion. Forms and systems have differed among various tribes and societies and throughout history. What should remain constant and not change as a result of changes in societies is one principal value: rulers should act according to justice. The Qur'an emphasizes this principle. (Shabestari 1377/1998, 60)

Shabestari continues to suggest that if a nation decides the principle of justice is best served through an elected form of government, then it is not only a rational move but also "a religious duty to form such an elective and consultative system" (60). The mundane realms, including the forms that the polity and religious expression might take, have their roots in human reason, culture, and mores. Even God himself recognized this, since "God has permitted the world to remain itself (in the secular sense of the term) and so has decreed the world to be the world" (67).

But what about those who claim that religions are complete and comprehensive, implying that they have to provide answers for every contingency? According to Shabestari, "The completeness of religion (*kamal-e din*) means that whatever God has sent to man is sent in its complete form and that the Prophet has delivered it as such . . . but it does not mean that it has covered every aspect of mundane existence. Certainly it does not mean that it should replace technology, science, or human thinking. This is a dangerous thought for both religion and the people of faith" (254–255). How does one guarantee that Shabestari's version of religious experience will prevail? He seems to have a great deal of hope for what he calls the "continuous functioning of independent reasoning" (*ijtihad-e mostamar*) in all fields of knowledge, including "theology and anthropology," provided independent reasoning is combined with the latest, "up-to-date findings of human knowledge and sciences" (93).

Though clearly his version of religion is far more democratic than the ruling version in Iran, he is tolerated by the authorities and is in less danger than other Islam-minded voices of the fourth generation. Further, his theory seems to suggest that if a jurist is an expert in the mundane matters of governance and is able to secure the support of the governed, then he could take part in any institution of power. This is evidently not the case for Soroush, for example, who seems to have continued Shari'ati's tradition of opposing any clericalism or clerically based religion.

ABDOLKARIM SOROUSH

Hossein Hajfaraj Dabagh, known as Abdolkarim Soroush, is possibly the biggest name in Islamic discourse in Iran. He was born in Tehran on December 16, 1945. It may be fate that his birthday coincides with that of Mowlavi/Rumi, the great Muslim mystic, and with Ashura, the day Imam Hossein and his family were martyred; he shows special reverence to both. He did his early schooling at Alavi High School, where he also taught. He then earned a pharmacology degree from Tehran University before going to London, where he pursued analytical chemistry along with the philosophy of science. He became attracted to the seventeenth-century Iranian philosopher Mulla Sadra, the last great Muslim philosopher, and wrote his first book about him.

I first learned of Soroush when I read this book in 1977. The writing revealed a person with a great appreciation for philosophy and an enormous talent for literature and Persian mystical poetry. Politically, he had become Khomeini's follower early in his life: "I got to know Khomeini before I knew Shari'ati, when I was a high school student . . . and when he was arrested" (Soroush 1376/1997, xxviii). He is referring to 1962, when Khomeini had his first showdown with the regime. Soroush even went to see him when he was freed, a year later. He felt closer to him later: "Years later, when I was at the university, I read his underground treatise on Islamic government and became one of his followers (*moqaled*)" (xxix). He confessed these words in 1992, but by 1997 he had gone through the metamorphosis with which I am concerned here. By 1997 he had turned against a juridical version of Islamic polity in both theory and practice.

In fact, there have been two distinct phases in Soroush's life. In the first, from his student days until the early 1990s, he was preoccupied with Islamic revival and the preservation of Islam, and he saw Khomeini as the best paradigm for uniting "philosophy, mysticism, and jurisprudence." This explains his quiet cooperation with the Islamic regime and his defense of Islam in the face of Marxism. He devoted most of his early works to the refutation of dialectical materialism, even on television, where he conducted debates with Ehsan Tabari (1917–1989), the ideologue of the Tudeh Party, and Farokh Negahadar of the Fada'iyan Marxist Guerrilla Organization. A book he published in 1980 branded Marxism a "Satanic ideology" (Soroush 1375/1996a, especially 39–70).

And yet Soroush changed when the Islamic regime brought about not a free and ethical society, but religious despotism, and even he was accused of having impure thoughts and ideas. What sparked the change was the publication in May 1988 of his essays on the "contraction and expansion of the creed (*shari'at*)," which appeared in the government-sponsored journal *Keyhan-e Farhangi* and were later collected in his magnum opus of the same name. The political establishment did not tolerate the publication of these works, so his followers had to give up the magazine, and they soon brought out a new one called *Kiyan,* which became the podium for the new Soroush, the defender of freedom. Here, not only did Soroush continue with his criticism of the traditional narrative of religion, but he also launched his defense of "democratic religious government" (Soroush 1375/1996b, 273–283). By this he means a society in which religion and democratic principles operate in congruity. It is a society in which religion is needed "to guide people and be the final arbiter in cases of conflict," and yet is one that relies on democratic principles: a "social understanding of religion [is] combined with rationality for people's satisfaction" (281). There is no contradiction between the two because both religion and democracy are universal values: God's revelation cannot be particular, and democracy does not have a religious or an irreligious form (Soroush 1382/2003, 1–5).

While Shabestari concentrates on freedom, Abdolkarim Soroush deals with all aspects of a contemporary secular world. His many volumes of writings and speeches deal with a variety of issues, but I concentrate on the following question, which appears repeatedly in his works: how can a religious-based polity deal with secularization? Unlike other prominent leaders of the Islamic movement, who concentrated on one area—Bazargan was primarily a man of science, Shari'ati a social scientist, Motahhari a man of philosophy, and the Khomeini of the elite a man of philosophy and mysticism—Soroush takes a multidisciplinary approach toward Islam and its place in the public sphere. According to Soroush, such an approach makes it possible for Muslims to live in a pluralistic world, since "the story of secularization amounts to the venture of nonreligious reason, and although not religious in character, it is not antireligious" (Soroush 1372/1993, 13). In his mind, wherever secularity is dominant, all emphasis will inevitably be on rights, scientific management, rationality, human progress, and worldly gain. As has happened in the West, such a world began with an introduction into the nature of things, and then the discussion shifted from concentrating on God to focusing on nature and natural rights (11). It is possible for a religious mind to live in such a world because none of these features contradict revelation.

Soroush is quick to point out that when secularity is combined with liberalism, problems can arise: "Any religious society that is bound by a creed cannot logically compromise with principles or derivatives of liberalism. The answers to many questions in a liberal context are derived from examination and experiment, whereas for a religious society, the answers to many questions are known ahead of time" (Soroush

1377/1998, 146). He sets out to explain how Muslims can accommodate the demands of secularization.

Soroush suggests combining three broad solutions. One is his controversial theory of the "contraction and expansion of religious knowledge." He proposes the study of modern sciences, both the natural and the social sciences, for ascertaining the principles of religion, instead of following traditional studies such as genealogy (*'elm al-rejal*), because the latter have lost their relevance. In 1991, when his theory of "the theoretical contraction and expansion of the creed (*shari'at*)" was shaping the debate among Islam-minded intellectuals in Iran, he summarized his main purpose for me as follows: "In one way or another, the revivalists before me wanted to reconcile tradition with change. . . . I argue that in order to solve the problem of the relation between tradition and change, we should separate religion from the understanding of religion. The first is unchanging, but the second changes. In fact, we should try to establish a constant exchange and interaction between the second and the other branches of human knowledge and understanding, such as sociology, anthropology, philosophy, history, and so on" (quoted in Rajaee 1993b, 114).[5] In a discussion with a group of seminary students, Soroush identified his argument as epistemological and theological and as applying to the fields of "jurisprudence (*usul*) and the science of interpretation (*tafsir*)" (Soroush 1370/1991a, 7).

The gist of what Soroush is saying is that "religion is complete and absolute, while the understanding of it is not." By the first, he means that "whatever God has deemed necessary, he has revealed, and in this sense [religion] has no shortcoming." And by religious understanding, he means that "what one gains from the text [the Qur'an] and the traditions [the ways of the Prophet and his household], and of course understanding refers to 'that' which is based [on] methodology" (7). Furthermore, religious understanding "is manufactured by humanity, just as it has constructed philosophy, medicine, psychology, or other areas of human knowledge. God has created nature, and both natural sciences are the result of human endeavors. Religion is descended from God, but religious studies and [their] understanding is a man-made phenomenon" (8). On the surface, the idea is simple, but it has far-reaching implications, two of which are worth mentioning. First, Soroush's idea allows for plurality. If one's knowledge of religion is temporal, one understanding is as valid as any other; thus, a plurality of interpretations would be inevitable, opening the door for democratization and political plurality. This is important in the case of Iran, where the clerical class claims that its understanding of religion is sacred and exclusively accurate. Since the official line dictates that only the clerical jurisconsults should rule, obeying the ruling elite is both a religious and legal duty. The second implication of Soroush's idea is that no particular group can or should claim special authority, a conclusion that threatens clerical rule.

Distinguishing between the changing and unchanging dimensions of religion is not a new concept among Muslims. For example, the Egyptian reformer and thinker Muhammad Abduh (d. 1905) introduced this idea before, but what differentiates Soroush's account is that he has abandoned the previously defensive or apologetic attitudes and instead actively rethought both Islam and modernity. He maintains a critical and imaginative perspective toward both. Soroush invites a complete revision of his fellow Muslims' understanding of secularity and Islam. Both Islam and secularity are complex categories, and it is wrong to assume that they cannot be rethought or renovated. There are many ways to understand each, and any representation of either Islam or the modern world is merely a narration of the people expressing it. This is certainly a postmodern interpretation.

The second idea relates to Soroush's understanding of the nature of religion. In the past few decades, a powerful trend of thought, claiming that Islam is a totalitarian ideology, has been argued among Muslims. Soroush challenges this narrative by claiming that religion is far greater than any ideological system, comparing religion to an ocean and ideology to a particular pool. Religions are mysterious symbols of truth not applicable to a particular historical epoch; they contain inner meanings and serve as criteria. In short, "religions are not manifestos, practical guides, plans for social engineering, or particular diet regimes, but rather are like waters that flow through rivers and waterways, but are not limited to them" (Soroush 1375/1996b, 130). Religions can be turned into ideologies, though at their own peril. An ideological religion may help you win a battle, but it will certainly make you lose the war. Humanity will prosper with the sense of awe that any religion offers, but not with the sense of struggle that an ideology provides (155). What is important about religion for Soroush, particularly in the second phase of his career, is the centrality of ethics and morality. This has become his new project.

After a few years of lecturing in Europe and America, Soroush inaugurated his public appearances with a series of talks on religious society and moral society. On one occasion he dealt with the question "whether a religious society is the same as a moral one" (Soroush 1383/2004b, 1). The reason such a question is important is that there can be a society without religion, but no society can exist without ethics. For example, "even the most liberal society, in which secularism is intrinsic, is based on a moral principle that I call here the principle of tolerance" (1). He goes further, arguing that "ethics and morality" make us human and distinguish us from other species, since "animals do not set priorities based on ethical distinctions (*tarjihaat*)" (2). Even religiosity should be based on ethics and morality in the sense of being more ethical than ir-religiosity, provided religious injunctions do not compromise principles of morality (2). Why is such a distinction necessary?

According to Soroush, there might be cases in which religious rituals and legal principles void of their moral and ethical aspects dominate, since "jurisprudence does not guarantee religiosity and morality" (3). He refers indirectly to the dominant practice in Iran, pointing out the ne-cessity for the "ethical cleansing and reconstruction" of contemporary Iranian society. He complains that the discussion of "rationality, tradi-tion and modernity" has imposed a "veil on more fundamental ques-tions" of ethics and morality: "Ethics has logical priority over religion and religiosity because we set our system and hierarchy of values before we embark upon the religious life or any other activity. . . . We have no right or duty to worship an unethical God" (Soroush 1383/2004a, 1). He even compares the issue of ethics to the air one breathes and the water one drinks, without which, life is impossible. The time has come to de-vise a system that eliminates unethical practices, including despotism, human-rights violations, lack of freedom, and intolerance. The reason these are so common in Iran is that people have lost the sense of unethi-cal practices being indecent or unseemly; so when "newspapers are shut down and their staffs lose their livelihoods, society does not feel that something indecent has happened" (2). In short, for him, religion has be-come intertwined with ethics to the point that "if ethics is removed from religion, it loses its categorization as religion" (Soroush 1382/2003, 4).

The third idea Soroush introduces is the notion of selection as a strat-egy for constructing a renovated religious narrative and society for Mus-lims today. Muslims should dare to choose from their own tradition as well as from those of others. In what he calls a "selective" approach, Soroush suggests that one should select the truth wherever it is found— in the West, among Muslims, or in any other tradition: "To select the truth requires insight and daring and it represents the noblest form of love toward the noblest lover" (Soroush 1373/1994, 250). This approach re-quires a critical mind that avoids any kind of generalization, positive or negative, about any particular tradition. Soroush entered into a heated debate with the powerful conservatives in Iran about the meaning of the West. Whereas conservatives propagated the idea that "the evil essence of the West" has threatened the sacred world of Muslims, Soroush discussed complexities both in the West and among Muslims. Both regions are marked by discord and collaboration, interactions between political actors, religious groupings, the presence of scholars and professionals, and so on (244).

Soroush's depiction of the complex world of Muslims and the distinction he makes between the essentials of religion and its accidental aspects are contrary to the views of those who consider Muslim society an undifferentiated mass blindly following the Islamic creed. His treatment of the West is similar for the modern and now globalized world. His careful reading of the evolution of modern science in the West is a serious attempt to depict the complex world that people often express with the overworked notion of "the West." For him, the latter represents dynamism, secularity, and progress, but this does not mean that one should prostrate oneself before it; instead, one should exercise the "art of analyzing it and learning from it" (239). The combination of the three ideas—the contraction and expansion of the religious creed; religion as mystery and not ideology; and the notion of selection—would enable Muslims to live within a secular framework. But while Soroush deals with generalities, our third thinker, Saeed Hajjarian, has more specifically examined the relation between Islam and republicanism.

SAEED HAJJARIAN

Hajjarian, an influential member of the Muslim revolutionaries in Iran, worked for the Ministry of Intelligence and was the deputy head of the Strategic Research Centre of the President's Office and special adviser to President Khatami. He began his training in mechanical engineering (BA, 1977) but changed direction both professionally and intellectually, finishing a PhD in political science at Tehran University in 2003. He was born in 1953 in a poor neighborhood of Tehran and became a political activist in his student days. His wife was arrested in 1975 and jailed until the revolution. A sympathizer of the mujahedin, he fought two battles, one against the shah and the other a difficult competition with the left, which was extremely powerful among students: "In each student election, all Muslims combined could not elect but at most one representative, while all the other seats went to the left" (Hajjarian 2004, interview).

Right after the revolution, Hajjarian joined the revolutionary committees, particularly in the Iranian navy, and attempted to preserve "official documents" from the revolutionary chaos (2004, interview). After he drafted a proposal for reconstructing and coordinating close to thirty intelligence agencies, he joined the newly established Ministry of Intelligence, where he worked for about five years as a deputy. His liberal and democratic tendencies were detectable in his work there. He proposed to make the ministry a democratic and responsive institution, dealing with intelligence and strictly accountable to the people (Baqi 1379/2000, 32–42). Indeed, he became "the theoretician and main founder of the Ministry of Intelligence" (Quchani 1382/2004, 52) before joining the Strategic Research Centre, where he still works.

At the same time, Hajjarian began publishing an influential sociopolitical biweekly called *Asr-e Ma* (Our Time) in October 1994. When I asked him what motivated him, he said, "After [president] Hashemi came to power and insisted on economic development, I argued with him that economic development would work only if it were contextualized within political development, but my argument fell on deaf ears. I concluded that he did not understand political development, so I decided to become a political activist" (2004, interview). He later helped publish the daily *Salam* and his own paper, *Sobheh Emrouz* (This Morning). While a member of the city council of Tehran, Hajjarian survived an assassination attempt on March 12, 2000, that left him half paralyzed. He continues to write and publish.

Hajjarian's main concern has been the process by which a religiously inspired polity might deal with republicanism. Like Shabestari and Soroush, he thinks the interaction between tradition and modernity, and now globalization, constitutes the gravest challenge for Muslims. The polity that can best deal with such a challenge is an Islamic republic, provided that the relationship between the tenets of Islam and the principles of republicanism is resolved and that a new legal framework, a "jurisprudence of the commonwealth" (*fiqh al-masleha*), is formulated and implemented (Hajjarian 1379/2000, 102–104). He articulates his mission as follows: "In our country, a revolution occurred in the name of religion, and [that revolution] even formed a polity. In effect, the sacred came to the public sphere in an age of secularism in the form of a revolution and a state. Naturally, the success or failure of a religious state, and more so the fate of the sacred, has become the main concern of Muslims" (10). How should one deal with this problem? When I asked him what he was after, he responded, "Finding the best path to political development within the culture of the Islamic Republic of Iran" (2004, interview). According to Hajjarian, history tells us that there have been two ways of reacting to this challenge: constitutionalism and republicanism.

Constitutionalism was born with the Magna Carta in 1215, when the English barons resisted the absolute power of King John and demanded "to participate in decision making" in accordance with "the taxes they were paying." A distinction between kingship and tyranny was written into the new charter, and many aspects of the "monarch's authority were delegated to Parliament" (Hajjarian 1379/2000, 47). Republicanism was born with the Declaration of the Rights of Man and Citizen in 1789 during the French Revolution. That revolution ushered in the age of representation and universal citizenship, whereby human beings "have rights, the most significant one being that of sovereignty [over themselves]" (48). At the beginning of the twentieth century, when Iran faced the challenge of modernity, people responded with constitutionalism: "The dominant discourse in the mind of Iranian intellectuals, even until the Islamic Revolution [1979], was that of constitutionalism," but that discourse proved unsuccessful (50). "The very revolution itself," Hajjarian says, "indicated that the crisis of legitimacy could not have been resolved by conditioning the absolute power of the ruler with a constitution" (50).

In his view, republicanism presents the most efficient solution. Not only can it solve the practical problems that Iran is facing today, but it also guarantees the preservation of the Islamic polity in Iran. The following passage offers a poignant approach to this issue: "If one accepts that Islam is a religion of justice, and if one further accepts that justice means paying everyone his or her due, then if a mature and rightful nation is not allowed the right to determine its fate through legal means, such a polity is not Islamic. In other words, if the Iranian regime after the revolution is not a republic (that is, if people do not determine their own fate), then it cannot be Islamic either" (190).

What is the basis of his claim? Like Kadivar, Hajjarian relies on the affirmative participation of the people. In the absence of the infallible leaders, "the criteria for both the Islamic and republic dimensions are the common customs and mores (orf-e 'am)," not the precedent of the jurists (foqaha) or that of the elite (various oligarchies) (2004, interview). For example, stoning may be sanctioned in jurisprudence, but because the Iranian public does not accept it, it is neither Islamic nor republican; it must be annulled owing to "Muslim liberal democracy" (interview).

Hajjarian identifies three trends in Iran's contemporary intellectual history. The first holds that tradition resembles a crumbling wall that should be destroyed completely. Criticizing or rethinking a tradition will not suffice; one has to eliminate it with "'a grenade of submission to the civilization of the Franks [Europeans].' [For the intelligentsia of the time] there was no other way but to establish a new civilization on the ruins of tradition" (Hajjarian 2000, 199). This trend originated in the aftermath of the wars between Iran and Russia (1813–1828) and became the dominant view until the first half of the twentieth century. The second trend was born after World War II. During this era, the West lost its legitimacy for many intellectuals, and the imperial and colonial dimension of modernism became a significant issue. The new trend emphasized a "resurgence of tradition," which included replacing the notion of "the deconstruction of tradition" with a "reenchantment" of tradition and the notion of a "return to the self" (200). Dependency theory and authenticity gave more substance to some of the arguments associated with this trend.

From here developed the third trend, which emerged after the Iran-Iraq War (1980–1988). Its proponents advocate a "reconstruction of tradition": "The main concern of this discourse emphasizes the presentation of a new narrative of the old tradition in such a way that it will be useful for our present condition without hiding its utilitarian reading of [the local] tradition" (201). Hajjarian thinks that he is advancing this idea. The method he proposes is to reach a synthesis between the "deconstruction and resurgence" of tradition: "It is possible to utilize the dynamic aspects of tradition in order to erect a new civilization process" (201).

Hajjarian makes intellectuals individually responsible for understanding the two worlds of tradition and modernity through a process of rethinking. Inspired by the four mystical intellectual journeys of Mulla Sadra, Hajjarian proposed a similar process for the new intellectuals in Iran. As he writes, a contemporary Iranian intellectual "has to prepare for a four-phase journey: the first is from tradition to modernity; the second is a journey within modernity; the third is the journey from modernity to tradition; and the final phase is the journey within modernity while staying faithful to one's tradition" (201).

This four-step process cannot occur unless it is self-motivated. Although personal dynamics and the interaction between modernity and tradition are present throughout the journey, tradition plays a strong role. It appears there is a break from the past, but in reality, there is a new form of continuity: "The agent-actors who are mature and responsible use outside sources without falling into either dependency or backwardness and will thus capture the treasure of development" (202). Contemporary demands of public life have altered Iranians. The mature population of Iran requires sophisticated and mature institutions, and putting them into place will complete the revolt of the masses in Iran (Hajjarian 1379/2000, 372–373).

As discussed above, the 2004 election marked the end of reform for many. However, this was not the case for Hajjarian and his cohorts, who are determined to create a modern Islamic state in Iran. Hajjarian continues to advocate "reform is dead, long live reform" because the process of creating a secular-Islamic state is too deep-rooted to be thwarted by one setback. The modernization of Iran, which affected only literature and education during the Pahlavis' rule, has now penetrated all aspects of Iranian life, and the process of constructing a new hybrid identity continues in art, society, family relations, political processes, and even individual relationships, as the new youth and women have taken over.

The irony of the modern situation is that the traditionalist segments of the Islamic revolution, through their instrumental use of the people during the war, have contributed more to the secularization and democratization of the polity than any other force. Whether the fourth generation of Islam-minded Iranians calls its polity theo-democracy or demo-theocracy or democratic-religious government, some congruence between Islam and modernity is unfolding. Abadgaran Iran-e Islami, the conservative coalition of the Developers of Islamic Iran, which gained the majority in Parliament, declares that it is committed to "guarding the revolution and the independence of the country." The coalition claimed the Seventh Parliament would be "the center of faith, wisdom, logic, and kindness, and a center for the defense of religion, ethics, freedom, and independence" (2005, www.abadgaran.ir/farsi/). On a more practical level, its members talk about a "regulated political development based on civil institutions," and about other principles, such as basic freedoms, individual and social rights, the centrality of the law, and social justice. In foreign policy, the coalition advocates "integrity, wisdom, and interest" as the bases for foreign-policy making, and it even talks about a "principled struggle against any form of violence and terrorism." But in practice, it has continued more or less with the reformists' policies.

I was not at all surprised when then–deputy president Abtahi suggested in a *Financial Times* article on March 15, 2004, that the new coalition was adopting most of the reformers' programs. The group seems to be hoping to move the country in the direction of Rafsanjani's constructive years as well as toward Khatami's plan of political development. The former insisted on economic development and the later on political evolution, but now the time has come to combine the two. The conservatives have changed their position from opposing to supporting development. Even the election of a conservative president in the summer of 2005 did not seem to change the course of reform. Just as the powerful wine of the complex Iranian society broke the bottle of the Pahlavis' extreme modernism, the same powerful wine will not tolerate the simplicity of radical conservatives' traditionalism and Islamism.

CONCLUSION

The Politics of Oscillation

Here is the irony of history. Nietzsche declared the death of the gods. But the dead gods got their revenge by reviving religion in form of ideology.

SAEED HAJJARIAN, *AZ SHAHED QODSI TA SHAHED BAZARI; ORFI SHODAN DIN DAR SEPEHR SIYASSAT* (FROM SACRED WITNESS TO PROFANE WITNESS: THE SECULARIZATION OF RELIGION IN THE POLITICAL SPHERE), 1380/1991

On September 14, 2005, the newly elected president of Iran, Mahmoud Ahmadinejad spoke to the General Assembly of the United Nations. When he returned to Iran, he reported to his religious mentor, Ayatollah Javadi Amoli, that when he "began with the words 'in the name of God,'" he saw that he became "surrounded by a light until the end [of the speech]." He added, "I felt it myself, too. I felt that all of a sudden the atmosphere changed there, and for 27–28 minutes all the leaders did not blink." In his estimation, the leaders of the world "were astonished as if a hand held them there and made them sit. It had opened their eyes and ears for the message of the Islamic Republic" (Internet site of Radio Free Europe, November 29, 2005).[1] He saw himself as the light in the midst of darkness where unbelief, secularism, and worldly powers dominate. He considered himself a child of light among the children of darkness.

What a contrast compared to the speech his predecessor made from the same podium five years earlier, on September 5, 2000. Khatami spoke of Iran not as a source of light entrusted with the mission of enlightening the modern age's ignorance, but as a country that has been a contributing part of human culture, imagination, civilization, and the struggle for freedom and emancipation. In the spirit of the "dialogue among civilizations," he saw his own task as enumerating Iran's contribution to the world, making a plea for understanding, and requesting, in what he called "the Cartesian-Faustian narrative of Western civilization," that the world take note of others and "begin to listen to other narratives proposed by other human cultures."[2]

These two episodes, both produced by revolutionary zeal, capture the heart of Iranian politics in the postrevolutionary era. They appear to have sought the same objective, namely, that Iran should become a world player and be taken seriously at the global level, but they approached this objective from different perspectives and through different methods: Khatami's belonged to a post-Islamist generation, and Ahmadinejad's voiced the concerns of Islamism.

This book focuses on these two trends, and more so, it narrates the story of Islam-minded Iranians in the past century as they have reacted to Iran's encounter with modernity. Islam-minded Iranians hoped to revive the basic tenets of Islam and embrace modernity. They aimed for a restoration of "Muslim politics," defined so as to reconcile the teachings of Islam with the imperatives of the modern world. Their activism culminated in the 1979 revolution, which resulted in the formation of a bicephalous entity. Indeed, the main slogan of the revolution read: "Independence, Freedom, and the Islamic Republic." The message was that henceforth Iranians would be masters of their fate and would restore the confidence whose loss, I claimed, was at the heart of revolutionary zeal. For a while there was a great hope that a new balanced polity in Iran, free from the yoke of both traditionalism and modernism, would emerge. As long as Khomeini was alive, he played an effective role as a relatively impartial father figure and arbiter. Though he tried to normalize revolutionary zeal, revolutions take a long time to unfold, and we have not yet seen the last phase of the revolution in Iran.

I concentrated on Islam-minded Iranians' quest because more than any other group, they appeared authentic, native, and sincere about succeeding. Would they be successful, or would their efforts be frustrated, like the efforts of the constitutionalists at the turn of the century or those of the nationalists in the mid-twentieth century? Karen Armstrong's insightful comment may serve as a signpost: "Time and again, when disaster had struck, the most devout Muslims had turned to religion, made it speak to their new circumstances, and the ummah had not only revived but had usually gone on to greater achievements" (Armstrong 2000, 152). In other words, Muslims have been able to rise from their own ashes, and Islam-minded Iranians are doing precisely that.

The Islam-minded Iranians' story displayed interesting twists and turns. It began defensively, but the success of the revolution has brought about a change toward thinking seriously about the place of Islam in the modern world and about the relation between Islam and republican discourse. Many may argue that the efforts of Islam-minded Iranians were doomed to fail from the start, owing to the very nature of religious epistemology. Since a religious cosmology circumscribes the horizon of human imagination with predetermined conclusions, there is always going to be a deadlock. Since religious frameworks accept reason only if it is conditioned by revelation, power, in practice, becomes the ultimate arbiter of all disputes, intellectual, cultural, or political. Even the most adamant religious voices supporting modernity did so by invoking either the principle of a lesser evil (*dafʿ-e afsad be fassed*), or secondary apparent principles (*usul saanavi-yeye zaheriye*). Furthermore, they argued that what motivated them was the welfare of Muslims.

I do not share such conclusions, because they underestimate human ingenuity and ignore the diversity, heterogeneity, multiplicity, and constructive tensions among the competing narratives that are the main feature of the human condition. There has never been one version of Islam, nor has there ever been just one version of modernity. Instead, one must speak the language of "Islams and modernities" (Azmeh 1993) or note various "social imageries" (Taylor 2004). I hope I have shown that the greatest enemies of progress have been extremists on both sides of the debate between Islam and modernity, for having reduced both to ideologies and the instruments of particular interests. The metamorphosis of Islamic discourse has resounded with a multiplicity of voices. While many see Islam in simplistic dichotomies, many others see the world of Islam as nuanced, complicated, and replete with both tensions and constant examinations and reevaluations. Can such a discourse respond to the political challenges presented by internal rivals and external enemies? What about the challenges of modernity, which in fact lie at the heart of these difficulties? Most importantly, can it successfully present any alternatives to the project of modernity? One can identify three justifiable positions in this regard.

First is the extreme position of those who believe in the Islamic power bloc. Interestingly enough, this is a position taken by the protagonists of Islamic discourse as well as its enemies. The arch-supporters of the discourse argue that their movement is successful and has been able to present a superior alternative to that of the Western modernity project.

In the words of Hojjati Kermani, "The Islamic Republic of Iran is a moral superpower in the world today" (Institute for Political and International Studies conference, July 9, 1996). Its enemies discuss the Islamic threat. From Bernard Lewis's important 1976 essay "The Return of Islam" to Samuel Huntington's much-debated article "The Clash of Civilizations," and to the latest commentaries on the Islamic threat, a common view is presented that Islam is a threat to the post-communist world order. In fact, Sir Alfred Sherman, one of Margaret Thatcher's advisers, wrote in 1993 that, "There is a Moslem threat to Christian Europe. It is developing slowly and could still be checked" (quoted in Halliday 1996, 184).

Second is the position of those who discuss the failure of the Islamic movement. In his recent book, *The Failure of Political Islam,* Olivier Roy boldly claims "the desert within" the Islamist movement; he thinks the movement has failed completely. It has failed on the intellectual level because it has fallen back on the traditional discourse presented by the old intelligentsia, that is, the ulama, which refuses innovation. It has failed historically because it has not been able to create a thriving and dynamic society in which each member feels that he or she has an active and meaningful role to play. It has failed politically because it has not been able to turn the Islamic world into a geostrategic factor in the international scene. However, Roy accepts that Muslim political activism will remain, since "re-Islamization has in no way changed the rules of the political or economic game" (Roy 1994, 26). He goes as far as to say that the "Islamic revolution, the Islamic state, [and] the Islamic economy are myths" (27). Obviously, I disagree with such a dismissive conclusion, but I agree with the general observation that the Islamists' attempts to present Islam as a straightjacket panacea have failed. In many ways, the tragedy of September 11, 2001, was both the peak and the beginning of the end of Islamism: it showed itself as explicitly contrary to the teachings of Islam, and yet it showed how easily Islam can be manipulated and associated with such a hideous act.

Both generalizations—regarding either the supremacy of Islam or its collapse—should be avoided. When Muslims become serious about tackling their problems independently, through solutions generated from within, they will naturally turn to their own heritage, which for the most part is an Islamic one. If they have become too zealous, they will suffer the consequences. Another French scholar, Gilles Kepel, is more perceptive about the unfolding of the Islamic movement. For example, his observation about the reason behind the Islamists' success might be applied to the emergence of the post-Islamist generation: the "successes of the Islamists are the clearest indication of the political, economic and social bankruptcy of the post-independence ruling elites" (Kepel 1994, 193). Similarly, the failure of the Islamist elites has given rise to a revisionist discourse that tries to give credit where it is due.

Muslims have displayed a great ability to contribute to the human heritage. They have a proud tradition that deserves to be revered, but they will do themselves a great disservice if they turn their tradition and religion into an all-purpose instrument. It is sobering to note, as Fred Halliday correctly observes, that "the rise of Islamic movements and the invocation of Islam as a justification for political action do not represent some general, trans-historical phenomena; they reflect particular forces within specific societies in the contemporary world" (Halliday 1996, 118). To apply the comment to the movement in Iran, specific forces with a sophisticated history of rich debate have led to what unfolded in that country. Thus, any attempt to present a general evaluation of the contemporary Islamic movement must address the following questions: Are Muslims resolute about assuming an active role in the public sphere? Do they have a realistic inventory of their own human condition and that of the world? Are they thinking of indigenous alternatives when seeking a new direction for Muslim civilization building? Insofar as Islamic discourse is concerned, my response to all three questions is a cautious yes.

I respond positively to the first question because the new generation of Muslims has shaken off the fear that had been inflicted on their psyches for so long. The notion of eroded confidence, with which this book began, is losing its intensity, and young Muslims are constructing a narrative "driven by a positive, mainstream vision" instead of one driven "by defensive fear" (Safi 2003, 1). The protagonists of the group call themselves progressives and are trying to free themselves from a siege mentality by "reclaiming the moral authority" of Islam (42). These positions resonate with the views of Hajjarian, Kadivar, and Soroush, for example, in their desire to revive an ethical and moral society in place of an oppositional and confrontational state.

The most significant reason for the emergence of this new progressive voice is the inability of the Islamic movement to deliver what it promised—an ideal community in which all other persuasions would welcome the Islamist polity. Within the Iranian context, the fourth generation has experienced many epochal developments. The following are just a few: it has witnessed and helped bring about the first classic revolution in the Middle East, which changed a 2,500-year monarchy into a republic; it has suffered through and participated in an eight-year war that incurred enormous human and material losses; and it has observed and even participated in the information revolution. On a more positive note, it has had the exuberance of the first national victory since the Irano-Russian wars (1805–1828), retaking its homeland from invading Iraqi forces (Rajaee 1383/2004: 244–246). Interestingly, though, even here the experiences of the emerging generation resemble the historical context of the first generation. They also experienced a revolution, a war, and the occupation of their country during World War I. Just as they were determined to take charge of their fate, so is the present generation determined to participate in the ongoing information revolution.

Regarding the second question—which concerns their understanding of the human condition, local and global—the new generations of post-Islamist and postmodern Islam-minded Iranians acknowledge the dismal conditions of underdevelopment, decadence, and corruption in their country. The writings of Akbar Ganji are a clear testimony to this awareness. He is not afraid to openly discuss the various dimensions of this situation, identifying Iran as a transitory society facing a host of problems: an identity crisis, inequality, intolerance, a battle of values, uncertainty about the future, poverty, addiction, embezzlement, the elimination of dissidents, and the encouragement of political fascism (Ganji 1379/2000b, 11). He goes on to address many of these concerns in detail and in terse, sharp, and bitter language. He does not feel the need to protect anyone or any group. He revealed many political maneuvers of former President Rafsanjani, thereby discrediting him and frustrating his attempt to regain control of the Iranian parliament. Ganji also disclosed many of the coalitions behind the "chain killing of the intellectuals" and linked them either to the officials of the Ministry of Intelligence or to parts of the judiciary (183–185, 271–273, 252–254, 276–279, 327–336, and 419–438).

This generation is conscious of its present and aware of its past. The Israeli scholar Haggay Ram, in his discussion of the use of Friday prayers in Iran, ends his book with the following words: "The American philosopher and man of letters, George Santayana is perhaps most famous for his aphorism, 'those who do not remember the past are condemned to relive it.' Our discussion in this study has shown just the opposite. The *Ulama* in revolutionary Iran have consciously striven to remember and to make their flock remember the past, with the unequivocal objective of reliving it" (Ram 1994, 234). The clergy, as well as the people at large, have become extremely interested in their history. Obviously, there is a powerful trend toward recognizing only certain aspects of Iranian and Shi'i history, to be put to parochial and particular ends, rather than learning objectively from history.

Both extreme secularists and extreme Islamists are guilty in this regard; they lack historical realism, and, more significantly, they refuse to accept history. But they are being pushed to the margins, and a new sense of historical consciousness is emerging. The Islamists are realizing that the "contemporary Muslim world is no more the medieval Muslim world than the European state according to Machiavelli was that of Thomas Aquinas" (Roy 1994, 16). Similarly, the proponents of secularism see that religion is an important component of Iranian identity, and its place in the public sphere has to be acknowledged and revered. They are discovering that Iranians have struggled, just like any other people in the world. Sometimes they have followed the tenets of their religion completely, sometimes they have deviated a little, and sometimes they have adopted other modes of thinking, but they have always strived for the betterment of their cultural milieu and acumen. This new, inclusive approach has relied on various sources, from the ancient Iranian worldview to Hellenic culture, Islamic doctrine, and the modern world. In the modern period, these other sources have colored the Iranians' world. The works of Soroush and Kadivar take historical conditions seriously and encourage realistic and complex thought; opportunism may bear short-term fruit, but it leads only to increased power, not statesmanship or civilization building.

Regarding the final question, which pertains to indigenous ideas, the new generation of Muslims seems to be serious about rethinking its own heritage and reevaluating the West and modernity so as to restore Muslim civilization once more. Whether they will be successful is hard to predict. The Canadian author Thierry Hentsch places the issue in another context: "Islam has no other limits, in the future, than those which Muslims themselves will impose upon it . . . No one knows what 'Muslim socialism' might become (or 'socialist Islam' for that matter), but nothing can prevent Muslims from attempting to build a new society (whatever its name or its sources of inspiration may be)" (Hentsch 1992, 199). The fourth generation in the Islamic discourse of Iran is doing precisely this, against all odds.

How can one be sure that the fourth generation will be successful and not be overtaken by a new wave of extremism? The election of President Ahmadinejad may present a case in point. The road to civilization production is tedious and hard. One may take one step forward and two steps back. Indeed, what happened in Iran in 2005 is consistent with the past two decades of the country's history. But taking a long-term view, one may note some degree of progress. First, the experiment with an Islamic revolution in the past two decades proved ineffective. Second, the poverty of any ideology is historically demonstrable, just as the experience of Nazism in Germany, Fascism in Italy, and Communism in the Soviet Union and China showed the inability of ideology to provide a solid ground for civilization production. Islamism proved that turning a religion into an ideology results in similar shortfalls.

For example, many Muslim voices are criticizing the Islamists for their lack of authenticity or moral roots within the Islamic tradition. What is interesting is that this line of thinking cuts across generations and intellectual approaches. Seyyed Hossein Nasr, one of the most eloquent voices of traditional Islam in the West and the president of the Foundation for Traditional Studies, and Mohieddin Mesbahi, a Muslim professor in Florida who expresses the views of the new Muslim generation, have made two similar critical observations. The first was uttered many years before the tragedy of September 11, 2001, and the second was uttered just over a month after those events. For Nasr, turning Islam into an ideology amounts to impoverishing spirituality:

> In those areas and among those groups where the Islamic religion has been reduced to Islamic ideology, often with the intention of preventing anything other than Islam from becoming the source for inspiration for human thought and action, there is a clear lack of spiritual beauty, of intellectual depth, and of traditional Islamic virtues, which have their root in the Qur'an and the very soul of the Prophet. (Nasr 1984, 283)

For Mesbahi, the same process utterly violates the meaning of religion, divorces it from ethics, and angers the creator:

> There was nothing Islamic in the September 11 acts. The perpetrators killed innocent people, committed suicide and did so by conspiracy and stealth; all three are strictly forbidden by both Islam's holy book and tradition; the perpetrators will not meet their Creator in heaven. The God of Islam is pretty unforgiving when it comes to the taking of innocent life. (*Miami Herald,* October 21, 2001)

Perhaps the eruption of extremism is part and parcel of the general emancipation of humanity, the revolt of the masses, and the indiscriminate empowering of globalization and modernity. At the same time, the voices of reason and the demand for a dialogue of civilizations may reveal the absurdity of extremism and force the paranoid voices of radicalism to the margin, allowing the emerging post-Islamist generation to formulate a more inclusive theology, polity, foreign policy, and Muslim politics.

NOTES

PREFACE AND ACKNOWLEDGMENTS

1. The Iranian historian Fereydun Adamiyat has devoted his life to the study of the intellectual history of Iran and has produced works that can be described as classics. In recent years the younger generation of Iranian scholars has done work on the twentieth century in particular. For example, see Akhavi (1980), Boroujerdi (1996), Chehabi (1990), Gheisari (1998), Nabavi (2003), and Vahdat (2002).

2. I had the good fortune to discuss with Professor Katuzian the very first ideas of this book and showed him my preliminary outline in 1990–1991, when I was in Oxford. He was kind enough to seriously review it and write a long report for me about each section. The original plan changed partly as a result of those constructive criticisms.

INTRODUCTION

1. In December 1977, President Carter described the Iranian regime: "Iran, because of the great leadership of the Shah, is an island of stability in one of the more troubled areas of the world. This is a great tribute to you, Your Majesty, and to your leadership, and to the respect and admiration and love which your people give to you" (Carter 1978, 2:2221). One week later, the same loving and admiring people clashed with the shah's forces.

2. The story of the Iranians' encounter with modernity is treated in my forthcoming work, *Authenticity and Modernity: Moments of Convergence in the Persian Question.*

3. There is the view that Reza Khan rose through the ranks of the military. There are two problems with this view: he was an officer in a small unit, and historically the military had never played a political role in Iran. The Pahlavi era, when outside powers and the military supplanted the social classes politically, is the only exception.

CHAPTER ONE

1. Growing up as a child, I never forgot how my grandmother would reproach me for using the pronoun "I" to identify myself. She would correct me by saying that "I" belongs to God only.

2. In a Persian work entitled *The Battle of Worldviews,* I have developed in detail a thesis regarding the distinction between the two patterns of thinking that contribute to development and state-building. While the battle of worldviews leads to a zero-sum game of war of all against all, the battle of ideas allows for intellectual interaction and political give-and-take.

3. I had access to the diary of Reza Khan's secretary, Suleyman Behbudi, and in it one sees how Reza Khan carefully monitored the life of the key players in Iranian politics, including Ahmad Shah, the last Qajar king.

4. *Bayt,* or household, is very important in a traditional setting. Each religious leader has elaborate offices attached to his home. The main function of this particular office is to collect special taxes and distribute them among students, a duty given to someone very trusted and close to a leader.

5. The essay begins with an interesting anecdote from the well-known man of tradition Abu-Horayre: "It is reported of Safein during the war that at the time of any meal he would go to Muawiyyah's camp, at the time of prayer he would go to Ali's camp, and when the war was on, he would sit aside and would be a spectator. When he was asked to explain this contradictory affair, he said: Muawiyyah's food is more elaborate, Ali's praying is more accurate, and being a spectator is more comfortable" (*Homayun* no. 5, 24).

6. This statement is probably a response to Sangelaji, who supported the idea of the separation between the two realms.

7. This claim is based on a Qur'anic verse: "Man shall have nothing but what he strives for" (Qur'an 53:39).

8. For example, there are other refutations, as follows: Mohammad Ali Hematabadi, *Resaleye Pasokhname Eslami; Rad Bar Asrar Hezarsaleh* [A Islamic Treatise of Response: Refuting 'The Secret of a Thousand Years'] (Tehran: Elmi, 1324/1945); and Muhammad Khalesizadeh, *Kashf al-Astaar; Javaab bar Asraar Hezaarsaaleh* [Revealing the Covered: A Response to 'The Secret of a Thousand Years'] (Tehran: Ardahaali, 1323/1944).

9. Ayatollah Abolqasem Khazali is currently a member of the Assembly of Experts, elected from Khorasan Province. He is also a member of the Guardian Council. Ayatollah Khazali was born in 1304/1925, moved to Mashhad in 1314/1935 to study, and finished high school there in 1321/1942. In 1327/1948 he moved to Qom to study with Burujerdi, Tabataba'i, and Khomeini. Since the revolution, he has become a prominent member of the establishment in Iran.

10. For example, there is Yadollah Sahabi, who was also an important member of the Bazargan-Taleqani group. He influenced a host of Iranians and attracted youth

to Islam. His son, Ezatollah, also became active and is one of the important voices of dissent in the postrevolutionary Islamic Republic.

CHAPTER TWO

1. A psychologist and the son of a cleric named Sheikh Mohammad Ebrahim, Nassereddin Sahabzamani had a large following. Bahar was an interesting intellectual with Tudeh connections; he came from a cultured family directly related to Malek as-Sho'ara Bahar, the participant observer and historian of the constitutional revolutionary period. Al-e Ahmad provides a very interesting case. He began studying theology, going to Najaf in 1943, but turned away and became a member of the Iranian Communist party. Later he abandoned them, established the "Third Way" with Khalil Maleki, and finally turned to religion in late life and performed the pilgrimage to Mecca.

2. James Bill, an American scholar on Iran, said the following about the book in 1967: "This book is a must for you—must be referred to in your study. Has already sold 18,000 copies here—just about a year old now—has created quite a sensation here" (from the copy of the note, in the author's possession). I am grateful to my friend Jallal Jalali for allowing me to copy this note. His copy of the book, purchased in an old bookstore in Princeton, had Bill's noted folded inside. I saw the note in Mr. Jalali's library in Washington, D.C., in 1986. There is no date on the note, but in a conversation with Jim Bill after I delivered a lecture at his university, he confirmed that the date was 1967 (Virginia, May 2001).

3. The debate over this book in Iran is interesting. In a society in which conspiracy theories rule and the assumption is that "big powers" run everything, the publication of a book openly critical of America meant something insightful. This book was "obviously commissioned and supported by the British to discredit America," (I remember hearing this among intellectuals in Tehran in the early 1970s.) The reason was to be found in the publication of a three-volume book on the story of Freemasonry that had been published a few years earlier, revealing the names of Iranian lodges and their members. The belief was that Americans had sponsored the publication of that book in order to discredit the British, and now the latter had struck back with a vengeance. On the other hand, in the aforementioned note, Jim Bill writes, "Some believe this book was done in line with the government policy of cooling relations with the U.S."

4. My reason for translation *marja'iyat* as "religious authority" is that this word, literally meaning "the source," refers to the highest office of religious authority for Shi'is to emulate in their daily lives. According to Shi'ism, either one is highly qualified (*mojtahid*) to licence and implement the Islamic injunctions independently, or one has to be a follower (*moqaled*). In the latter case, one looks for a source of emulation, that is, the *marja'* (the office of the *marja'iyat*).

5. The others on the list were, in order, (2) Mohammad Reza Golpayegani, (3) Kazem Shari'atmadari Tabrizi, (4) Abdolnabi Araki, (5) Mohammad Mohaqeq Yazdi, (6) Abasali Shahrudi, (7) Shahab ad-Din Mar'ashi, and (8) Murteza Langarudi. This list is important because it shows that Khomeini had already achieved a high scholarly stature and social position before he became actively engaged in political struggles with the shah.

6. I was in Iran in 1978–1979 and observed how most members of the elite of the shah departed months before the king finally had to leave the country. Even during the trial of some members of the old regime, all responsibility was passed on to the shah himself, including the duties of his prime minister of thirteen years, Amir Abbas Hoveida.

7. Ayatollah Sadr said that he was present when Khomeini did his best to gently help a bug fly out of a room rather than kill or hurt the insect, yet when informed about the killing of more than 5,000 [revolutionaries estimate] people in the June 1963 uprising, Khomeini said without any remorse that Islam was in need of more blood.

8. Nader Naderpour was not very sympathetic to religious discourse and its clerical proponents. Note his poem called "Qom," written long before the revolution: "Thousands of women / Thousands of men / The women in veil / The men in cloaks / A single gold dome / With old storks / A joyless garden / With a few scattered trees / Devoid of laughter / Silent / A half-filled courtyard pool / With greenish water / Some old crows / On piles of rocks / Crowds of beggars / Every step of the way / White turbans / Black faces."

9. Two of the founders of the organization claim these publications as theirs, but according to the subtitle of the journal *Be'sat*, it was "the internal publication of the of Qom seminary students," and among organization members it was referred to as "the secret publication of the Qom seminary."

10. This society met for over two years, and the "ninety one talks" presented there were later published in three volumes (Jahanbakhsh 2001, 60).

11. It is still a controversial book, even after three decades. On one of my last research trips to Iran, in the summer of 2004, I picked up a book of more than 600 pages dedicated to the fate of Najafabadi's book, appropriately titled *The Story of the Book "Shahid Javid."* See Haj Sheikh Reza Ostadi, *Sargozasht-e Shahid Javid* (Tehran: Qods, 1382/2003).

12. Seyyed Hossein Nasr told the author in Ottawa (spring 2003) that he had been present when Shari'ati compared Imam Hossein to Che Guevara. He added that Shari'ati left Ershad and never returned to that institution.

13. One of the most contentious questions in Muslim history has been how to define a Muslim. Many of Shari'ati's critics accused him of not being strongly committed to the daily observation of Islamic rituals and legal duties. Here, my emphasis for a Muslim is on the philosophical commitment to Islamic ontology and cosmology.

14. Other radical Muslims, such as the members of the Egyptian Islamic Movement, also call jihad the forgotten duty that has to be revived.

15. The other founders of the organization included Ayatollah Mahmoud Taleqani (d. 1979), Rahim Ata'i (d. 1977), and Yadollah Sahabi (d. 2001).

CHAPTER THREE

1. Some refer to this group as the New Left (*Chap-e Jadid*), which does not accurately reflect its views. In many ways, it resembles the New Right in other places, including Europe and the United States.

2. This is a daily founded in fall 1998 by Abdollah Nuri, Khatami's first minister of the interior, who lost his vote of confidence. The name is significant: It is the name of the third month of the Iranian calendar, corresponding to May/June, the month during which Khatami was elected president. The first issue, published on December 3, 1998, declared its primary mission as promoting Khatami's mandate: civil society, political development, and political participation.

3. A technical term originating from the Greek, "androlepsia" refers to capturing foreign citizens and holding them for ransom or compensation in retaliation for acts committed by the foreigners' compatriots or home country. The Iranians who kidnapped the American diplomats were seeking the return of the shah by America.

4. The publication is owned by Ansar Hezbollah, one of the most radical Islamists in the country. Note the headline: "Development and Cultural Liberalism" ("Tose'e va Liberalism Farhangi").

5. This is striking, since *nafsaniyat* is a special notion in Muslim philosophy, denoting carnality, sensuality, and the vanity of passions. It was quite intentional for Davari to equate it with the notion of subjectivity.

CHAPTER FOUR

1. Here I concentrate on the debate within and among the political elite of the society, otherwise I would spend a whole section on the debate on the nature of despotism or on why Iran has stayed behind while others move ahead. In the late 1990s and early 2000s, works such as *Jame'eshnasi Nokhbeh Koshi* (The Sociology of Elite Killing) by Ali Rezaqoli (Tehran: Nashr-e Ney, 1378/1999) and *Jame'eshnasi Khodemaani* (Commonsense Sociology) by Hassan Naraqi (Tehran: Nashr-e Akhtaran, 1380/2001) became best-sellers.

2. For example, Montazeri is prepared to tolerate a diversity and multiplicity of voices in Islam and has even given controversial legal rulings on contemporary issues. The case of the contemporary Iranian Baha'is is important to note. While he accepts that the first generation of Baha'is committed apostasy by leaving Islam, the present generation could not be considered apostates because they had not chosen their religion, thus they should be considered members of another religion.

3. Though the documents have not been entirely disclosed, Montazeri objected to Khomeini's orders to kill many people in 1988, including many former members of the leftist People's Mojahedin organization who had not even finished their sentences, but were called back to be killed. Three memoirs have dealt with this issue. One, by Ahmad Khomeini, is entitled *Ranjnameh;* one by Mohammad Reyshahri is entitled *Khaterat-e Siyassi;* and the third is Montazeri's, which has been published on the Internet. Appendix 153 of the last memoir contains Montazeri's letter to Khomeini about the mass killing of dissidents in the summer of 1988.

4. I discuss Burujerdi in Chapter One. Ayatollah Khoei, a prominent source of emulation in Shi'ism at the same time as Khomeini, insisted on education and the cultural dimension of Islam, whereas Baqir Sadr was a Shi'i leader in Iraq until his assassination, in 1980, and introduced many new ideas in Islamic jurisprudence.

5. Soroush first introduced this idea in a set of articles in a cultural monthly called *Keyhan-e Farhangi* in 1988–1990, but it became the most debated issue in the 1990s, forcing Soroush to elaborate on his point in a volume of more than 600 pages. The Council on Foreign Relations commissioned a study of it: Valla Vakili, *Debating Religion and Politics in Iran: The Political Thought of Abdolkarim Sorush* (New York: Council on Foreign Relations, 1997).

CONCLUSION

1. The URL for this report is http://www.rferl.org/features/features_Article .aspx?m=11&y=2005&id=184CB9FB-887C-4696-8F54-0799DF747A4A (accessed December 1, 2006).

2. Khatami's speech can be found at http://www.iranian.com/Opinion/2000/ September/Khatami/ (accessed January 30, 2007).

REFERENCES

INTERVIEWS WITH THE AUTHOR

Note: The identities of some interviewees have been shielded, either for security reasons or from requests for anonymity.

Ashtiyani, Seyyed Jalaledin; Mashhad, 1990.
B——, Kazem (a close relative of Ayatollahs Hae'ri and Isfahani); Tehran, May 2004.
Badkobeei, Ayatollah Hassan; Arak, April 16, 1990.
Bazargan, Mehdi; conversations from 1987 to 1992.
Bodala, Hossein; Qom, November 1990.
Boroujerdi, Mahmud; Tehran, April 1992.
Davari, Reza; Tehran, March 1990, June 1995, and May 2004.
Ebrahimi-Dinani, Gholamhossein; Tehran, throughout the 1990s and in May 2004.
Faqihi, Ali Asghar; Tehran, 1990, 1992, and 1995.
Fardid, Ahmad; Tehran, May 1982.
Hajjarian, Saeed; Tehran, May 2004.
K-A, Hossein (a high government official); Tehran, 1987.
Kadivar, Mohsen; Tehran, May 2004.
M-J, Mohammad (a young clergyman who served as a high official and an ambassador); Tehran, 1990.
Mahdavi-Damghani, Mahmoud; Mashhad, June 3, 1990.
Mehryar, Mohammad; Isfahan, August 2, 1990.
Montazeri, Ayatollah Hossein-Ali; Qom, May 2004.
Pahlavan, Changiz; Tehran, spring 1992.
Pasandideh, Morteza; Tehran, spring and summer 1990.
Reza, Enayatollah; Tehran, spring 1992.
Sabet-Rasekh, General Yadollah; Isfahan, July 31, 1990.
Sadr, Ayatollah M. R.; Tehran, April 8, 1990.
Shabestari, Mohammad; Tehran, 1990 and 2001.
Shams, Shams ed-Din; Tehran, January 26, 1990.
Soroush, Abdolkarim; Tehran, 1990, and Princeton, 2003.

SOURCES IN PERSIAN

Aabaadiyaan, Hossein. 1376/1999. *Andisheye Dini va Jonbeshe Zed-e Rezhi dar Iran* [Religious Thinking and the Tobacco Movement in Iran]. Tehran: Mo'assesse-ye Motale'at-e Tarikh-e Mo'asser-e Iran.

Abdi, Abbas, and Mohsen Gudarzi. 1378/1999. *Tahavolat-e Farhangi dar Iran* [Cultural Evolution in Iran]. Tehran: Entesharat-e Ravesh.

Adamiyat, Fereidun. 1340/1961. *Fekre Azadi va Moqadameye Nehzate Mashrutiyate dar Iran* [The Idea of Freedom and the Beginning of the Constitutional Movement in Iran]. Tehran: Sokhan.

———. 1360/1981. *Tahlili az Shuresh bar Emtiyazname-ye Rezhi* [An Analysis of the Uprising against the Reggi Concession]. Tehran: Payam.

Afshari, Alireza. 1379/2000. *Mardi baraye Tamam Tarikh* [A Man for All History]. Tehran: Nashr-e Marsa.

Alavi, Seyyed Abas. 1328/1950. *Bayane Haqayeq* [Explicating the Truth]. Tehran: Lajneye Melli.

Alavi, Seyyed Hossein. 1354/1975. *Aya Sobh Nazdik Nist? Goftari Piramune Vujude Mobarake Imam Zaman.* [Isn't the Dawn Approaching? On the Existence of his Holiness the Imam of the Age]. Isfahan: Khatam.

Al-e Ahmad, Jalal. 1364/1986. *Namehaye Jalal Al-e Ahmad* [The Letters of Al-e Ahmad]. Edited by Ali Dabashi. Tehran: Entesharat-e Peik.

———. 1375/1996 [1341/1962]. *Gharbzadegi* [Weststruckness]. Tehran: Ravaq.

Aryanpour, Yahya. 1350/1971. *Az Saba ta Nima; Tarikh-e Sadopanjah Sal Adab-e Farsi* [From Saba to Nima: A Hundred Years of Persian Literature]. 2 vols. Tehran: Kharazmi.

Ashuri, Daryush. 1383/2004. *Ostureye Falsafe dar Mian Ma* [The Myth of Philosophy among Us]. N.p.: Nilgon.org.

Badamchian, Assadollah, and Ali Banaei. 1362/1983. *Hay'atha-ye Mo'talefe-ye Eslami* [The Coalescing Islamic Societies]. Tehran: Entesharat-e Owj.

Bahar, Mehdi. 1344/1965. *Miraskhar-e Este'mar* [The Inheritor of Colonialism]. Tehran: Amir Kabir.

Bahar, Mohammad Taqi. 1323/1944. *Tarikh-e Mokhtasare Ahzab-e Siyassi dar Iran* [A Short History of Political Parties in Iran]. Vol. 1. Tehran: Amir Kabir.

Bahsi darbareye Marja'iyat va Rohaniyat [A Discussion of Religious Authority and the Clergies]. 1341/1962. 2nd ed. Tehran: Enteshar.

Bani Sadr, Abolhassan. 1360/1981. *Kheyant be Omid* [The Betrayal of Hope]. Paris: published by the author.

Baqi, Emaddodin. 1362/1983. *Dar Shenakht Hezb-e Qa'edin Zaman, Mossum be Anjomane Hojjatiye* [On Introducing the Party known as the Hojjatiye Association]. Tehran: Entesharate Rahe Mojahed.

———. 1379/2000. *Baraye Tarikh; Goftegu ba Said Hajjarian* [For History: An Interview with Saeed Hajjarian]. Tehran: Nashr-e Ney.

Barzin, Said. 1374/1996. *Zendeginameye Siyassi Mohandes Mehdi Bazargan* [A Political Biography of Mehdi Bazargan]. Tehran: Nashr Markaz.

Bazargan, Mehdi. 1341/1962. "Entezare Mardom az Maraje'" [The People's Expectations of the Religious Authorities]. In *Bahsi darbareye Marja'iyat va Rohaniyat*, 103–129.

———. 1344/1965. *Mazhab dar Orupa* [Religion in Europe]. Tehran: Sherkate Enteshar.

———. 1355/1976 [1341/1962]. *Marz Miyane Din va Omur Estemaei* [The Boundary between Religion and Social Issues]. Houston: Pakhshe Ketab.

———. 1356/1977 [1343/1964]. *Modafe'at* [Defense]. Belleville, Ill.: Nehzate Azadi Khareje Keshvar.

———. 1357/1978 [1335/1957]. *Rah Tey Shodeh* [A Path Taken]. Houston: Pakhshe Ketab.

———. 1362/1983. *Shoura-ye Enqelab wa Doulat-e Mowaqat* [The Revolutionary Council and the Provisional Government]. Tehran: Nehzat-e Azadi.

Behnam, Jamshid. 1375/1996. *Iranian va Andisheye Tajadod* [Iranians and the Idea of Modernity]. Tehran: Nashr Farzan.

Bist-o-Hasht Hezar Ruz Tarikh-e Iran [Twenty-eight Thousand Days of Iranian History]. 1309/1930. Tehran: Ettela'at.

Bistomin Salgarde Nehazate Azadiye Iran [The Twentieth Anniversary of the Freedom Movement of Iran] 1362/1983. Tehran: Nehzat-e Azadi.

"Chardah Qarn Rahbaran Shi'a." 1340/1962. *Khandaniha* 22 (46): 23–34.

Daftar-e Rahbari. 1375/1996. *Hadith-e Vellayat; Majmu'eye Rahnemudhaye Maqam Mo'azam-e Rahbari* [A Collection of the Speeches of the Leader]. Vol. 1. Tehran: Sazman-e Madarek-e Enqelab-e Eslami.

Davani, Ali. 1360/1981. *Nahzat-e Rohaniyun-e Iran* [The Clerical Movement of Iran]. 11 vols. Tehran: Bonyad-e Imam Reza.

———. 1371/1992. *Zendegani Zaeim Bozorg 'Alam Tashyu,' Ayatollah Burujerdi*. [The Life of the Great Leader of Shi'ism, Ayatollah Burujerdi]. Revised ed. Tehran: Nashr Motahar.

Davari, Reza. 1357/1978. *Vaz'e Konunt-ye Tafakor dar Iran* [The State of Contemporary Thought in Iran]. Tehran: Soroush.

———. 1364/1985. *Nassionalizm, Hakemiyat-e Melli va Esteqlal* [Nationalism, National Sovereignty, and Independence]. Isfahan: Entesharat-e Porsesh.

———. 1373/1994. *Falsafe dar Bohran* [Philosophy in Crisis]. Tehran: Amir Kabir.

Dehgan, Ebrahim. 1331/1953. *Noore Mobin* [The Clear Light]. Arak: Farvardin.

Dolatabadi, Yahya. 1309/1930. "Name az Bruksel" [Letter from Brussels]. In *Bist-o-Hasht Hezar Ruz Tarikh-e Iran* [Twenty-eight Thousand Days of Iranian History]. Tehran: Ettela'at.

———. 1336/1957. *Tarikh-e Mo'asser ya Hayat-e Yahya* [A Contemporary History or the Life of Yahya]. 4 vols. Tehran: Eqbal.

Edareye Kole Qavanin, comp. 1369/1990. *Surat-e Mashruhe Mozakerate Baznegariye Qanun-e Assasiye Jumhuriye Eslami* [Proceedings of the Review of the Constitution of the Islamic Republic of Iran]. 4 vols. Tehran: Adareye Tabloqat va Entesharat.

"Enqelab Islami; Dastavardaha va Tahdidha" [The Islamic Revolution: Accomplishments and Challenges]. 1375/1997. *Sobh: Political, Cultural, Social and Economic Monthly* 2, no. 67 (Esfand/February–March).

Eshkevari, Hassan Yusefi, ed. 1373/1995a. *Naqd-o Barrassi-ye Jonbesh-e Eslami Mo'asser; (1) Mossahebe ba Mohandes Mehdi Bazargan* [A Critical Review of the Contemporary Islamic Movement, No. 1: An Interview with Mehdi Bazargan]. Tehran: published by the editor.

———. 1373/1995b. *Naqd-o Barrassi-ye Jonbesh-e Eslami Mo'asser; (3) Mossahebe ba Dr. Abdolkarim Soroush* [A Critical Review of the Contemporary Islamic Movement, No. 3: An Interview with Dr. Abdolkarim Soroush]. Tehran: published by the editor.

———. 1373/1995c. *Naqd-o Barrassi-ye Jonbesh-e Eslami Mo'asser; (5) Mossahebe ba Ostad Mahammad Mojtahed Shabestari* [A Critical Review of the Contemporary Islamic Movement, No. 5: An Interview with Professor Mohammad Mojtahed Shabestari]. Tehran: published by the editor.

Eslami-Nadoushan, Mohammad-Ali. 1362/1993. *Goftim-o-Nagoftim* [Told and Untold]. Tehran: Yazdan.

Faiz, Abbas. 1349–1350/1970–1971. *Ganjineye Asar Qum* [A Collection of Qom's Stories]. 2 vols. Qom: published by the author.

Fardid, Ahmad. 1381/2002. *Didar-e Farahi va Fotuhaat-e Aakhar-e Zamaan* [The Divine Encounter and Illuminations at the End of Time]. Tehran: Moassesseye Farhangi va Pazhuheshi va Chap van Nashr-e Nazar.

Fateh, Mostafah. 1310/1932. *Rah-e Pishraft* [The Path to Progress]. Tehran: Matbaeiye Soroush.

Ganji, Akbar. 1379/2000a. *Aalijenab-e Sorkhpush va Aalijenab-e Khakestari* [His Eminence Red and His Eminence Gray]. Tehran: Tarh-e No.

———. 1379/2000b. *Tarikkhane-ye Ashbah* [The Darkroom of the Ghosts]. Tehran: Tarh-e No.

———. 1381/2002. *Manifest-e Jumhurikhahi* [The Manifesto of Republicanism]. Unpublished manuscript in author's possession.

Golmakani, Hooshang. 1377/1999. "Az Khoshunat va Ta'asob ta Modara va Mehrvarzi" [From Violence and Fundamentalism to Tolerance and Kindness]. *Kiyan* 8 (Bahman–Esfand/February–March): 4–5.

"Gozareshi az Fa'aliyate Anjoman" [A Report on the Activities of the Association]. N.d. Internal handwritten report, in author's possession.

Hairi, Abdul-Hadi. 1367/1988. *Nakhostin Ruyarueihaye Andishegaran Irani ba Doruyeye Tamadon-e burzhuvazie Gharb* [The Early Encounter of Iranian Thinkers with the Two-Sided Civilization of the Western Bourgeoisie]. Tehran: Amir Kabir.

Hajjarian, Saeed. 1379/2000. *Jomhuriyat: Afsunzedaei az Qodrat* [Republicanism: The Disenchanting of Power]. Tehran: Tarh-e No.

——. 1380/2001. *Az Shahed Qodsi ta Shahed Bazari; Orfi Shodan Din dar Sepehr Siyassat* [From Sacred Witness to Profane Witness: The Secularization of Religion in the Political Sphere]. Tehran: Entesharat-e Tarh-e No.

Hakamizadeh, Ali Akbar. 1322/1943. *Asrare Hezarsaleh* [The Secret of a Thousand Years]. Tehran: Parcham.

Hedayat, Mehdiqoli. 1346/1967 [1329/1950]. *Khaterat va Khatarat* [Memoirs and Challenges]. Tehran: Zavar.

Hojjati-Kermani, Ali, comp. 1368/1989. *Be'sat; Organ Makhfi-e Daneshjuyan-e Houze-ye 'Elmiye-ye Qum dar Salhaye 1342–44* [Be'sat: The Covert Organ of Students at the Qom Seminary in the Years 1342–44/1963–65]. Tehran: Suroush.

Honarmand, Manuchehr. 1351/1972. *Pahlavism: Maktab-e No* [Pahlavism: The New School]. Tehran: n.p.

Iqbal, Abbas. 1326/1937. "Ma va Tamadon-e Orupaei" [We and European Civilization]. *Yadegar* 5 (4): 1–7.

Izadi, Mohammad. 1359/1980. *Gozari bar Zaendegi va Andisheha-ye Faqih Aliqadr Ayatollah Montazeri* [A Review and Look at the Life of the Exalted Jurist, Ayatollah Montazeri]. Tehran: Nehzat-e Zanan-e Mosalman.

Kadivar, Mohsen. 1378/1999. *Hokumat-e Vallae'i* [Government as Guardianship]. Tehran: Nashr-e Ney.

——. 1379/2000a. *Daghdaghe-ye Hokumat-e Dini* [Preoccupations with Religious Government]. 2nd ed. Tehran: Nashr-e Ney.

——. 1379/2000b. *Hokumat-e Entesabi* [Government by Appointment]. Tehran: Nashr-e Ney.

——. 1380/2001. *Nazareye-haye Dolat dar Fiqh-e Shi'a* [Theories of the State in Shi'i Jurisprudence]. 5th ed. Tehran: Nashr-e Ney.

——. 1382/2003. "Andisheye Siyassi-ye Akhond Khorassani" [The Political Ideas of Cleric Khorassani]. Paper presented at a conference in Tehran dealing with the intellectual foundation of the Constitutional Revolution; copy in the author's possession.

Kasravi, Ahmad. 1336/1957. *Din va Jahaan* [Religion and the World]. 3rd ed. Tehran: Paayedaar.

——. 1355/1976 [1325/1946]. *Zendegani Man; Doureye Kamel* [My Life: Complete Series]. Tehran: Entesharat Bonyad.

——. 1357/1978. *Dar Peiraamun-e Taarikh* [On History]. 2nd ed. Tehran: Jaar.

——. 1358/1979. *Ma Che Mikhahim: Goftaarhaaei az Maahnaameye Peymaan* [What We Want: Essays from the Monthly *Peymaan*]. Tehran: Roshdiye.

——. 1363/1985 [1340/1961]. *Tarikh-e Mashrute-ye Iran* [A History of Iranian Constitutionalism]. Tehran: Amir Kabir.

Kazemi, Moshfeq. 1303/1924. "Enqelab-e Ejtemari, Zarurat-e Diktator" [Social Revolution, the Necessity of the Emergence of a Dictator]. *Name-ye Farhangestan* (Urdibehesht/May): 11–15.

Khamenei, Ali. 1365/1986. *Gozareshi az Tarikhe va Oza'e Kononiye Hozeye 'Elmiy-eyye Mashhad* [A Report on the History and Contemporary Condition of the Seminary of Mashhad]. Mashhad: Astane Qods Razavi.

———. 1375/1996. *Farhang va Tahajom-e Farhangi* [Culture and Cultural Assault]. Tehran: Vezarat-e Ershad Eslami.

Khomeini, Ruhollah. 1321/1943. *Kashf-e Asrar* [Revealing the Secret]. Tehran: Islamiyeh.

———. 1361/1982. *Sahifeye Noor* [The Book of Light]. 21 vols. Tehran: Vezarat-e Ershad Eslami.

———. 1367/1989. *Ava-yi Tawhid* [The Sound of Monotheism]. Tehran: Ershad.

Khosroshahi, Seyyed Hadi. 1375/1996. *Fada'iyan Islam; Tarikh, Amalkard, Andishe* [The Devotees of Islam: History, Actions, and Thought]. Tehran: Entesharat-e Ettela'at.

Mahbubi-Ardakani, Hossein. 1368/1989. *Tarikh-e Mo'assessat-e Tamadoni-ye Jadid dar Iran* [A History of the Institutions of Modern Civilization in Iran]. 3 vols. Tehran: Tehran University Press.

Mahiyat Zed Enqelabi Anjoman Hojjatiye ra Beshenassim [Getting to Know the Counterrevolutionary Nature of the Hojjatiye Association]. 1360/1981. Tehran: n.p.

Maki, Hossein. 1357/1978. *Tarikhe Bist Saleye Iran* [A Twenty-Year History of Iran]. 8 vols. Tehran: Amir Kabir.

———. 1358/1979. *Modarres, Qahreman-e Azadi* [Modarres: The Hero of Freedom]. 2 vols. Tehran: Bonyade Tarjomeh va Nashr-e Ketab.

Mehrizi-Tabataba'i, Sadreddin. 1351/1972. *Hamasye Javid* [The Eternal Epic]. Qom: Elmiye.

Mesbah Yazdi, Mohammad Taqi. 1360/1981. *Pasdari az Sangarhaye Eideologic* [Guarding the Ideologic Fronts]. Qom: Mo'assesseye dar Rah-e Haq.

———. 1381/2002. *Negahi Gozara be Nazariye-ye Velayat Faqih* [A Short Overview of the Theory of the Guardianship of the Jurisconsult]. Qom: Mo'assesseye Amuzeshi-Pazhuheshi Imam Khomeini.

———. 1381/2003. *Tahajom-e Farhangi* [Cultural Assault]. Qom: Imam Khomeini's Educational and Research Institute.

Montazeri, Hossein-Ali. 1379/2000. *Mabani Feqhi Hokumat-e Eslami* [The Juridical Foundation of Islamic Government]. Edited and translated from the Arabic by Mohammad Salavati. Vol. 2 (of 6). Tehran: Sarabi.

Moqadaszadeh, Seyyed Mohammad. 1335/1956. *Rejale Qom va Bahsi dar Tarikhe Aan* [Notable Men of Qom and a History of That City]. Tehran: Mehr-e Iran.

Moradiniya, Mohammad Javad, ed. 1374/1995. *Khaterate Ayatollah Passandideh* [Ayatollah Passandideh's Memoirs]. Tehran: Hadith.

Mosaddeq va Nehzat Melli Iran [Mosaddeq and the Iranian Nationalist Movement]. 1357/1978. N.p: Etehadiyeye Anjomanhaye Eslami Daneshjuyan dar Europa.

Motahhari, Morteza. 1341/1962. "Mazaya va Khadamate Ayatollah Burujerdi." In *Bahsi darbareye Marja'iyat va Rohaniyat,* 234–249.

———. 1357/1978. *Adl-e Elahi* [The Divine Justice]. Qom: Sadra.

———. 1372/1994 [1349/1970]. *Khadamat-e Motaqabel-e Islam va Iran* [Mutual Contributions of Islam and Iran]. Qom: Sadra.

———. 1376/1997 [1351/1972]. *Mas'ale-ye Hejab* [The Question of Women's Coverings]. Qom: Sadra.

———. 1382/2003 [1353/1974]. *Nezam-e Hoquqiye Zan dar Islam* [The System of Women's Rights in Islam]. Qom: Sadra.

———. n.d. *Piramun Enqelab-e Eslami* [On Islamic Revolution]. Tehran: Sadra.

Musavi-Makoei, Mir-Assadollah. 1376/1998. *Dabirestan-e Alborz va Shabaneruziye Aan* [Alborz High School and its Boarding System]. Tehran: Nashr-e Bisotun.

Mussavi, Mir Hossein. 1364/1985. "Roshanfekran-e Maghruq dar Falsafe-ye Gharbi" [The Intellectuals Overtaken by Western Philosophy]. *Faslname-ye Honar* 2:39–49.

Na'ini, Mohammad Hossein. 1334/1955. *Tanbih ul-Umma va Tanzih ul-Mella* [The Admonition of the Umma and the Refinement of the Nation]. Tehran: Enteshar.

Najafabadi, Saleh. 1349–1970. *Shahid-e Javid* [The Immortal Martyr]. Qom: Sadra.

Nateq, Homa. 1368/1990. *Iran dar Rahyabi-ye Farhangi, 1834–48* [Iran on the Threshold of Cultural Renovation, 1834–48]. Ottawa: Pegah.

Nehzat-e Azadi-ye Iran. 1364/1985. *Safahati az Tarikh-e Mo'asser-e Iran, Asnad-e Nehzat-e Moqavemat-e Melli* [Pages from the Contemporary History of Iran: Documents of the National Resistance Movement]. 5 vols. Tehran: Nehzat-r Azadi.

Nooriala, Esmaeil. 1357/1978. *Jame'eshenasi Tashayo'* [The Sociology of Shi'ism]. Tehran: Entesharat-e Qoqnus.

Pahlavi, Mohammad Reza. n.d. *Majmue'ye Ta'lifat, Notqha, Mosahebeha va Bayanante Mohammad Reza Shah* [The Collected Works, Speeches, Press Conferences, and Sayings of Mohammad Reza Shah]. 10 vols. Tehran: Keyhan.

Pahlavi, Princess Shams. 1327/1948. "Khaterat." *Ettela'at Mahane,* Urdibehesht/May.

Quchani, Mohammad. 1382/2004. *Naziabadiha* [People from Naziabad]. Tehran: Nashr Sarabi.

Rahamni, Qodratollah. 1382/2004. "Karnameye Rob-e Qarn Jumhuri Eslami dar Goftegu ba Ayatollah Hashemi Rafsanjani" [The Record of a Quarter Century of the Islamic Republic in Conversation with Ayatollah Rafsanjani]. *Keyhan* (from January 31 to February 24).

Rah-e Mossaddeq [Mossaddeq's Path]. 1374/1985. 5 vols. Tehran: Nehzat-e Azadi.

Rajaee, Farhang. 1364/1985. "Akhlaq, Elm, va Zendegi-e Daneshqahi" [Ethics, Science, and Academic Life]. *Nashr-e Daneshqahi* (Urdibehesht/May): 12–21.

———. 1376/1998. *Ma'reke-ye Jahanbiniha: dar Kheradvarzi Siyassi va Hoviyat-e Ma Iranian* [The Battle of Worldviews: On Political Rationalism and Our Iranian Identity]. Tehran: Ehya'e Ketab.

———. 1383/2004. *Moshkeleye Hoviyat-e Iranian Emruz* [The Problem of Contemporary Iranian Identity]. Tehran: Nashr-e Ney.

Razi, Mohammad. 1332/1953. *Asarolhojja, ya Tarikhe, va Da'eratolma'ref Hozeye Elmiyeye Qom* [The Clergies' Contribution, or the Chronicle and Encyclopedia of Qom's Seminaries]. Qom: Darolketab.

————. 1358/1979. *Sheykh Mohammad Bafqi*. 2nd ed. Qom: Shahid Gomnam.

"Rohaniyat dar Iran" [Clergies in Iran]. 1313/1935. *Homayun* no. 2: 3–4.

Rouhani (Ziyarati), Seyyed Hamid. 1362–1364/1983–1985. *Barrassi va Tahlili Az Nehzat-e Imam Khomeini* [An Overview and an Analysis of Imam Khomeini's Movement]. 2 vols. Tehran: Amozeshe Enqelabe Eslami.

Rudi-Kadivar, Zahra, comp. 1379/2000. *Bahaye Azadi; Defa'iyat-e Mohsen Kadivar dar Dadgah-e Vizheye Rohaniyat* [The Price of Freedom: The Defense of Mohsen Kadivar in the Special Court of the Clergy]. Tehran: Nashr-e Ney.

Saalnaameye Paars [Paars Annals]. 1306–1333/1927–1954. Tehran: Paars.

Sadiq, Eissa. 1352/1973. *Yadegar-e Omr* [Memories of a Life]. 2 vols. Tehran: Dehkhoda.

Sangelaji, Shari'at. 1321/1942. *Kelid Fahm Qur'an* [The Key to the Understanding of the Qur'an]. Tehran: Danesh.

————. 1322/1943. *Tawhid, Ibaadat, Yektaparasti* [Monotheism, Prayer, and Worshiping the One]. 2nd ed. Tehran: Chap-e Majlis.

Sarza'im, Ali. 1381/2002. *Daramadi be Barrasiye Tahlili Tarikhi Mo'assesseye Farhangi-ye Alavi* [An Introduction to the Historical Analysis of the Cultural Institution of Alavi]. Unpublished manuscript in author's possession.

Seyri dar Zendegani Ostad Motahhari [A Review of the Life of Motahhari]. 1382/2003. Qom: Sadra.

Shabestari, Mohammad Mojtahed. 1377/1998. *Hermonotik, Ketab, va Sonat* [Hermeneutics, Scripture, and Tradition]. 2nd ed. Tehran: Entesharat-e Tarh-e No.

————. 1378/2000. *Iman va Azadi* [Faith and Freedom]. 2nd ed. Tehran: Entesharat-e Tarh-e No.

————. 1381/2002. *Naqdi bar Qara'at Rasmi az Din: Bohranya, Chaleshha, Rahhalha* [A Critique of the Official Reading of Religion: Crisis, Challenges, and Solutions]. Tehran: Entesharat-e Tarh-e No.

————. 1383/2004. "Adonis's Conversation with Shabestari." Reprinted from *al-Hayat* (April 4, 2004) on http://emruz.info.

Shari'ati, Ali. 1347/1969. *Islam-Shenassi* [Islamology]. Mashhad: Chapkhaneye Tus.

————. 1357/1979. *Majmu'eye Asaar* [Collected Works]. 35 vols. Tehran: Daftar-e Tanzim-e Majmu'eye Asaar Dr. Ali Shari'ati.

————. n.d. *Ensan va Islam* [Man and Islam]. Tehran: Sherkat-e Sahami-ye Enteshar.

Soroush, Abdolkarim. 1370/1991. "Qabz-o Bast dar Mizan Naqd-o Bahs" [Contraction and Expansion at the Level of Criticism and Discussion]. *Kiyan* 1 (2): 1–8.

————. 1372/1993. "Ma'na va Mabnay-e Seckularizm" [Meaning and the Foundation of Secularism]. *Kiyan* 26:1–6.

————. 1373/1994. *Tafaroj Son'* [A Journey to the World of Technology]. Tehran: Sertat.

————. 1375/1996a. *Eideology-ye Sheitani* [Satanic Ideology]. Tehran: Serat.

————. 1375/1996b. *Farbahtar az Ideology* [Broader than Ideology]. Tehran: Serat.

———. 1376/1997. *Qesseye Arbab-e Ma'refat* [The Story of the Masters of Understanding]. Tehran: Serat.

———. 1377/1998. *Razdani, Roshanfekri va Dindari* [Knowing the Secrets, Intellectualism, and Religiosity]. Tehran: Serat.

———. 1382/2003. "Democracy Dini va Gheyr-e Dini Nadaarad" [There Is No Religious and Irreligious Democracy: An Interview with Soroush]. *Sharq* 1:8–9.

———. 1383/2004a. "Bazsaazi vs Shostoshuye Mojaddad Akhlaqi" [Ethical Cleansing and Reconstruction]. *Emruz* (24 Mordad/August 14); available at http://emruz.info.

———. 1383/2004b. "Jame'eye Dini va Jame'eye Akhlaqi" [Religious Society and Ethical Society]. *Bamdad* (15 Mordad/August 5).

Taleqani, Mahmoud. 1334/1955. "Moqadima" [Introduction to *Tanbih ul-Umma va Tanzih ul-Mella,* by Mohammad Hossein Na'ini]. Tehran: Enteshar.

"Tarikhcheye Hozeye 'Elmiye-ye Qom" [A Short History of Qom Seminary]. 1340/1961. *Maktab-e Eslam* 3 (4): 42–51.

Yadname-ye 20th Saal-e Ta'sis-e Nehzat-e Azadi [The 20th Anniversary of the Formation of the Freedom Movement of Iran]. 1362/1983. 2nd ed. Tehran: Nehzat-e Azadi.

Zarshenas, Shahriyar. 1373/1995. "Bahar Enqelab va Nur-e Velayat" [The Spring of the Revolution and the Light of Guardianship]. *Mashreq* 1:2–3.

Zibakalam, Sadeq. 1377/1998. *Ma Cheguneh Ma Shodim; Reisheyabi Ellal-e Aqab-mandegi dar Iran* [How Did We Become Who We Are: An Inquiry into the Root of Iranian Backwardness]. Tehran: Rozaneh.

SOURCES IN OTHER LANGUAGES

Abbott, Walter, ed. 1966. *The Documents of Vatican II.* New York: Guild Press.

Abrahamian, Ervand. 1982a. *Iran between Two Revolutions.* Princeton, N.J.: Princeton Univ. Press.

———. 1982b. *Radical Islam: The Iranian Mojahedin.* London: I. B. Tauris.

———. 1988. "Ali Shari'ati: Ideologue of the Iranian Revolution." In Lapidus and Burke, 289–297.

Ajami, Fouad. 1981. *The Arab Predicament.* New York: Cambridge Univ. Press.

———. 1986. *The Vanished Imam: Musa al-Sadr and the Shi'a of Lebanon.* Ithaca, N.Y.: Cornell Univ. Press.

Akhavi, Shahrough. 1980. *Religion and Politics in Contemporary Iran: Clergy-State Relations in the Milani Period.* Albany: State Univ. of New York Press.

Al-e Ahmad, Jalal. 1982. *Gharbzadegi (Weststruckness).* Translated from the Persian by John Green and Ahmad Alizadeh. Costa Mesa, Calif.: Mazda Publishers.

Algar, Hamid. 1988. "Imam Khomeini, 1902–1962: The Pre-Revolutionary Years." In Lapidus and Burke, 263–288.

———. 1991. "Religious Forces in Twentieth-Century Iran." In *The Cambridge History of Iran,* vol. 7: *From Nadir Shah to the Islamic Republic,* edited by Peter Avery, Garm Hambly, and Charles Melville, 732–764. Cambridge: Cambridge Univ. Press.

Amanat, Abbas. 1997. *Pivot of the Universe: Nasir al-Din Shah Qajar and the Iranian Monarchy, 1831–1896.* Berkeley and Los Angeles: Univ. of California Press.

Anderson, Benedict. 1983. *Imagined Communities: Reflections on the Origin and Spread of Nationalism.* London: Verso.

Aneer, Gudmar. 1985. *Imam Ruhullah Khumaini, Sah Muhammad Riza Pahlavi, and the Religious Traditions of Iran.* Uppsala, Sweden: Acta Universitatis Upsaliensis.

Arjomand, Said Amir. 1981. *The Shadow of God and the Hidden Imam.* Chicago: Univ. of Chicago Press.

———. 1984. "Traditionalism in Twentieth Century Iran." In *From Nationalism to Revolutionary Islam,* edited by Said Amir Arjomand, 195–232. Albany: State Univ. of New York Press.

Armstrong, Karen. 2000. *Islam: A Short History.* New York: Modern Library.

Ashraf, Ahmad. 1971. *Iran: Imperialism, Class, and Modernization from Above.* Ph.D. diss., New School for Social Research (New York).

———. 1990. "Theocracy and Charisma: New Men in Power in Iran." *International Journal of Politics, Culture, and Society* 4, no. 1: 13–151.

———. 1995. "From the White Revolution to the Islamic Revolution." In *Iran after the Revolution: Crisis of an Islamic State,* edited by Saeed Rahnema and Sohrab Behdad, 21–44. London: I. B. Tauris.

Avery, Peter. 1965. *Modern Iran.* London: Benn.

Ayoub, Mahmoud. 1978. *Redemptive Suffering in Islam: A Study of the Devotional Aspects of "Ashura" in Twelver Shi'ism.* The Hague: Mouton.

Azimi, Fakhreddin. 1989. *Iran: The Crisis of Democracy.* London: I. B. Tauris.

Azmeh, Aziz. 1993. *Islams and Modernities.* New York: Verso.

Bakhash, Shaoul. 1984. *The Reign of the Ayatollah: Iran and the Islamic Revolution.* New York: Basic Books.

Banani, Amin. 1961. *The Modernization of Iran, 1921–1941.* Stanford, Calif.: Stanford Univ. Press.

Berkes, Niyazi. 1964. *The Development of Secularism in Turkey.* Montreal: McGill Univ. Press.

Binder, Leonard. 1988. *Islamic Liberalism: A Critique of Development Ideologies.* Chicago: Univ. of Chicago Press.

Black, Anthony. 2001. *The History of Islamic Political Thought: From the Prophet to the Present.* New York: Routledge.

Boroujerdi, Mehrzad. 1992. "Gharbzadegi: The Dominant Intellectual Discourse of Pre- and Post-Revolutionary Iran." In Farsoun and Mashayekhi, 30–56.

———. 1996. *Iranian Intellectuals and the West: The Tormented Triumph of Nationalism.* Syracuse, N.Y.: Syracuse Univ. Press.

Braudel, Fernand. 1994. *A History of Civilization.* Translated from the French by Richard Mayne. New York: Penguin.

Brown, Carl L. 1984. *International Politics and the Middle East: Old Rules, Dangerous Game.* Princeton, N.J.: Princeton Univ. Press.

Burke, Edmund III. 1988. "Islam and Social Movements: Methodological Reflections." In Lapidus and Burke, 17–35.

Carter, Jimmy. 1978. *Public Papers of the President of the United States, 1977.* 2 vols. Washington, D.C.: Government Printing Office.

Chehabi, H. E. 1990. *Iranian Politics and Religious Modernism: The Liberation Movement of Iran under the Shah and Khomeini.* Ithaca, N.Y.: Cornell Univ. Press.

Cottam, Richard. 1989. "Inside Revolutionary Iran." *Middle East Journal* 43 (2): 168–185.

Curzon, George N. 1966. *Persia and the Persian Question.* 2 vols. London: Cass.

Dabashi, Hamid. 1993. *Theology of Discontent: The Ideological Foundations of the Islamic Revolution in Iran.* New York: New York Univ. Press.

———. 2000. "The End of Islamic Ideology." *Social Research* 67 (2): 475–518.

Diba, Farhand. 1986. *Mohammad Mossadegh: Political Biography.* London: Croom Helm.

Dorraj, Manuchehr. 1988. *From Zarathustra to Khomeini: Populism and Dissent in Iran.* Boulder, Colo.: Lynne Rienner.

Ehteshami, Anoushirvan. 1995. *After Khomeini: The Iranian Second Republic.* New York: Routledge.

Elshtain, Jean Bethke. 1993. *Democracy on Trial.* Concord, Ont.: House of Anansi Press.

Enayat, Hamid. 1980. "The Resurgence of Islam." *History Today* (February): 16–27.

———. 1982. *Modern Islamic Political Thought.* Austin: Univ. of Texas Press.

———. 1983. "Iran: Khumayni's Concept of the 'Guardianship of the Jurisconsult.'" In *Islam in the Political Process,* edited by James Piscatori, 475–518. Cambridge: Cambridge Univ. Press.

Farmanfarmayan, Hafiz. 1968. "The Forces of Modernization in Nineteenth-Century Iran: A Historical Survey." In *Beginning of Modernization in the Middle East: The Nineteenth Century,* edited by William Polk and Richard Chambers, 115–151. Chicago: Univ. of Chicago Press.

Farsoun, Samih K., and Mehrdad Mashayekhi, eds. 1992. *Iran: Political Culture in the Islamic Republic.* London: Routledge.

Feldman, Noah. 2003. *After Jihad: America and the Struggle for Islamic Democracy.* New York: Farrar, Straus and Giroux.

Fischer, Michael. 1980. *Iran: From Religious Dispute to Revolution.* Cambridge, Mass.: Harvard Univ. Press.

Fischer, Michael, and Mehdi Abedi. 1990. *Debating Muslims: Cultural Dialogues in Postmodernity and Tradition.* Madison: Univ. of Wisconsin Press.

Floor, Willem. 1980. "The Revolutionary Character of Iranian Ulama: Wishful Thinking or Reality?" *International Journal of Middle East Studies* 12 (4): 501–524.

Foran, John. 1993. *Fragile Resistance: Social Transformation in Iran from 1500 to the Revolution.* Boulder, Colo.: Westview.

———, ed. 1994. *A Century of Revolution: Social Movements in Iran.* London: UCL Press.

Fuller, E. Graham, and Ian O. Lesser. 1995. *A Sense of Siege: The Geopolitics of Islam and the West.* Boulder, Colo.: Westview.

Gellner, Ernest. 1984. Foreword to *From Nationalism to Revolutionary Islam,* edited by Said Amir Arjomand, vii–xi. Albany: State Univ. of New York Press.

———. 1992. *Postmodernism, Reason, and Religion.* London: Routledge.

Ghani, Cyrus. 2000. *Iran and the Rise of Reza Shah: From Qajar Collapse to Pahlavi Power.* London: I. B. Tauris.

Gheissari, Ali. 1998. *Iranian Intellectuals in the Twentieth Century.* Austin: Univ. of Texas Press.

Green, Jerrold D. 1993. "Ideology and Pragmatism in Iranian Foreign Policy." *Journal of South Asian and Middle Eastern Studies* 17 (1): 57–75.

Hairi, Abdul-hadi. 1977. *Shi'ism and Constitutionalism in Iran: A Study of the Role Played by the Persian Residents of Iraq in Iranian Politics.* Leiden: Brill.

———. 1982. "Ha'eri." In *The Encyclopedia of Islam.* New ed., supplement 5–6, 342–343. Leiden: Brill.

Halliday, Fred. 1996. *Islam and the Myth of Confrontation: Religion and Politics in the Middle East.* London: I. B. Tauris.

Hentsch, Thierry. 1992. *Imagining the Middle East.* Translated by Fred A. Reed. Montreal: Black Rose.

Hobsbawm, Eric. 1987. *The Age of Empire, 1875–1914.* London: Weidenfeld and Nicolson.

Hodgson, Marshall. 1974. *The Venture of Islam: Conscience and History in a World Civilization.* 3 vols. Chicago: Univ. of Chicago Press.

Jahanbakhsh, Forough. 2001. *Islam, Democracy, and Religious Modernism in Iran, 1953–2000: From Bazargan to Soroush.* Leiden: Brill.

Katouzian, Homa (Mohammad-Ali Homayun). 1981. *The Political Economy of Iran, 1926–1979.* London: Macmillan.

———. 2000. *State and Society in Iran: The Eclipse of the Qajar and the Emergence of the Pahlavis.* London: I. B. Tauris.

Kazemi, Farhad. 1984. "Fada'iyan-e Islam: Fanaticism, Politics, and Terror." In *From Nationalism to Revolutionary Islam,* edited by Said Amir Arjomand, 158–176. Albany: State Univ. of New York Press.

Keddie, Nikki R. 1972. *Sayyid Jamal ad-Din "al-Afghani": A Political Biography.* Berkeley and Los Angeles: Univ. of California Press.

———. 1981. *Roots of Revolution: An Interpretive History of Modern Iran.* New Haven, Conn.: Yale Univ. Press.

———, ed. 1983. *Religion and Politics in Iran: Shi'ism from Quietism to Revolution.* New Haven, Conn.: Yale Univ. Press.

——. 1999. *Qajar Iran and the Rise of Reza Khan, 1796–1925*. Costa Mesa, Calif.: Mazda Publishers.

Kepel, Gilles. 1994. *The Revenge of God: The Resurgence of Islam, Christianity, and Judaism in the Modern World*. University Park: Pennsylvania State Univ. Press.

——. 2002. *Jihad: The Trail of Political Islam*. Translated by Anthony F. Roberts. Cambridge, Mass.: Harvard Univ. Press.

Khomeini, Ruhollah. 1980. *Islam and Revolution I: Writings and Declarations of Imam Khomeini (1941–1980)*. Translated by Hamid Algar. Berkeley, Calif.: Mizan Press.

Kramer, Martin, ed. 1987. *Shi'ism, Resistance, and Revolution*. Boulder, Colo.: Westview.

Kynsh, Alexander. 1992. "Iran Revisited: Khomeini and the Legacy of Islamic Mystical Philosophy." *Middle East Journal* 46 (4): 631–655.

Lambton, A. K. S. 1964. "A Reconstruction of the Position of the Marja' Taqlid and the Religious Institution." *Studia Islamica* 20:115–135.

——. 1992 (1970). "Persia: The Breakdown of Society." In *The Cambridge History of Islam*, vol. 1A, edited by P. M. Holt, A. K. S. Lambton, and Bernard Lewis, 430–467. Cambridge: Cambridge Univ. Press.

Lapidus, Ira M., and Edmund Burke III, eds. 1988. *Islam, Politics, and Social Movements*. Berkeley and Los Angeles: Univ. of California Press.

Lawrence, Bruce. 1989. *Defenders of God: The Fundamentalist Revolt against the Modern Age*. San Francisco: Harper & Row.

Ligabo, Ambeyi. 2004. "Report Submitted by the Special Rapporteur on the Right to Freedom of Opinion and Expression [in Iran]." Addendum (E/CN.4/2004/62/Add.2), 1–25. New York: United Nations.

Litvak, Meir. 1998. *Shi'i Scholars of Nineteenth-Century Iraq: The 'Ulama of Najaf and Karbala*. Cambridge: Cambridge Univ. Press.

Lockhart, Laurence. 1958. *The Fall of the Safavi Dynasty and the Afghan Occupation of Persia*. Cambridge: Cambridge Univ. Press.

Lorentz, John H. 1974. "Modernization and Political Change in Nineteenth-Century Iran: The Role of Amir Kabir." Ph.D. diss., Princeton University.

——. 1995. *Historical Dictionary of Iran*. Lanham, Md.: Scarecrow Press.

Luciani, Giacomo, and Hazem Beblawi, eds. 1987. *The Rentier State*. New York: Croom Helm.

Mahdavy, Hossein. 1970. "Pattern and Problems of Development in Rentier States: The Case of Iran." In *Studies in the Economic History of the Middle East*, edited by M. A. Cook, 382–420. Oxford: Oxford Univ. Press.

Mallat, Chibli. 1993. *The Renewal of Islamic Law: Muhammad Baqer as-Sadr, Najaf, and the Shi'i International*. Cambridge: Cambridge Univ. Press.

Marty, Martin E., and R. Scott Appleby, eds. 1992. *Fundamentalisms and Society: Reclaiming the Sciences, the Family, and Education*. Vol. 2 of *The Fundamentalism Project*. Chicago: Univ. of Chicago Press.

Mashayekhi, Mehrdad. 1992. "The Politics of Nationalism and Political Culture." In Farsoun and Mashayekhi, 82–115.

———. 2000. *The Persian Sphinx: Amir Abbas Hoveyda and the Riddle of the Iranian Revolution*. Washington, D.C.: Mage.

———. 2001. "The Revival of Student Movements in Post-Revolutionary Iran." *International Journal of Politics, Culture, and Society* 15, no. 2: 283–313.

Milani, Abbas. 1996. *Tales of Two Cities: A Persian Memoir*. Washington, D.C.: Mage.

Milani, Mohsen. 1992. "Shi´ism and the State in the Constitution of the Islamic Republic of Iran." In Farsoun and Mashayekhi, 133–159.

———. 1994. *The Making of Iran's Islamic Revolution: From Monarchy to Islamic Republic*. 2nd ed. Boulder, Colo.: Westview.

Moin, Baqer. 2000. *Khomeini: Life of the Ayatollah*. New York: St. Martin's.

Moslem, Mehdi. 2002. *Factional Politics in Post-Khomeini Iran*. Syracuse, N.Y.: Syracuse Univ. Press.

Mozaffari, Mehdi. 1993. "Changes in the Iranian Political System after Ayatollah Khomeini's Death." *Political Studies* 41 (4): 611–617.

Nabavi, Negin. 2003. *Intellectuals and the State in Iran: Politics, Discourse, and the Dilemma of Authenticity*. Gainesville: Univ. Press of Florida.

Najmabadi, Afsaneh. 1987. "Depoliticisation of a Rentier State: The Case of Pahlavi Iran." In *The Rentier State*, edited by Hazem Beblawi and Giacomo Luciani, 211–227. London: Croom Helm.

Nasr, Seyyed Hossein. 1984. "Present Tendencies, Future Trends." In *Islam: The Religious and Political Life of a World Community*, edited by Marjorie Kelly, 275–292. New York: Praeger.

———. 1996. "Mulla Sadra: His Teachings." In *A History of Islamic Philosophy*, edited by S. H. Nasr and O. Leaman, 1:643–662. London: Routledge.

———. 2003. *Islam: Religion, History, and Civilization*. San Francisco: Harper-San Francisco.

Nawid, Senzil K. 1999. *Religious Response to Social Change in Afghanistan, 1919–1929: King Aman-Allah and the Afghan Ulama*. Costa Mesa, Calif.: Mazda Publishers.

Parsa, Misagh. 1994. "Mosque of Last Resort: State Reform and Social Conflict in the Early 1960s." In *A Century of Revolution: Social Movements in Iran*, edited by John Foran, 135–159. London: UCL Press.

Polanyi, Karl. 2001 [1944]. *The Great Transformation: The Political and Economic Origins of Our Time*. Boston: Beacon.

Poullada, Leon B. 1973. *Reform and Rebellion in Afghanistan, 1919–1929: King Amanullah's Failure to Modernize a Tribal Society*. Ithaca, N.Y.: Cornell Univ. Press.

Rahman, Fazlur. 1982. *Islam and Modernity: Transformation of an Intellectual Tradition*. Chicago: Univ. of Chicago Press.

Rahnema, Ali. 2000. *An Islamic Utopian: A Political Biography of Ali Shari´ati*. London: I. B. Tauris.

Rahnema, Ali, and Farhad Nomani. 1995. "Competing Shi'i Subsystems in Contemporary Iran." In *Iran after the Revolution: Crisis of an Islamic State,* edited by Ali Rahnema and Farhad Nomani, 65–93. London: I. B. Tauris.

Rajaee, Farhang. 1983. *Islamic Values and World View: Khomeyni on Man, the State, and International Politics.* Lanham, Md.: Univ. Press of America.

———, ed. 1993a. *The Iran-Iraq War: The Politics of Aggression.* Gainesville: Univ. Press of Florida.

———. 1993b. "Islam and Modernity: The Reconstruction of an Alternative Shi'ite Islamic World View in Iran." In *Fundamentalisms and Society: Reclaiming the Sciences, the Family, and Education,* edited by Martin E. Marty and R. Scott Appleby, 103–125. Chicago: Univ. of Chicago Press.

———. 1994a. "Intellectuals and Culture: Guardians of Traditions or Vanguards of Development." In *Culture, Development, and Democracy: The Role of the Intellectual; A Tribute to Soedjatmoko,* edited by Selo Soemardjan and Kenneth W. Thompson, 39–52. New York: United Nations Univ. Press.

———. 1994b. "The Social Origins of Political Elites in Iran: A Historical Review." *Iranian Journal of International Affairs* 6, no. 1–2: 1–27.

———. 1999. "A Thermidor of Islamic Yuppies? Conflict and Compromise in Iran's Politics." *Middle East Journal* 53, no. 2 (Spring): 217–231.

———. 2000. *Globalization on Trial: The Human Condition and the Information Civilization.* Ottawa: IDRC; West Hartford, Conn.: Kumarian.

Ram, Haggay. 1994. *Myth and Mobilization in Revolutionary Iran: The Use of the Friday Congregational Sermon.* Washington, D.C.: American Univ. Press.

Richard, Yann. 1988. "Shari'at Sanglagi: A Reformist Theologian of the Rida Shah Period." In *Authority and Political Culture in Shi'ism,* edited by Said Amir Arjomand, translated by Kathryn Arjomand, 159–177. Albany: State Univ. of New York Press.

Riggs, Fred W. 1964. *Administration in Developing Countries: The Theory of Prismatic Society.* Boston: Houghton Mifflin.

Roy, Olivier. 1994. *The Failure of Political Islam.* Translated from the French by Carol Volk. Cambridge, Mass.: Harvard Univ. Press.

———. 1998. "Tensions in Iran: The Future of the Islamic Revolution," *MERIP [Middle East Research and Information Project] Report* 28 (2): 38–40.

Rubin, Barry. 1980. *Paved with Good Intentions: The American Experience and Iran.* New York: Oxford Univ. Press.

Sachedina, Abdulaziz. 1981. *Islamic Messianism: The Idea of the Mahdi in Twelver Shi'ism.* Albany: State Univ. of New York Press.

Sadri, Mahmoud. 2001. "Sacral Defense of Secularism: The Political Theologies of Soroush, Shabestari, and Kadivar." *International Journal of Politics, Culture, and Society* 15 (2): 257–270.

Safi, Omid, ed. 2003. *Progressive Muslims: On Justice, Gender, and Pluralism.* Oxford: Oneworld Publications.

Samii, Abbas William. 1994. "The Role of SAVAK in the 1978–1979 Iranian Revolution." Ph.D. diss., Cambridge University.

Sanghvi, Ramesh. 1968. *Aryamehr: The Shah of Iran; A Political Biography*. London: Macmillan.

Sarabi, Farzin. 1994. "The Post-Khomeini Era in Iran: The Elections of the Fourth Islamic Majlis." *Middle East Journal* 48 (1): 89–107.

Sayyid, Bobby S. 1997. *A Fundamental Fear: Eurocentrism and the Emergence of Islamism*. New York: Zed Books.

Schahgaldian, Nikola B. 1989. *The Clerical Establishment in Iran*. Santa Monica: RAND Corp.

Schirazi, Asghar. 1993. *Islamic Development Policy: The Agrarian Question in Iran*. Translated from the German by P. J. Ziess-Lawrence. Boulder, Colo.: Lynne Rienner.

Shayegan, Daryush. 1992. *Cultural Schizophrenia: Islamic Societies Confronting the West*. Translated from the French by John Howe. London: Saqi Books.

Shepard, William. 1989. "Islam and Ideology: Toward a Typology." *International Journal of Middle East Studies* 19 (3): 307–336.

Siavoshi, Sussan. 1990. *Liberal Nationalism in Iran: The Failure of a Movement*. Boulder, Colo.: Westview.

Skocpol, Theda. 1982. "Rentier State and Shiʿa Islam in the Iranian Revolution." *Theory and Society* 11 (3): 265–283.

Sreberny-Mohammadi, Annabelle, and Ali Mohammadi. 1994. *Small Media, Big Revolution: Communication, Culture, and the Iranian Revolution*. Minneapolis: Univ. of Minnesota Press.

Taleqani, Mahmoud. 1983. *Islam and Ownership*. Translated from the Persian by Ahmad Jabbari and Farhang Rajaee. Costa Mesa, Calif.: Mazda Publishers.

Taylor, Charles. 2004. *Modern Social Imaginaries*. Durham, N.C.: Duke Univ. Press.

Tocqueville, Alexis de. 1955 [1856]. *The Old Régime and the French Revolution*. Translated by Stuart Gilbert. Garden City, N.Y.: Doubleday.

Vahdat, Farzin. 2000a. "Post-Revolutionary Discourses of Mohammad Mojtahed Shabestari and Mohsen Kadivar: Reconciling the Terms of Mediated Subjectivity, Part I: Mojtahed Shabestari." *Critique: Critical Middle Eastern Studies* 16 (Spring): 31–54.

———. 2000b. "Post-Revolutionary Discourses of Mohammad Mojtahed Shabestari and Mohsen Kadivar: Reconciling the Terms of Mediated Subjectivity, Part II: Mohsen Kadivar." *Critique: Critical Middle Eastern Studies* 17 (Fall): 135–157.

———. 2002. *God and Juggernaut: Iran's Intellectual Encounter with Modernity*. Syracuse, N.Y.: Syracuse Univ. Press.

Wolin, Sheldon. 1973. "The Politics of the Study of Revolution." *Comparative Politics* 5 (3): 343–358.

INDEX

Adamiyat, Feridun, 8, 20, 247
Aghajari, Hashem, 200, 207
Ahmadinejad, Mahmoud, xi, 237, 238, 243
Alavi High School, 70, 86, 128, 142, 146, 147–148, 226
Al-e Ahmad, Jalal (1923–1969), xv, 8, 48, 51, 79, 96, 102–103, 109, 182, 249n1
Ali Akbar Bahramani. *See* Hashemi Rafsanjani
Amanullah Khan (1892–1960), 45–46
America. *See* United States
Amir Kabir, Mirza Taqi Khan (1807–1851), 7, 36, 208
Arak, 53, 54
Arani Taqi, 48
Ataturk, Mustafa Kemal Pasha, 44–45, 109

Bahaism, 51, 71, 85–86, 251n2 (Ch. 4)
Bahar, Mehdi, 21, 102, 104–105
Bazargan, Mehdi (1907–1995), 8, 16, 25, 32, 74–78, 79, 83–84, 92, 114, 126, 141, 151, 221
  and Freedom Movement of Iran, 142–143
  and role of clerics, 108
Britain/British. *See* Great Britain
Burujerdi (Mohammad Hossein Tabataba'i) (1875–1961), 64, 65, 67, 68–74, 85, 147, 209, 215, 252n4

and cultural activism, 71–74
and political quietism, 69–70
and rapprochement of Shi'ism and Sunnism, 72

Carter, Jimmy, 98, 247
Cold War, 99–100, 154
Constitutional Movement. *See* Constitutional Revolution
Constitutional Revolution (1905–1911), xiii, 8, 20, 23, 29, 53, 54, 81, 178

Dabagh, Hossein Hajfaraj. *See* Soroush, Abdolkarim
Davar, Ali Akbar, 34–35
Davari, Reza, 185–190
democracy, 184, 213
Devotees of Islam. *See* Fada'iyan Islam
Din va Danesh High School, 142

Ebadi, Shirin, 203
Enayat, Hamid, 12, 44, 64, 131, 132

Fada'iyan Islam, 39–40, 42, 69, 70, 82
Fardid, Seyyed Ahmad (1912–1994), 102–103, 150, 171, 181–185
Fayziyeh Seminary, xiii, 53, 56, 78, 111
freedom, 76, 84, 140, 145, 222–224
Freedom Movement of Iran, 95, 142–143, 145, 156

Ganji, Akbar, 200–201, 242
Gharbzadegi, x, 17, 51, 86, 102, 182, 184,
    186, 190
  characteristics of, 103
  definition of, xv
globalization, 203
Great Britain, 9, 20, 28, 37, 38, 55, 98,
    249n3
Guardianship of the Jurisconsult, 23, 111,
    121, 122–123, 175, 207, 210–211, 219

Ha'eri Yazdi, Sheikh Abdolkarim
    (d. 1937), 27, 52, 55–56, 69
  cultural activism of, 60–64
  life of, 53–54
  political positions of, 57–60
Hajjarian, Saeed, 1, 194, 196–197, 205,
    206, 231–235, 237, 241
Haj Seyyed Javadi, Ali Asghar, 106
Hakamizadeh, Ali Akbar (d. 1988), 49,
    52, 60, 64, 65–66, 74
Halabi, Sheikh Mohammad Zakerzadeh
    Tavalaei, 85, 88
Haqqni School, 173, 179–180
Hashemi Rafsanjani, Ali Akbar, 151, 154,
    155–156, 159, 163, 196, 206
Hey'atha-ye Mo'talefe-ye Eslami, 123–125
Hezb-e Mellal Eslami (Islamic Nations
    Party), 70, 126, 157
Hojjati-ye Association, 71, 83, 84–89
Homayun (monthly from Qom), 54, 56,
    60–65, 72
Hosseiniye-ye Ershad, 128, 142, 146–147,
    250n12
Huyser, Robert E., 9

ideology, 4, 134
Ijtihad, 23, 107, 215, 225
Imam Hossein, 132–133
Iran, xi, 19, 21, 48, 105, 141, 183, 189, 201,
    230, 238
  and Americanization, 46, 94, 96
  circle of power in, 199
  and coup of 1953, 91, 92

dependency of, on oil, 92–93, 97
  and hostage crisis in (November
    1979), 164
  and identity, 7, 31, 94, 96, 116, 129, 143
  intellectuals in, 35, 208, 215, 233, 234
  and intellectual killings, 169–171
  and Iran-Iraq War (1980–1988), 18,
    153, 154, 158, 164, 168, 234
  and Islam, 129–130
  June 1963 uprising in, 95
  and modernization/modernity, xi, 29,
    41, 47, 51, 62, 94
  political factions in, 157–162, 198–199
  population of, 202
  power structure in, 93, 97
  radical right in, 155–159
  social classes in, 8, 38
  westernization of, 29, 31–32, 35, 36, 37,
    46, 60, 61, 62, 78, 92, 94, 97, 106, 115,
    126, 147
Iranian Communist Party. See Tudeh
    Party
Iranian Revolution. See Islamic
    Revolution
Islam, 5, 10, 19, 43, 75, 80, 107, 120, 127,
    143, 156, 191, 207, 220, 244
  and governance, 216
  as ideology, 4, 137, 148, 229
  and juridical narrative, 121, 149
  and monarchy, 90, 122
  and nationalism, 129–130
  and politics, 81
  of Qom, 52, 57, 68, 110, 172, 208
  and republicanism, 231, 232, 239
  and secularity, 229, 232
  social mission of, 140
  of Tehran, 64, 74, 78, 110, 123, 126, 180
  women's rights in, 24, 130–131
Islamic movement, 10–21, 24
Islamic Republic of Iran, 22, 99, 121, 147,
    151, 153–154, 177, 178, 184, 189–190,
    196, 200–201, 207, 211, 215, 216, 218,
    220, 237, 238, 240
Islamic Revolution (1979), x, 6–10, 65,

97–98, 104, 122, 128, 149, 158, 165, 238
impact of, 189
and struggle of right and wrong, 125
Islamic yuppies, 207
Islamism, x, xi, 4, 5, 11, 18, 19, 150, 171–172, 191, 236, 238

Jameye Rohaniyat-e Mobarez-e Tehran, 123, 125–126, 155, 157, 159
Janati, Ahmad, 158, 172, 204
Jihad, 119, 140, 250n

Kadivar, Hojjatoleslam Mohsen, 25, 194, 205, 208, 214–221, 233, 241, 243
Kashani, Ayatollah Abolqasem, 40, 42
Kasravi, Ahmad (1890–1946), 25, 49, 50–51, 62, 65, 70, 102, 166, 173
Kazemi, Zahra, 202–203
Khamenei, Ayatollah Seyyed Ali, 72, 164, 168, 169, 174, 200
Khatami, Mohammad, xi, 8, 158, 162, 171, 173–174, 194, 195–196, 202, 235, 237, 251n14
Khomeini Ruhollah Musavi (1904–1989), xi, 1, 15, 16, 22, 23, 41, 64, 65–67, 90, 95, 98–99, 110–123, 128, 141, 151, 164, 174, 177, 201, 209, 210, 216, 219, 226, 227, 252n3
death of, 151–152
debating Hakamizadeh, 65–67
desire of, to become king, xii
to the elite, 116–120, 175, 227
on government, 23, 121, 122–123
and June 1963 uprising, 111–112
and Khomeinism, 113
marriage of, 115
to the masses, 120–121
and Mojahedin, 121–122, 145–146
in Paris, 113–114
philosophy of, 118–119
and Plato, 118, 120
and return to Qom, 172
in Turkey, 112, 115–116

Khorasani, Mohammad Kazem, 69, 217, 218
Kiyan, 205, 206, 227

liberalism, 140, 227

Majma'e Rohaniyun-e Mobarez-e Tehran, 155, 157, 158
Makhmalbaf, Mohsen, 194, 208
Maktab-e Islam, 71, 180
Marxism, 48, 80, 122, 226
Mesbah Yazdi, Ayatollah Mohammad Taqi, 172–174, 210
modernism, 4, 5, 11, 17, 19, 37, 46, 62, 126, 147, 191
modernity, 4, 5, 15, 19, 43, 135, 171, 189, 191, 207, 222, 245
Montazeri, Ayatollah Hossein-Ali, 25, 205, 208, 209–214, 252n3
Mosaddeq, Mohammad (1882–1967), 7, 8, 9, 28, 40–42, 47–48, 84, 89, 101, 142, 217
Motahhari, Morteza (1920–1979), 24, 69, 107–108, 126, 127–131, 137–138, 217, 227
Mulla Sadra (d. 1642), 117–118, 182, 226, 234,
Muslim politics, 5, 10, 11, 20, 238

Na'ini, Ayatollah Mirza Hossein, 49, 69, 79, 81–82, 217, 218
National Front, 42, 84, 95, 99
National Resistance Movement, 83–84, 142
Navvab Safavi, Mojtaba (1923–1956), 70, 173
Nuri, Abdollah, 162, 173, 207, 251n2 (Ch. 3)

Pahlavi, Muhammad Reza, xi, 9, 28, 37–42, 68, 85, 92, 97, 152
and the Azerbaijan crisis, 38–39
and the "great civilization," 94, 96
and Pahlavism, 94
and reform from above, 93, 111

Pahlavi, Reza Khan (Shah), 9, 27, 28, 30–37, 44, 46, 57, 78, 79, 152, 168, 247n3, 248n3
    and change of alphabet, 36–37
    and modernism, 31–32, 33
    policies of, 29
    reliance of, on army, 9, 33
Pahlavi dynasty, 1, 7, 9, 20, 88, 153, 192, 236
People's Mojahedin Organization, 122, 142, 143–145, 252n3
post-Islamism, 5–6, 22, 24, 208, 238, 240, 245

Qajar dynasty, 28, 58
Qom, xi, xii, xiii, 2, 16, 27, 52, 53, 57, 58, 59, 60, 64, 65, 68, 72, 78, 89, 98, 111–113, 115, 172, 208, 214

Rafsanjani. See Hashemi Rafsanjani, Ali Akbar
reform and restoration, 18, 22, 204, 206, 207
religion, 12, 63, 76, 220, 222, 228, 229
    and ethics, 230
    in Europe, 76–77
    and freedom, 223–224
    and politics, 77–78, 193, 197
    and religious despotism, 82
    and science, 127
revivalists, 17–18
revolution, 15, 18, 169, 184, 189

Sadr, Mohammad Baqir (d. 1980), 215, 217
Safavid dynasty, xiii, 7, 43, 53, 138
Sangelaji, Shari'at [Mirza Rezaqoli] (1890–1944), 49–50, 61
SAVAK (Iranian Secret Police), xv, 98
Shabestari, Mohammad Mojtahed, 193, 205, 221–225
Shahid Javid, 132, 250n11
Shari'ati, Ali (1933–1977), 8, 16, 126, 131–141, 226, 250nn12,13

Shari'atmadari, Ayatollah Mohammad Kazem, 64, 74, 250n5
Shi'ism, 1, 17, 18, 20, 27, 50, 51, 52, 66, 67, 77, 88, 107, 108, 111, 122, 124, 131, 138, 140, 174, 184, 210–211, 216, 249n4
    and clerics (ulama), 3, 8, 20, 55, 56, 66, 115, 137–138, 140, 143, 172, 214, 228
Soroush, Abdolkarim, 15, 16, 25, 148, 166, 205, 225–231, 243, 252n5
Soviet Union, 48

Tabataba'i, Mohammad Hossein, 106–107
Tahajom Farhangi Gharb. See Western cultural onslaught
Taleqani, Mahmoud (1910–1979), 74, 78–83, 126, 251n15
Taqizadeh, Seyyed Hassan, 27, 33, 47
Tehran University, xiii, xiv, 36, 39, 48, 52, 74, 75, 99, 144, 181, 185, 199, 226, 231
Tudeh Party, 40, 48–49, 61, 79, 102, 104, 226

United States, 9, 28, 42, 71, 91, 92, 93, 96, 98, 101, 102, 104, 165–166, 170, 180, 204, 249n3

Vatican II, 101
Velayat-e Faqih. See Guardianship of the Jurisconsult

West, the, 34, 84, 102, 103, 105, 106, 110, 141, 152, 166, 182, 186–188, 204, 231
Western cultural onslaught, 166, 167, 168–169
Westernization. See modernism
Weststruckness. See Gharbzadegi

Yazdi, Ibrahim, 156